MAD DOGS AND ENGLISHMEN

An Expedition Round My Family

Ranulph Fiennes

WINDSOR
PARAGON

First published 2009
by Hodder & Stoughton
This Large Print edition published 2010
by BBC Audiobooks Ltd
by arrangement with
Hodder & Stoughton

Hardcover ISBN: 978 1 408 48607 8
Softcover   ISBN: 978 1 408 48608 5

British Library Cataloguing in Publication Data available

Printed and bound in Great Britain by
CPI Antony Rowe, Chippenham and Eastbourne

MAD DOGS AND ENGLISHMEN

For my Lollick, with love

CONTENTS

Foreword   xiii

1   The Conquest that Nearly Wasn't   1
2   Stolen from the Saxons   10
3   Riding to Jerusalem   21
4   A King's Ransom   29
5   'Across the reeds at Runnymede'   45
6   Marriages of Convenience   55
7   Dangerous Liaisons   63
8   Fiennes on Both Sides   84
9   Founder's Kin   104
10   Once More Unto the Breach   118
11   Murdered by a Mob   131
12   Winter of our Discontent   151
13   The Sun of York   165
14   Twisletons and Tudors   178
15   Death of a Deer Hunter   187
16   Stately Homes of England   206
17   Begging for a Barony   216
18   A Failed Poisoning   242
19   The Small Room with No Ears   256
20   Old Subtlety   271
21   Adultery at the Castle   291
22   Restoration and Elopement   305
23   Ride a Cock Horse   320

24 Fiennes vs. Fiennes   341
25 Bankers, Bubbles and Bonnie
        Prince Charlie   348
26 Riot and Romance   369
27 A Dandy Road to Ruin   392
28 Uncle Geoffrey in Zulu Land   415
29 Eustace and Winston   434
30 Colonel of the Greys   456

Our national characteristics   469
Acknowledgements   470
Picture Acknowledgements   472
Sources   473

The Romans first with Julius Caesar came,
Including all the nations of that name
Gauls, Greeks, and Lombards, and, by
    computation,
Auxiliaries or slaves of every nation.
With Hengist, Saxons; Danes with Sueno came,
In search of plunder, not in search of fame.
Scots, Picts, and Irish from the Hibernian shore,
And conquering William brought the Normans
    o'er.
All these their barbarous offspring left behind,
The dregs of armies, they of all mankind;
Blended with Britons, who before were here,
Of whom the Welsh ha' blessed the character.
From this amphibious ill-born mob began
That vain ill-natured thing, an Englishman.

From 'The True-Born Englishman'
by Daniel Defoe

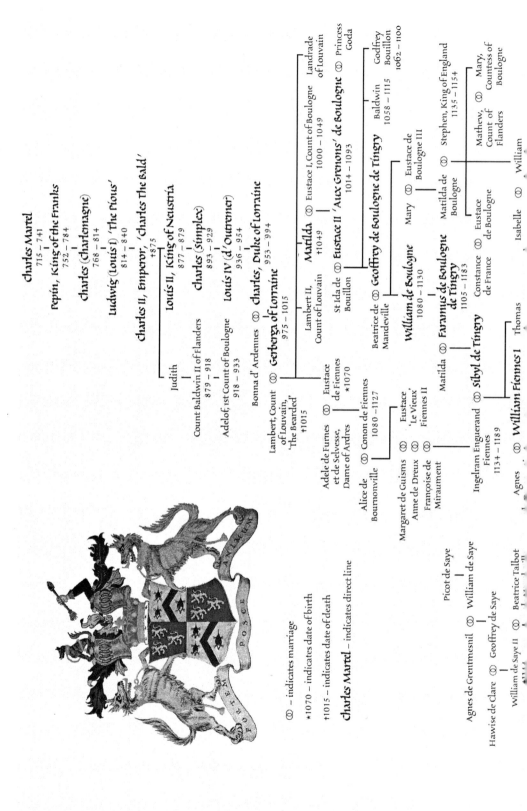

Charles Martel
715 – 741

Pepin, King of the Franks
752 – 784

Charles (Charlemagne)
768 – 814

Ludwig (Louis I) 'The Pious'
814 – 840

Charles II, Emperor, 'Charles The Bald'
†875

Louis II, King of Neustria
877 – 879

Charles (Simplex)
893 – 929

Louis IV (d'Outremer)
936 – 954

Judith

Count Baldwin II of Flanders
879 – 918

Adelof, 1st Count of Boulogne
918 – 933

Bonna d' Ardennes ⊕ Charles, Duke of Lorraine
953 – 994

Lambert, Count of Louvain, 'The Bearded' †1015 ⊕ Gerberga of Lorraine
975 – 1015

Eustace de Fiennes *1070

Lambert II, Count of Louvain

Matilda †1049 ⊕ Eustace I, Count of Boulogne 1000 – 1049

Landrade of Louvain ⊕ Princess Goda

St Ida de Bouillon ⊕ Eustace II 'Aux Grenons' de Boulogne 1014 – 1093

Baldwin 1058 – 1115

Godfrey Bouillon 1062 – 1100

Beatrice de Mandeville ⊕ Geoffrey de Boulogne de Tingry

Mary ⊕ Eustace de Boulogne III

Matilda de Boulogne ⊕ Stephen, King of England 1135 – 1154

Mathew, Count of Flanders ⊕ Mary, Countess of Boulogne

William de Boulogne 1080 – 1130

Constance de France ⊕ Eustace de Boulogne

Isabelle ⊕ William

Adele de Furnes et de Selvesse, Dame of Ardres ⊕ Conon de Fiennes 1080 –1127

Eustace Le Vieux', Fiennes II

Alice de Bournonville

William de Boulogne de Tingry 1105 – 1183 ⊕ Faramus de Boulogne de Tingry

Matilda ⊕ Sibyl de Tingry

Margaret de Guisms ⊕
Anne de Dreux ⊕
Françoise de Miraument ⊕

Ingelram Enguerand Fiennes 1134 – 1189

William Fiennes I

Thomas

Agnes

⊕ – indicates marriage

*1070 – indicates date of birth

†1015 – indicates date of death

Charles Martel – indicates direct line

Picot de Saye

William de Saye

Agnes de Grentmesnil ⊕ Geoffrey de Saye

Hawise de Clare ⊕

William de Saye II ⊕ Beatrice Talbot

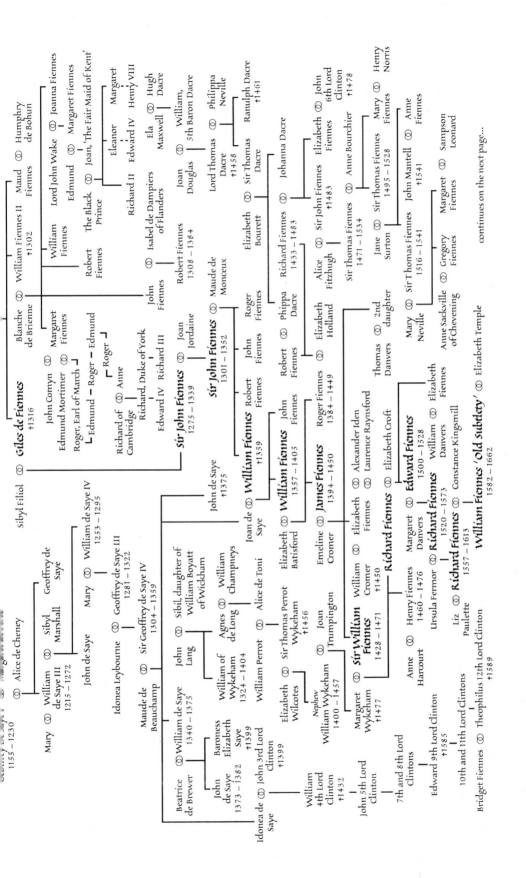

continues on the next page...

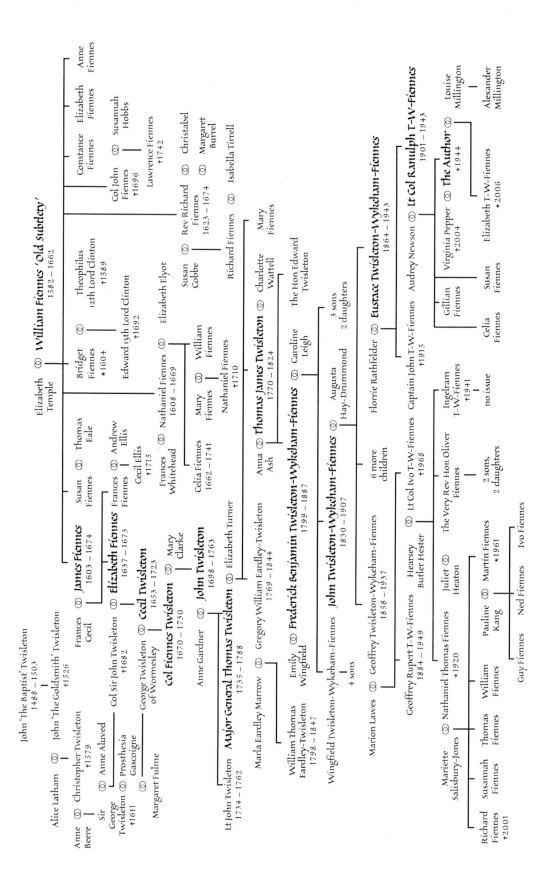

FOREWORD

My grandfather was born the second son of a family that has lived for six hundred years and twenty-one unbroken generations in the same house, Broughton Castle in Oxfordshire. This book is the record of my family and, through them, a simplified squint at the history of my country, England, warts and all, from its beginnings until 1944 when I was born. Churchill wrote: 'There is a forgotten, nay almost forbidden word which means more to me than any other. That word is England.' I go along with that.

I have spent fifty years of my life returning to England from abroad, and every now and again visiting the family at Broughton, as my father did before me. I always knew that just under the roof there was a secret tower room, 'a small room with no ears' they called it, where the leaders of the opposition to Charles I, including John Hampden and John Pym, had plotted against the king with the powerful 8th Lord Saye and Sele and I knew that the 1st Lord Saye and Sele had been beheaded by Jack Cade, the leader of the Peasants' Revolt. But beyond that, I had no knowledge of family history.

That all changed last year when I started to sift through often conflicting historical opinions alongside the voluminous family documents lent me by my cousin Nat, the 21st Lord Saye and Sele. I then became aware that one or two of my ancestors had played roles that almost certainly changed the course of English history.

On past expeditions and this year on Everest I have often conjured up the image of my father, my grandfather and long lines of Fiennes watching my flagging efforts and I pressed on because I didn't want to let them down. I never knew my father, much less the forty earlier generations, but since writing this book those vague shadows down the ages have for me become living people.

Ranulph Twisleton-Wykeham-Fiennes
written from Base Camp, Everest, May 2009

THE CONQUEST THAT NEARLY WASN'T

Many English people today point to Norman ancestry and boast, 'My lot came here in 1066.' Quite why that should be a point of pride rather than of shame, when one considers how those same ancestors behaved, is questionable and, as I shall reveal, the Fienneses are as guilty as anyone. Geoffrey Twisleton-Wykeham-Fiennes, Lord Saye and Sele (yes, that's just one man) writing in his book, *Hearsay*, in 1830 offers us a corrective viewpoint however.

'Your family history goes back a long way,' remarked a casual acquaintance to me.

'Yes,' I replied, my bosom heaving with pride, 'we came over with the Conqueror.'

'Ah!' he said. 'We were waiting for him.'

The 'English' who were sharpening their weaponry in anticipation were still a mongrel mix, a genetic goulash of a dozen racial origins who had arrived from what we now call Germany and the Low Countries of Belgium and Holland and the English language derives from these illiterate and pagan tribes, the Jutes from Jutland, plus the West Saxons (Wessex), the East Saxons (Essex) and the South Saxons (Sussex) from Old Saxony. The name England derives from the land of the Angles, a Germanic people from Angeln, now southern Denmark. Over the fifth, sixth and seventh centuries regional groupings of settlers fought each other for land and established their own kingdoms of East Anglia, Essex, Mercia (in the midlands), Sussex and Wessex.

By the eighth century a pecking order had emerged. Offa of Mercia (757–96) became direct ruler of all but the Wessex and Northumbrian provinces and was on 'My dearest brother' terms when addressing the most powerful man in Europe, his trading partner, the Frankish Emperor Charlemagne. And this is the point where I can introduce my family for the first time, as Charlemagne was my direct ancestor going back thirty-nine generations. In fact we have been traced back two generations more through his father Pepin the Short to Charles Martel, Charlemagne's grandfather and my great-to-the-power-of-forty-one grandfather. But it was to be a couple more centuries before we set foot on English soil and in that time Offa and his descendants had to cope with a brand new threat, the Vikings.

The English hero who stemmed the Viking invasions was Alfred the Great who penned the Danes into the so-called Danelaw along the eastern seaboard of England. Alfred was lauded as 'Engele hirde, Engele dirling'—shepherd and darling of England. It was his grandson, Edgar, who divided England into counties whose boundaries remained in place until 1974. He also started the tradition at coronation rituals of the great cry of fealty 'Long live the king, may the king live forever' which we still use in the twenty-first century.

The Danes made nuisances of themselves in

Europe as well, laying siege to Paris and settling in the rich Frankish region which became known as Normandy, the land of the Norsemen. One of their villages was Fiennes, but more of that later.

No sooner had Alfred's successors thought the Viking problem had been settled than fresh waves of invasion panicked Edgar's son Ethelred the Unready into ordering all Danish men in England to be killed. A great many were massacred but the new Danish forces soon ousted and exiled the witless Ethelred whose unfortunate career I would not have mentioned had he not been a relation by marriage. His daughter Goda married my great-to-the-power-of-thirty grandfather, Eustace II of Boulogne.

The man who stepped into the power vacuum, King Canute, was luckily for us an anglophile and a sadly misunderstood one in popular mythology. When he let the waves on a beach near Chichester wash over his royal feet he was in fact demonstrating to his foolish courtiers the limit of human and kingly powers, not attempting to rule the tides. He did rule both England and Denmark pretty successfully from 1016 until his death in 1035.

His two sons, one of whom was an alcoholic, died a few years later, at which point the Wessex dynasty was restored to the English throne in the person of the late King Ethelred's son, Edward the Confessor, whose sister Goda, you will recall, was married to my cousin Eustace of Boulogne. I'm calling him my cousin Eustace because I am going to get sick of referring to various ancestors as ancestor this and ancestor that through the rest of this book. 'Cousin' is a much more user-friendly and less pompous general term.

During the reign of Canute and sons, Ethelred's immediate family had been in exile at the Norman court for twenty-five years, so when young Edward the Confessor found himself back in England as reigning monarch, he brought with him a goodly number of Norman friends, many of whom he appointed to senior positions of power, much to the annoyance of various influential English and Danish nobles, especially Lord Godwin, Earl of Wessex, the most influential noble in England.

An unhealthy power struggle now developed between the party of Edward, supported by the Dukes of Normandy, on the one hand, and Godwin of Wessex, the eminence grise behind the English throne—the man who would be king and was raising troops against Edward. It was this situation which sowed the seeds for the Norman invasion of Britain. Godwin bullied Edward into marrying his daughter, Edith. Edward, king in name only, had always loathed Godwin for having his teenage brother murdered, and he made sure that Edith remained childless by packing her off to a nunnery and taking a vow of celibacy himself.

At this point Edward's brother-in-law, my cousin Eustace, came, albeit unwittingly, to the king's assistance. Eustace had been having an eventful time in France rebelliously fighting against the forces of his overlord, the Emperor and, as if that were not enough grief, finding himself being excommunicated by the Pope for remarrying to too close a relation. Chastened, he begged forgiveness of the Emperor and prudently retreated for a spell to the friendly court of his English former brother-in-law. The two men were united in their hatred of Godwin and when Godwin's men killed twenty of Eustace's men in an affray at Dover, it was the last straw and the king had a perfect excuse to exile Godwin and his sons for not seeing the culprits were brought to justice.

But only a year after the Dover brawl the Godwins were back with a large Flemish army lent them by the Count of Flanders. Earl Godwin and sons once again became the power in the land and King Edward a mere puppet king who was anyway by then getting old and interested only in his pet royal architectural project of building Westminster Abbey.

No written evidence remains but during Godwin's brief exile, King Edward is said to have invited his friend, Duke William of Normandy, to his court, where he promised to make him heir to the throne of England. Nevertheless, on his deathbed only a year later Edward recommended to his council of nobles that Godwin's eldest son, Harold, should be his successor.

Another incident, of which there is also no written evidence, occurred during the year before Edward's death. Harold Godwinson, shipwrecked off Normandy or—less likely—sent there as an emissary to confirm Edward's promise of the succession to William, found himself in William's hands where he was forced over the bones of a saint to swear allegiance to the Duke of Normandy. The pictorial version of Harold's Oath is to be viewed on the Bayeux Tapestry which depicts Harold's ship sailing to France, his capture there by William's men, his joining William to fight the Duke of Brittany and, significantly, a friendly scene where Harold is thanked for his help prior to

5

his making his oath of allegiance to William.

Edward died in 1066, the last of twenty-five kings of the Wessex dynasty, all of whom had lived in England. Harold Godwinson, an Anglo-Saxon-Scandinavian with no blood claim to the throne, but the mightiest earl in the land, was immediately proclaimed King of England.

Storm clouds gathered at once to the north and the south of the realm. King Harald Hardrada of Norway, a six foot four professional fighter of great military experience and with a clear claim to the throne of England due to his descent from King Canute, mustered his forces on the Norse island of Orkney. Duke William of Normandy worked feverishly on the Norman coast to prepare a fleet of over four hundred ships with which to attack from the south.

A good number of these vessels, according to historians, are likely to have been on loan from my cousin, Eustace of Boulogne, who was to ride beside Duke William in the heat of battle and carry his standard. Another strand of our family tree comes into the picture at Hastings. This was a Norman neighbour of Eustace's called William de Saye (from the village of Saye, near Argentan), who is described in all our medieval documents as 'companion of the Conqueror'.

Harold collected his 3,000 strong force of axe-men, or house-carls, and some 12,000 part-time soldiers (who owed the king forty days a year of armed service) and manned the beaches of the south coast. But bad weather delayed the Normans' attack and Harold's men began to wander off to tend their late summer harvests.

At this point came news that the Norwegian

army, augmented by the forces of Tostig, the disaffected exiled brother of Harold, had landed north of York. Deciding that this northern threat was the more serious, Harold force-marched his men, recruiting more en route, for 190 miles in less than five days. At the ensuing Battle of Stamford Bridge, Harold's Anglo-Danish forces thoroughly defeated the Norwegians on 25 September. Victory celebrations must have been short-lived because William's army landed at Pevensey only three days later. So Harold turned back south, his force depleted and exhausted, to meet the well prepared Norman army a few miles north of Hastings. Here he gathered his men along the crest of a hill and formed a wall of shields.

Duke William initially divided his force into three groups, with Bretons on the left, his own Norman contingent in the centre and, on the key right flank, the main force of knights and mercenaries under my cousin Eustace. Harold's army was initially successful in holding off the first Norman attacks, but then a great many of his men broke ranks to pursue the Normans back down the hill. This was a costly mistake. The best known historian's description of the great battle, the last time England was ever successfully invaded, was by William of Poitiers, chaplain to Duke William. He describes the aftermath of the error by Harold's men.

The Normans then surrounded several thousands of their pursuers and rapidly cut them down so that not one escaped. Heartened by this success, they then furiously carried their attack on to the main body of the English host, which even after their losses scarcely seemed diminished in number. The English fought confidently with all their strength . . . so closely massed together that even the dead had not space in which to fall . . . There were present in this battle: Eustace, count of Boulogne; William, count of Evreux; Geoffrey, count of Mortagnet . . . Haimo of Thouars; Rodulf of Tosny . . .

But some of those who retreated took courage to renew the struggle on more favourable ground . . . These people, descended from the ancient Saxons (the fiercest of men) are always by nature eager for battle, and they could only be brought down by the greatest valour. Had they not recently defeated with ease the King of Norway at the head of a fine army?

The duke . . . did not turn from his course when he saw these enemy troops rallying . . . Armed only with a broken lance he was more formidable than others who brandished long javelins. With a harsh voice he called to Eustace of Boulogne, who with fifty knights was turning in flight, and was about to give the signal for retreat. This man came up to the duke and said in his ear that he ought to retire since he would court death if he went forward.

If William had listened to Eustace's assessment of the situation the whole outcome of the Norman invasion might have been different. Duke William's historian continues.

But at the very moment when he uttered the words Eustace was struck between the shoulders with such force that blood gushed out from his mouth and nose, and half dead he only made his escape with the aid of his followers . . . In this dangerous phase of the battle many Norman nobles were killed . . .

The bloodstained battle-ground was covered with the flower of the youth and nobility of England. The two brothers of the king were found near him, and Harold himself stripped of all badges of honour could not be identified by his face, but only by certain marks on his body.

The Battle of Hastings and the events leading up to it are beautifully depicted on the Bayeux Tapestry, which is some two feet high by 230 feet long and is believed to have been commissioned either by William the Conqueror's wife or by his half-brother, Bishop Odo of Bayeux, or by his army chief, my cousin Eustace of Boulogne. Whoever inspired it, the tapestry disappeared for 500 years, turned up in Bayeux, was almost used as a cover for an ammunition wagon during the Civil War, and was removed to Paris by the Nazis. It is now back in its museum in Bayeux and cousin Eustace is depicted on it proffering his unheeded advice.

The Normans had arrived in style. They would make the Saxon English suffer for many a long year. As far as the family is concerned, it is at this point that we started to spend our time in England from our Boulogne base just over the Channel. The words of Daniel Defoe, in his 1703 poem 'The True-Born Englishman', are appropriate:

And here begins our ancient pedigree,
That so exalts our poor nobility:
'Tis that from some French trooper they
  derive,
Who with the Norman bastard did arrive . . .

2

STOLEN FROM THE SAXONS

Today, 934 years after the battle of Hastings,
people still believe that the French conquered
England on that fateful day in 1066. But, as we
have seen, the two countries' leaders were as
un-French and un-English as most of their soldiers.
Duke William, whose nickname back home was the
Bastard, was the great-great-grandson of Viking
raider, Hrolf, whilst King Harold Godwinson's
grandfather, Wulfnoth, had once destroyed most of
the Saxons' royal navy. It was a case of one group
of Viking vandal descendants clashing with
another, something which both groups' ancestors
had been doing all over Europe and back in their
own Scandinavian homelands for centuries.

However, the genuine Wessex Saxons in
Harold's army had been in England long enough to
claim to be English, and their royal family had
eventually, with interruptions, achieved a unique
English way of living under Edward the Confessor
and his dynastic predecessors. This fledgling
nation was to be ruthlessly disrupted by the
Normans, and it would take some 350 years before

their DNA, their customs and their language eventually emerged with those of the Romano-British, the Anglo-Saxons and the Anglo-Vikings to form an island people quite distinct from their contemporaries in France, Germany or Scandinavia. They had by then earned a name of their own, the English.

I picture liquid grey cement, representing the pre-Romano-Britons, revolving slowly in a mixer, and a pigment of imperial Roman purple being added to the mix. Then a blood-red dye to represent the Saxons and Vikings. And finally blue for the Normans. Eventually the cement attains its own distinct hue, unlike any other, and none of the separate additives are now recognisable in the hardened cement. At that point we have, for the first time, the English.

Daniel Defoe summarised this cement-mix result in 'The True-Born Englishman':

But grant the best, how came the change to
    pass,
A true-born Englishman of Norman race?
A Turkish horse can show more history,
To prove his well-descended family.
Conquest, as by the moderns it is expressed,
May give a title to the lands possessed:
But that the longest sword should be so civil
To make a Frenchman English, that's the
    devil.
These are the heroes that despise the Dutch,
And rail at new-come foreigners so much,
Forgetting that themselves are all derived
From the most scoundrel race that ever lived;
A horrid crowd of rambling thieves and

drones,
Who ransacked kingdoms and dispeopled
  towns,
The Pict and painted Briton, treacherous
  Scot,
By hunger, theft, and rapine hither brought;
Norwegian pirates, buccaneering Danes,
Whose red-haired offspring everywhere
  remains,
Who, joined with Norman-French, compound
  the breed
From whence your true-born Englishmen
  proceed.

The post-Hastings Bastard, now King of
England and Duke of Normandy, was well aware
that he could never enjoy a peaceful holiday, since
his subjects on either side of the Channel were
both troublesome by nature and constantly
threatened by their neighbours. He would have to
travel back and forth to assert his presence as
much in Rouen and Boulogne as in London and
York. The key to keeping the lid on such a
situation was to have eyes, ears and loyal allies
everywhere.

Loyalty, William knew well, was a fickle beast at
a time when neighbour fought neighbour and built
castles for fear of predatory brothers or even sons.
In Normandy he had spent his adult life at war
with ever shifting alliances in and around his duchy
and often against his official liege lord, the King of
France. So he had developed a pyramid system of
vassals, of barons, knights and serfs, which he
quickly (he did everything quickly) replicated with
brutal efficiency in England.

England's Roman, Saxon and Viking invaders had let the local leaders retain a good deal of their land and local authority, providing they paid tax to their new landlords and behaved themselves. The Norman invaders, however, intended to remove every last vestige of self-esteem and power from the natives of England. William marched his army from Hastings to London and had himself crowned King of England on Christmas Day 1066 in Westminster Abbey, even as his men burnt down Saxon homes in the vicinity.

The Norman army that remained in England the year after Hastings was made up of less than 8,000 men, but by the end of the twenty-one years of William's rule, some 5 per cent of the two million people in England were Gallic immigrants approved of or appointed by William to rule the natives with a rod of iron and by way of a rigid caste or feudal system. Many English Saxons escaped Norman oppression by emigrating, some to Nova Anglia, New England, an area which was later known as the Crimea on the Black Sea coast, and thousands responded to a recruiting drive to join the Varangian Guard of the Eastern Emperor in Constantinople.

Just as the Senate of Rome logged the name and status of each and every citizen in town, so William instituted his own census of Saxon England, the Domesday Book. His tax assessors recorded the wealth of every hamlet (some 13,000 settlements) down to the last goat and a measured tally of every productive acre, so that an unavoidable tax burden could be levied. One observer wrote at the time: 'So very narrowly did the King have his new land investigated by his inquisitors that there was no single hide nor acre of land, nor indeed . . . one ox or one cow or one pig which were left out and not recorded; and all these records were brought to him afterwards.'

Norman barons controlled the Welsh Marches, but the more inaccessible reaches of western Wales remained the land of the native British. The Scots succumbed from time to time to the Normans, but never for long, and even in southern England there were occasional revolts. One of these was spearheaded by my feisty ancestor, Count Eustace of Boulogne, who clearly felt badly treated by William, and his grievances were well known. So when the men of Kent decided to revolt while the king was abroad, they invited Eustace over with a force of Boulogners. (They knew him well due to his original fracas with Godwin thugs in Dover in 1051, which had caused Harold Godwin's temporary exile.) This was an extremely rash move, and it misfired at the outset because, although Eustace's men successfully occupied Dover town, they failed to overcome the garrison of Dover Castle. Eustace then sensibly retired back to Boulogne with his tail between his legs and, unsurprisingly, had various of his English lands forfeited by an apoplectic King William. Given to him by a grateful post-Hastings Conqueror and known as the Honour of Boulogne, they constituted a huge chunk of English land. After his failed invasion of Kent, Eustace made no further attempts to seize any part of England from King William. Some years later, and no doubt to ensure his loyalty, William gave him back most of his confiscated properties, including a huge collection of estates and manors that were part of the

14

Honour of Boulogne.

For Anglo-Saxons all over England life under the Normans grew ever more miserable. If the serfs had always had a hard life, they were now hammered into the soil. To meet the Norman levies meant toil without respite. The best land was taken from its Saxon owners and given to Normans, whether they wished to live there permanently or, like my ancestors, the Fiennes, the Sayes and the Counts of Boulogne, to be absentee landlords. Domesday reveals that half the value of all England was in the hands of a mere two hundred men, including cousin Eustace. So much rental did this earn that Eustace introduced a standard of his own into England for weighing the moneys due to him. Some statistics from the Domesday Book reveal the truly ruthless nature of William's acquisition policies. He stole 5,000 estates from their Saxon owners and gave them to his barons. By 1087 when he died, only two out of the 190 big estate owners in England were Saxons. Only a hundred out of 1,400 medium-size estates were still Saxon owned. Many small holdings were confiscated and then leased back to their owners for rental. And of the sixteen bishops in all England, fifteen were Normans.

In exchange for their huge new Saxon estates and the acquired titles that went with them, the Norman barons had to remain utterly loyal to William and provide him with a set number of armed knights whenever he needed to raise an instant army. If they failed to come up with the goods, their land was confiscated.

In 1069 the citizens of York welcomed a Danish army as liberators from the Norman tyranny, so

William rushed north to crush the rebels. His reputation alone must have impressed the Danes, for they fled before he arrived. The chronicles told of the vengeance exacted by the king: 'It was horrible to behold human corpses decaying in their houses, the streets and on the roads, swarming with worms whilst they were consumed by corruption with an abominable stench . . . There was no village inhabited between York and Durham; they became lurking places for wild beasts and robbers and were a great dread to travellers.'

The Normans in England during William's reign did not mingle or intermarry, spoke only French, tore down Saxon churches and imposed sky-high taxes. Saxons were now second-class citizens who were shunned socially by their Norman overlords. My Norman ancestors were clearly members of a nasty and arrogant bunch, and I feel, when I read about their behaviour, rather like Germans of my generation must feel about their Nazi forebears. All families have cupboard skeletons, and we had our fair share, alongside our saints and heroes.

*   *   *

The Twisleton and the Wykeham family branches stayed away from the Fienneses for quite a while, so I will concentrate at this point on Fiennes, Saye and Boulogne. The Counts of Boulogne took their name from their city, and the villages of Fiennes and Saye also became family names.

Normandy was divided into counties which waged constant war between themselves. These included Guisnes county, within which the town of

Guisnes fought against the town of Ardres. Both had a castle and an army and both had supplies of rich young heiresses of great interest to the nearby village of Fiennes. Especially to the senior family there, who had taken on the village name as their surname, a fashionable thing to do. This family had become one of the twelve top baronies of Guisnes county, and their alpha male was, at the time of King William's death, Seigneur Eustace de Fiennes. There were a lot of Eustaces about at the time, which confuses things, but this one did well on the First Crusade and, as a local hero on his return, had no difficulty gaining the very profitable hand in marriage of Dame Adele of Ardres. Their son, Conon de Fiennes (1099–1127), failed to find a wealthy bride, but his eldest son, yet another Eustace but with the nickname of 'Le Vieux', the Old, focused on Guisnes and came up with a five-star lady named Margaret, who gave birth to one of our top heiress-grabbers, Ingelram Fiennes (1134–89), who married the sole heiress of the Counts of Boulogne.

Ingelram's father, Eustace Le Vieux, squandered some of the family fortune by terminally drilling an opponent at a local jousting tournament, which was not the done thing and the equivalent today of killing a man in a boxing match. As a penance Eustace founded the magnificent, but expensive, Abbey of Beaulieu, not far from the village of Fiennes. In the year 2001 there were 821 people living in Fiennes, which is about halfway down the main road from Calais to Boulogne. Turn left at the Fiennes signpost and you will enter the region once covered by the Forest of Fiennes and overlooked by Mount

Fiennes, from which, on a clear day, you can see the coastline of England.

To keep up with Guisnes and Ardres the Fiennes family built our own modest castle in the forest in 1049. It was burnt down in 1320 but rebuilt. Then in 1543 Henry VIII of England razed it to the ground, since when our only castles have been in England.

The very first Fiennes who, according to the family, went to England and settled there was John, who fought so well at Hastings that the Bastard honoured him with the accolade of Constable of Dover Castle and Warden of the Cinque Ports. This was a hereditary title, so the next three generations of John's family proudly retained it. Sadly, a close inspection of medieval records reveals no trace of any of these four Fienneses, and the 21st Lord Saye and Sele, my cousin Nathaniel Fiennes, believes that they probably never existed but were the complex invention of one James Fiennes (the 1st Lord Saye and Sele) in the 1440s, who was, for unconnected reasons, hanged, drawn and quartered. This James was an avid social climber and by suggesting that four of his forebears were Wardens of the Cinque Ports he would have gained much prestige. If he did indeed mastermind such a fraud, it clearly worked well for him, since he eventually became Lord High Treasurer of England before his gory demise.

Going back to ancestors who definitely did exist, you will remember cousin Eustace of Boulogne who tried to persuade the Bastard to retreat during the battle of Hastings and the following year conducted his own failed invasion of England.

18

Eustace's eldest son, Geoffrey, more than made amends for his father's bad judgment by marrying the daughter of Geoffrey de Mandeville, a close companion and trusted adviser of King William who was given vast English estates stolen from the Saxons. Not only did Geoffrey win back the remainder of the lands his father had forfeited by his invasion stunt, but he further inherited, according to the Domesday records in 1086, major estates in eleven different counties. He styled himself Baron of Tingray and Lord of Clapham.

*   *   *

Meanwhile, his fellow barons resident in England were hard at work building formidable castles throughout the land from which they could dominate the locals. The most impressive of these was the Tower of London, built mostly of white stone from Caen in Normandy. From such centres, French culture was slowly but surely to become the culture of England and the way by which the new master race would eradicate the ways of the old Anglo-Saxon elite. Normandy and England were both now ruled by an aristocracy of Anglo-Normans, who moved between their estates in both countries, taxing and exploiting both sets of serfs. They were the new governing class of England, and, in the words of the contemporary historian Orderic Vitalis, 'The native inhabitants were crushed, imprisoned, disinherited, banished and scattered beyond the limits of their own country.'

The English language remained the tongue of the suppressed masses, but a well-educated Anglo-

Norman who settled in England and stayed all his life there would be trilingual. His French would be fluent, he would know church Latin and he could understand English. The fact that, 350 years later, English had become the tongue of English royalty was purely because the vast majority of the island's inhabitants spoke it and their Norman overlords made no effort to penalise those who did. Nowadays the French, threatened by 'franglais', doubtless consider this to have been an extremely bad error and missed opportunity.

Half a dozen years after Hastings, William began to spend more and more time back in Normandy fighting various of his neighbours, including the King of France and, intermittently, his own rebellious elder son, Robert. On one of these campaigns, in 1087, William died of wounds, having appointed his second son, William, King of England.

Norman records of William's deathbed words include the confession: 'I persecuted the native inhabitants of England beyond all reason. Whether nobles or commons, I cruelly oppressed them; many I unjustly disinherited; innumerable multitudes, especially in the county of York, perished through me by famine and sword . . . I am stained with the rivers of blood that I have shed.'

The Bastard was buried in Caen, so corpulent that when the attendant bishops tried to force his body into the royal sarcophagus, his entrails burst forth and the resulting pestilent stench caused panic amongst the mourners, many of whom fled the ceremony.

3

RIDING TO JERUSALEM

Despite the treasonable behaviour of his eldest son, Robert, King William left him the Duchy of Normandy. His second son, William, was speedily crowned King of England, and the third son, later to become Henry I, received 'innumerable treasures'. This turned out to be a recipe for fraternal strife and, quite possibly, murder.

The coronation of William II went ahead without immediate complaints from any meaningful party, but a powerful grouping of Anglo-Norman barons broke into open revolt in 1088. A firm reaction by King William won the day, but the unrest continued to simmer and major trouble was on the verge of exploding into civil war in 1095.

The main aim of the barons was straightforward. They wanted their king, whether Robert, William or even Henry, to be monarch of both England and Normandy. Since Robert, the eldest son, was clearly dissatisfied with his father's deathbed decision to give him the duchy not the kingdom, the barons reckoned he would cause endless trouble (and war taxes for them to stump up) until such time as he could win the crown.

Their rationale made sense. The historian Vitalis quoted the most powerful of the rebel magnates, the late king's half-brother, Odo of Bayeux, as saying, 'How can we yield good service to two distant and mutually hostile lords? If we serve Duke Robert well, we will offend his brother, William, who will confiscate our land in England. On the other hand, if we obey King William, Duke Robert will do likewise with our Norman properties.'

There would doubtless have been civil war between the two brothers sooner or later, but for Robert's personal and heroic desire to be a crusader hero. To raise a meaningful army of his own with which to carry out this ambition, he would need a great deal of money, and his surprise method of raising the funds was to sell Normandy to brother William in 1095, the year of the First Crusade.

By the time he disappeared in a cloud of dust towards the Holy Land, Robert had already lost chunks of the Bastard's hard-won French territory to the King of France. Once William II took over the duchy, he waged war on France until he had restored all his father's French territories to their former frontiers and England and Normandy were once again a single sea-split land. Known as Rufus, due to his red hair, William II ruled his dominions with the same dedicated cruelty as had his father, the Bastard. He was not religious, and treated the church with contempt as a bottomless source of taxes. Even his barons received short shrift, for he preferred to give royal favours to the captains of his mercenary armies. He never married and his court was said to squirm with 'fornicators and sodomites'. He died, most conveniently, in the year 1100, which averted the long-postponed but imminent civil war with brother Robert, who was by then on the long journey back from his highly successful crusade.

Rufus died on a New Forest stag hunt, killed by a stray arrow. These things can happen in field sports even today. But murder conspiracy tales were soon rampant, with the chief suspect being William's younger brother Henry, who happened to be hunting in the same woods on the same day. Whether implicated in the king's death or not, Henry, knowing that brother Robert was heading home from Palestine, rode post-haste to Winchester to seize the Royal Treasury and thence to Westminster Abbey, where he had himself crowned Henry I of England, on the principle that possession is nine-tenths of the law.

William II's corpse did not explode, as had his father's, but the clergy refused to bury it in royal Winchester due to the bloody and sacrilegious nature of his thirteen-year rule.

The key factor that saved England from civil war between brothers Robert and Henry was and remained the First Crusade, and my family was into crusading in a major way. The response to Pope Urban II's call to arms was not only far greater than he had expected, it also proved uncontrollable, for he had loosed a vicious genie which stirred the worst leanings of the Franks, the latent bloodlust of their Viking forebears, and their subsequent actions were to horrify the Pope. Styling themselves pilgrims, they sewed crosses on their cloaks and marched away for hundreds of miles to lands and sights beyond their wildest dreams. They came from all levels of society: monarchs, bishops, knights, peasants and clerks. Their aim was indeed to fight the forces of evil, but they were themselves a devilish brew. The advance waves of some 60,000 fighting men, many with their families in tow, set out for the East in the spring of 1096 and, that autumn, another 100,000 in five armies followed their trail. Among their leaders were the charismatic preacher Peter the Hermit and the robber baron Count Emich from Germany, notorious for his cruelty, in charge of 20,000 men.

Peter the Hermit's message to aspiring crusaders was as anti-Semitic as anti-Muslim and posed the point that to march thousands of miles to kill the Antichrist in Jerusalem made no sense if you spared the killers of Christ, the Jews, back home. So the likes of Count Emich's army conducted widespread purges in Germany before their crusading marches began. Jews whose families had lived peacefully in their European homes for centuries were offered a choice of baptism or death. Most chose the latter and were burnt to cinders. Many family members killed each other to prevent any abandonment of the faith. All over Europe, wherever a crusading army gathered together, its first act was to kill any Jews within reach.

The first army to leave France in the summer of 1096 was led by two members of the family of my ancestors, Godfrey de Bouillon and his brother Baldwin de Boulogne. Their parents were Eustace de Boulogne (of Hastings and Dover fame) and his wife Ida of Bouillon. Being direct descendants of Charlemagne helped Godfrey and Baldwin as leaders of often fractious armies of proud Franks. Cousin Godfrey's background was military with a good deal of campaigning against the Pope during a papal war with the Bouillon region, a complex affair which even involved Godfrey fighting battles in Italy.

However, when the Pope proclaimed the crusade, Godfrey signed up and mortgaged much of his property to pay for the 40,000 knights and foot soldiers he would command. Many were armed mercenary bands of Germans, Walloons and Flemings. His army moved with speed and efficiency. In Hungary, like many other crusader leaders, he had trouble preventing his men from pillaging from the locals, their fellow Christians. But he still arrived at Constantinople in the vanguard and was the first crusader general to take an oath to the Byzantine Emperor who ruled there. Other lesser leaders heading for the Holy Land that summer included Eustace Fiennes, the husband of Dame Adele of Ardres, and Seigneur of the Fiennes Castle. Eustace was twenty-six years old.

For two years the crusaders fought the Muslim occupants of the Holy Land, many of whom were Fatimids from Egypt. Godfrey and Baldwin were at the forefront of the fighting, alongside Count Raymond of Toulouse, another Frank. In 1098 they successfully laid siege to Edessa, where Baldwin of Boulogne remained as commandant. Later in the year they took the major city of Antioch, where Godfrey fell out with some of the other leaders. He remained there whilst most of the army moved on south down the Mediterranean coast. For a while the local Sunni Arabs offered no resistance, for they feared the Fatimids, who were Shias, more than they feared the Christians.

Godfrey joined his army to that of William II's brother, Duke Robert. Together they reached Tripoli in early May, then on to Beirut, Jaffa and

Bethlehem. On 6 June they came at last to Jerusalem and learnt that the Fatimid commandant had poisoned nearby springs, burnt crops and expelled all Christians from the city. The gathered crusaders had struggled in all weathers from towns as far away as York or Hamburg, but they were still a long way from victory as they gazed at the high walls of the Holy City, the final goal of their long march. They had yet to cleanse Jerusalem of the Devil.

It is a sad reflection on human nature that Muslims, Christians and Jews, despite sharing the origins of their religions as People of the Book, have spent so much energy over so many centuries trying to eliminate each other, and are still at it today.

The crusaders, led by men of varying degrees of religious fervour or none, clearly believed that the only good Muslims were dead ones. The siege wore on through the hot month of June. Ladder-scaling attacks failed as boiling oil, rocks and flaming arrows rained down from the Fatimids along the battlements. The Egyptians' rigorous scorched-earth policy carried out over a wide area outside the city walls proved effective, and the crusaders' food supplies dwindled so that speedy success became critical. They convened a council and decided to build mobile siege towers. There was no available wood as the Fatimids had taken care to burn all nearby forests, but the timbers of two Genoese ships that had recently brought the crusaders some supplies were torn apart and three attack-towers were fashioned, which proved crucial in finally breaking the siege on 15 July 1099.

The Franks, with cousin Godfrey and his knights

leading the way, swarmed through the city, hacking the inhabitants to death. Nobody but the garrison commander and his personal escort was spared. Blood, according to one participant, the chronicler Fulk, sloshed ankle-high around the corpse heaps in the stone alleys of the city. Fulk wrote:

At the noon hour with trumpets sounding and with great commotion, the frenzied Franks broke into the city, and the pagans, demoralized, began to flee. Some Saracens, Arabs and Ethiopians fled to the tower of David, others to the temple of Solomon, where a great battle followed. They could not escape our gladiators. Those who fled to the roof were shot by arrows. Some ten thousand were killed in this temple alone. We spared the life of none of them, neither woman nor child.

During this massacre, cousin Godfrey stripped off his armour and walked unarmed and barefoot through the carnage to pray in the Church of the Holy Sepulchre.

After the last inhabitant lay dead or herded into groups ideal for slavery, the crusaders plundered the empty houses. Fulk wrote:

They took whatever they found. Thus many poor men became rich. Our footmen discovered the Saracens had swallowed gold coins. So they burnt great heaps of bodies so that the stomachs and intestines of the dead released the precious metal into the human ashes. Afterwards the clergy went chanting to the Lord's glorious temple. It was the eleven hundredth year of our Lord when the people of Gaul, the Franks in their might, took the city, 285 years after the death of Charlemagne and twelve years from the death of William I of England.

The crusaders counted over 40,000 Muslim corpses after the massacre. They herded all the Jewish survivors together into one of the synagogues and burnt every last one to death. Then they all gathered in the Church of the Holy Sepulchre to give thanks.

Of their various army leaders, the crusaders selected cousin Godfrey to be Jerusalem's new ruler. He nominated the city as capital of the whole country, and was installed as the first 'Christian King of the crusader Kingdom of Jerusalem'. Over the next year he forced the Saracen strongholds of Ascalon, Arsuf and Caesarea into submission and rebuilt the city of Jaffa as a port of arrival for crusader reinforcements. In 1100 he died, struck by an arrow according to Arab legend, but more likely by one of the many exotic diseases rife at the time.

By the end of the twelfth century cousin Godfrey was a legend among crusader descendants all over Europe. Tasso made Godfrey the hero of his epic poem *Gerusalemme Liberata*. In his *Divine Comedy*, Dante sees the spirit of Godfrey in the Heaven of Mars with other 'warriors of the faith'. Godfrey is depicted in Handel's opera *Rinaldo* as Goffredo. In 1848 a statue of him was erected in the Royal Square in central Brussels, as Godfrey was born on the Belgium side of the French border and in 2005 he was voted seventeenth in the Greatest Belgian contest, a public vote of national heroes in French-speaking Belgium.

When he died, his title of King of Jerusalem passed to his warrior brother, Baldwin of Boulogne, which kept the Holy City in the family for a while longer.

4

A KING'S RANSOM

When King William II died in the New Forest, his brother Robert became the rightful heir to the throne of England. But Robert was in the wrong place at the wrong time, being on his way back home from the capture of Jerusalem, which gave younger brother Henry his chance to leap in. Henry I, nicknamed Henry Beauclerc because of his learned ways, was the first King of England to speak English fluently.

Just a few weeks after Henry's coronation, Robert arrived back in Normandy, flushed with his crusading successes. Most of England's Anglo-Norman barons supported his claim to the throne, but a powerful minority, as well as the leaders of the church, preferred Henry. Civil war was only averted by the cunning politics of Henry. Robert would keep Normandy and be paid the huge annual sum of £2,000 by the king.

Fearing that, despite this agreement, brother Robert would sooner or later gather forces and funds sufficient to invade England, Henry set about enfeebling those barons known to support Robert, such as the powerful Marcher lords, the Mortimer family who straddled the Welsh border. He then began to woo the loyalty of many of the magnates (who William Rufus had alienated) by increasing their lands or handing out titles and other favours. He married Matilda, the daughter of a Scottish noble with no Norman blood, who bore him a son and a daughter. He later became infamous for extra-marital activities, resulting in over twenty illegitimate children, including a number of daughters who were to prove extremely useful when Henry needed to neutralise potential rivals. At least seven of Henry's bastard daughters were married off to likely threats, such as the King of Scotland and various French regional dukes. The historian, William of Malmesbury, summed up this royal tactic as sex 'for politics not pleasure'. One hopes Matilda found this an acceptable practice.

By 1106 Henry was ready to deal with brother Robert, so he invaded Normandy and, at the Battle of Tinchebray, captured him and took over the duchy. England and Normandy once again shared the same ruler, and Henry ensured that Robert would never again be a threat by locking him up in Cardiff Castle, where he learnt Welsh from his jailer and died twenty-eight years later. Some say he was murdered.

One of Henry's contemporaries wrote of him: 'God endowed him with three gifts, wisdom, victory and riches, but these were offset by three vices, avarice, cruelty and lust.' An example of his cruelty was when, at the tender age of twenty-one, he took a rebellious citizen of Rouen up a castle tower and threw him out of the window to his death on the cobbles far below.

After taking Normandy from Robert, Henry spent less and less time in England, which was possible thanks to the efficient and sophisticated system of government he left there, especially the apparatus for gathering the taxes he needed for his wars with Normandy's ever-aggressive neighbours. These included the King of France and the Counts of both Anjou and Flanders.

Keen that his only legitimate son, William, should be his heir, he had him groomed and educated to that end. In 1120 the king, his heir and many senior barons sailed back to England after a campaign. Young William sailed on the speedy 'White Ship' and handed out generous supplies of wine to the crew. Racing to catch up with the king's vessel, the White Ship's skipper hit a rock in the dark and only one passenger survived to describe the death of Henry's heir.

Henry's final years were heavily involved with his attempts to secure the succession of his dynasty for his surviving, legitimate child, his daughter the Empress Matilda. On her husband the Emperor's death and under threat from powerful forces in Flanders, he secured a new marriage deal for her with the Count of Anjou's heir, Geoffrey Plantagenet. The marriage went ahead, but without the approval of many of the Anglo-Norman barons, so when, in 1135, Henry suddenly died of food poisoning in Normandy, my ancestors in Boulogne were able to stir up big trouble. Let me explain.

Henry had a favourite nephew to whom he had given land and great wealth, Count Stephen of

Blois, Matilda's first cousin, who clearly planned to grab nice uncle Henry's throne as soon as he died. The fact that Henry was not all that far from Boulogne when he died of food poisoning, and so news of his demise reached Stephen quickly, and that Queen-to-be Matilda was away with her husband Geoffrey in distant Anjou, all added up to a wonderfully coincidental opportunity for Stephen to hop on a speedy ship from Boulogne to London, where he knew he had the key support of the magnates. This worked well and Stephen, the grandson of William the Conqueror but nonetheless a clear usurper of the crown which Henry I had appointed for his daughter Matilda, was duly crowned King of England. He claimed that Henry had actually changed his mind on his deathbed and named him, Stephen, as heir. Very cheeky.

Where my relations enter the story is through the Counts of Boulogne. Cousin Eustace had three sons. We have met the two who went crusading but not his eldest son, Eustace III, who married Princess Mary of Scotland (the daughter of King Malcolm III) and produced a daughter confusingly also called Matilda, who in 1125 married Count Stephen of Blois, who ten years later usurped the English crown.

This not only makes Eustace's daughter the Queen of England, but it also complicates any précis of the next few years of English history by giving both the chief contenders for the crown the same name. To get round this confusing issue, I will follow the historians in calling my ancestor King Stephen's wife and loyal supporter, Queen Matilda, whilst Henry I's daughter and legitimate heir to his throne, is the Empress Matilda. At the time of Stephen's seizure of the crown, our Matilda was heavily pregnant with yet another Eustace of Boulogne. A few months later she joined Stephen in London and was crowned his queen.

Stephen set about the difficult job of placating his many and various enemies in England and France, doing everything he could to avoid open warfare. He allowed powerful barons to get away with murder and, even worse, to steal lands considered to be under royal ownership. To keep his rival and cousin, Empress Matilda, quiet, he accepted highly unfavourable terms in a treaty with her husband, Geoffrey Plantagenet of Anjou. In England he weakly gave way to all those with local pretensions to power. Anarchy ruled throughout the land, well portrayed in the Anglo-Saxon Chronicle.

> When the traitors perceived that he was a mild man, and a soft, and a good, and that he did not enforce justice, they did all wonder. They had done homage to him, and sworn oaths, but they no faith kept; all became forsworn, and broke their allegiance, for every rich man built his castles, and defended them against him, and they filled the land full of castles. They greatly oppressed the wretched people by making them work at these castles, and when the castles were finished they filled them with devils and evil men . . . never was there more misery, and never acted heathens worse than these. At length they spared neither church nor

33

churchyard, but they took all that was valuable therein, and then burned the church and all together. Neither did they spare the lands of bishops, nor of abbats, nor of priests; but they robbed the monks and the clergy, and every man plundered his neighbour as much as he could. If two or three men came riding to a town, all the township fled before them, and thought that they were robbers. The bishops and clergy were ever cursing them, but this to them was nothing, for they were all accursed and forsworn, and reprobate. The earth bare no corn, you might as well have tilled the sea, for the land was all ruined by such deeds, and it was said openly that Christ and his saints slept. These things, and more than we can say, did we suffer during nineteen years because of our sins.

This horrific state of affairs had already begun when Empress Matilda arrived in England to claim her throne in 1139. At the time of her arrival, Stephen was in a good position to seize and imprison her, but instead of confronting her feeble force with his army, he merely had her escorted to the south-west to Bristol, the seat of her brother, Robert of Gloucester. From then on there were, to all intents, two rival royal courts in England. Matilda and her brother began at once to ferment rebellion wherever they could. Civil war would ravage the land for the next nine years.

Empress Matilda's forces soon held sway in most of the west country, and in 1141 at the battle of Lincoln her forces captured King Stephen, imprisoning him in Bristol, her headquarters.

Stephen's fickle brother, Henry of Blois, the papal legate, went over to Empress Matilda's side and helped her gain the key support of London—just. A few weeks later Stephen was deposed and the empress entered London in triumph.

Cousin Matilda of Boulogne, aka the queen, surrounded herself in this time of trouble with her close family, including cousin Faramus of Boulogne, putting him in charge of the royal family affairs as Comptroller of the Household, whilst Stephen languished in jail. She then rallied as great a force of loyalists as she could in the short time that remained before the date when the empress, then styled by a clerical council as 'the Lady of the English', was to be officially crowned in Westminster Abbey.

Fortunately for Stephen and Queen Matilda, the empress was hoist by her own rapacious petard. In no time at all, and ignoring the peace conditions laid down by the papal legate to woo the Londoners, she squandered their support so that when Queen Matilda's force arrived and marched towards the city, the Londoners took up arms and forced the empress out. She was soon captured, but escaped by riding away from her captors at full speed, sitting astride like a man.

Stalemate ensued until, later that year, Robert of Gloucester, chief ally and brother to the empress, was captured by loyalists. She had no choice but to agree to a prisoner swap. The king for her brother. In double quick time the deposed Stephen was re-crowned at Canterbury Cathedral and the civil war flickered on in a see-saw fashion. The empress, as brave as she was proud, became quite a legend when she escaped Stephen's men on two further occasions: once from Devizes dressed up as a dead body, and then in 1142 from Oxford Castle 'gliding over the snows in a pure white gown'.

The trouble with civil wars is you find you have family on both sides. Two of my relatives, William de Saye and his brother-in-law Geoffrey de Mandeville, the Earl of Essex, were loyal soldiers of the empress, but both were killed in 1141 when attacking King Stephen's fortress at Burwell, near Cambridge. William's son Geoffrey de Saye may have been a chip off the old block when described as, *'vir in armis strenuus sed in mundanis rebus minus sapiens et incircumspectus'*, meaning 'strong as a fighter but thick and rash in worldly matters'.

Stephen was grateful to those of his wife's relations who had remained loyal during his time in prison, and cousin Faramus, made Constable of Dover Castle and Warden of the Cinque Ports, was given lands in England which later ended up with his Fiennes descendants. Our family still owns a watercolour dated 1837, before Dover Castle was extensively rebuilt, showing the Fiennes Tower.

Over in Jerusalem meanwhile, a half century had passed since the victorious First Crusade. Cousins Godfrey and Baldwin de Boulogne, successive rulers of the city, were long gone, and Saracen raiders were overrunning crusader lands. When in 1144 the Pope called for a new crusade, Stephen wisely stayed out of it, but some 50,000 French and German crusaders, at vast cost to their nations' coffers, finally reached Damascus in 1147. Meeting a superior Muslim force before they could even begin their conquest plans, they were forced into an ignominious retreat.

This failed crusade did have an indirect effect on English history because, by sod's law, both the beautiful French Queen Eleanor of Aquitaine and her husband's uncle were on the crusade and had an affair, which naturally upset the King of France, who divorced his wife. Eleanor, clearly not a woman to waste time, married again eight weeks after the divorce, the then main rival of King Stephen of England, Henry, the son of Empress Matilda.

Henry had control of both Anjou and Normandy and now, by marrying Eleanor, also Aquitaine. Encouraged and financed by the feisty Eleanor, Henry took his army to England in 1152. There he found an ongoing situation of stalemate between pro- and anti-Stephen barons, which seemed insoluble until, in 1153, Stephen's eldest son and heir, Eustace of Boulogne, died suddenly.

The long drawn out civil war and resultant anarchy which had so ravaged England for nearly two decades had made most of the barons on both sides keen for peace, and a treaty was signed between the two contenders for the throne: one the grandson of Henry I, the other his nephew. It was agreed that Stephen, by then a sick and weary man, would keep the crown until he died and that Henry would be his heir. Stephen died of a heart attack a year later and Henry II took the throne. His father's family name of Plantagenet now became that of the English monarchy, a dynasty that would rule through fourteen kings over three hundred years.

From a family point of view, the close relationship of Faramus with King Stephen, through his wife Matilda, had for the first time given us a solid base and extensive lands in England to add to those in Boulogne. But a likely problem, common to all times of leadership change, was that the new King Henry would wield a new broom to sweep out the favourites of his predecessor and give their lands to his own cronies. Faramus ran that risk.

*   *   *

Henry II was the most powerful monarch in all Europe, with territory stretching between the borders of Scotland and Spain. Indeed, he ruled far more of France itself than did its nominal king. He established reforms of government and is still regarded by many historians as the founder of English common law. Henry II fathered eight children with his beautiful wife Eleanor, who had been accused by her previous husband, the King of France, of being barren. But his four sons were truly a Devil's brood, as nasty as their father was clearly likeable.

Richard, the eldest, later called Richard Lionheart, was happy only when at war. The fourth and last son, John, was born when his mother was forty-five, by which time Henry had already willed all his vast territories to his three elder sons. He nicknamed him John Lackland, which must have seriously irked the lad. In 1185 he was promised Ireland—a poisoned chalice if ever there was one. All four sons caused Henry trouble throughout his highly successful thirty-four year reign. On occasions Richard fought alongside his father against his brothers. The middle two died in 1183 and 1186 which cleared the ground, but not enough for Richard who correctly feared the king preferred his younger brother John and might will him the throne. In 1189 he allied himself with the French king and defeated Henry's army at the Battle of Ballans, forcing his father to name him officially as heir apparent.

A twist in the tail of this whole sorry family saga was when, not long after Ballans, as a sick Henry lay dying at his castle in nearby Chinon, he learnt that son John, his favourite, had secretly allied himself with his enemies. Despite his highly successful reign, both in military and in governmental terms, he died an unhappy man. Even his wife Eleanor betrayed him and plotted with their sons against him. He had her imprisoned and thereafter, according to well documented legends, kept his mistress, Rosamund Clifford, hidden within a forested labyrinth at Woodstock in Oxfordshire where Queen Eleanor's agents eventually tracked her down and had her poisoned.

Henry never cleansed his court nor the baronage of the favourites of his predecessor and longtime rival, the late King Stephen. So cousin Faramus lost none of the privileges gained through Stephen's patronage. Indeed, he remained a favourite of King Henry, who granted his daughter, Sibyl of Boulogne, many rich estates in England, including those of Ash, Martock and Widdicombe in Somerset. Faramus also retained lordship of Clapham and Carshalton in Surrey. Faramus, like other Anglo-Normans, still spent a good deal of time in France, where he was a close friend and adviser of Stephen's surviving son, William of Boulogne.

Since Sibyl was the only surviving child of

Faramus, she inherited much land in England and France, which all passed on her marriage to her husband, Ingelram de Fiennes, the son of Eustace le Vieux, who founded Beaulieu Abbey in penance for killing a jousting opponent. Thanks to Ingelram, the Boulogne inheritance was now subsumed into the Fiennes family. It would require a few more decades for us to take over the Sayes.

*   *   *

The year before Henry died, the Holy Roman Emperor led the Third Crusade to the Holy Land to rescue Jerusalem from Saladin. The siege of the coastal port of Acre early in 1189 became one of the longest sieges in history and killed at least three of my ancestors. Over the next three years of siege and counter-siege and squabbles among the crusader leaders the situation in the Holy Land was at stalemate. The tide finally changed in favour of the crusaders when, in the summer of 1191, fresh armies arrived, including a hundred ships and 8,000 men, led by the English King Richard I who, three years earlier, had succeeded his father, Henry. Richard's entire adult life had involved fighting, very often against his father and brothers as well as the King of France, and the crusaders could have found no better military leader to pit against the wily Saladin.

Richard's crusader knights included Sir Ingelram Fiennes, his cousin Tougebrand Fiennes, and John Fiennes. All were killed during the crusade and John's family gave the land in England where they buried his heart to the citizens of London; a place now known as Finsbury Square.

Richard sent envoys to Saladin once he was sure the 5,000-strong Acre garrison was on its last legs following a major battle on 11 July. Saladin agreed to surrender the city on various conditions, and Richard's victorious armies entered the gates. At this point an apparently minor squabble occurred when Richard noticed the flag of Leopold, Duke of Austria flying over the city. He had it torn down, since he believed the Austrians had done little to help during the siege. Leopold's revenge was later to affect English history.

Saladin agreed to swap 1,600 Christian prisoners for 2,700 of the captured garrison but, when the return of some of the Christian leaders was delayed, Richard massacred over 2,000 prisoners, including many women and children, the story of which act of cruelty was told and retold by Muslims down the centuries.

Acre became the new capital of the crusaders in the Holy Land, and Richard went on to other major victories against Saladin's forces. Jerusalem, however, remained in Muslim hands. Acre would remain a Christian redoubt for one hundred years until 1291 when a force of Egyptian troops attacked and massacred the garrison. A few months later the last of the Crusaders was driven from the Holy Land.

During his ten-year reign, King Richard I of England, who spoke only French, spent just six months in England. Yet for his derring-do he has become, like King Arthur and Robin Hood, a romantic and essentially English hero. Does he deserve such reverence? His reign began with the sorry death of his father Henry II, an extremely good king, to whom he had behaved with determined disloyalty for many years.

Richard was crowned in Westminster Abbey, and the ceremony sparked a London mob to attack the local Jews. They knew the new king was off to save Jerusalem and, like crusade-enthusiasts all over Europe, they confused Muslims with Jews; all Christ-killers from their warped viewpoint. Richard's reaction was revealing. He had the London Jew-killers executed and allowed one Jew, who had survived by submission to conversion, to return to his own religion. This and his consistent treatment of both Jews and Muslims throughout his reign showed that he was neither anti-Semitic nor anti-Islam. The Jews were simply better than other Europeans at lending money, and the Muslims were merely another military enemy like, often enough, the French.

After Richard's successful siege of Saladin's forces at Acre, his army headed towards the main target of Jerusalem, harassed all the way by the Saracens, by thirst, disease, great heat, snakes, spiders and scorpions. Over the next year his men advanced twice to within sight of the Holy City but retreated on both occasions as they were too weak to take it.

It was time for Richard to cut his losses, particularly as back home his former partner in arms, the wily King Philip of France, was in cahoots with Richard's treacherous younger brother John. Philip wanted to expel the English from Normandy. John wanted the English throne. So Richard negotiated the Treaty of Jaffa with Saladin in 1192 which allowed Christian pilgrims safe entry to the Holy City in future. This was not exactly a triumph but it was better than nothing and the king set off to sort out home affairs.

Forced by a storm to land near Venice, he decided to travel overland via Austria to avoid hostile French territory. All went well until the royal party were recognised not far from Vienna and word of their presence reached Leopold, Duke of Austria. His men captured and imprisoned Richard, demanding a fortune in ransom money for his release. The politics of Europe were complex, and the Emperor of Germany soon paid up a large sum in order to gain a much larger one from the next bidder. Richard then languished in a German castle for some eighteen months, during which time John tried hard to ferment rebellion in England, whilst Philip successfully took over big chunks of Richard's French empire.

The German emperor set the ransom at the equivalent of three tons of silver, or the total of three years of England's entire tax yields. Luckily for Richard, this was an amount that Philip and John, who would have loved to have transferred Richard into a French prison for life, could not sensibly afford. Somehow Richard's agents in England raised enough tax to pay the ransom and Richard agreed to an oath of alliance with his emperor captor. Once the money was handed over, Richard would be released.

A trusted group of barons under Chancellor William Longchamp, the bishop Richard had left in charge of his government in England, travelled to Germany in February 1194 with the ransom chests. My ancestor William de Saye II, his son Geoffrey and his father-in-law Geoffrey de Mandeville escorted the ransom out and the king back.

After a tumultuous English welcome, a re-crowning ceremony, a day's hunting in Sherwood Forest where, myth has it, he greeted Robin Hood, and a remarkably generous pardon of his treacherous brother John, Richard was off to Normandy to sort out his nemesis, King Philip of France. Both Geoffreys went too and stayed with him for his next four years of warfare, diplomacy, bribery and force of personality, by the end of which he had regained from the French king almost all the territory he had lost during his eighteen months in prison.

In the spring of 1199, during a minor siege operation, Richard was hit by a crossbow bolt and died of gangrene poisoning. He left his empire to his brother John, who had fought beside him over the past four years, together with three-quarters of his fortune. The rest he willed to loyal members of his retinue and to the needy. Although he spent a mere six months of his ten-year reign in England, he had selected a group of mostly brilliant ministers to govern in his absence. Despite the heavy taxation imposed to fund his crusading and Normandy campaigns, and despite the best efforts of John to cause trouble, the majority of the barons remained loyal to their absent king, and a highly efficient system of central government developed that was the envy of Europe.

'ACROSS THE REEDS AT RUNNYMEDE'

King John is portrayed by many teachers of English history as the worst of our kings by far—lecherous, treacherous, ugly and cruel. He had his men locate the money hoards of Jews by extracting their teeth, one by one, until they came clean and coughed up. On his accession he had only one obvious family rival, his twelve-year-old nephew Arthur, whose support lay with the barons of the Anjou region. At first Philip of France was friendly and the two kings signed a treaty of no interference the one with the other. But neither man trusted the other, and in 1202 the French armies poured into Normandy and Philip declared that the rest of John's lands in France were henceforward the property of Arthur.

John, with an army of mercenaries, managed to defeat and imprison his nephew in a tactical campaign worthy of his brother Richard, and gained some territory at the same time. But not for long. Philip's pressure was constant, and John resorted to murder, for he could see no chance of peace whilst Arthur still lived. History does not record quite how young Arthur died, but monastic chronicles relate that John ordered the baron in charge of the prison to blind and castrate the child and when this order was ignored, John himself, after a drunken dinner, murdered his nephew and dragged his body, lashed to a rock, into the Seine, where it was later found and recognised by a fisherman.

Philip gnawed away at the rest of John's Norman lands until, by the end of 1208, all Normandy was French, save for the Channel Islands. John, based back in England, reacted by confiscating the English lands of those who had accepted Philip as their king, an act which turned many of them from ambivalence towards him to outright hostility.

More to the point, he fell foul of the Pope, not the first English King to do so and by no means the last. John's choice for the prime job of Archbishop of Canterbury clashed with the Pope's nominee and, when John refused to accept the latter, the Pope excommunicated John and thus the English church for the next five years. This meant no official weddings, funerals or baptisms in churches, but nobody seemed to mind much.

Philip's invasion plans, now blessed by Rome, grew sufficiently ominous to alarm John into submitting to the Pope and even, in 1215, taking an oath to lead a papally-blessed crusade. This adroit move made England a bad place to invade if you feared, as the French did, papal wrath. Free from excommunication, John took his mercenaries back to France, where he did well for a while, but then suffered a catastrophic loss to Philip's forces at the battle of Bouvines. With very little land left outside England, John had no choice but to agree to a five-year truce with Philip and, back home, to concentrate on the threat of a major rebellion by hostile barons. There were several reasons for their unease, especially after John's major defeat in France.

Since the Norman Conquest, Anglo-Norman

barons, including my Fiennes, Boulogne and Saye ancestors, had happily owned lands in and received annual income from various parts of England, whilst mostly basing themselves in Normandy. Now that their ancestral homes on the continent were owned by the French king, they had to make up their minds. Some stayed in France and lost their English properties, whilst others became solely English and wound up their affairs in Normandy.

Many officials who had enjoyed positions of power in Norman castles now headed for England and found a job shortage, which was exacerbated by John's habit of preferring jobs for his boys, meaning the officers of his many mercenary groups from various parts of France. To these foreigners he gave key castles, shires and other rich pickings.

The severance with Normandy also caused many barons to refuse to supply John with soldiers to fight outside England. This included involvement in the Fourth Crusade, which John had avoided and which had a poor attendance by the English. My ancestor Ingelram Fiennes I, the son of Eustace le Vieux, did join a Flemish contingent under Philip of Flanders and took his son, Thomas Fiennes, with him. This was a sad waste of Fiennes blood on a worse than pointless cause.

This Fourth Crusade was a shameful business. It was not even fought to kill Muslims or to recapture Jerusalem. The crusaders didn't get that far. Instead they set about destroying their fellow Christians, the Greek orthodox church in Constantinople. Ingelram disappeared during the crusade, and I imagine Thomas did too, since no record was ever traced of what exactly happened to either of them.

On the more positive side of military matters, John is often credited (as are three or four other kings) with having founded the English navy. Knowing that Philip was preparing a fleet to invade England, John had his own custom-built ships made in various ports and, in 1213, destroyed a major part of all Philip's navy with a surprise attack on the harbour of Damme, near modern-day Bruges. He seized three hundred French ships, a goodly haul for no loss of life.

John also built up an alliance with those French and Flemish coastal fiefs that had proved friendly to previous English kings. The most important of them was clearly Boulogne, the land of my ancestors. William Fiennes, grandson of Sibyl of Boulogne, had recently married Agnes de Danmartin, the sister of Count Renaud of Boulogne, and the count was a key ally of the English who, a year before the attack on Damme, came to London and paid homage to King John.

Philip was aware that the Counts of Boulogne were traditional anglophiles and, therefore, a weak French link and thought to put this right by marrying into the family. Arrangements were at one point made for his marriage to Maud of Boulogne, but the Boulogne marriage never came to fruition and, since the province was key to his plans for the invasion of England, Philip invited Count Renaud of Boulogne to a meeting at Vernon to woo him as an ally. This failed to work, for Renaud and his neighbour, the Count of Flanders, both visited King John in Lambeth in 1212 and again in 1214 and pledged themselves to a coalition with him. Philip's army attacked the Count of Flanders, but thanks to cousin Renaud's firm alliance with John, Philip never gained the best harbours for an invasion of England.

Early that year, John began to find out exactly which of the English-based barons he could count on. William Fiennes, Baron of Martock in Somerset, was a loyal supporter but John nonetheless reserved the power to take any Fiennes properties away at any time. William had been granted Martock in the first place as a favour from William of Boulogne, the son of King Stephen. But William, like many other barons, although a natural loyalist, was unhappy about the way he was so heavily taxed. So he wavered.

His cousin and friend, the hugely wealthy Geoffrey de Mandeville, Earl of Essex, was, however, virulently anti-John and, along with the Bishop of Hereford, sparked off a civil war by marching on the royalist castle at Northampton on 2 May 1215.

John, with his professional mercenary army, could have crushed the rebels at that point, and the Northampton garrison held out with ease. But John had no wish to provoke trouble, so he offered the rebels the chance of arbitration via a court with four of their men and four of his, plus a papal deputy to chair the event. He further promised to arrest none of them nor confiscate their land. He then offered the two leaders, de Mandeville and the Bishop of Hereford, personal olive branches, by promising to withdraw the huge fines he had recently imposed on them. Both men turned down the king's offer, for they and their rebel colleagues had the bit between their teeth and were spoiling for a fight. Two days later John ordered their estates to be seized, and the civil war began.

*　　　*　　　*

The general conception of many people today is that King John and his immediate cronies, with mercenary support, faced the massed aristocracy of England, but this is not the reality. At the time only forty barons and their vassals supported the rebels, and they came from different, often dispersed counties. Fathers, sons and brothers were in many cases split for or against the rebels. Even William Marshall, England's most respected warrior and statesman, loyal at all times to his monarch, had a son amongst the rebels.

The king's support came largely from the south-west and the midlands, but the most influential group were neutralists who, through the Archbishop of Canterbury, hoped to avoid war through discussion. Things may well have been different if John had had some dynastic rival hovering in the wings, but his own two sons were mere children, and no other figurehead existed for the rebels to promote. So they championed a new focus for their uprising; a people's charter, to right the wrongs to which they had been subjected by John, by Richard and by Henry II, mainly through unbearably heavy taxation for the endless Plantagenet wars.

John's patience grew thin, and he called up more mercenaries, this time from Wales, but after the rebels had occupied London William Marshall and the Archbishop of Canterbury rode back and forth between king and rebels to effect a meeting and a truce. This eventually worked in the form of an agreed safe passage for all concerned to a wide

50

Thames-side meadow called Runnymede.

The meeting began on a glorious June day, and some say a thousand people attended. The twenty-five barons' or signatories' self-appointed task was to gain the king's agreement, seal and subsequent adherence to their charter of rights. Peace, it was hoped by the neutralists, would be the result. John hoped merely to gain time by affixing his seal and then ignoring it. The barons, believing he would either refuse to sign or sign and then renege, were ready for battle to follow.

The charter, possibly the work of the archbishop himself and his legal advisers, formed a legal and constitutional document which bound the king and all his successors to fully respect the liberties of his subjects, as stated in the charter's sixty-three clauses. These included forty-nine specific grievances. Once the full text had been prepared in the Royal Chancery and sealed with the Royal Seal, copies of this Magna Carta were sent out all over the land.

Four of the originals survive to this day, two in the British Library, one in Salisbury, and the other in Lincoln Cathedral. In 1987, the two hundredth anniversary of the American constitution, the Dean of Lincoln, my cousin Oliver Fiennes, younger brother of Lord Saye and Sele and descendant of the signatory Baron Saye, arranged to exhibit his cathedral's eight hundred-year-old copy of the charter all over the United States, where (since it forms the basis of the American Bill of Rights) it received great acclaim and interest. Cousin Oliver raised funds for Lincoln Cathedral on the side by selling tea imported by the very firm whose tea had been thrown into Boston Harbour back in 1773.

Cynics like to point out that the barons were actually only wanting an agreement to preserve their own baronial rights and to hell with the serfs. This is, of course, true, and the three members of my family who were signatories at Runnymede would surely agree and see nothing wrong with that. They were the rebel leader, Geoffrey de Mandeville, Henri de Bohun of Hereford and Baron Geoffrey de Saye (who had helped ransom King Richard from the Germans eleven years earlier).

The cynics notwithstanding, the Magna Carta, as the charter came to be called, is recognised worldwide as being the most significant and earliest influence on the historical process which led to the rule of constitutional law today. Government must be responsible to the governed. It also famously proclaimed: 'We will sell to no man, we will not deny or defer to any man either justice or right.'

It is still referred to in the twenty-first century as the bedrock of various legal arguments. In the year 2003, in the international court case of the Chagos islanders, compulsorily removed from their islands by Britain to facilitate the US military base on Diego Garcia, the islanders' counsel used the argument of 'unlawful exile', which he claimed was 'based on rights derived from Magna Carta'.

On leaving Runnymede the cunning John sent messages to the Pope complaining about the barons' infringement of his rights as the Pope's man in England, and in due course received exactly the papal reply he had hoped for which completely annulled the charter, 'this shameful and demeaning agreement, forced upon the King by violence and fear', and threatened anyone who might impede King John's papally-approved royal powers.

John had clearly signed and sealed Magna Carta under duress, and English custom as well as the law recognised that oaths taken in such a manner were meaningless. The majority of the barons in the country were not at Runnymede and would have been shocked, if they had been, by the revolutionary nature of the conditions forced on their king by the charter. There was also a large section of the aristocracy with personal and dynastic interests which dictated their loyalty to the monarch and to his young son and heir.

The man with a weak but existing link to the throne, who the rebels now chose to support, was King Philip of France's son Prince Louis, who built up a fleet across the Channel. John also sent for more mercenary troops from the continent to strengthen his army. By September 1215, awaiting his new troops at Dover, John listed the barons he believed to be on his side, including Baron William Fiennes. William had, however, decided to join the standard of Prince Louis, so John had him blacklisted as 'being with the King's enemies' and confiscated his properties in Somerset. William's cousin, and arch-enemy of John, Geoffrey de Mandeville, was killed at that time in a jousting match.

Since his new navy had been so successful at Damme, John decided to cross the Channel and bottle up Louis with his fleet in Calais. But a storm ruined his plan and, in May 1216, Louis landed unopposed and laid siege to John's headquarters in Winchester. William Fiennes, soon after joining Louis's army, decided for reasons unknown but, judging by other accounts of the time, due to the great arrogance of the French prince, to switch back to supporting King John. As a result, in September John gave him back his Somerset possessions.

By then the two armies were circling each other like snarling cats, neither with a clear advantage. In October 1216, crossing a swollen tidal river by the Wash, John's wagons containing the royal treasure and crown jewels were snatched away by the current. That night John went down with a severe attack of dysentery and soon died.

Had he lived and defeated the rebels, John would certainly have rendered Magna Carta a toothless and soon to be forgotten event. But his successors were to reissue the charter, slightly modified but legally binding. Within fifty years of John's death the first real English Parliament was to emerge.

John's loss of Normandy led to his title being altered from that shared with his Norman predecessors of 'King of the Anglo-Normans' to 'King of England'. English Normans were now simply English, even though their switch from use of the French tongue would take a touch longer. Normandy was now just another French province and England an isolated kingdom with no meaningful empire. However, in the year 2009, over two million British people own French properties, and, in the Channel Islands, the Queen of England still has the title of Duke of Normandy. After the loss of Normandy, some Fienneses and some Sayes saw themselves as solely French, whilst others became truly English citizens, and I will now, with one or two exceptions, focus on the English branch.

6

MARRIAGES OF CONVENIENCE

The rebel barons of England failed to capitalise on the death of King John because his nine-year-old son Henry III was crowned with alacrity by the royalist clique with solid support from two main areas of England, the south-west and the midlands.

The chief authorities in the land, Hubert de Burgh and William the Marshal, were sound strategists, knew their barons and saw that the young prince was a feeble-minded child who would be putty in the hands of his enemies if given sole charge of the country. With this in mind, de Burgh and the Marshal ensured that Prince Henry remained under close tuition (their shorthand for supervision) until he was in his mid-twenties. They also reissued the Magna Carta soon after Henry's accession, despite the fact that it had been annulled by the Pope, which adroit move pulled the carpet from beneath the feet of those barons with rebellious inclinations.

One of the young Henry's most faithful supporters was my great to the power of twenty-four grandfather, Ingelram Fiennes II. In King John's reign he had held the top post of Constable of Dover Castle, and on Henry's accession he was made a Knight of the Bath and became the highest paid official in the royal household. Ingelram's second son Giles married Sibyl, the beautiful eleven-year-old daughter of the Filiol family who owned the manor of Old Court in Wartling, near Pevensey. On the night of 30 August 1223, seven years into Henry's reign, Sibyl was kidnapped by thugs and for three years was taken from one hiding place to another by a suitor named Richard Pageham, who had, so he said, been previously promised her hand in marriage by her parents. In the subsequent court case Pageham defended his actions by claiming that Sibyl's parents had given him 'the marriage, guardianship and nourishment' of Sibyl, after her father's death, for the sum of two hundred marks, of which he had already paid six marks. Perhaps Pageham was robbed of his rightful nuptials by my ancestor, Giles, her parents deciding he was a better bet for their daughter's future.

The case dragged on for years and is the first detailed record I can find of a personal event in the life of one of my early ancestors' families. Whatever its outcome, elder brother William was to become a favourite, like his father Ingelram, of King Henry III, who appointed him to oversee the education of his heir, the young Prince Edward.

Since most of the Anglo-Norman barons had spent much of their time (and now all of their time) in England for the past two hundred years, they not only felt English rather than French, but they were no longer much interested in the goings-on over the Channel. They became inward-looking and scarcely minded when Prince Louis, on becoming King Louis VIII of France, captured the remaining English possessions of Poitou and La

Rochelle. Now only Gascony remained as 'English' land in France.

Henry would, in due course, try to defend Gascony, but back in 1225 he and his advisers were focused entirely on home affairs, in particular their attempts to avoid rebellion by the troublesome barons. To this end they proclaimed, with much song and dance and 'by the king's own spontaneous good will', a new and generous version of Magna Carta, and this 1225 charter was officially lodged in the statutes of the realm.

Henry III's heir, Prince Edward, was born in Westminster and named after the king's favourite saint, the last of the Anglo-Saxon kings, Edward the Confessor. Giles Fiennes, son of Ingelram, was brought up and educated alongside the young prince. In 1254, aged only fifteen, Prince Edward was sent to Spain to marry the nine-year-old Eleanor of Castile, and shortly before this arranged marriage King Henry gave him Gascony, the last remaining English province in France, along with parts of Wales and Ireland. Edward spent 1255 in Gascony and, when he left, Henry put his chancellor, Michael Fiennes, in charge there with his brother, Baldwin Fiennes, and a small army.

To keep Louis of France from predatory moves in the direction of Gascony, Henry agreed the Treaty of Paris with the French king and was, as a result, able to concentrate on the long festering trouble with the barons which by 1259 was about to burst into a new civil war. A sworn confederation of the most influential barons in England was mobilising its local armies against the government, and their main grievance, which had simmered and flared for nigh on a quarter of a century, was Henry's choice of advisers from a family circle, most of whom were recently arrived from the continent. It was the familiar old grudge against immigrants taking native jobs. Of course, the vast majority of these 'foreigners' were in reality Normans or Anglo-Normans switching their permanent domicile from France to England. But Prince Edward's young wife, Eleanor of Castile, naturally brought with her to her strange new country as many of her own friends and relatives as possible, the majority of whom were found positions of influence and wealth.

Ingelram Fiennes (whose mother was Eleanor's great aunt) would also count as a foreigner as far as the barons were concerned, and he rubbed a good deal of salt into their wound by marrying his son and heir, William Fiennes, to Blanche, the first cousin and personal friend of Prince Edward's wife Eleanor. Once settled into the ways of the English court, Eleanor generously and actively arranged top-class marriages for her Fiennes kin. This she continued to do for the rest of Henry's rule and well into her husband's.

Although the barons' anger was largely fanned by Henry's nepotism, it was a specific scheme, encouraged by the Pope, to make his second son Edmund into the King of Sicily that finally caused the barons to take the government out of Henry's hands. Henry's folly was to tell the Pope that he would finance the conquest of Sicily. A crippling tax burden on the barons would be the only way he could go ahead with such a plan, and this was the final straw.

Civil war did not break out at that point, which

was a miracle partly due to Henry's non-aggressive, some say weak, character. An elected body, the Council of Twenty-four under the moderate guidance of the baronial leader Simon de Montfort, took all governmental decisions out of reach of the king, which can clearly be described as a revolutionary process. It was known as the Provisions of Oxford, and arranged for all Henry's Sicilian-linked debts to be met by the English taxpayer in exchange for a raft of reforms. For five years de Montfort and his barons fought the royalist clique by parliamentary means, but the king's intransigence eventually led to open civil war.

One of de Montfort's main supporters and planners was his son Henry, who, on a cross-Channel mission for his father, was arrested by William de Saye III, the Constable of Rochester Castle, and shut up in a Boulogne jail. Political pressure by the barons soon freed this young de Montfort, who returned to England in time to join his father's victorious army at the Battle of Lewes in 1264, where he fought against his neighbour, Sir Giles Fiennes.

Fighting valiantly by the side of Prince Edward was William de Saye, Lord of Sele (a village in Kent), who was famous for having captured six knights single-handed at the Battle of Saintes. At Lewes his fighting prowess was clearly not enough to prevent de Montfort's men winning the day and imprisoning Prince Edward as a hostage to guarantee the king's future subservience to the dictates of Parliament.

For the next sixteen months de Montfort assured himself a place in English history by inventing and establishing the first elected and regional parliamentary democracy, while he himself remained content with the role of merely guiding the government, and with the modest title of Steward of England. Nonetheless many barons soon began to feel that he was swinging too far to the left (in today's parlance) and feared that they had unleashed a popular force that might quickly threaten their own positions of power. So, when Prince Edward escaped and raised a royalist army, de Montfort's baronial force was severely depleted. The two armies met at Evesham, where it was noted that cousin Ingelram Fiennes 'distinguished himself by his valour'. Prince Edward's much larger force annihilated the parliamentarians, and when the royalists located de Montfort's body among the heaped corpses of his men, a thunderstorm raged whilst they cut off his head, his limbs and his testicles as trophies to award to the main royalist generals.

De Montfort's head was displayed on London Bridge until it rotted, but his legacy to the English people lasted down the centuries, for it provided the first glimmerings of true democracy without the trauma of a bloody revolution. There would be another ten Plantagenet kings but, in terms of their post-1264 autocratic power, they would be as impaired as the genitalia-reduced de Montfort.

*   *   *

For the last seven years of his reign King Henry lapsed slowly into senility, and England was ruled by Prince Edward or, in his absence, his well-chosen ministers. He focused on reconciling the king and the barons, relieving the populace most affected by the years of bad harvest and famine and adopting most of de Montfort's social reform programmes.

Once Prince Edward was confident that even the most troublesome barons were quiescent and the populace reasonably content with their government, he decided to indulge in his long-cherished wish to join a crusade to the Holy Land. He took 1,000 soldiers, including 150 selected trusted knights, and appointed his most loyal supporters to responsible positions in government during his absence. These included, as his chancellor, Michael Fiennes, the brother of King Henry's senior official, Ingelram Fiennes.

Prince Edward and Eleanor set off on crusade in August 1270 with the intention of joining up with the crusading army of the French King Louis IX, St Louis, in the Holy Land. Louis and his impressive French army landed in Tunis and did well against their Muslim opponents until, stricken by a virulent plague, they ran out of steam and, when Louis himself succumbed to the plague, his entire army surrendered. One French general described the onset of this plague: 'The skin became covered with black and earth-coloured spots, just like an old boot . . . the flesh on our gums began to rot away.' One of St Louis' close companions on this disastrous eighth and last crusade was William Fiennes, who is shown in the crusade records as having 'nine knights' and as having 'dined in the King's lodging'.

When Prince Edward's tiny contingent of knights arrived in Acre, there was no longer a French force to join. Nonetheless he stayed in the

Holy Land for over a year, making minor raids, supported by the Fiennes brothers William and Giles after Louis's death. Much of the crusade would have involved heat, disease and boredom, but excitements did occur, including a near-successful attempt on Prince Edward's life by an assassin, an agent of a secret order of Shiite Muslims. Eleanor is said to have sucked the poison from her husband's stab wounds and saved his life.

Back in England, after a reign of fifty-six years, King Henry III died, his last few years spent focused entirely on the rebuilding of Westminster Abbey as a memorial to its original founder, his hero Edward the Confessor.

Ingelram Fiennes, and his brothers Baldwin and Chancellor Michael, had all served Henry with loyalty and distinction throughout his struggles with the barons and his various campaigns in Gascony. The highs and the lows of what being in the constant service of a medieval monarch might involve can be seen from the family records of another kinsman, William de Saye III. He distinguished himself on expeditions in France, he witnessed charters and agreements, parcels of his lands were confiscated one minute and restored the next, he was allowed weekly markets and annual fairs, he was granted the right to hunt the wolf, hare, fox, cat and otter in certain of the king's forests 'if he take none of the king's deer', he was ordered to join the king's army at Shrewsbury, summoned to Windsor, to Westminster, to Oxford with horses and arms, he fought in the Battle of Lewes. He died in 1272, the same year as the king he had served so well for over forty years, and his heir was his son, William de Saye IV.

7

DANGEROUS LIAISONS

Prince Edward was heading slowly home from his crusade when news reached him of his father's death. He took this in a very relaxed way and did not rush back home, as might have been expected. He had, after all, been proclaimed king in his absence, the barons had sworn allegiance to him, there was no rival claimant to his throne, and he was enjoying himself with his beloved Eleanor in interesting places. Everywhere he went he was acclaimed as a great crusader and 'the best lance in the world'.

He lingered in Italy, Sicily, southern France and Paris, and finally arrived in London to be crowned two years after his father's death. A good many kings, before and after him, would have sped home apprehensive of being usurped, but Edward I's position was unusually secure for a medieval monarch. He was an energetic leader with charisma and a violent temper. Capable of cruelty, arrogance and intolerance, he was also a faithful husband and, above all, a good, successful king. England was ruled in his initial absence by his nominees, and he had chosen well for they acted as his loyal regents and Edward I returned in 1274 to a peaceful realm.

Even before his crusading prowess, Edward had gained a reputation as a brave and skilled martial arts fighter. Tournaments were then, as football matches are today, highly popular spectacles, but jousting was dangerous even for the great and the bold. Henry II of France, for example, died when the splinter from a shattered lance pierced his eye. And the Earl of Salisbury killed his own son in a 'friendly' joust.

The Fiennes family, though not yet entwined with the Sayes, were doing well in their adopted land of England. Giles Fiennes, who had for so long enjoyed his enviable position in King Henry's household, benefited further through the marriage of his son, sister and daughters to various wealthy personages. Son John married the daughter of the Head Forester of Windsor Forest, and thereby gained an estate in Berkshire and two in Oxfordshire. Sister Maud married Humphrey de Bohun, Earl of Hereford and Essex and Constable of England. Maud Fiennes is referred to in the royal records as 'the noble damsel Maud, cousin of Queen Eleanor', and Eleanor, who appears to have personally arranged the match, agreed to pay Humphrey de Bohun £3,000 in instalments for which Maud's brother, William Fiennes, was to reimburse her. The fruits of Maud's marriage to this noble earl included two sons, who between them were to be largely responsible for a major defeat of the English army. But more of that later.

Giles's elder daughter, Margaret Fiennes, married Edmund Mortimer, and their eldest son Roger would later murder King Edward II. Their daughter would marry the Black Prince. Giles's second daughter, Joanna Fiennes, married Lord John Wake, Earl of Kent, and their daughter Margaret would later marry Edmund, Edward I's younger brother.

King Edward spent a great deal of time riding

around his kingdom with Queen Eleanor in the baggage train. Despite this state of almost continuous travel, she bore him thirteen children, of whom four were sons. Three of these died young, and the youngest (Edward II to be) was born in Wales during one of his father's ongoing Welsh campaigns. He was known as Prince Edward of Caernarfon and grew up to be a foppish wimp. One of his guardians was Giles Fiennes' son, John, who the prince described in a letter in 1305 as *'consanguineus et alumnus meus'*—'my cousin and teacher'.

*   *   *

King Edward's first priority was to mould the disparate parts of his kingdom into a single country under the rule of the crown, starting with Wales, whose leader, Prince Llewelyn I, was killed by Edward's men in 1282. The reason no previous English army had finally crushed the Welsh was mainly due to the mountainous terrain in the north, but Edward did not let this deter him. His navy blockaded the North Wales coast and his army was as big or bigger than any previously assembled in Britain by a king; over 15,000 men including 9,000 from South Wales.

Llewelyn's main supporter, Rhys Vychan, quickly surrendered to Humphrey de Bohun, Maud Fiennes' husband, who passed him on to the Tower of London for safekeeping.

In the king's army during the Welsh campaigns were two more of my kin. Giles Fiennes (whose swans were all stolen from his Wartling manor while he was away) and William Saye's younger brother, John.

Llewelyn's brother, Dafydd, carried on fighting, but was caught the next year and executed. The chronicles described his death, the first British political prisoner to be hanged, drawn and quartered.

David was first drawn as a traitor, then hanged as a thief. Thirdly he was disembowelled alive and his entrails burnt as an incendiary and a homicide. Fourthly his limbs were cut into four parts as the penalty of a rebel. His right arm was sent to York, the left arm to Bristol, the right leg with hip to Northampton and the left leg to Hereford. The villain's head was bound with iron bands lest it should fall to pieces from putrefaction. This head was stuck upon a long spear for the mockery of London.

With both rebel leaders dead, Edward ensured that the status of Wales as an independent principality came to an end, and its land, like all England's, was divided up into shires ruled by English law. To ensure against further trouble, Edward built eight great castles along the Welsh border.

In 1286 he turned his attention to his lands in Gascony in the far south of France. He spent the next three years living there and avoided war with his arch-enemy Philip IV, the King of France, until in 1294 the latter brazenly attacked Gascony and forced Edward into a series of skirmishes which reclaimed only a part of the province for England, and an uneasy peace ensued. Edward's army in

Gascony was led by his brother Edmund (married to Joanna Fiennes), whose close adviser, one of his officers, was William Saye.

*   *   *

Although Edward is remembered today as the Hammer of the Scots, he never actually managed to subdue them, as he so successfully had the Welsh. The royal house of Scotland had intermarried with my ancestors when Eustace III of Boulogne had wed a daughter of King Malcolm III of Scotland. (Their daughter Matilda had then married King Stephen of England.) Malcolm III's descendant, Malcolm IV, had a great great granddaughter who, King Edward I hoped, would marry his own son, Prince Edward, and thereby secure a family pact between the two countries.

When this plan failed to materialise, various Norman-Scottish barons who controlled lowland Scotland disputed which of them should inherit the throne of Scotland; the Bruce clan being the chief claimants. When their current king, Alexander of Scotland, died, the claimant barons called on King Edward I to arbitrate as to which dynasty should take over the Scottish monarchy. Edward duly nominated John Balliol as being the closest relative to royalty, and he was crowned. One of Edward's unnecessarily arrogant terms imposed on Balliol was that he should make no legal decision of any import without his, Edward's, advice. This naturally offended the proud Scottish barons who soon felt that Balliol should rebel against Edward. They therefore tried to put Robert Bruce (grandfather of King Robert the Bruce) on the

67

throne whilst Edward was busy in Gascony in 1296.

Balliol decided to invoke the French on to his side against Edward; the Auld Alliance. With this in place, he felt strong enough to face Edward, so he renounced all previous agreements that he had made with the English. A furious Edward I, back from Gascony, caught up with Balliol's supporters in their stronghold, the border town of Berwick-upon-Tweed. When Balliol refused to parley, Edward stormed the town and, in the accepted practice of the time, spent three days killing over 7,000 of the inhabitants. Giles Fiennes was there, and I sincerely hope that he took no part in the killings. It was Britain's worst ever massacre, and Edward only called off his killers on watching a defenceless woman being hacked to death.

Balliol himself, a weak and vacillatory man, left Scotland and, after a brief sojourn in the Tower of London, retired for good to France. At this stage, instead of placing one of the other Norman-Scottish claimants on the vacant throne, Edward stupidly appointed three English bureaucrats as regents. He then left them to it.

A year later an outlaw knight, William Wallace (who has today, thanks to Mel Gibson's *Braveheart* film, greatly boosted the popularity of the Scottish National Party), raised the Scottish standard and reconquered the entire country, bar one or two border towns, within a year.

A few months later Edward was back with an army of 25,000 soldiers and defeated the Scots at the battle of Falkirk. Wallace escaped but was captured eight years later and executed in London. He became a Scottish martyr and has never been overshadowed by his successor, the next Scottish 'rebel' Robert the Bruce, himself a descendant of Norman invaders, who after a long and arduous campaign would finally defeat the English. But not until after the death of Scotland's nemesis, King Edward I, the Hammer of the Scots.

Lord John Wake, the eldest son of Joanna Fiennes, who, like Giles Fiennes, had been present at the massacre of Berwick, was a captain under the Bishop of Durham during the battle of Falkirk where he was killed. Joanna's sister, Margaret Fiennes, chose unfortunate husbands, the first being John Comyn of Badenoch, the Red Comyn, nephew of the exiled Balliol and possible claimant to the Scottish throne, who was murdered in a church by Robert the Bruce shortly before the latter was crowned King of Scotland. Margaret Fiennes' next husband was the youngest son of King Edward I, Edmund, who was beheaded in the reign of Edward III. Margaret's daughter Joan married Edward, Prince of Wales who died in 1376 and by whom she was mother to King Richard II who was executed at Pontefract Castle.

Despite all the husbandly deaths, Margaret Fiennes still managed to spawn the kings who led both the House of York and the House of Lancaster.

When Robert the Bruce defied Edward in 1306 the English king was sixty-eight years old and sick. But he raised another army and headed north yet again. He made it as far as Carlisle, where he died. Prince Edward of Caernarfon, his only son, was quickly crowned, but he was far too feeble a character to continue the Scottish campaign.

With Edward I and, some years previously, his wife Eleanor both dead and buried, the close relationship between the royal family and the Fiennes family wavered for a while but, unfortunately for the new king, Edward II, did not entirely vanish.

In England Edward I is still remembered as a great king. He maintained both the spirit of Magna Carta and many of the additional canons introduced by his old and vanquished enemy, Simon de Montfort, which expanded the number of people summoned to the parleys or Parliaments that Edward held twice a year. The motive behind many of Edward I's laws and his setting up of ever larger assemblies was the need to collect huge sums of money for his Welsh, French and Scottish campaigns. This worked well to begin with, but by the latter part of his reign, failed miserably to the point where, in chronic debt, he was refused help by the clergy, the Archbishop of Canterbury threatened him with excommunication, and the barons, some of whom refused to fight for him, began to mutter mutiny. Nonetheless he introduced many good new laws and promoted both the uniform administration of justice and the exposure of abuse by officials.

In terms of foreign conquests, always of importance to the reputations of medieval kings, Edward I held Wales, but not Scotland, and lost very little land in France, which was not difficult since, after his father Henry's reign, there was very little left to lose. In 1303 he successfully arranged a treaty with the French whereby the previously confiscated parts of Gascony were all restored to English rule, but his various attempts to spin a web of alliances to balance the power of France were generally ill-conceived or unlucky, and one, with the traditional allies of England, Boulogne and Flanders, ended with his earning the sobriquet *'perfidus anglorum rex'*, the perfidious King of England, when he did a political about-turn, leaving both provinces at the mercy of the French.

Boulogne was soon to become an integral part of France, but the Flemings revolted in 1302 and, at the Battle of Courtrai, the 'Battle of the Golden Spurs', they astounded everyone by defeating a French army that included 2,000 mounted knights, the flower of the French cavalry, with a ragbag of Flemish foot soldiers armed with long spears. Helped by marshy ground, the Flemings not only withstood the French attack, but routed their fabled knights. They took no prisoners, and some contemporary accounts put the overall casualties at 10,000 dead, which included about 40 per cent of the aristocracy of France. One Fiennes who died that day on the French side was that William, son of Ingelram, who all those years before had accompanied Prince Edward and Queen Eleanor on their first crusade to the Holy Land. Flanders never became a part of France, and the date of the Battle of Courtrai is still celebrated in modern-day Belgium as a national holiday.

*   *   *

Edward II began his reign aged twenty-three, popular enough with his people but hampered by the legacy his father had left him, which consisted of huge debts, a war with Scotland which looked unwinnable and, worst of all, great expectations that he would be as powerful a character as his father.

He started badly by promoting the son of a Gascon noble named Piers Gaveston to ever more exalted positions of power and wealth in England. Rumour was rife that Edward was not only gay but, worse still for a king, on the receiving, passive end of a loving relationship with Gaveston. The more outrageous the favours, especially the Earldom of Cornwall, that Edward bestowed on this 'foreigner', as the Barons scathingly termed him, the more unpopular both men became.

A suitable marriage seemed to the king's dwindling band of loyal supporters to be the best way of ousting Gaveston and, at the same time with luck, cementing a sound relationship with some powerful royal family. When Edward II was still a young prince, his father had betrothed him to Philippa, a daughter of the Count of Flanders, and, when she had died young, to her beautiful sister Isabella.

At this point we need to take a closer look at John Fiennes, the son of William who was killed at the battle of Courtrai, for John was to become the lover of Isabella. His father William, who had gone to the crusades first with Saint Louis and then with Edward I, had taken the French side when trouble with the French reignited, and Edward had confiscated his land. A little later peace broke out and William was given back his land. After his death at Courtrai, there were disputes as to whether his son and heir, John, should inherit his English lands because, the records state, he was born 'beyond the seas' and had spent much time in France. All we know of son John (who did get his father's lands at some point) was that as a young man he was unruly when visiting his properties in the English west country. There exists a record of King Edward I writing to the Bishop of Exeter asking him to be gracious to John when John comes to ask for a pardon for 'breaking up the Bishop's property'. A further record, a few years later, accuses John with a gang of others of breaking John de Foscle's dyke at Asherugge in Wiltshire and felling his trees.

Both John and his brother Robert were involved in the post-Courtrai period, fighting for the French against frequent border raids by the ebullient Flemings. On one occasion French troops under John's command cornered and destroyed a large group of raiders. Following negotiations to end the fighting, John, acting for the French, became very friendly with the Count of Flanders, the father of Isabella, then betrothed (in lieu of her dead sister Philippa) to Edward II. John, therefore, saw quite a lot of Isabella.

At the same time, the King of France was using John as a royal commissioner to negotiate with King Edward about various disputes. At Broughton Castle, the Fiennes home for the past six hundred years, there is a record of a letter, in French, from John to the King of England on behalf of Philip of France.

At some point John Fiennes fell in love with Isabella of Flanders, the story of which may well have shocked both French and Flemings and is well described by the chronicle of Brother Mineur of Ghent. Luckily for John, his affair and subsequent marriage worried neither Philip nor Edward because, in a separate treaty, they betrothed each other's children to one another, Isabella of France to Prince Edward of England.

From then on John became a favourite of King Philip, and when Edward II wished to do business with the Count of Flanders, he treated John as the count's equal.

In 1308, a year after Edward II became king, he went to France to marry Isabella and made the serious mistake of appointing Piers Gaveston as regent in his absence. This naturally infuriated the barons and was not improved by the arrogant behaviour of Gaveston. Soon afterwards and not far short of open rebellion, the barons enforced Gaveston's exile.

Edward somehow wheedled the return of Gaveston in 1309 to be his main man in Ireland, where he did surprisingly well subduing minor insurrections. But back in England he was as arrogant as ever, and this time the full hatred of the barons was directed by the most powerful magnate in the land, the Earl of Lancaster, who determined to control the king and to preserve baronial powers. In 1311 he and his councillors drew up a series of ordinances to achieve his aims. The king spent the rest of his life trying to circumvent or ride roughshod over such curbs on his powers.

In 1312 one of Lancaster's cronies murdered Gaveston. He was mourned only by the king. In the words of a chronicler: 'Anon he had home his love Piers of Gaveston and did him great reverence and worshipped and made him great and rich. Of this doing fell villainy to the lover, evil speech and backbiting to the love, slander to the people, harm and damage to the realm.'

Gaveston's murder saved the land from almost certain civil war. Edward must have, briefly at least, climbed into bed with Isabella long enough to conceive a son and heir—or maybe John Fiennes did it for him. In any event, another little Prince Edward was born to the joy of the nation. Meanwhile, trouble a plenty was brewing north of the border, and Edward was lucky that the ever opportunistic Philip of France was focused on home matters at the time, busy annihilating the Knights Templar.

Whilst that was going on in France, Edward finally gathered an army to crush Robert the Bruce, who, ever since his murder of Margaret Fiennes' first husband, John Comyn, had gradually reduced virtually all the English strongholds north of the border, save for a few great castles. His initially small band of followers might be described as forerunners of the SAS, for they disdained sieges, preferring silent night raids with ladders, which proved highly successful, and his popularity helped swell his forces into a real army.

The most important stronghold that did not succumb to the Bruce's ladder-by-night methods was Stirling Castle, which the Scots therefore had to besiege in the traditional cumbersome manner. Edward's aim was to crush the Scottish army and to relieve Stirling Castle, and he set out northwards with confidence. Disaster ensued. The two armies met in a wood two miles from the castle and on a part of the Forth plain dissected by marshy streams. A place called Bannockburn. Not good for heavy cavalry, but a big plus for the Scottish army.

The Scots fielded a mere third the strength of Edward's force, but by clever tactics, a forest of sharp stakes held by foot soldiers, and especially by using the local geography in the same way as the Flemish had against the superior French force at Courtrai, they won the day with a massive victory, well followed up by efficiently killing off the vanquished English as they retreated through enemy country.

Edward II himself is surprisingly reported to have 'fought like a lion'. Parted from his shield-bearer, he lost his horse only to grab another and head anew for the heart of the fray. But once defeat was obvious, he and a small group managed to retreat to the still English-held redoubt of Dunbar, and thence by ferry to the border at Berwick.

Maud Fiennes, as you may recall, had married Humphrey de Bohun, Earl of Hereford during Edward I's reign. They had two sons, the elder of whom, another Humphrey, commanded the English army at Bannockburn and was captured by the Scots. His younger brother Henry was also partly responsible for the outcome of the battle by having himself sparked off an ill-timed and disastrous cavalry charge which turned possible success into a massacre of English knights.

Whether or not this can be said to have altered Anglo-Scottish history, who can say? But Robert the Bruce managed to ransom Humphrey for £200,000, a vast sum, plus the return from England of his own queen, his sister and his daughter. Once Robert the Bruce was crowned, the Scots would remain firmly independent for three hundred years until King James VI of Scotland became James I of England, at which point both nations were ruled from London by Scotsmen (just like nowadays).

Edward's tiny force arrived back in London

where the king's main opponent, the Earl of Lancaster, bound Edward to adhere minutely to the ordinances that he and his cronies had previously installed in Parliament but which the king had, prior to the disaster of Bannockburn, largely ignored. Lancaster was not interested in the good of the country at large so much as the retention, and indeed the increase, of his personal powers. But he was a skilled PR man and for a while he was backed by the barons, the church and the people. He appointed himself as King's Councillor, checking every move the king made. Monarchical power was then at a very low ebb.

In October 1321 an event occurred which sparked off Edward's escape from the puppet string controls of Lancaster. Queen Isabella, on a personal pilgrimage to Canterbury, desired to spend a night at Leeds Castle in Kent. To her understandable anger, the governor of the castle, Lord Badelsmere (or rather his wife, since he was away at the time) refused her entry to the castle due to fear of Lancaster's reaction. He might, she presumably thought, assume that the Badelsmeres were in secret cahoots with royalty and sack her husband from his job.

A furious Isabella told her escort to storm the castle. They were unsuccessful and six were killed. Isabella complained to Edward who sent the ever-faithful Geoffrey de Saye to arrest and try all those responsible for the Isabella incident. One way or another the king found himself unexpectedly the popular man of the moment with many normally neutral barons right behind him due to this apparently minor event of discourtesy against the monarch. His force laid siege to Leeds Castle which surrendered in a week. Badelsmere and sixty-three of his garrison were hanged.

Minor clashes followed shortly between King Edward's group and the mixed forces of Lancaster, the Mortimers of the Marches, and others of the king's enemies. In May 1322 both armies had swollen and met up at Boroughbridge, north of York. The result gave Edward his first meaningful victory over his key opponents. He had Lancaster executed, along with his chief associates and all those previously implicated in the murder of Piers Gaveston. Others, including Roger Mortimer, captured just prior to Boroughbridge, were imprisoned in the Tower. Mortimer was the son of Margaret Fiennes, and Edward would have done well to have executed him while he had the chance. Another bitter enemy of the king was Lord Thomas Wake, the son of Joanna Fiennes, Margaret's sister, but he also escaped arrest.

Edward generously rewarded those few individuals who had remained constantly loyal through the dark Lancaster years, including Geoffrey de Saye, who had been at Edward's side since he was a prince in his teens and fought for him both against the Scots and against Lancaster. In 1318 Geoffrey had briefly been jailed 'for consorting with the outlaw Robert Coleman', but Edward soon had him released and fully returned to royal favour.

Also loyal to Edward, and to his father before him, with a few exceptions over the years, was Giles Fiennes who had arrived in England as a young, penniless cousin of Queen Eleanor, bride of Edward I, and had been appointed to her household. By the time of his death, just prior to Boroughbridge, his descendants were well established with at least six large estates in England. He was the first Fiennes to establish himself as an English, rather than an Anglo-Norman, resident. After him there were English Fiennneses and French ones. You had to make your mind up quickly or it was made up for you. The records note: 'Moreover, John Fiennes had the living of the manor of Wendover but, being afterwards attainted for adhering to the French, he lost all.'

Edward used his post-Boroughbridge success and his recovery of power to repeal those of Lancaster's ordinances that had rendered him virtually impotent, but not those that favoured the populace in general. Unfortunately, Edward adhered to the rule that leopards never change their spots. He developed an unnaturally close friendship with an adviser, Hugh Despenser and his son (Hugh Junior) in much the same manner as he had with Gaveston. The Despensers were given wealth and power. A chronicler of that time, one Lanercost, observed that the young Despenser became 'the apple of the king's eye'.

A group of barons forced the Despensers into exile, as they had Gaveston. And, as before, Edward managed subsequently to retrieve and reinstate both men, gaining many powerful enemies thereby. The most venomous of these was Edward's own wife, Isabella, known to all as the 'she-wolf of France'. She plotted, with great diplomacy and secrecy, the downfall of the Despensers, even writing to the Pope to have them excommunicated, but that didn't work.

Her next ploy was to release from the Tower the

man with whom at some point she had fallen in love, Roger Mortimer, the son of Margaret Fiennes. Isabella's co-conspirator, Bishop Orleton of Hereford, hired two Londoners who smuggled liquor and a rope to Mortimer's prison. After ensuring his guards were drunk, Mortimer abseiled the outer wall of the Tower and fled to his uncles, John and Robert Fiennes, in France, both of whom at that time had their English lands confiscated by Edward for 'adhering to the French'.

Edward II wrote letters to each of the Fiennes brothers, addressing them as 'my kinsman' but using strong language to persuade them to give Mortimer up. The king knew both brothers well, and in 1309 he had paid Robert five years' rental in advance for the use of his estate at Wendover. The records show no response from Robert, whose 'warhorse was confiscated'.

Back in England, Queen Isabella, who clearly hated her husband Edward as much as she did his right-hand man Despenser, carried out stage two of her plot. Edward obviously had no idea of what she had in mind, for he sent her as his ambassadress to parley with her brother, King Philip of France. He even, very stupidly, allowed her to take their son Edward, the heir to his throne, with her. Once there she persuaded Philip to restore Gascony and Ponthieu to the English. Whilst the details of this treaty carried on over the next year, she remained in France making love to Margaret Fiennes' son, Mortimer, and plotting with him and with his uncles, the Fiennes brothers, the overthrow of her husband and the crowning of her son.

John and Robert agreed to raise a force to help

her and Mortimer invade England, whilst they raised their main army in Holland. In 1326 their invasion force landed in Suffolk and, with a rapidly growing army, marched on London where they occupied the Tower once Edward II, and the hated Despensers had fled to the west country. Despenser aides unfortunate enough to stay in London were killed. The head of one was sliced off with a butcher's knife and sent to Isabella, who thanked the donor with a dignified speech of gratitude. She then promoted the two locals who had helped Mortimer escape the Tower, one becoming Mayor and the other Constable of the Tower.

Edward's party sought sanctuary in Bristol, which surrendered to Isabella, so they fled by ship bound for the Despensers' island of Lundy. But the wind blew them back to Wales, where they were soon captured. The Despensers were executed, the younger being hanged, drawn and quartered with an added twist. The Froissart chronicle reported: 'His member and testicles were first cut off because he was a heretic and a sodomite even if, it was said, with the King.'

Edward was imprisoned initially in Kenilworth Castle, and in 1327 was forced to sign his own abdication in favour of his son, the thirteen-year-old Prince Edward, who was very much under the control of his mother and her lover Mortimer and clearly unaware that their next move was secretly to murder his father. Edward was moved from Kenilworth, where his captors were friendly, to Berkeley Castle where they were not. His new custodians had both been captured at Boroughbridge and owed their release from prison to Isabella.

Edward's last months at Berkeley were for a long time kept secret from the public, but it was clear to Isabella that he must die. Soon after she and Mortimer gained power as regents for her son Edward III, the country and a growing number of barons realised that the new outfit was just as bad as the Despensers had been. A growing move in sympathy for the imprisoned Edward II gathered strength, so the latter's speedy death became vital to Isabella.

In September 1327 Edward's death from illness was announced, and his body was given to an official group of Bristol worthies to check that he had not been murdered. The truth came out slowly. Geoffrey le Baker's Chronicle reported:

> His wife Isabella was angered that his life which had become most hateful to her should be so prolonged. She asked advice of the Bishop of Hereford, pretending that she had had a dreadful dream . . . that her husband would at some time be restored to his former dignity and would condemn her, as a traitress, to be burned or to perpetual slavery. The bishop of Hereford was feared . . . And so letters were written to Edward's keepers. [These men] believed that the favour of Isabella and the bishop made them secure [and they] took control of the castle . . .

Then began the most extreme part of Edward's persecution . . .

He was shut up in a secure chamber, where

he was for many days and almost suffocated by the stench of corpses buried in a cellar hollowed out beneath him. Carpenters who worked beneath the window of his chamber heard his laments. When his warders perceived that the stench alone was not sufficient to kill him, they seized him on the night of 22 September . . . and held him down. They thrust a plumber's soldering iron, heated and red hot, guided by a tube inserted into his bowels and thus they burnt his innards and his vital organs . . . He shouted aloud so that many heard his cry both within and without the castle and knew it for the cry of a man who suffered violent death. Many in both the town and the castle of Berkeley were moved to pity for him.

There were rumours that Roger Mortimer was himself among the murderers, but there was no proof. I prefer to believe that he had no involvement in the cruel details of Edward's demise. Isabella, in widow's weeds, attended the lavish funeral of her late husband, and ruled the land with Mortimer, the son of Margaret Fiennes.

Under Edward II the people were far better off than under his father, with less taxation, far less conscription and no foreign service. In short, Edward II did not deserve his horrible death.

8

FIENNES ON BOTH SIDES

Prince Edward, son of the late King Edward II, grew up in the constant company of his adulterous mother and her murderous lover. Yet he was to flower into a great king, Edward III, who ruled for fifty years almost without civil strife. His secret was largely to recognise the monarchical limitations laid down by successive Parliaments over the past century and, above all, to keep the barons on his side. A seemingly simple recipe, but in fact one requiring endless tact, cunning and diplomacy. And bags of self-confidence, which Edward possessed from birth. He was well educated by tutors, especially by Richard of Bury (whom he later promoted to Bishop of Durham) who clearly honoured study:

The value of books cannot be expressed . . . Yet a lazy youth will lounge over his book and, in mid-winter, when his nose is oozing mucus, he does not think of wiping it, but allows it to drop on the page before him. If only he had a cobbler's apron in front of him, instead of a book! His nails are black with dirt, with which he marks any passage that strikes him. He sticks in straws to remind him of the bits he had to learn by heart, so that the book becomes so stuffed it tears away from its binding. He eats fruit and cheese over it, and drinks wine, all of which leave their traces;

and, always chattering, he waters the page with his spittle.

Edward, luckily and unlike his late father, was keen on and excelled at the martial arts. He would need above all to be a great military leader. The contemporary Chronicles of Froissart summed up the ideal English monarch:

The English will never love and honour their king unless he be victorious and a lover of arms and war against their neighbours and especially against such as are greater and richer than themselves. Their land is fuller of riches and of goods when they are at war than in peacetime. They take delight and solace in battles and slaughter; they covet and envy other men's wealth beyond measure.

Only a year after his coronation in 1327, the teenage King Edward III was forced to sign a treaty with King Robert the Bruce, giving him full sovereignty and Scotland full independence. He said at the time that he found this deeply humiliating. In 1330 Roger Mortimer, son of Margaret Fiennes, made it obvious that he would stop at nothing short of the crown, when he successfully conspired to have Edward's uncle, the Duke of Kent, a potential future royal claimant but a harmless popular character, executed on a trumped-up charge of treason.

Young though he was, Edward III was no fool and he made the first move with a night raid on Nottingham Castle when his mother and Mortimer were over-nighting there. He killed their two room guards and personally arrested Mortimer in his bedroom, and in front of Queen Isabella denounced him for murder and other crimes. Mortimer was sent to the Tower and Isabella into comfortable, but carefully observed, retirement in Norfolk.

Mortimer was hanged, drawn and quartered in front of a huge crowd of enthusiastic voyeurs at a specially erected gibbet at Tyburn, which, from that day, became London's favourite and official place of execution.

Edward was too shrewd to kill off Mortimer's allies, or even those who were known to have been involved in murdering Edward II. These were men, or friends of men, whom the king would have to work with and fight beside. He wanted as few enemies as possible. In this he did remarkably well, having over the next forty years virtually no disagreements with great barons.

*   *   *

The Fiennes and Saye fortunes were definitely in the ascendant in Edward III's reign, during which they intermarried to become a powerful family entity. Geoffrey de Saye, son of the Geoffrey who was always loyal to Edward II, had two daughters, one of whom, Idonea, married John, Lord Clinton, who was one of Edward III's greatest warriors. And Geoffrey himself became Edward's Admiral of the Fleet, as well as a great land general at such battles as Crécy. His daughter, Joan, became the sole heiress of the Saye fortunes, and she married William Fiennes. During Edward III's reign the Fiennes family absorbed the name and fortunes of the Sayes through the marriage of Joan and William. The Wykehams would come next.

One family problem was caused in 1337 when Edward declared war on France and laid claim to the French throne. The last links whereby Fiennes members could happily feel both Norman and English were irrevocably split, at which point Ingelram's son Giles elected to be English, whilst his brother William's family became wholly French.

Ingelram's daughter Maud had married Humphrey de Bohun, the Constable of England, and their daughter Mary married King Henry IV. Mary's sister Eleanor (also granddaughter of Ingelram Fiennes) married Thomas of Woodstock, the youngest son of Edward III.

Not long after Ingelram's two sons went their separate ways, and during Edward's reign, one descendant, Geoffrey de Saye, was Admiral of the English fleet and the other, Constable Robert Fiennes, commanded the French army. On 5 March 1327 John Fiennes having 'declared for the French', Edward III promptly removed his estates at Martock and elsewhere and his manors were 'granted to other more faithful subjects of the house of Plantagenet.'

*   *   *

In 1338 the French King Philip VI was preparing to invade England. Naval raids took place at Portsmouth, Southampton, Dover and even up the Thames, and as a result deep stakes were placed along the riverbed against future attacks by the London route. Early in the summer of 1340 spies reported to Edward that a great armada of French, Spanish and Genoese ships were massing in the Channel port of Sluys, prior to invasion. The first big military move of the so-called One Hundred Years War had begun, and Edward ordered his Admiral, Geoffrey de Saye, grandfather of William Fiennes (my great to the power of twenty grandfather) to prepare the southern fleet for war. Edward and most of his court, including his queen, sailed with the fleet.

Against the advice of his spies, Edward ordered the fleet to attack without delay. The French ships, joined to one another by rope walkways, never left the Sluys channel into which the English sailed. Most of Edward's ships, square-rigged and oar-steered, were known as cogs. They had small crews of five and carried up to thirty soldiers. The chronicle of Geoffrey le Baker describes the battle.

The whole fleet gave a terrible shout, and a shower of arrows out of long wooden bows so poured down on the Frenchmen that thousands were slain . . . At length they closed and came to hand blows with pikes, poleaxes, and swords, and some threw stones from the tops of ships, wherewith many were brained . . . many of the Frenchmen abandoned their ships and leapt overboard . . . during the night thirty ships . . . fled away . . . The fight continued all night, and in the morning, the Normans being overcome and taken, there were found in the ships four hundred men slain . . . The number of ships of war that were taken was about 230 barges; the number of enemies that were slain and drowned was

about 20,000, and of Englishmen about 4,000
. . .

No member of the French king's court dared give him the news from Sluys. Finally the king's jester was ordered to tell him, which he did by saying, 'Our knights are much braver than the English.' 'How so?' asked Philip. 'Because,' replied the jester, 'the English do not dare to jump into the sea in full armour.' In fact, many of those French soldiers who managed to swim to the shore were then killed by the hostile Flemings. The victory at Sluys gave Edward control of the Channel throughout his reign and enabled his forces to attack along the French coast as and when he wished.

His army was based on that of his grandfather, Edward I, who, for the first time, had paid his men wages to ensure that they turned up when needed, trained and equipped, and they did not disappear whenever some distant female or harvest needed attention. Edward III honed this professional system. Under him all ranks received daily wages. Thus his kingly ally, Edward Balliol, King of Scots, had fifty shillings per day, his eldest son, the Black Prince, got twenty shillings, down to an archer at six pence daily and ordinary foot soldiers at two. The majority of his unprofessional troops were from Wales and Cheshire and most were either archers or men-at-arms who wore intricate armed suits made up of more than two dozen separate items. Carrying a sword and a dagger, they were highly effective so long as they remained upright, but, once fallen, they usually needed help to stand up. Falling in bogs or shallow water, they would often drown.

The secret of much of Edward's military success lay in the six foot long wooden bow fashioned of oak or yew or maple, which could fire four hundred yards with relative accuracy, but only in the hands of an archer who had developed his skill over many years. To this end, English and Welsh villagers were encouraged to practise archery from an early age. Other nations, including the Scots, never indulged in this remarkable skill that built up the great, but lopsided, often body-deforming, muscle, needed to exert the necessary hundred-pound 'tug' on the bowstring. The government passed many laws forbidding such village sports as football and cockfighting, expressly because they distracted people from archery practice.

Because the French authorities forbade French peasants to carry any weapons of war, they never developed a force who could use longbows. The practical range of the crossbow, far easier to use with accuracy, was a mere hundred yards, and the act of reloading it was far slower. An experienced longbow archer could loose off an arrow every five seconds, which was six times quicker than a crossbow. To protect them from cavalry charges, they also carried long pointed stakes. Siege guns and simple cannons were just emerging but were of no import during Edward III's reign, other than for scaring all horses within earshot.

*   *   *

Nine years after the original declaration of war, in 1346, Edward launched his first major attack on northern France, with the idea of luring the French army into direct confrontation there, which would draw them away from the English lands in the south. One of his three chief advisers was the Earl of Warwick, whose son-in-law was Admiral Geoffrey Saye of Sluys fame, and one of his best army commanders-to-be, although only sixteen at the time, was his eldest son, Edward the Black Prince, whose great great grandfather was William Fiennes. Their forces laid waste to the countryside and plundered churches, anything to provoke a response.

When the French king finally did get his act together, he was quickly successful in raising a huge force of 80,000, including Genoese specialist crossbowmen, the cream of the French cavalry, together with forces from Bohemia, Germany, Savoye and Luxembourg.

Edward's army consisted of 4,000 knights and men-at-arms, 7,000 Welsh and English archers, and 5,000 Welsh and Irish spearmen. Additionally, there was a tiny contingent of cannoneers who lugged five cannons with them and a supply of stone cannon balls, the predecessors of today's Royal Artillery. Realising that direct confrontation with such a numerically superior force was a bad idea, Edward decided to retreat towards the coast. The Seine got in the way, for its bridges were either destroyed or heavily defended. Not far from Paris one bridge was repaired and crossed, but the river Somme then caused a similar problem. Edward followed its course north to the sea and crossed the river mouth at low tide, just evading the French who advanced along the far bank.

Edward's army halted on a ridgeline between two villages, one named Crécy. He commanded from the hilltop. My relations were well represented that day. The Black Prince commanded the division of archers in the front line, assisted in command by the Earl of Warwick, and Geoffrey Saye fought alongside the king.

On the French side, Robert Fiennes was a senior captain who would soon rise to command the entire French army. Robert was the son of the John Fiennes who had incurred the displeasure of Edward II and, having had his English estates confiscated, had settled in the old Fiennes territory of Fiennes and Guisnes. When Edward III had laid siege to the key city of Amiens, Robert was the senior French army captain who forced the English to yield, not only at Amiens, but soon thereafter at Rheims, Tonnerre, Auxerre and Regennes. He met most of the costs of these campaigns himself, went bankrupt and, by the time of Crécy in 1346, appealed to the French king, who appointed him Constable or commander-in-chief of the French army, a job with a salary.

First to attack at Crécy were the massed ranks of the Genoese crossbowmen whose weapons fired iron bolts, stones or lead bullets with a flat trajectory that could pierce armour. The British longbowmen used high trajectory metre-long arrows which descended on their targets at an angle in showers. Horses were easy targets. At Crécy the average rate of fire was thirty seconds between each crossbow shot. The 15,000 Genoese crossbowmen were tired after their long march and before they advanced there was heavy rain with thunder and a terrible eclipse of the sun. Froissart tells us a great flight of noisy crows hovered over the battalions. Then the sun came out and shone into the eyes of the French. The Genoese advanced with great shouting but the English, quietly, rose up, stepped forward and let their arrows fly, 'so thick it seemed as snow.'

Froissart also explains that the rain had the instant effect of making the archers unhitch their bowstrings (a three-second job) to keep them dry inside their hats, but the unwieldy crossbow strings could not be so easily kept dry, became loose and lost effectiveness.

The Genoese, with serious losses, sensibly retreated, but the heavy cavalry had begun a mighty uphill charge and rode down a great many of the Genoese, contemptuous at their cowardice. Horses stumbled in deep bloody mud, knights in heavy armour floundered among dying Genoese, and the heaps of bodies grew higher as successive flights of metal-tipped arrows found new targets.

Nonetheless, at one point King Edward received a breathless messenger from his sixteen-year-old son clad in black armour and thenceforth called the Black Prince. He and my kinsman Warwick needed support. The king surveyed the battle scene below and asked if his son was wounded. No, he was told, and so he replied to the messenger, 'I am sure he will repel the enemy without my help. Let the boy win his spurs.'

The battle continued far into the night, but at midnight King Philip VI of France abandoned the carnage, and his surviving knights and men-at-arms went with him. The English army stayed on their ridgeline until, cautiously at dawn, they could be sure the French had truly gone. I call the two armies French and English, as did the chronicles, but in truth they were clearly European and

British.

Once Edward was certain that the French had not rallied, his men swarmed over the battleground. Those knights too wounded or crushed beneath dead horses were unable to be carried off for ransom, and the vast majority of the wounded not worthy of ransom were murdered where they lay by men with long daggers. These were inserted either through visor slits into the eyeball and brain, or through the armpit into the heart.

With an eye to ensuring maximum ransom revenue and good public relations back home, Edward arranged a meticulous tally of the dead by two nominated lords with three heraldic experts and their secretaries. The result of their grand post-mortem was a report that eighty battle standards, eleven princes, three archbishops, 1,200 noble knights and 30,000 common soldiers had been identified. When the English moved away towards Calais, their target, they flew the eighty French standards which caused ignorant onlookers to believe that their own king's forces had won at Crécy.

The battle enhanced King Edward's warrior reputation and that of his young son. The Black Prince was titled Prince of Wales and Duke of Cornwall, but he spent most of his life fighting in France, and French was his first language. At Crécy he chose for his battle standard the family crest of the dead King of Bohemia who had fought well, despite being totally blind, lashed to his horse and to those of two 'guide-dog' knights on either flank. The Bohemia crest of three white feathers is still that of today's Prince of Wales, as well as the

Welsh Rugby Football Union. The Black Prince made sure that, on their return to South Wales, his brave Welsh bowmen were each given an acre of land, made freemen and exempted grazing tax for their cattle.

But first Edward's victorious army had to begin their siege of the fortified deep-water port of Calais, a convenient day's sail from Dover and a key position from both a military and commercial viewpoint. Calais was defended with a tidally-fed double ditch and high double walls, well built and strongly garrisoned. Edward surrounded and blockaded Calais for eleven months until, all supplies gone and the citizens starving, they desperately needed their king to relieve them. But Philip's memories of Crécy kept him firmly in Paris, and eventually the Calais garrison commander faced the hard fact that if he didn't surrender, the inmates would die slowly of hunger. On the other hand, surrender, according to the rules of war of the period, entailed the massacre of all citizens if their town or fortress had held out for any length of time.

Froissart's Chronicle tells the famous story of the garrison commander pleading for clemency for Calais, of the toing and froing of fruitless emissaries, and eventually Edward's deciding that if six leading burghers brought him the keys of the city and the garrison, 'I will do with those six as I please, but the rest I will spare.'

The chronicler continues:

Finally the town's wealthiest citizen, Master Eustace de Saint Pierre came forward saying, 'It would be a terrible thing indeed to allow so many to die when there appears a means to avoid such misfortune. An act of such merit would surely find favour in Our Saviour's eyes. Let me be delivered into the King of England's hands.' Other greatly respected citizens volunteered to accompany Saint Pierre, including Jean d'Aire, brothers Jacques and Pierre de Wissant, Andrieu d'Andres, and [the youngest of them] Jean Fiennes.

When the six heroic burghers of Calais knelt before the king bare-headed, barefoot and with halters around their necks, they so impressed everyone present by their bravery that all begged the king to show them mercy. But he was adamant they should die in recompense for grievous English losses over the course of the siege.

At this point, the Queen of England, Philippa, who was present during these events, was moved to intercede. Though she was pregnant at the time, she fell to her knees before the king and weeping said, 'My lord, since I crossed the sea to join you, at great danger to myself, I have never asked of you a single favour, but now I ask you in all humility, in the name of the Son of the Blessed Mary and by the love you have for me, to have mercy on these six men.'

The king remained silent for a time and finally spoke saying, 'My lady, I might wish you were anywhere but here. Nevertheless I cannot refuse your request, though it be against my will. These men are yours to do with what you like.' And with that the queen thanked her husband the king and had the halters taken from the necks of the prisoners. They were presented new clothes and fed an ample dinner. Whereupon they were given safe passage through the English army and released to freedom.

In 1888 the famous French sculptor Auguste Rodin completed a life-size bronze grouping of the Burghers of Calais, the original of which still stands in the centre of Calais, but copies can be admired in London in the gardens below the Houses of Parliament, and also in Paris, New York, Washington, Jerusalem, Tokyo, Canberra and Copenhagen. In the year 2000 I went to look at one of Rodin's representations of my distant French kinsman, who was in his day as famous as his contemporary cousin, Constable Robert Fiennes. He helped to save King Edward from ordering a major massacre.

Calais remained a key English possession until 1558, but the war elsewhere in France continued, and this benefited those of my ancestors with military careers on both sides. Especially Captain Robert Fiennes who, the week after the Battle of Crécy, was sent by King Philip to defend the nearby key town of St Omer. When an English-allied force from the Flemish army came his way, Robert ambushed them, killing seven hundred. Fiennes together with the Governor of St Omer made continued raids on the English lines of communication. One night, not long after Calais was taken by the English, the two men plotted to attack the town by a sudden night raid.

97

Unfortunately they were betrayed, and according to Froissart:

> The King of England was informed of the conspiracy and came into Calais with three hundred men-at-arms and six hundred archers. The English knew that a large detachment of French remained at the bridge at Nieulay under the command of Robert Fiennes. The King put to flight or killed the crossbowmen of St Omer. He then came to the bridge believing he would seize it with ease. But Fiennes and his small troop fought through the night. Later, when his enemies increased, Fiennes sounded the retreat and returned to St Omer. This attempt against Calais failed but gave Fiennes, the future Constable, the occasion to show his valour.

Froissart uses the term Constable of France for the commander-in-chief of the French army. The position was vacant for a while after the battle of Calais, where Constable Raoul Eu was captured and taken to England for ransom. Whilst there, in loose captivity, he took an enthusiastic part in many court activities, especially the jousting. Word got back to King Philip and when the Constable did return to Paris, he was tried for treason and beheaded. Nonetheless Constable of France was the summit of ambition for a French soldier, and my French cousin Robert Fiennes was helped to achieve the honour by Raoul Eu's execution.

*   *   *

Edward III's personal popularity in England, just prior to his Crécy campaign and the subsequent success at Calais, had been waning due to his government's methods of raising money. There was also hostility to the expansion of compulsory military service. Victory at Crécy and Calais, however, renewed his popularity and put the brakes on growing parliamentary opposition, at least for as long as his French campaigns continued to succeed. Sadly a new threat was soon to cut short the national mood of post-Crécy jubilation.

The Black Death ravaged England in three separate pandemics during Edward III's reign. The bacteria-carrying flea was hosted by rodents, especially by the large black rat, and the symptoms included swollen glands which oozed pus and blood in the armpits, neck and groin, followed by heavy bleeding under the skin. Hence the 'black' appearance of victims. Accompanying tumours or 'buboes' could grow to the size of apples overnight. Excruciating pains and vomiting of blood, which drove people mad, preceded death within a week. A mutated sister bacillus was hosted by human fleas causing additional septicaemia, and this would kill in less than two days. A third variety went for the lungs and was spread by the breath of the victim. The speed of the plague's onset, the terrible pain and the grotesque appearance of the victims all made it especially terrifying.

The disease was first spotted in central Asia in 1338, whence it spread inexorably through China and India. In 1346, the year of Crécy, a Mongol army besieging a Crimean port used the old tactic of catapulting decomposing bodies over city walls to infect the inhabitants. From the Crimea the plague spread within a year through all of Italy and soon reached Paris. In 1348 a French sailor arrived in Melcombe, near Weymouth, and brought the plague to England. It thrived in the warm summer weather and the pneumonic variety flourished in winter with much sneezing. By early 1349 Edward was forced to cease his military activities altogether, and even had to close Parliament, since it was unsafe to go to London like most towns, a centre of infection.

The Archbishop of Canterbury was an early victim. The aristocracy death rate was relatively low due to their more spacious houses shared with fewer rats. Nonetheless, 27 per cent of the English nobility and 40 per cent of the clergy were to die over the next three years, as did half the population of Britain; as many as two million people. In winter the plague dropped away, since fleas rest up in the cold, but in spring they were hopping about again from ratty host to human. Throughout Europe one third of the population died over four years; some twenty-five million people. The plague killed like no other illness. Boccaccio wrote of what he saw: 'Victims often ate lunch with their friends and dinner with their ancestors in paradise.'

Rural records tell of 5,000 sheep dying of starvation on a single estate where all the farmhands and the owner had died. Animal corpses littered the land. Cattle ran wild over untended crops. Nobody blamed the rats, they looked for culprits in society at large. Preacher Thomas Brinton wrote: 'We are not constant in faith . . . for that reason there exists in England . . . so cruel a pestilence, so much injustice, so many illegitimate children—for on every side there is so much lechery and adultery that few men are contented with their wives but each man lusts after the wife of his neighbour or keeps a stinking concubine.'

England recovered very slowly from the plague, partly because other epidemics followed in the ensuing years, but with fewer workers to till the land, the common people demanded and got higher wages, despite the barons. In France this same wages issue caused peasant rebellions and large areas of France became ungovernable. The man charged with dealing with this problem there was Robert Fiennes, in the years before he was made Constable.

*   *   *

The old French King Philip VI, died in 1350, and his successor, King John II, renewed hostilities against English territory in southern France. By 1355 the Black Prince was again at war in Gascony and the Mediterranean provinces, ravaging the land and gaining rich plunder and a Europe-wide reputation as a great warrior. In 1356 he decided to emulate his father's strategy of a decade earlier; that of causing so much damage that the French would confront him in a major battle which he, the Black Prince, was confident of winning. He left Bordeaux with an army of 10,000 soldiers, only three hundred of whom were mounted, soon to be pursued by the French king with 50,000 men. They met at the village of Poitiers with the Black Prince's men positioned on high ground approachable only up a single hedge-bound lane.

What followed was in many ways a carbon copy of the Battle of Crécy some nine years before. Once again the retreat of the first French attack clashed with the advance of the next. Once again the longbow arrow proved superior to all other missiles and, as before, French casualties were enormous, and the jewel in the crown of the entire battle for the Black Prince was the capture of John, King of France, who was taken to England and only released after a treaty was signed at Calais by both kings, a huge ransom was paid and the English gained full sovereignty over all their current possessions in France. In return, Edward renounced his claim on the French throne. The various talks and transactions that sealed this deal in the late 1350s were conducted, on behalf of the French king and his dauphin, largely by Constable Robert Fiennes, who travelled back and forth between his Guisnes headquarters and London.

In 1360 Edward III gave Robert Fiennes leave to travel all over the English possessions in France as a troubleshooter to negotiate problems and flare-ups. But when the estates of Fiennes and Guisnes were included in areas given to the English by King John of France, Robert refused to pay homage to the English and was briefly imprisoned in England before becoming Governor of Languedoc and retiring.

In the decade after Poitiers, King John died and his successor, Charles V, soon broke the treaty, and the war rumbled on. King Edward was growing old and less energetic but the Black Prince was as active as ever, although successes came less easily and less often. Nonetheless the long years of victory in France had given the English great self-confidence. The fighters who won the victories were men of every class, from humble village archers to lance-bearing nobles. A chronicle of 1373 stated: 'the English are so filled with their own greatness and have won so many big victories that they have come to believe they cannot lose. In battle, they are the most confident nation in the world.'

That may well have been true at the time, but the situation reversed over the next five years. Queen Philippa, loved by her nation and, above all, by her husband, died and Edward was never his energetic, decisive self again. He relapsed slowly into senility, and the Black Prince, a sick man for many years, died in 1376, a year before his father. It is easy with hindsight to focus on the bad times of any monarch, especially one who survived as long as Edward. His dotage saw the French regain nearly all the territory he had won for England in his glory years, but his capture of Calais was a longstanding and precious prize. Under Edward, trade prospered and increased, the language of English flowered, as did a great sense of nationhood, despite the horrors of the Black Death. He had also bucked the Plantagenet curse of civil war, thanks to his pragmatic and sensitive policies. His successor, the son of the Black Prince and great grandson of Joanna Fiennes, was crowned Richard II at the tender age of ten.

9

FOUNDER'S KIN

Richard II's rule was to be bedevilled at different times by his uncles, since they and their children would always have an eye on the throne. To have been royal with no uncles must have been wonderful in medieval times. Richard's grandfather, Edward III, was to blame for a great deal of strife by siring twelve children, seven of whom were male and likely, if they reached adulthood at the time of the Black Death, to be itching to get their claws on the crown. It was one of Richard's four uncles, John of Gaunt, Earl of Lancaster, who acted as his regent until he was twenty-four.

Somehow through a natural propensity for peace which clearly did not come from his father, the Black Prince, Richard managed to avoid civil war for all but the last few days of his reign. But following his twenty-two-year reign, the bloody War of the Roses, fought between the dynasties of two of his uncles (both directly descended from the Fiennes sisters Margaret and Joanna), would rage for over eighty years.

The Fiennes family members most involved with King Richard were the inmates of Herstmonceux Castle; an expensive place to run. To glimpse the finances of the estate of Herstmonceux (which looks pretty much in the twenty-first century as it did then, a unique red-brick crenellated manor, now called a castle), I am including text from a local record of the mid-1350s. The Fiennes inmates at the time were William, whose father had inherited Herstmonceux from his heiress wife, Maud Monceux, and Joan Saye, an heiress of the Saye fortunes. William and Joan lived well and he served King Richard loyally as a rural bureaucrat. His jobs included serving on the Sussex commission for ditches and dykes, being Sheriff of Sussex and Surrey and, for many years, Constable of Pevensey Castle until, in 1399, the French invaded Pevensey and he surrendered it. His brother Robert had the hazardous job of Collector of Taxes for Sussex.

William died in 1361 and an 'inquisition' held after his death found that at Herstmonceux:

> there are 350 acres of arable land lying in the marsh, of which two parts can be sowed yearly, and that an acre is worth 9d a year, beyond the reprises, producing altogether £13 2s 6d; there are 199 acres of arable land, two-thirds of which can be sowed every year, of which each acre is worth 4d when sown, when not sown 3d, as pasturage for beasts; the other third is worth 2d an acre as pasture; there are 10 acres of meadow, worth 10s a year, the value of an acre is 12d and no more, because it is often flooded, and cannot be mown except in a dry season; 20 acres of bush, worth 3s 4d a year, for pasturage of sheep and other beasts; 8 acres of bush called Bemsell [a small farm in the northwest part of the parish of Watling is still known by the name of Bemsells]. Another farm not very far distant bears the name of Prinkle [one of the

jurors on the inquisition held on the death of John de Fiennes, in 1251, being Alan Prinkle] worth nothing because they are copse, and were cut down before William's death; 80 acres of arable called Lewstrode, worth 20s a year; the price of a acre is 3d for pasture, because it cannot be sown and 'is overgrown with heath'. And they say that the rents from the free tenants and 'nativi' there amount to £17 16s 4d, and the labour of the bondsmen is worth 58s.

While William and Joan Fiennes lived out their rural existence in Sussex, Joan's sister, Idonea Saye, had married a career soldier who spent his life fighting for the Black Prince in Scotland and France and, to a lesser extent, for King Richard in the same countries. This was John, the 3rd Lord Clinton, whose family adopted the Saye title for several generations. Lord John was a senior commander in the English army at the time when the Constable of the French army was Robert Fiennes. As far as I can trace, there is no record of the two meeting up at the same battle. Both of them would have spoken French as their first language. But in England English was gaining ground slowly.

In 1330 a Chester Monk named Ranulf Higden wrote a history book in which he comments:

[The] corruption of the mother-tongue is because of two things. One is because children in school, contrary to the usage and customs of all other nations, are compelled to abandon their own language and to construe their lessons and their tasks in French, and have since the Normans came to England. Moreover, gentlemen's children are taught to speak French from the time they are rocked in their cradle . . . and rustic men want to make themselves like gentlemen, and strive with great industry to speak French, in order to be more highly thought of.

John of Trevisa, another Chester monk who taught French and translated much of Higden's writing into English, wrote that French was 'much in use before the first plague [the Black Death] and since has somewhat changed . . . in the ninth year of Richard II, in all the grammar schools of England children are abandoning French, are construing and learning in English.' Under the cultured King Richard, such poets as Chaucer were encouraged and patronised. More practically, Richard's Statute of Pleading decreed: 'The king hath ordained that all pleas in the courts of the realm shall be pleaded, defended, debated and judged in the English tongue.'

As early as John's reign when Normandy was lost, the barons who committed themselves and their families to England, began also to adopt the English language and by 1400, the year Richard II was murdered, England's new king, Henry IV, would be a native English speaker for the first time.

Despite his ongoing efforts for peace Richard continued to have trouble in France and Scotland where victories of the calibre of his father and grandfather were a thing of the past. But he was an arrogant man and, like his great grandfather,

Edward II (but without the homosexual factor), he favoured certain nobles above all others and caused enemies by promoting them unreasonably.

Then there was the uncle problem. Richard had only to look over his shoulder to spot one or another lurking in predatory mode. There was John of Gaunt, of the House of Lancaster, the Duke of Gloucester (who he eventually had executed), and the Duke of York, largely harmless but not to be trusted when it mattered most. There were many reasons for the unrest Richard faced, but few were of his own making. The feudal system was declining. Vassals enjoyed protection from their barons in return for their work and, if needed, their military service. But by Richard's day, compulsory enlistment had rendered much of this system obsolete.

The immediate cause of the uprisings, now known as the Peasants' Revolt, was the unprecedented level of taxation. The 1380 poll tax was three times higher than that of the previous year and, for the first time, taxed both rich and poor at the same rate. This was both unfair and extortionate, especially when viewed in conjunction with the Statute of Labourers which pegged wages to pre-Black Death levels. The peasant could not win, so he naturally revolted. Manors were attacked, officials beaten up or murdered. In Cambridge university archives were burnt, Norwich Castle was taken over, mobs of several thousands marched on London, mainly from Essex and Kent, and for several days mayhem ensued. Key buildings were ransacked and burnt, officials and foreigners were beheaded, prisoners were released from jails, and legal documents destroyed.

The chief leaders of the mob were a Lollard preacher, John Ball, and a Maidstone ex-soldier, Wat Tyler. As many as 60,000 rioters were involved, and one group gained entry to the Tower of London where they seized the chancellor, the Archbishop of Canterbury and the treasurer. All three were beheaded and their heads joined others displayed on Tower Bridge.

The king, only fourteen years old at the time, was not considered by the mob to be behind their troubles. He was, they felt, being duped by the regent, John of Gaunt, and his government. Gaunt was away in Scotland, so the young King Richard agreed to meet the rioters at Smithfield. A 20,000 strong armed crowd gathered to meet the king who, with sixty retainers, bravely rode towards them. Wat Tyler's ensuing insolence towards Richard infuriated the Mayor of London, who stabbed and killed him on the spot. Not, you would think, a wise action in the circumstances. King Richard somehow stilled the fury of the armed mob with promises that all their demands would be met as soon as possible. Ten days later with his army around him, Richard felt safe enough to revoke all his promises and execute those rebels who were traceable. He had proved, even at fourteen, that he was no pushover. The poll tax was reintroduced at a more realistic level, so in one way the peasants achieved their objective.

John of Gaunt returned from Scotland, once the English mobs were safely out of the way, and continued his reign. Four years later he involved English soldiers in protecting Portugal from a Spanish invasion, and cemented an Anglo-

Portuguese alliance with a Treaty of Friendship which has endured for six hundred years and was last invoked in 1982 during the Falklands War. Gaunt's daughter married the Portuguese king, and their son, Henry the Navigator, became a famous sponsor of the nautical exploration which paved the way for the Portuguese empire.

One of the commanders of the English force who fought the Spanish for Portugal was Gaunt's highly capable general, Lord John Clinton, husband of Idonea Saye, who died on campaign at the end of Richard II's reign. His grandson would later hand over the title of Lord Saye to the Fiennes family.

*   *   *

Although, in Richard II's reign, our family's main home was Herstmonceux in Sussex, the manor in Oxfordshire where the family lives today was first purchased in 1377 by Richard II's chancellor, whose name was William of Wykeham. This house, Broughton Castle near Banbury, was to be inherited by Wykeham's nephew's great granddaughter, Margaret, who became Margaret Fiennes.

William was born into a farmer's family in the village of Wykeham in Hampshire and became a clerk in Winchester, graduating to be a clerk of the works for royal properties. At some point he oversaw building work at Windsor Castle and impressed Edward III, who liked and promoted him to Bishop of Winchester and eventually to chancellor of England. When Edward grew senile and his brother John of Gaunt became regent,

William resigned after various disagreements with Gaunt. He had many ups and downs during the period of political turbulence between King Richard's troublesome uncles, successive Parliaments and loyal king's men, but when Richard eventually emerged from beneath the wing of Gaunt, William again became chancellor. He was clearly lucky not to be in that position during the Peasants' Revolt, or he would have lost his head and my family would never have inherited Broughton Castle.

William's main drive, especially after he resigned the chancellorship for a second time, was the furtherance of clergy education. Once he became one of the richest men in the kingdom, he founded Winchester College and New College, Oxford, to consolidate a firm link between public schools and universities. He made both places of learning available through scholarships granted to the 'poor and indigent'. He established the academic layout of large quadrangles surrounded by arched cloisters and, more than anyone else, he promoted the perpendicular style of architecture, strengthening the culmination of the gothic style. Although he hoped that his new schools would produce generations of learned and competent clerics, able to act independently of influential and often corrupt barons, William did not neglect the education of his own heirs.

To this end, he invented *Consanguineus Fundatoris* (Founder's Kin), a process by which his heirs into perpetuity could gain favourable rates for education at Winchester and New College. Sadly this excellent system ended in 1868 after only five hundred years, so I just missed out (by eighty-eight years) and had to go to Eton instead. During the centuries between the entry to Winchester College of the first Fiennes in 1465 until the Founder's Kin arrangement ceased, a total of fourteen Fiennesès or Twisletons entered the college. Of those fourteen, one died in school and another was drowned during a holiday. Since then, when Fiennesès had to pay up like anyone else, fifteen of them have been educated there, one of whom was head boy. Nathaniel Fiennes, Lord Saye and Sele, the current owner of Broughton Castle and William's heir, used to be a member of the College's governing body.

*   *   *

As for William of Wykeham, he was well out of it when he resigned the chancellorship for the last time, as things went from bad to worse between the king and his wicked uncles. In 1397 Richard's position was sufficiently secure for him to arrest the Dukes of Warwick and Arundel and exile his uncle, the Duke of Gloucester, to Calais where he was mysteriously murdered. With his main rivals now gone and his regal powers restored, he made friends with Uncle John of Gaunt again and appointed him his chief adviser. All went well until, in February 1399, Gaunt died and his son, Henry Bolingbroke (named after the village where he was born), claimed the vast Lancastrian wealth and estates which King Richard badly wanted for himself. Both men plotted in secret, but for a while were openly cordial to one another.

The king, making the first move, managed to have Bolingbroke permanently exiled to France, and, feeling at last completely safe at home, led an army to Ireland to deal with ongoing troubles there. This was definitely a mistake. Over in Paris Henry Bolingbroke made his move. He was, after all, the grandson of Edward III, as was Richard II, but he clearly shared more of that powerful king's aggressive genes than did Richard. Together with a substantial French army, Bolingbroke landed his fleet in Yorkshire, where the Percy dynasty of Northumberland rallied their considerable forces to his cause. They were then joined by various Lancastrian forces, and by the time King Richard heard the bad news and embarked from Ireland in July, Bolingbroke had time to muster further support in the south and west of England.

Richard's army had to stay and maintain the status quo in Ireland, so he had hoped to raise new forces in his traditional recruiting ground of Cheshire and North Wales. But the astute Bolingbroke knew this and reached Chester first. Richard then found himself, with only a small band of loyal supporters, stranded in North Wales. Surrounded by the forces of Bolingbroke, he could only surrender, and was taken to London where Bolingbroke and a quickly assembled Parliament accused the king of having broken his coronation oath and ruled for his own pleasure and not by the laws of England. He was forced to abdicate and the vacant throne passed to Henry Bolingbroke as King Henry IV of England.

Richard was imprisoned in Yorkshire and he died there in February 1400 aged thirty-three. Some say that, heartbroken, he starved himself to death, but the more likely explanation is that he was starved or suffocated to death on the new

113

king's orders. His body was brought to London and buried without ceremony. Richard's death at the hands of his cousin created the seeds of the dynastic instability which would, in due course, explode into the Wars of the Roses.

Henry Bolingbroke of the House of Lancaster, murderer and usurper of his cousin Richard and now King Henry IV, hurried to make it appear to the nation that his four sons had been involved in the coup, lest they later turn against him and take a 'holier than thou' line to depose him. He obviously feared that usurping, like abusing, might run in families. The Fiennes connection to King Henry IV was through his wife, Mary de Bohun, whose grandmother was Maud Fiennes, the sister of the William Fiennes killed at the Battle of Courtrai.

*　　　*　　　*

Henry IV was residually less Norman than his predecessors, in that he was the first English king since the Conquest to have been born on English soil to an English father and an English mother. Further, on the day of his coronation he made his induction speech, the first post-Conquest monarch to do so, in English, not French. The long-lasting habit of most aristocratic and bureaucratic conversations being in French was at last fading away, slowly but surely. One reason was the sense of English patriotism engendered by the many wars against the French and their identification as the number one enemy. The other reason had to do with the Lollards, the religious sect who had first appeared in Richard II's reign with their anti-papal, keep-religion-simple message and the

Wycliff translation of the Bible into English which helped standardise midlands English as a dialect more and more people began to accept. The great writer of this new midlands English was Geoffrey Chaucer whose patronage by Richard II was one thing continued by Henry IV who doubled Chaucer's salary as court poet on the day of his coronation.

As things turned out for Henry the threats to his throne came not from his four sons but from Scotland, Wales and the north of England who sometimes even managed to liaise with each other, though not very efficiently. The Percys of Northumberland who had helped Henry achieve the throne grew resentful and over-ambitious. Their great champion, Harry Hotspur, was eventually put down by Henry's even more famous son and heir, Prince Hal of Shakespearean history fame, at the Battle of Shrewsbury. Although only sixteen at the time, the prince led the king's forces in an uphill attack on Hotspur's men, while they concentrated on mounting charges at King Henry's royal standard, knowing that to kill or capture the king would win the day. But the cunning Henry had dressed several of his own knights in royal surcoats to confuse the issue, which clearly worked well. In the thick of battle Hotspur was killed and the Percy rebellion crushed.

Prince Hal also led campaigns against Owain Glyndŵr (Shakespeare's Glendower) who at one point had managed the improbable feat of uniting the whole of Wales under his leadership. From Glyndŵr Prince Hal learnt about guerrilla tactics, as year after year the English army tramped aimlessly through endless rain and fog in search of

115

an enemy that would only skirmish, then fade away.

Many of Henry IV's best army leaders during his Welsh campaigns were the sons of King Richard's top army men, who clearly saw no problem working for the great usurper. One of these was William Clinton who, with no legal basis, called himself Lord Saye, which had been the title of his mother, Idonea Saye, and which should have gone to the Fiennes family who had previously inherited the Saye fortunes. At the time, William Fiennes lived peacefully at Herstmonceux Castle, where he remained a loyal subject of Henry IV, the Sheriff of Sussex and Surrey and busy with 'several royal commissions to view the banks, sea-coasts and marshes of Pevensey, Hailsham, Hoo and adjacent parishes in order to draw up the ordinances for Pevensey Marsh'.

Henry's policies towards the French were very different from the appeasement strategy of Richard II. Henry was convinced that, as King of England, he had taken over the Plantagenet claim to the throne of France. Once his home-grown troubles were quelled therefore, he turned his attention to gaining territory and glory in France. He was not bothered by the twenty-eight-year truce that Richard had engineered, since the French had already ignored it when, a few years back, they sent an army to help Owain Glyndŵr.

France, Henry knew, was engaged in three or four regional civil wars, the two main rivals in which were the Burgundians and the Armagnacs. King Charles VI was a mere figurehead who, medically insane, was incapable of sorting out the murderous strife between those of his various relatives who led the two warring dynasties. The great province of Brittany was also split between two rival groupings, so England was in a wonderful position to create alliances which would tip the balance of power in favour of one or other faction in return for land which Henry thought of as being his by traditional rights.

There was a period in the middle of his reign when two separate groups formed a council to decide such things as the best policy to follow in France. One group consisted of the king and his key advisers, and the other slightly bigger cabal was led by Prince Hal and his young colleagues. The older group favoured the Armagnacs and Prince Hal preferred the Burgundians. In 1410 the king believed that he and his advisers could do without Prince Hal's help, so he disbanded the council and thereafter decided French policy by himself.

Prince Hal became famous for his enjoyment of London's dens of iniquity and of wine, women and song. After all his teenage years spent marching through rain-sodden Wales, he deserved to sow his oats, but the king disapproved. The prince was ever-popular and there were, after 1410 when Henry fell ill, rumours of disloyalty. Twice there were open rows between father and son. But when an undiagnosed illness finally killed the king in 1413, Prince Hal was still as loyal and obedient a son as any monarch could wish for. French chronicles relate the dying Henry saying to the Prince:

'How shall you have any right to this Crown when, as you know, I never have?'

'My Lord,' Prince Hal replied, 'as you have kept and guarded it by the sword, so do I intend to guard it all my life.'

Prince Hal, the grandson of Maud Fiennes, was crowned, in the midst of a snowstorm, as King Henry V.

10

ONCE MORE UNTO THE BREACH

Things were pretty good for most people in England at the time Prince Hal was crowned. The barons were peaceful, the rash of plagues had all but gone away, harvests were mostly good, and the government had reduced taxes to a reasonable level. Because of the plagues, there were fewer workers and the government was no longer trying to keep wage levels down to force peasants to remain as feudal serfs. Forced to pay more, it now suited many landowners to rent out land to peasants, who were, therefore, able to grow prosperous and better fed. Henry V was a lucky king to walk into such a placid scenario.

There was just one small blot on the landscape. The Lollards were increasing in number and spreading their heresy to all classes. Like his father before him, Henry believed in burning all Lollards who would not recant at the stake. A story told often about Henry and the Lollards involved a clothworker who was being burned in the royal presence. As the flames licked up the man's legs, he screamed for mercy. Henry ordered the fire to be put out and waited for the man to escape his fate by recanting. But, when he didn't, Henry had the fire relit and watched him burn to death.

Otherwise, England was at peace with itself for once, which enabled Henry to plan that which medieval English kings were seemingly designed for: to wage war on France. In Henry's case he had learnt to fight as a prince in many a long campaign in Wales, and an arrow scar down one side of his face was a reminder of his great victory at Shrewsbury. War would mean the chance to reclaim those continental parts of his rightful inheritance that his French cousin Charles VI, mad as he was, held tantalisingly across the Channel. He knew that both church and Parliament would support him and that circumstances were just right, due to the ongoing French civil war.

The barons, he knew, would salivate at the thought of a French war. They had been denied such fun throughout the reign of the pacifist King Richard, yet war was what they were trained and yearned for. It meant adventure, romance, glory and plunder. Especially in France.

And not only the barons looked forward to war. There were in England a great many outlaws on the run for whom military service was the only way they might redeem themselves in the eyes of the law. In some of the English armies of the fifteenth century, up to 5 per cent of the soldiers were murderers officially seeking a pardon. There was none of the ancient problem such as King Harold's army faced in the days of the Conquest, when men deserted in droves at the season of harvesting crops, because Henry's fighters were for the most part the landed classes and their servants, not field labourers. Three-quarters of all Henry's army were his archers, most of whom were professionals a great deal of their time. Then there were the cannon fodder troops from Ireland who, often enough, fought barefoot with great ferocity using daggers as their only weapons. As for the fully armoured men-at-arms (mostly dismounted in battle in Henry's day due to the ever-increasing vulnerability of horses to modern weaponry), their equipment was hugely elaborate and costly. From his all-enclosing helmet and visor to his steel-encased feet, a man-at-arms was completely sheathed in overlapping sections of plate armour. His eye slit was minimal, and only his arms and legs could move, puppet-like but sufficiently to wield his sword and his dagger. If he fell over, it would take two men to stand him up again, and if he fell into a puddle, he was likely to drown.

Henry planned his invasion of France down to the last detail. A huge amount of back-up equipment was involved, and to get it all across the Channel with the army meant a great many boats. These he simply requisitioned from every port in England. His eventual invasion fleet consisted of 1,500 vessels, including Dutch, Venetian and Genoese mercenary ships, a fleet twelve times the size of the Spanish Armada. Henry's entire army numbered at the outset some 10,000 men, or one per cent of the population.

Three Fiennes relations fought for Henry V at Agincourt: the same self-styled Lord Saye who had fought for Henry's father in Wales, and two Fiennes brothers from Sussex, the sons of William of Herstmonceux. The elder son, Roger, Sheriff of

Sussex at the time, was given £1,086 to pay for himself and a company of eight men-at-arms and twenty-four archers to present themselves to the fleet at Southampton. This Roger was to spend a great deal of time serving Henry in France over the next ten years.

His younger brother, James, led a 'lance', or small section of infantry in the division headed up by the king's brother, Humphrey, Duke of Gloucester, and James outshone his brother to the extent that Henry later awarded him the lordship of Court-le-Courte, the governorship of Arques and captain-generalship of various key towns along the River Seine. He was later to build the beautiful manor of Knole in Kent with the spoils of Agincourt and its aftermath.

The army landed unopposed on the north bank of the Seine and close by the walled city of Honfleur, which Henry considered as the key to Normandy. He sent his favourite brother, the Duke of Clarence, to block the far side of Honfleur and positioned his siege guns to batter its great walls from the north. Sapper groups began to tunnel under the walls with explosives, but the French dug counter-tunnels and fierce underground fights ensued where the skills of English archers were redundant. The city moat, wide as a lake, made ramming tactics unfeasible. Pontoon-mounted scaling ladder attacks were met by showers of burning sulphur and lime or scalding streams of hot oil from the battlement guards above.

In the English siege camps along the salt marshes of the Seine estuary, dysentery struck, and hundreds died of the bloody flux. Fortunately for

Henry, the town ran short of supplies, one of the key towers was taken, no relief army turned up and, five weeks after the siege began, the garrison surrendered.

Henry now had his foothold in Normandy, but his army, ravaged by sickness, was too weak to march on Paris. So he decided to march east to his only other secure base, the port of Calais some 160 miles away. His 6,000-strong force managed seventeen miles a day, baggage trains and all, and did well until they reached the Somme, when they found every bridge destroyed and every ford heavily defended. Food began to run out and the rain poured down, as it would five centuries later. The miles went wearily by as the weakened men toiled along the south bank of the river, searching upstream for a crossing point, but always losing ground to their goal of the coast and Calais. Soon a French force as big as theirs appeared on the far riverbank and shadowed their progress inland.

Wet, cold, sick and hungry, the English marched on, their prospects dire. It looked as though Henry had made a horrible tactical error. Hundreds of men had crutch-rot, a condition from which I have suffered for hundreds of miles man-hauling in the polar regions. This can result from walking when there are no washing facilities and one is suffering from diarrhoea. Henry's soldiers cut the backs out of their breeches to stop the bloody flux rotting the leather.

On this long and fearful march, James Fiennes was with the king's brother, the Duke of Gloucester, as was the king himself and various royal favourites, including William Wykeham, the heir of ex-chancellor William of Wykeham.

William was only seventeen at the time, but his uncle Thomas had died at the siege of Honfleur, so he took command of the family standard and led his archers on towards Calais. One outcome of James Fiennes of Sussex and young Wykeham from Hampshire sharing such memorable circumstances may well have been the subsequent marriage, twenty years later, of James's son to William's daughter and heiress, resulting in the Fienneses inheriting Broughton Castle.

As the long hellish march continued and bridge after bridge bristled with French troops, making, one imagines, gallic gestures, Henry may have regretted his decision to head for Calais. But what other option did he have after the long and disease-stricken Honfleur siege? He could hardly have taken his army straight back to an expectant England. His prestige would have sunk below zero with sullen soldiers, angry barons and an uppity Parliament, truly a potential rebellion scenario. On top of which, any future invasion of France would be well nigh impossible to finance. So the march to Calais, however disastrous its outcome, might yet be preferable to having gained Honfleur and then fleeing home.

At some point Henry received local information which led him to cut away from the river where it performed a great loop, thereby gaining ground on the French on the other bank. Then, when the English reached the river again at the end of its loop, they found and crossed two bridges that were intact. This involved feverish work destroying local wooden houses to provide solid approaches to the bridges, for the French had broken up the previous causeways. One can imagine Henry's apprehension as this work went on since, at any minute, the French army might arrive on the far bank before the English could cross. But their luck stayed good, they crossed and must have slept greatly relieved on the northern bank. That night, although they could not know it, the two armies camped only seven miles apart. Henry gave his exhausted men a rest day and sent out scouts to search for the French. Calais, he knew, was still a full eight days' march away.

The two armies then marched along on parallel roads but in the same direction until, converging near the village of Agincourt and from high ground, the English gained their first view of the enemy. They were shocked and dispirited by the sheer size of the French host of some 27,000 soldiers. The French continued northwards until, just ahead of the English, they deployed right across the approach roads to Calais and just outside Agincourt. The English camped a mile short of the enemy lines on the eve of the Feast of St Crispin. They were truly exhausted. Their mood must have been sombre as they camped, having seen the size of the army blocking their escape route. They were outnumbered more than four to one. Henry ordered silence in his camp. Then he moved around the groups of wet, hungry men with words of exhortation. Shakespeare's later version of his speech on the eve of battle was to make Henry famous down the centuries.

The rain poured down all night, but ceased at dawn when Henry rode down his lines. For four hours the armies faced each other 1,000 yards apart in a wide, muddy field with a slight dip between them and woods to either flank of the

English. Six thousand men, mostly archers, against 25,000 men mostly men-at-arms with 1,200 cavalry behind them.

Henry made the first move, for his men were cold, wet and hungry. He gave the order 'Banners advance', his men cheered, drums beat and pipes played. Leaning with the weight against their bows, his archers loosed their first arrows to goad the French cavalry into a charge. Once the charge began, the archers planted sharpened stakes ahead of them and continued to shoot as the cavalry lumbered towards them through deep mud. Unable to pass the stakes, the cavalry wheeled about, but their subsequent rally blocked the oncoming waves of men-at-arms, struggling through the mud to reach the English. So the French living piled up on the French dead and when the English archers ran out of arrows they set about the French with axes and swords taken from the corpses, then sorted the living from the dead to keep the live for ransom.

One problem that the French men-at-arms clearly had at Agincourt was that their pages were left behind, leaving nobody to help them up when they tripped or overbalanced. If two men fell onto a third, the man beneath was likely to die, such was the weight of the plate armour. During the battle, the Duke of York, fighting in the front line, was pushed over and others fell on top of him. When the battle ended and his body was found, he was uninjured, but was dead from suffocation. He was the last of Edward III's grandsons.

As the English took their prisoners, a sudden new danger arose. French cavalry had successfully raided Henry's baggage train and carried off his crown, whilst others had rallied in a force still bigger than the entire English army and were spotted gathering for a new attack. Henry, realising that thousands of French men-at-arms, fallen but uninjured, could yet pose a big threat in any new battle, gave the immediate order that no Frenchman was to be left alive. Wholesale throat-cutting and eyeballing ensued, much to the displeasure of Henry's troops who lost fortunes in potential ransom fees. But they went ahead with the mass killings, saving only the likes of the Dukes of Orleans and Bourbon and other royal personages.

For reasons unknown, the new cavalry attack never materialised and the battle was over. That night the English set off for the safety of Calais where, after two weeks of rest and care of their wounded, they set sail for England.

Less than 1,000 Englishmen were killed at Agincourt, but 10,000 Frenchmen died in the battle, including three dukes, ninety lords and 1,560 knights—over half the nobility of France. This was surely England's greatest hour of triumph in the Hundred Years War. Back in England, King Henry and his men could do no wrong. Eighty years after Agincourt, an Italian visitor was recorded as saying: 'the English are great lovers of themselves . . . They think there are no other men than themselves, and no other world but England. And when they see a handsome foreigner they say that "he looks like an Englishman."'

In the year 2008 a group of French academics met in Agincourt on St Crispin's Day for a conference to mark the 593rd anniversary of the battle. They ridiculed the idea that it was a heroic

English victory against overwhelming odds, saying the size of the French army had been grossly exaggerated and that the English had behaved 'like war criminals', setting fire to prisoners and killing French noblemen who had surrendered. In fact, Agincourt was, as Henry himself was quick to realise, just a small, if successful, beginning to his quest to become King of France. At a cost of a quarter of his army lost, mostly to sickness, he had merely captured one town and won a single battle.

Over the two years following Agincourt, Henry prepared for his second invasion by diplomacy, using as his main lever the ongoing civil war between the Burgundians in the north and east and the Armagnacs or House of Valois, in the south and west. Both sides vied for the favour of the mad French king and whichever of his sons was his dauphin at the time (they died off one by one). Henry eventually chose the Burgundians for an alliance, and only planned his next move secure in the knowledge of Burgundian aid, or at least their non-interference with his planned annexation of Normandy. His enemy would be narrowed down to the armies of the Armagnacs, and the dauphinists.

The Count of Armagnac was now also Constable of the French army, the position previously held by Robert Fiennes, and he attempted to forestall Henry's invasion by retaking Honfleur, having blockaded the mouth of the Seine. In August 1416 one of Henry's brothers, the Duke of Bedford, with a large English fleet, won the Battle of the Seine and lifted the siege. Henry then took Caen, after which other lesser towns yielded like falling dominoes, so that, by November 1416, he controlled all of Lower

Normandy and could move on to the challenge of Rouen.

The garrison at Rouen knew the English were coming and burnt all the churches, abbeys, manors, castles, villages, harvests and barns, until a blackened wilderness surrounded the city for miles around. All families who could not prove they could provide for themselves for at least ten months were exiled. Several thousand died of starvation as a result.

One of Henry's fears had come to pass, for Paris had fallen to his former ally the Duke of Burgundy, who now felt powerful enough to ignore his truce with England and send troops to help hold Rouen. The city lies on the east bank of the Seine and its walls were five miles long. Henry never succeeded in a direct assault, but after six months the garrison were starving, holding out only because they believed the Duke of Burgundy would soon arrive with his main army to relieve them. But he never did, and inside the city the cost of a cat was ten times that of a mouse, whilst shoes made of leather were boiled and chewed. Finally, in January 1418 the garrison surrendered and Henry's men entered in triumph. Normandy could now be said to be the property of the English king 'Henry the Conqueror', 352 years after William the Conqueror and the Battle of Hastings.

Henry's two successful invasions gained Normandy, but he had yet to achieve his ultimate aim of gaining the crown of France. A third invasion would be needed and, before that, a great deal more diplomacy, particularly when he learnt the Burgundians and Armagnacs were about to bury their differences in an anti-English alliance. A grand meeting was fixed between Burgundy and Armagnac to agree terms. The Duke of Burgundy duly arrived at the rendezvous, in the centre of a bridge over the river Yonne, expecting to meet the dauphin. Instead the dauphin's Armagnac soldiers hacked off half of the duke's head with an axe.

Nothing could have helped Henry more, throwing as it did the Burgundians straight into his arms. A further outcome of the duke's murder was that the French Queen Isabella, the Burgundian figurehead, betrothed her daughter Catherine to Henry. She loved her daughter but detested her son, the dauphin, leader of the Armagnacs. In May 1420 Henry married Catherine of France and co-signed with her mother, the queen, the Treaty of Troyes which made him the next King of France as soon as mad King Charles VI died. Until then he would act as regent. The only drawback to the treaty was the promise Henry had to make to continue war against the southern territories still held by the dauphin. But, so what? Henry was King of France and England, and his new wife was young, beautiful and quickly bore him a son.

Henry and the new Duke of Burgundy were highly successful in their ongoing joint campaigns, but Henry's brother, the Duke of Clarence, was operating with a small force near Baugé in Maine when a dauphinist Scottish-French army of 5,000 blocked his way near Tours. Clarence rashly attacked when his archers under Lord Salisbury were still hours away, and was massacred. Clarence was Henry's favourite brother and trusty comrade-in-arms and, although the battle was in itself minor and led by the Scots, its effect on the morale of the dauphinists was great, for it was the first time in the Hundred Years War that the English had suffered a straightforward defeat in open battle.

The dauphin promoted the Scottish victor of the Battle of Baugé, the Duke of Buchan, to be the Constable of his army: a unique honour for a foreigner. At one point, due to the tiny force left to Lord Salisbury with which to defend Normandy, the dauphin may well have been able to retake much of the province. But he never pressed his attack, and Salisbury held out until he was reinforced.

In the spring of 1421 Henry set out from England for his third and last campaign. This was not, technically, an invasion force, since he was after all regent of France. He landed at Calais with 4,000 men, his aim being to defeat a powerful dauphinist counter-offensive and to subdue a minor regional rebellion. The successes that followed were as brilliant as ever, with no open battles but several hard sieges of diehard garrisons, such as Maux. But his main aim, to lure the dauphin into a major battle, never worked, and in 1422 he became too ill to ride a horse. By August that year he was confined to bed, probably with severe dysentery, at the Castle of Vincennes, where he spent his last three weeks putting his dominions in order and securing the inheritance of the baby son, his heir, whom he had never seen. His funeral cortege moved slowly and in great style through Normandy. The Normans would long remember the passing of King Henry the Conqueror.

11

Murdered by a Mob

Henry VI was born in July, only six months before his father, Henry V of England, and mad King Charles of France both died, leaving their thrones to him. He became the only monarch ever to be crowned king of both countries. However, King Charles's exiled and dispossessed son, the dauphin, was shortly to proclaim himself the rightful King of France and to dedicate his reign not just to getting Henry out of the way but to ridding France of the English once and for all.

English successes in France to date had been largely due to brilliant commanders but, more so, to clever manipulation by the English of the ongoing civil war between two royal dynasties, the Burgundians and the House of Armagnac (Valois), both having reasonable claims to the French throne. However, the rumblings of civil war in England between two similarly royal-contending dynasties, the Houses of Lancaster and of York, both claiming the right to the throne of England, allowed the French to slowly turn the tables and to rid France of the English. The seeds of this civil war were sewn largely by the unfortunate Henry VI, not through aggression on his part but through his very weakness and ineptitude, for he was as feeble a character as his father, Henry V of Agincourt, had been ultra-efficient and powerful.

During Henry V's final three weeks on his deathbed in France, he had made meticulous plans for his succession. He specified that his brother, the Duke of Bedford, was to be young Henry VI's regent in France and Normandy, that his brother, the Duke of Gloucester, was to be regent in England, and that his uncles, the Duke of Exeter and Bishop Beaufort, would be Henry VI's tutors.

This initially worked well, and in France, despite the loss of the ever-victorious Henry V, things carried on normally, even though there was a serious lack of troops to man the garrisons of the many hundreds of castles and fortified towns held by the English. Bedford and Talbot were the two great English generals of the time and, in the wings, the Earls of Salisbury and Warwick.

One great battle of the period was fought at Cravant in Normandy between a fairly small English/Burgundian allied force under Salisbury against a mixed Scottish/Armagnac army. Some 4,000 Scots were killed and 2,000 Frenchmen. By the mid 1420s a constant stream of Scottish reinforcements were joining the Armagnacs to fight the English, and in April 1424 the Earl of Douglas led an army of 6,500 Scotsmen against an English force. The dauphin later gave the earl the title of Duke of Touraine. At the subsequent Battle of Verneuil, Bedford and Salisbury defeated a Franco-Scottish force twice the strength of their own army and annihilated the Scottish contingent of 6,000. French writers of the time described the battle as another Agincourt.

All went well under the young Henry VI's regents, or at least it did so for the first five years of his reign. And for the Fiennes clan of the period, things were also looking up. Two successive William Fienneses had lived at

Herstmonceux Castle and both had been Sheriffs of Sussex and Surrey. The younger William had surrendered Pevensey Castle to French raiders some twenty years before the start of Henry VI's reign, but that had not affected his high standing in royal eyes. He had two sons, Roger and James, and passed all his lands to Roger, the elder son, who joined the royal household, took over as Sheriff of Sussex, was knighted, and spent many years as the influential Treasurer to Henry VI's household.

He and his younger brother James had both done well at Agincourt for Henry V and on subsequent campaigns, but James, who set out in life with no land, was extremely ambitious. He is my great to the power of eighteen grandfather, and I have to admit that both written history and William Shakespeare make him sound the sort of man who would and did do anything in the pursuit of power. He attended the young King Henry VI at his coronation in Paris, and was made Commissioner of the Peace for Kent, a lifelong appointment. At the time he began to cultivate and promote friends and relations into a veritable Kent mafia that would eventually affect English history.

The wealth James Fiennes made from his French campaigning helped him purchase two great estates in the south-east that are open to the public today: Knole, near Sevenoaks, and Hever at Penshurst. But the more James had, the more he wanted. Whenever he could he used his big brother Roger's influence, and that was considerable, especially after he had organised the marriage of the young Henry VI to a niece of the King of France, Margaret of Anjou. Before long both Fiennes brothers were Members of

Parliament, representing Kent and Sussex.

Whilst these two Fiennes stars were in the ascendant, the English situation in France was deteriorating fast. The rot set in when a teenage peasant girl from eastern France, Joan of Arc, became the talisman of the dauphin's army with her 'divine voices'. Agincourt became merely a nightmare of the past for the French. The English were no longer invincible. This ensured that it would only be a matter of time before the Burgundian/English alliance collapsed, as the Duke of Burgundy always sought the stronger side. However, the alliance was still in place when, after a string of minor victories, Joan of Arc was captured by the Burgundians, sold to the English for 16,000 francs, condemned as a heretic by the French church and burnt at the stake. Joan's main beneficiary was, of course, the dauphin who, despite several reversals due to brilliant generalship by the likes of Lord Talbot, spent the next quarter century driving the English out of every corner of France, save for the port of Calais. In this he was greatly helped by one Jean Bureau, an expert designer of artillery who changed the face of siege warfare and, at length, rendered obsolete the previous advantages of the English longbow.

When the French captured the key town of Pontoise, they slaughtered five hundred English soldiers in the garrison and ransomed their commander, John Fiennes, the 6th Lord Clinton, who had married Elizabeth Fiennes, the granddaughter of that Roger Fiennes who was treasurer of the royal household. Like his father before him, this Clinton styled himself as Lord

Saye. But the exorbitant ransom that John Clinton had to pay to escape the French clutches (twice, because he was later recaptured!) crippled his finances and, to retrieve his fortunes, he sold the title of Lord Saye to the Fiennes family, where it had rightly belonged since one of the William Fienneses of Herstmonceux had married Joan de Saye almost a century before.

The senior Fiennes who should have taken over the Lord Saye title from the Clintons was Roger, the royal treasurer, since he was the elder brother. But the ever ambitious James was, by the time of Pontoise, a close favourite and adviser of Henry VI, who agreed that he, James, should become Lord Saye. James added the name of his estate village, Sele, to his title, and so was officially thereafter Sir James Fiennes, the 1st Lord (or Baron) Saye and Sele.

In 1440, the new Lord Saye and Sele, James Fiennes, began a meteoric rise to the dangerous heights of political power in England. His methods may be described as occasionally dubious. He and his elder brother Roger were members of the inner circle surrounding the king, led by the Earl of Suffolk. James spent a great deal of time working with the king on two of the latter's more praiseworthy projects: the foundation of Eton College and King's College, Cambridge. In 1444 James became chamberlain to the queen, Margaret of Anjou, who was, much of the time, a powerful influence on the king. James received many other offices, wardships, estates and annuities to add to his growing wealth and influence. He was appointed Constable of both Pevensey and Rochester Castles. The same year the Archbishop of Canterbury gave him various church lands by the king's order, and recorded these appointments as 'havyng consyderacion how the seid James stondyng aboute the Kyng as he dooth, may dayly proufyte our church and us'.

The tangled plotting of different advisers to King Henry VI was further complicated in the mid-1440s when the king began to experience periods of madness. The Earl of Suffolk's influence vied with that of the regent, the Earl of Gloucester, and when the latter's star waned, Suffolk went in for the kill, successfully persuading Parliament to arrest and imprison Gloucester for his failed policies in France. James Fiennes was Suffolk's main crony and, when Gloucester died mysteriously in prison, he was accused of his murder. But nothing was proved and James, who had served alongside Gloucester at Agincourt, profited hugely from his death, since the day after its occurrence he petitioned successfully for various offices held by the duke.

His royal wages were greatly increased and he became chamberlain of the royal household, which gave him control over access to the king and membership of the Continual Council. For a period he became Constable of the Tower of London, whilst all the while adding to his web of influential friends in Kent, a regional mafia involved in heavy extortion of taxes and dubious landgrabbing tactics.

Many historians later accused Roger Fiennes of extortions in Kent alongside his brother, but his actions suggest that he had no sympathy with James's greedy and aggressive behaviour. There is no evidence of his ever lining his own pockets, nor did he have himself ennobled. Indeed, Roger resigned from his influential position at court at the exact time when James and the Duke of Suffolk reached the peak of their power on the back of policies which Roger clearly detested.

On the wider political front, Suffolk and James tried to buy peace with France through mediation and by marrying King Henry VI to a French royal. They pushed a plan to surrender Anjou and Maine, providing they could keep Calais, Gascony and Normandy. Such appeasement was loathed by supporters of the possibly murdered Duke of Gloucester, including Roger Fiennes who had risked his life over the years to retain such French territories.

When the Suffolk policies collapsed in ruins and the French grabbed back everywhere but Calais, the vengeance of Parliament was immediate. The king tried to save Suffolk from execution by banishing him, but he was intercepted by a mob of Kentish sailors during his cross-Channel escape and was clubbed to death. To be fair to Suffolk and James Fiennes, their peace policy, with hindsight, looks to have been the most sensible option. If the English had retained Calais, Normandy and Gascony, they would have kept control of the Channel and the wool and wine trades. The alternative course was war, which may have looked good at the time but was an expensive no-win solution. As it was, the peace policy appeared to have allowed France to throw out the English, and James, with Lord Suffolk dead, must have known his days were numbered. But he did not go without a struggle.

The king appointed James lord high treasurer,

to which the Commons responded by moving to have him arrested, and his fate was sealed by his past shady dealings in Kent. But the men of Kent were not the only folk in England with grudges to bear. In a world already ravaged by the Black Death, there followed outbreaks of plague, disastrous famines, wet summers, cattle and sheep epidemics and a slump in wool prices. Private armies of disbanded soldiers, most but not all owned by local barons, roamed, bullied and wrecked many local economies. King Henry VI, insane and weak, appeared to do nothing to alleviate the misery of his people.

In June 1450 a great crowd from all over Kent county met together on the road to London. Their aim was to punish those in government who caused their tribulations and, in their own words, to free the good king from the trickeries of these false ministers. The ringleader of the march on London was one Jack Cade whom history records as having been a part of the household of close Fiennes relations in Kent, but was often described as a mere peasant. Mere peasant he could not have been, bearing in mind the efforts made after his death to declare officially that 'his blood was corrupt'. Two years after his death, the king ordered that his goods should be forfeited, including his lands, rents and possessions. Had he been low-born, no such act of attainder would have been made. He himself claimed to be called John Mortimer, the family name of the Duke of York.

In July 1450 Cade's mob came to London, and the king, 'dredying the malice of the peple', committed James Fiennes to the Tower as a sop to the rebels who in a 'dyrge made by the comons of

Kent in the tyme of their rysynge' wrote:

'So pore a kyng was never seene
Nor richere lordes alle bydene;
The communes may no more.
The lorde Say biddeth hold hem downe,
That worthy dastarde of renowne,
He techithe a fals loore.'

James is berated in better prose and verse when he features in Shakespeare's *King Henry VI, Part 2*, where in true Elizabethan royalist style he is afforded the dignity of afflicted nobility whereas Cade is merely comic relief:

Thou hast most traitorously corrupted the youth of the realm in erecting a grammar school: and whereas, before, our forefathers had no other books but the score and the tally, thou has caused printing to be used; and, contrary to the king, his crown and dignity, thou hast built a paper-mill. It will be proved to thy face that thou hast men about thee that usually talk of a noun and a verb, and such abominable words as no Christian ear can endure to hear. Thou hast appointed justices of peace, to call poor men before them about matters they were not able to answer. Moreover, thou hast put them in prison; and because they could not read, thou hast hanged them; when, indeed, only for that cause they have been most worthy to live.

Shakespeare replies for James Fiennes with the words:

I sold not Maine, I lost not Normandy;
Yet, to recover them, would lose my life.
Justice with favour have I always done;
Prayers and tears have moved me, gifts could
    never.
When have I aught exacted at your hands,
But to maintain the king, the realm, and
    you? . . .
Have I affected wealth or honour?
Are my chests fill'd up with extorted gold?
Is my apparel sumptuous to behold?
Whom have I injured, that ye seek my death?
These hands are free from guiltless blood-
    shedding,
This breast from harbouring foul deceitful
    thoughts.
O, let me live!

At the Guildhall mock-trial James was accused
of many things, including murder. The record
states that he 'knowlachyd of the dethe of that
notabylle and famos prynce the Duke of
Glouceter'. The Bury Parliament 'was maad [set
up] only for to sle the noble duke of Gloucestre,
whoz deth the fals duke of Suffolk . . . and ser
Jamez Fynez lord Say . . . hadde longe tyme
conspired and ymagyned.'

He requested a proper trial, but the mob,
enraged and beyond the control of anyone or
anything but their immediate bloodlust, dragged
James on foot to Cheapside, where they hacked off
his head halfway through his confession and before
'the priest could shrive him'. His head was then
impaled on a long spear and paraded ahead of

Cade 'as he rode, like a lordly captain, thro' every street.'

At Mile End, James's son-in-law, William Cromer, the much hated Sheriff of Kent, was also decapitated, his head mounted on another spear and the mob then 'made both hedes kisse to gider'. James's body was stripped, tied to a horse's tail and dragged naked, 'so that the flesh clave to the stones all the way from Chepe to Southwark'. At London Bridge the two heads were rammed on to spikes and the bodies hanged and quartered.

Documents that Nat and Mariette Fiennes lent me from Broughton indicate a sub-plot behind the Cade killing of James Fiennes. For anyone interested in conspiracy theories this one rates a great deal more likely than most of those suggested for the deaths of Kennedy, Princess Diana or Michael Jackson. If you can't abide a touch of 560-year-old forensic dabbling, then simply skip the next page or so. The facts and deductions are as follows:

FACT Sussex records state: 'Cade drew with him a great company of tall [important] personages and vagrant persons from Kent, Sussex and Surrey . . . These musters were levied by the Constables . . . We have by name four hundred Sussex men . . . Lord Saye [James Fiennes] was unfavourably known here as having acquired his title by grant from his kinsman John Clinton of Sussex and it will be seen that the neighbours of Clinton and the men living closest to Fiennes's eldest brother Sir Roger and to Thomas Dacre, in whose service Cade had been, were the strongest in the list of Cade's Sussex men.'

DEDUCTION James's Sussex relations did not

141

approve of him. His unpopular reputation and his closeness to the hated Suffolk were perhaps reflecting on them and they wanted him sacked but not killed.

FACT Of the Kent rebels with Cade only one was a knight, John Cheney, who was at the forefront of the rebellion. He shared a common Saye ancestry with James and his great grandmother was James's grandmother.

DEDUCTION Cheney was in league with the above Sussex Fiennes plotters and for the same reason.

FACT The above Fiennes plotters would also have received an unpopular backlash from the fact that the hated James and Suffolk clique was closely associated with yet another relation of theirs, Sir John Saye, the only man to be Speaker of the House of Commons in both a Lancastrian and a Yorkist Parliament, 'related to James Fiennes, Lord Saye and Sele, in whose company he is often recorded . . . brother to William Saye, Dean of St Paul's. Close associate to the Earl of Suffolk.' This Sir John was a favourite of both Henry VI and Edward IV, but in 1450 was 'attacked by the Cade rebels and in 1451 the Commons demanded his banishment from Court'.

FACT In addition to targeting James and his cousin John Saye, Cade's other main target was, as we have seen, William Cromer, Sheriff of Kent, who was married to James's daughter.

DEDUCTION A powerful group of the Fiennes/Saye/Dacre clan in Sussex and Kent were fed up with three family members who, as extortioners and cronies of Suffolk, were getting them a very bad name. So their plot was as follows.

They were influential enough to have friends in

court and learnt of the king's plan to help Suffolk escape by sea. So they paid men to bludgeon Suffolk to death during his secretive flight. These same men were later listed as Cade followers.

Next the plotters instructed Cade (who had once worked for Thomas Dacre) to extract James from his refuge in the Tower and then to select Robert Danvers, the Recorder of London, as the man to judge James.

They selected Danvers because he was part of their plot, being brother-in-law to James's daughter Jane. Danvers would ensure that James, John Saye and Cromer were removed from their high-profile jobs but not actually killed.

All went well with the plan until Cade lost control of his mob. John Saye was indeed sacked but both James and Cromer were murdered. The plotters, fearing discovery, decided to have Cade silenced so, when Cromer's widow married the new Sheriff of Kent he was tasked to find and kill Cade, which he speedily did.

Many historians proffer the theory that Cade aka Mortimer was put up to the rebellion against King Henry's ruling clique in order to make way for a rival group under Richard Duke of York, whose family name was Mortimer. But the Fiennes versus Fiennes plot that I offer here is based on no less circumstantial evidence.

THE FIENNES VERSUS FIENNES PLOT

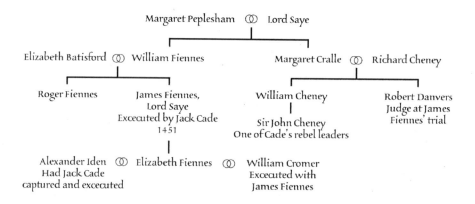

After the Cade revolt, English reverses continued apace in France, and soon after the final English bastions of Rouen and Castillon were lost, Roger Fiennes, ten years of whose life had been spent fighting for Henry V, died at his moated home, Herstmonceux Castle, which he had rebuilt and crenellated at a total cost of £3,800. At the time this was considered to be the greatest brick building in England since Roman times. Unaltered, in the twentieth century it would become the Royal Observatory in lieu of Greenwich when the London lights became too bright in the night sky for observation of the stars. When Herstmonceux also became too bright at night, the Observatory moved to the Canary Islands, and Herstmonceux became a Canadian-funded international study centre.

I believe that Roger was always as strait-laced as James was wily. Both brothers were for a long period full-time courtiers of Henry VI and both received many royal gifts as a result. One record of the Treasury from the 1440s records. 'An ouche [brooch] garnished with a baleys and a saphyr and

144

six perles yeven by us to Sir James Fenys on New Yere's Day and an ouche of gold with, in the middle, a fleur de lys yeven at the same time to Sir Roger Fenys, tresorier of our household.' Both men had sons who were to shine in their separate fields with no adverse effects from James's lamentable end.

* * *

After 1453 Henry VI and his successors had little to worry about in France, but troubles at home soon made up for the next sixty years of peace with the French. The Wars of the Roses did not begin with a bang, nor were the warring parties divided along clean lines, although they clearly fought to place a Lancastrian or a Yorkist on the throne of England. Henry VI, the Lancastrian was directly descended in an unbroken male line from Edward III's third son. The claimant who was to take Henry's throne from him was Richard, Duke of York, who was descended from Edward III's second son, but through two women. In the male only line, he was also descended from Edward's fifth son.

Quite who was the more legitimate contender and why is a matter long fought over by historians, but at the time of the Wars of the Roses both sides were certain that their king was the rightful heir. Both dynasties originated from the same family and both dynasties were at some point mothered by Fiennes DNA. On the Lancastrian side, Henry VI's grandmother was Mary, the granddaughter of Joan Fiennes. On the Yorkist side the soon to be King Edward IV was the direct descendent of

BOTH THE HOUSES OF YORK AND LANCASTER WERE

AT SOME POINT MOTHERED BY FIENNES DNA

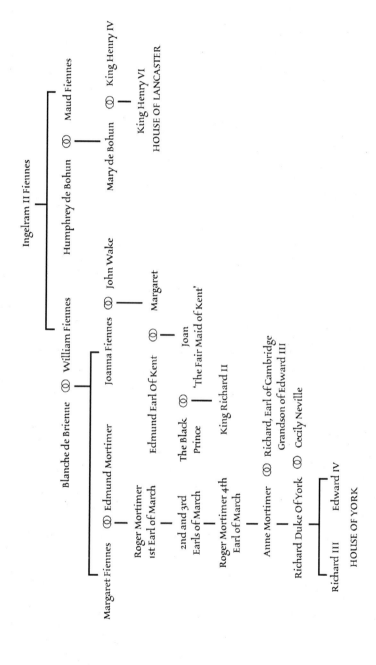

Margaret Fiennes.

Although the Lancastrians could trace their descent back to Edward III, they were clearly already usurpers since their Henry IV had murdered the Yorkist ancestor Richard II. Richard of York's advantage was that he was more popular in England than the weak King Henry. One of the Cade rebellion's demands had been his installing as Henry's chief adviser, in place of Edmund, Duke of Somerset, who had just been promoted chancellor.

Richard realised that Somerset would sooner or later have him banished or executed on some pretext or other. So he struck first, arriving outside London with a small force and loudly proclaiming that he wished only to oust Somerset, not the king. This did not work, and Richard, who then disbanded his men, would almost certainly have been done away with but for the fact that his ten-year-old son, Edward of York, with a sizeable force from the Welsh borders, marched to his father's rescue.

Richard had married a Neville, one of two powerful families from Northumberland. They and the Percy dynasty hated one another, and the two families were to fuel the coming civil war. The Percys supported the Lancastrians and the Nevilles pushed for the rise of the House of York, with Richard as their great white hope.

In 1453 Henry VI became temporarily insane, due to madness in his maternal family, and his wife Queen Margaret took over the reins of England alongside Somerset. These two became implacable enemies to Richard and his young son, Edward. Early in 1455 King Henry's insanity disappeared

147

long enough for him to regain power, causing Richard and his supporters, in fear of their lives, to raise an army which confronted the king's forces at St Albans, the first battle of the Wars of the Roses. This was in reality a one-hour skirmish, but the Duke of Somerset was killed and the king was captured.

Once again Richard was in charge and his main men, Salisbury and Warwick, got the top jobs. King Henry, weak and verging on new bouts of insanity, would surely have accepted the situation, but not his feisty Queen Margaret who plotted constantly to ensure that when her mad husband died, her young son Edward, and not the hated Richard of York, would take over.

The two armies clashed again at Northampton in 1460, and in no time the Lancastrian army dissolved, King Henry was once again in Richard's hands and, for a while, things seemed little changed. The mad Lancastrian King Henry was on the throne with a Yorkist government ruling the land in his name. But then Richard's personal ambitions to usurp and rule without awaiting Henry's demise grew too strong. He found soon enough that the country was not quite ready to remove its rightful king, but Parliament did sign an agreement that, on Henry's death, Richard's dynasty, not Henry's, would succeed.

This was too much for Queen Margaret. Her husband might be mad and accept whatever humiliation Richard threw at him, but she would somehow ensure that her son remained heir, as was his birthright. She raised support in Scotland and in the Lancastrian northlands, so Richard went north to deal with her. Overconfident and somewhere near Wakefield, he found himself with few troops and surrounded by a large Lancastrian force. He was killed, along with the Earl of Salisbury and others. Their heads were paraded on poles and then planted on the battlements of York.

A few days later Richard's son and heir, Edward of York, heard the news. His father, brother, uncle and cousin were all dead. He himself defeated a force of largely Welsh Lancastrian supporters near Hereford before heading for London. Meanwhile, the queen's large army of northerners behaved like Viking raiders as they also advanced on London over a wide front, looting, raping and causing devastation wherever they went. Known or suspected Yorkists were tortured and killed. The queen could not control her army, so, on reaching London, she camped on the outskirts. This allowed Edward of York, and his cousin and main supporter the Earl of Warwick, to outflank the queen's wild horde and secure the capital, the centre of power.

This time there was no beating around the royal bush. A speedily convened council agreed that Edward of York, who was neither mad nor in charge of an army of rapists, should be king in place of the mad King Henry and his haughty wife. So King Edward IV, only twenty years old, became the first Yorkist king. But there were now two reigning monarchs, a situation that would need speedy resolution.

Edward and Warwick sped north a week after the coronation to deal once and for all with Queen Margaret, her son and their army. The two armies, each numbering over 40,000, met at Towton in Yorkshire on 29 March 1461 in a blinding snowstorm. This was to be the bloodiest battle, since Roman times, ever fought on British soil, and the dead were counted at almost 30,000. Roger Fiennes of Herstmonceux's only son, Richard and his wife and Johanna's uncle Ranulph of Dacre were commanders of a large Lancastrian army at Towton. In the filthy weather, the Lancastrians manned the high ground so that the Yorkists had to climb to get at them. There were crude firearms around, but the main groups of fighters on both sides were still archers and dismounted men-at-arms.

A strong cold wind appears to have been the deciding factor of the day, blowing from behind the Yorkists as they toiled uphill. Their wind-blown arrows went that little bit farther and killed Lancastrians whose arrows, fired into the wind, fell short of their Yorkist targets. Present day archaeologists claim to have found the very first battlefield bullet, and have worked out that a total of over a million arrows were loosed in the first few hours of the battle. Rather than risk slow attrition, the Lancastrians advanced downhill and soon lost their uphill advantage. Close-quarter fighting was intense. Bodies had to be moved simply to get at the enemy as the hours of slaughter continued. Eventually Yorkist reserves arrived and outflanked the Lancastrians, who began to flee.

No quarter was given, no prisoners were taken and thousands of Lancastrians were slaughtered as they tried to escape. Yorkist horsemen rode them down for many miles through the night and the following day. My kinsman and namesake, Ranulph of Dacre, died at some point in the battle. At rivers with broken bridges hundreds of bodies piled up in the frozen water. Somehow King Henry, Queen Margaret and the Duke of Somerset survived and fled to Scotland. But their army was no more.

Edward IV and the man whose support had proved crucial, Warwick the Kingmaker, were soon back in London and feeling secure. For a while there was peace. King Edward must have had a sense of humour, for he appointed as Commissioner to 'look into the extortions in Kent' by the late beheaded James Fiennes and his crony, Cromer, the sheriff, none other than James's only son William Fiennes, 2nd Baron Saye and Sele. William must have done well, as he soon became vice-admiral and senior adviser to Warwick the Kingmaker.

12

WINTER OF OUR DISCONTENT

The immediate aftermath of the bloody Battle of Towton saw Yorkist King Edward IV, direct descendant of Margaret Fiennes, fairly secure on the English throne, backed by his cousin and main adviser, Warwick the Kingmaker, a slimy character, who was the father-in-law of Geoffrey de Saye and grandfather of William Fiennes, my great to the power of twenty grandfather. In 1465 mad King Henry was captured in the north and locked up in the Tower of London. Although his queen and young son were still at large, an imprisoned mad king was better than a loose one, so Edward felt a good deal more secure. He gave the most powerful three positions in England to three men whom he trusted. Two of them were to let him down badly, Warwick the Kingmaker and his youngest brother, the slippery Duke of Clarence. The third, who remained loyal, was the eldest of his brothers, Richard, Duke of Gloucester.

Edward gratefully rewarded all those who had led his forces at the key Battle of Towton, including William Fiennes whom he knighted and made a Privy Councillor. Aged twenty-four, he had taken his beheaded father's title and so was the 2nd Lord Saye and Sele. He had also taken over various appointments his late father had held, including Constable of Dover Castle and Warden of the Cinque Ports, Sheriff of Kent and Sussex, and was owner of many estates in both counties.

However, William was as pro-Yorkist as his father and uncle Roger had been Lancastrian. He did a number of things which seemed to indicate that he was ashamed of the way his father had behaved. He sold his hereditary title of Constable of Dover Castle to the Duke of Buckingham and the superb manor and estate of Knole to the Archbishop of Canterbury. He sold the manor of Sele, and even Hever Castle (which his father had bought from Sir John Fastolf, Shakespeare's Falstaff) to Sir Geoffrey Boleyn, whose lovely granddaughter Anne would later be discovered at Hever and fatally courted by Henry VIII before giving birth to Queen Elizabeth I and losing her head. Many documents by various historians state that William sold his estates because he was twice held captive and ransomed whilst fighting in France for the king. But this is clearly a case of mistaken identity, since his cousin, Lord John Fiennes Clinton, *was* captured twice by the French, did become poor through paying ransom and did sell off the title of Lord Saye to William's father as a result.

Another reason for selling off estates in Sussex and Kent may well have been his acquisition of Broughton Castle through his marriage to Margaret Wykeham. The Wykehams were ardent Lancastrians, but nonetheless seemed to approve of young William. Our family has since that time lived in Broughton Castle for twenty-one unbroken generations and, from time to time, included the name of Wykeham as part of our surname. Broughton Castle came to public attention in 1999 when the film *Shakespeare In Love*, recipient of thirteen Oscar nominations, was filmed there with the titular role being played by my cousin, Joseph Fiennes. The castle was chosen for the film because it provided exactly the right period setting, complete with crenellated gatehouse overlooking the moat. Little is known of its early history save that in the Domesday Book it was owned by the Saxon thane, Turgot, and was later given by William the Conqueror to a Norman knight, Berenger de Todenai. He sold it to a family called de Broughton, who sold it to William of Wykeham, who sold it, over six hundred years ago, to us.

With Edward firmly on the throne, the country became relatively peaceful. History has portrayed England at the time of the Wars of the Roses as a land laid waste by civil strife and widespread carnage, but the reality was very different. There were battles, and I list them below, but their effect on the general population was minimal. There

153

were exceptions, such as the last march of Queen Margaret's northern troops towards London, which ravaged the land over a wide front, but usually battles were short and affected few folk beyond the battlefield.

According to Shakespeare, the Wars of the Roses (white for York and red for Lancaster) got its name one morning when Richard of York met King Henry's men, the Duke of Suffolk and the Earl of Somerset, whilst they were walking round a rose garden in the Inns of Court. They argued. Richard said, 'From off this brier pluck a white rose with me.' And Somerset responded, 'Let him that is no coward nor But dare maintain the party of the truth, Pluck a red rose from off this thorn with me.'

THE WARS OF THE ROSES
Major Battles

King Henry VI's Reign

1455	St Albans	won by Yorkists
1459	Blore Heath	won by Yorkists
1459	Ludford Bridge	won by Lancastrians
1460	Northampton	won by Yorkists
1460	Wakefield	won by Lancastrians
1461	Mortimer's Cross	won by Yorkists
1461	Second St Albans	won by Lancastrians
1461	Ferrybridge	won by Yorkists
1461	Towton	won by Yorkists

King Edward IV's Reign

1464	Hedgeley Moor	won by Yorkists
1464	Hexham	won by Yorkists
1464	Edgecote Moor	won by Lancastrians

1469	Losecote Field	won by Yorkists
1471	Barnet	won by Yorkists
1471	Tewkesbury	won by Yorkists

King Richard III's Reign
| 1485 | Bosworth | won by Lancastrians (Tudors) |

King Henry VII's Reign
| 1487 | Stoke | won by Lancastrians (Tudors) |

The reasons that the Wars of the Roses involved few folk other than the direct protagonists were many and various. Most of the fighting was done by the noble families and their retainers. There was no conscription-raised army at the time, other than the soldiers of Calais. There were no long sieges involving troops, sometimes for many months, living off pillage and looting for miles around the city under siege. Great massacres of troops, other than at Towton, did not automatically follow a victory, since fleeing troops were not usually hunted down and the victors were often content to lop off only the heads of the opposing leaders. The overall death toll of executed aristocrats during the Wars of the Roses totalled nine dukes, a marquess, twenty-four barons, twelve earls, a prince and a king. Another factor which was important to both sides was to avoid upsetting the population for fear of losing their backing, and this was very easy to do, so both armies tended to behave well rather than alienate the locals.

In England in the fifteenth century the Wars of

the Roses usually involved small armies, 5,000 men at most per side, and confrontation on some unpopulated moor or open fields. So many of the major historic buildings of the era, such as Roger Fiennes' Herstmonceux or William Fiennes' successors' Broughton, had thin walls, large windows and minor crenellations, since no foreign invasions were feared, nor sieges from neighbouring barons.

The main chronicler of the period, Philippe de Commynes, Councillor to the King of France, wrote that, 'Of all the countries which I have known, England is that wherein public affairs are best conducted and managed with least destruction to the people.'

After the anarchy of mad King Henry VI's rule, the baronial mayhem, lack of police force and very little law, Edward IV took care to tour the country from end to end and to sit on the bench himself at assizes. He left what fighting had to be done in the lands of Lancastrian sympathisers, mainly the north and Welsh borders, to his trusted generals like Warwick. He made a successful truce with Scotland and considered alliances either with France or with their great enemy, Burgundy.

Warwick advised the king to marry the sister of the French queen, and thereby become allied to France against Burgundy. To the horror of Warwick and his supporters, the king in 1464 admitted in public that he could not marry Warwick's target bride, or anyone else for that matter, since he had already secretly married the beautiful daughter of an English duchess. This girl, Elizabeth Woodville, was descended from the French Dukes of St Pol, but was of no value at all in terms of a political marriage.

Robert Fiennes who, as the commander of the French army, had fought the English at the Battle of Poitiers, had died childless, so his inheritance as the senior French Fiennes had passed to his niece, Jeanne, and thence to the Dukes of St Pol and to Richard Woodville, the father of King Edward's surprise bride, Elizabeth, who, whether the Earl of Warwick liked it or not, was already the Queen of England.

Warwick took this very badly. He had loudly and in public proclaimed his initiative in arranging with the French king for Edward's French marriage. Now Edward's secret marriage made him look a fool, and his full support of Edward veered through 180 degrees to hatred. The members of Queen Elizabeth's family, the Woodvilles, were numerous and ambitious, and Edward helped many of them to positions of influence and power that upset Warwick still further, for he began to sense his uniquely powerful status was on the wane. King Edward's views on England's best foreign policy, especially with France, were also diametrically opposed to those of his chief foreign adviser, Warwick. The two men may have been cousins, but they were increasingly at odds.

Quietly, the worried Warwick the Kingmaker made his plans. If he could make one king, he could make two, and maybe he could even end up king himself. Secretly he approached the king's youngest brother, the Duke of Clarence, a sly serpent of a man who was deeply envious of his big brother Edward. Warwick was also aware that Edward's honeymoon period with his people was over, signs of Lancastrian conspiracies were abroad again, and both Warwick and Clarence were sufficiently two-faced to switch overnight from their previously ardent Yorkist loyalties to wooing their old enemies.

In June 1469 Warwick, Clarence and a mix of Lancastrian rebels marched on London, defeated a royal force at Northampton and locked King Edward up in Warwick Castle. This was a difficult time for many ardent Yorkists, including cousins William Fiennes of Broughton and Richard Fiennes of Herstmonceux, both of whom had fought for King Edward and for the Kingmaker. William Fiennes had fought for the king in England and France and been appointed Lord High Admiral of the Fleet for the major invasion of France that never happened. At home his perks included Commissioner for Sewage in Sussex.

William's cousin, Richard, being Lord of Herstmonceux in that south-east heartland of rural whingers (which produced both Wat Tyler and Jack Cade), was a valuable noble to be kept happy by any sensible London-based monarch. So he was elevated to the royal inner circle as Chamberlain to Edward's wife, Queen Elizabeth, made a member of the Privy Council, Sheriff of Surrey and Sussex, and Constable of the Tower of London.

Before he died, Richard's father, Roger, had rebuilt Herstmonceux as the very first redbrick castle in England, widened the moat and carved above the gateway the three lions rampant of Fiennes supported by wolfhounds. Unlike cousin William's Broughton Castle, which sported crenellated battlements but was soon to be proved useless as a defensive bastion, Herstmonceux was built to withstand aggression and guard the approaches to London from the coastline of the Pevensey Marshes.

The Lord Dacres of Fiennes lineage now owned a huge swathe of the Herstmonceux region, with many manors and villages. To name but a few, these included Arthington, Dacre, Risk-Oswald, Blackhall, Farlam, Branhanwarp, Lasingby, Brampton, Burgh-upon-the-Sands, Ayheton, Roucliss, and Glassenby, and 300 acres of land with 200 acres of pasture, 40 acres of wood and 50 shillings in rent in Newbigging, Mesdale and Starhull; also Castell-Harriot in Cumberland, Barton and Holf in Westmorland, Holbeche in Lincoln, plus Halton Fishwick, Relette and Eccleston in Lancashire.

There was one problem, however. The Dacre heiress, Richard's wife Joan, had even greater estates in the north, but disputes about these arose with one of her uncles called Humphrey who contested the inheritance so hotly that King Edward eventually, with the wisdom of Solomon, split the barony in two, so that Richard Fiennes ended up as the 1st Lord Dacre of the South, and Humphrey Dacre's dynasty became the Dacres of the North.

The northern Dacres had emerged from the mists of Cumberland where they were a rough bunch known as the Devil's Dozen for their exploits at avenging Scottish raiders and were ranked with the Nevilles and Percys as great defenders of the borderlands. Ranulpho de Dacre and his grandfather were both Sheriffs of Cumberland and Yorkshire and Governors of Carlisle.

Ranulpho had three sons, William who fought at

Neville's Cross and was Sheriff of Dumfries, next was Ranulph II who was Warden of the West Marches but was murdered in bed, and lastly his little brother Hugh who was locked up in the Tower of London for murdering his brother. For some reason Hugh was released and became 4th Baron Dacre. His son William, the 5th baron, married the daughter of the Earl of Douglas, a family who had led Scottish armies against the English in France, and the 6th baron married a Neville whose sons all died, leaving the Dacre estates to Joan, who passed the southern lands by marriage to Richard Fiennes of Herstmonceux.

Joan's uncle, Ranulph, was killed at Towton. He, like his niece's husband and rival claimant to the Dacre wealth, Richard Fiennes, was a Lancastrian, but when his claim to the title was ready, Edward the Yorkist was on the throne, and poor Ranulph's claim failed dismally. Seven years later when his younger brother, Humphrey, renewed the claim, Edward had grown mellow, so Humphrey was pardoned with the words, 'The seid Humphrey is as repentaunt and sorrowful as eny creature may be of all which the seid Ranulph or he have doon or comitted.'

Edward still had the problem of two lords with the same title sitting in the Lords glaring at one another, so the records quote the king's judgement as: 'Richard Fenys shall be reputed, held, named and called Lord Dacre . . . Humphrey Dacre shall be reputed, held, named and called Lord Dacre of Gilsland and have, use and keep the place in parliaments next adjoining beneath the said place that the said Richard Fenys . . . now hath and occupieth.'

The Fiennes Dacres thus gained the superior spot in the lordship stakes, which must have made Roger and Joan a touch less miserable at losing all the northern Dacre estates to Uncle Humphrey. To summarise the status of the two cousins: William Fiennes, who was my great to the power of seventeen grandfather, did well under Edward IV and sat in the Lords as the 2nd Lord Saye and Sele of Broughton, while Richard Fiennes prospered equally as the 1st Lord Dacre of Herstmonceux.

*   *   *

King Edward IV himself, however, was by 1469 in bad trouble. The Kingmaker, having locked him up in Warwick Castle, proceeded to wreak vengeance on everyone he considered his enemy, including Edward's wife's father and brother. Heads were lopped off left, right and centre. The Kingmaker was clever enough to know that the English masses were definitely not ready for him to usurp their rightful monarch, so he kept Edward cooped up and had him sign the many edicts that he, Warwick, issued for Parliament to pass.

Edward, for his part, bided his time. He knew that the Lancastrians would jump at this major split at the Yorkist helm. When they did, up north, Warwick found that, without the king's presence, he simply could not raise a strong enough force to fight the Lancastrians. So he let Edward out of prison and the two cousins made a show of togetherness. Warwick, with the king's approval, went north and smashed the rebels. Edward grabbed his chance, gathered all his own supporters around him and returned to

Westminster and to full regal power. His attitude to the traitors Warwick and his own brother Clarence was, surprisingly (and foolishly) forgiving. This merely resulted in their taking advantage of his clemency to raise another army of rebellion, this time in Lincolnshire, cunningly hiding their treachery from Edward until the very last minute. The king's army, equipped now with powerful artillery, defeated these new rebel forces at Huntingdon in March 1470. Warwick's hopes of ousting the king for whom he himself had fought since youth, and had put on the throne ten years before, had come to nought.

But he did not give up. With the slippery Clarence in tow, he proceeded to reverse all his past loyalties and turned to his previous enemies to aid his next step. He announced to England's current arch-enemy, the King of France, that he was prepared to work for the restoration of the mad King Henry, who was still languishing in the Tower of London where Warwick had imprisoned him ten years before. A more odious example of two-faced treachery would be difficult to devise, even in a work of fiction. The French king, Louis XI, welcomed the Kingmaker's offer to put back on the English throne the mad King Henry, whose wife, Queen Margaret, was French. Queen Margaret had spent decades loathing Warwick, but buried her hatred for this chance of revenge on Edward IV and the possibility of her seventeen-year-old son (another Edward) becoming king. Warwick's French-aided army landed near Plymouth and soon cobbled together a force of some 30,000 from Wales and various English counties. Edward IV, weary from fighting

Lancastrian rebels in the north, found himself heavily outnumbered in Doncaster, and was forced to flee with a small band of supporters, including his faithful brother, Richard of Gloucester, and his ever-loyal supporter, William Fiennes, Lord Saye and Sele. They made it, just, to the relative safety of Burgundy, whilst Warwick was, once again, in charge back in London.

The Lancastrians who had helped him did not trust Warwick an inch. But nor did the Yorkists. So his new government included a mixture of both groups, and he removed poor mad Henry from the Tower to reinstall him as king (the only monarch in English history to be recycled in this manner).

The tit-for-tat fight between Yorkist King Edward IV and the Lancastrian-cum-Yorkist Kingmaker continued as soon as Edward mustered some thirty-six ships and 2,000 men with which he landed at Ravenspur on the Humber with William Fiennes, as ever, at his side. Gradually Edward's force grew to some 6,000 men, and at Coventry he was joined by his ever-treacherous brother Clarence with a further 4,000 men from the west country. This Clarence army was actually on its way to join Warwick in order to fight Edward, but Clarence changed his mind at the last moment.

The brothers embraced, apparently forgetting their past enmity, and so arm-in-arm, as it were, with brothers Gloucester and Clarence, Edward entered London in triumph where, the mind boggles, he met up with the 'other king', mad Henry, who shook hands with him and is quoted as having said, 'My cousin of York, you are very welcome.' To avoid King Henry falling into the hands of others, Edward kept him at his side when his army of 10,000 confronted the Kingmaker's force of 15,000 at Barnet on the Great North Road. At dawn and in thick mist, Edward's men attacked, and in less than four hours routed the Lancastrians. John Warkworth, the official chronicler of this key Battle of Barnet, wrote: 'and of King Edward's party was slain the Lord Cromwell, heir to the Earl of Essex, Lord Berners, Lord Say and divers other to the number of 4,000 men.' And so cousin William, Lord Saye, was killed in the heat of the battle, as was Warwick the Kingmaker, with whom he had once fought side by side against the French.

Edward had no time to mourn lost friends nor to savour his victory, for another Lancastrian army under Henry VI's wife Margaret and young son Edward had landed from France and was en route to meet up with Welsh reinforcements. Edward once again exhorted his weary men and met the queen's forces at Tewkesbury. Richard of Gloucester, Edward's loyal brother, saved Edward from certain defeat at one point, and their artillery did much deadly work. The Lancastrians fled, but many were caught and put to the sword. Queen Margaret was locked in the Tower, her son lay dead at Tewkesbury, as did her greatest general, Earl Somerset.

Back in his long-time prison in the Tower, poor mad Henry VI was soon reported to have died of melancholy. But when his bones were exhumed in 1910, forensic evidence concurred with the theory of most fifteenth-century chronicles, that the old king's dented skull and hair remnants were matted with blood, evidence of a violent death. Only King Edward would have had the motive and the right of access to carry out Henry's murder, but there was never proof that he did so. Either way, the main Lancastrian royal line was now extinct. The civil war seemed over and England settled down to a strife-free existence for the next twelve years.

13

THE SUN OF YORK

In the fifteenth century it was still common for people to die early. William and Margaret Fiennes of Broughton lost their first son, Richard, while he was still being schooled at Winchester. Their second son, Henry, died at twenty-three, leaving only their youngest son, Richard, who inherited their estates as the 4th Lord Saye and Sele at the age of five. King Edward IV, you will remember, had two younger brothers: the Duke of Clarence who was as slimy as a greased snake, and Richard, Duke of Gloucester, who was everything anyone could wish for in a brother. This Richard was utterly loyal to King Edward throughout the latter's life, and young Richard Fiennes was lucky enough to have him as his guardian and custodian. England's history was soon to be steered by Richard of Gloucester, a man who, thanks to Shakespeare turning him into a murdering hunchback, is still thought of as the ultimate villain. This, in my opinion, is grossly unfair.

After their twin victories at Barnet and Tewkesbury, Edward and Richard ruled supreme, the one as king, the other as Constable and

Admiral of England. Richard Fiennes' father, William, would almost certainly have been his Vice-Admiral had he not been killed at Barnet. Edward was amazingly merciful to his defeated Lancastrian foes, those who had survived the war, fining them heavily rather than chopping their heads off.

The most troublesome areas of England were traditionally Kent and the north, so Edward placed his most trusted and capable men in both places. The Fiennes Dacres of the South retained the offices of Sheriff in Sussex, Surrey and Kent, and the Dacres of the North the governorship of Carlisle. Above him, as supreme Commander of the North, Richard of Gloucester dealt successfully with King James III of Scotland's intermittent raids. A marriage fixed between James's and Edward's children also helped.

After a few years Richard had tamed the north and decided to marry his childhood sweetheart, Anne, a daughter of the dead traitor, Warwick the Kingmaker, and extremely wealthy by inheritance. Richard's brother Clarence was at the time determined to grab the Warwick riches for himself and complained to his elder brother, King Edward. The latter, keen to avoid strife between his younger brothers, allowed Richard to marry Anne, but gave many of Richard's best estates and influential titles to Clarence as a heavyweight sweetener.

But, as a chronicler of the day put it: 'Clarence was born with a sour taste in his mouth and no amount of goods or honours could sweeten it.' True to his reputation for treachery, Clarence proceeded to conspire with King Louis XI of

France and various Lancastrian magnates in exile to remove Edward from the throne. Both Edward and Richard, ever ready to forgive their brother Clarence for his intermittent acts of treason, did so again, but decided to make war on France anyway, starting by wooing the two provinces currently at odds with the French king: Brittany and Burgundy. In 1472 Edward sent a small army to help the Duke of Brittany, but it returned when the duke's nerve went and he sued for peace with King Louis.

In 1475 Edward signed a treaty with the Duke of Burgundy that they would attack France in tandem. So Edward raised an army of 11,000 men, landed at Calais and awaited the army of Burgundy. They camped for a couple of nights on the Agincourt battlefield, but things did not go to plan. A Fiennes descendant, the Count of St Pol, who had agreed to help Edward, changed his mind and fired artillery at the English instead. The armies of Brittany and Burgundy never materialised, so Edward made peace with Louis XI and withdrew his great army without involvement in a single battle or siege. Not very glorious but politically sound; since King Louis agreed in return to pay Edward a huge annual pension, to marry his heir to Edward's daughter and to act with England in trade and in war.

With a rare trouble-free vista at home, up north and in France, Edward IV now enjoyed himself to the full. He grew fat through gross addiction to good food and wine and he ravished pretty much anything female that came his way, married or single, for he was a great charmer, handsome in an increasingly pudgy sort of way, and notably oversexed. Despite all this, he was a dedicated and effective monarch. He built many great palaces, libraries and chapels, some rated now as the very best examples of the English Gothic style. He started the first Royal Library and patronised William Caxton.

Sound financial management and solvency were hallmarks of Edward's reign, and his interest in the finances of the realm extended to encouraging extensive wool exports. This would form the basis of the Fiennes family business and that of their Northampton neighbours, the Spencers of Althorp, for generations to come. Edward's business acumen resulted in him becoming the first king for a very long time who did not have to beg cash from Parliament. As a result he never summoned one for six years, preferring a centralised monarchical government.

There was the odd hiccup in this unnatural medieval calm, as when the French urged their Auld Alliance partners the Scots into some border raids, quickly put a stop to by Richard. Then Clarence overstepped the mark yet again. This time the King had had enough. Clarence was arrested and placed in the Tower, the death sentence was pronounced and Clarence, according to tradition, was found drowned in a barrel of Malmsey wine.

Richard of Gloucester, according to the chronicles, was 'overcome with grief for his brother and thenceforward came very rarely to Court'. He preferred to stay up north where, for twelve years, he ruled the roost on behalf of the king. Edward IV was definitely set for a long, fine rule when his physical over-indulgence did him in and, without much warning, he fell gravely ill in the spring of

1483. His son, Edward, was but twelve at the time the king took to his deathbed, 'neither worn out by age [he was forty-four] nor yet seized with any known kind of malady'. He was compos mentis enough to appoint his beloved brother, Richard of Gloucester, as Protector of the Realm to be regent of all England until young Edward V was old enough to take over.

King Edward's sudden death put the fear of God into many Woodville relatives of his widow, Queen Elizabeth, who had been placed in positions of influence as royal favourites. The queen attempted to persuade the ruling council to pass a resolution that Richard of Gloucester should head, but not dominate, a body to be known as the Regency Council. A situation quickly arose where, with the late King Edward freshly buried, Richard of Gloucester headed towards London with a band of supporters, and the young Prince Edward, with his Woodville uncle Lord Rivers did likewise.

These two groups met up en route and agreed to arrive in London together as joint guardians of the prince. But the Duke of Buckingham, a peer whose treacherous potential was rivalled only by that of the late Clarence, somehow managed to persuade Richard that if he arrived in London with Rivers, he would be arrested once the Woodville clique had the prince under their wing. Persuaded to strike first, Richard arrested Rivers, then took the prince under his own protection. He and Buckingham, supported by the people of London, ousted the queen and the Woodville faction. They promised the people that they would soon have young Edward crowned.

The queen's supporters and the late Edward's key advisers, under the leadership of Lord Hastings, were deemed by Richard to be conspiring against him. He had Hastings executed and then sent both his nephews, the young prince and his brother, into that part of the Tower of London which, at the time, served as a royal residence. He then spread word that his late brother, King Edward, whose loyal servant he had been down the long years, had already been contracted to marry another woman when he married Queen Elizabeth. Were this true, the two princes in the Tower would be bastards and their uncle Richard would have the greater claim to the throne.

With help from the cunning machinations of the Duke of Buckingham, himself third in line for the throne, Richard engineered the switch from mere protector or regent to being crowned King Richard III and successor to the brother he had served so long and so loyally. No proof has ever been produced, but there is little doubt in the minds of most historians that Richard ordered the secretive murder of his two nephews in the Tower at some point soon after his coronation. In 1674 workmen demolished a staircase in the Tower of London and found a chest with the skeletons of two children aged ten and twelve. Forensic evidence does not point the finger of guilt at Richard of Gloucester, nor at any other specific character, but he and Buckingham are the most likely suspects.

It is easy to shake one's head in disbelief at how easily kings could be usurped and loyalties switched throughout medieval times and irrespective of so-called Lancastrian or Yorkist attachments. Family loyalty often took a poor second place to self-preferment. Uncles, brothers and cousins often enough fought and killed one another. Sudden treacherous turnabouts of whole armies were common. For Richard to switch from ultra-loyal subject to murderer and usurper more or less overnight does however seem out of character, but may well have happened because of the influence of the snake-tongued Duke of Buckingham. Whether or not this was the case, as soon as Richard III was King of England he appointed the duke as Constable and Great Chamberlain.

*　　*　　*

The new king set out at once on a royal tour of the south. Having been the de facto and popular ruler in the north for over a decade, he felt no need to make his presence felt in those parts. But he did choose York for the investiture of his own dynasty, his son (another Edward), as the Prince of Wales.

Very quickly, whilst Richard's royal tour trundled on, a rolling conspiracy gathered force down south. Where else, but in Kent! Part Lancastrian aficionados, part Edward IV's old friends and long-time advisers, part Woodville clan survivors, part ever-discontented Kentish men. All these elements came together and were stirred into outrage by the ever-growing rumour that King Richard had murdered the princes.

In order to stand any chance of removing the usurper Richard from the throne, the conspirators needed a suitable royal claimant of their own, and such a man they found in the twenty-seven-year-old Henry Tudor, the sole surviving heir to the claims of the House of Lancaster. Henry Tudor's grandfather, Owen, was a Welsh squire with no royal blood, but his grandmother had been Queen Catherine of England, widow of Henry V. Although the daughter of mad King Charles VI, she had not returned to France when Henry V died, but had retired to Wales as wife of Owen Tudor. Her grandson Henry was pretty much forgotten until, after the Lancastrian defeat at Tewkesbury back in 1471, he became the Lancastrians' last real royal claimant and so was taken to Brittany for safety.

The key link between the anti-Richard plotters in England and Henry Tudor over in Brittany was the ultimate traitor himself, the Duke of Buckingham. The duke, as Constable of England and Richard's right-hand man, was playing a long game. He considered his own royal claim more legitimate than that of King Richard or of Henry Tudor, but he needed to pretend loyalty to both. First he got rid of the Princes in the Tower through his influence over Richard of Gloucester. Next he was to oust Richard by backing Henry Tudor. For sheer effrontery and KGB-like covert plotting it would take some beating. But the best laid plans fall foul of spies, and King Richard's intelligence network soon knew of Buckingham's involvement with the Henry Tudor plot.

The various conspiring groups on both sides of the Channel agreed upon a simultaneous uprising to take place in October 1485, but swift moves by Richard cornered Buckingham, who was betrayed by his own servants and executed in September. Henry Tudor, who had set sail from Brittany with fifteen ships and 5,000 men, survived a major storm but found none of the support he expected, so he turned about and went back to his Breton refuge. The Buckingham revolt was over without a shot being fired.

Shakespeare goes well over the top in his caricature of Richard as Crookback Dick, the evil murdering hunchback, devoid of any redeeming feature. Others even accuse Richard of previously murdering Henry VI, but offer no evidence. I have read a great deal about Richard and come to the conclusion that he was a touch strait-laced, capable of a modicum of what we now call cruelty, as seen from an age where the death penalty is frowned on, and no great long-term strategist. But on the plus side, we have a great deal to thank him for. In the two years of his reign and with a group of able advisers, he concentrated on improvements to government with constructive, far-reaching results. He was a just man, as can be seen from the judicial records of the three northern counties that he ruled so successfully for over a decade. He introduced a good many new laws, including that juries must be kept free from intimidation, that individuals arrested merely on suspicion of a crime must be allowed bail, and that property buyers must be protected from malpractices such as gazumping. These laws, aimed often at corrupt and unjust nobles, showed that Richard had no compunction about upsetting the powerful en route to improving social justice. His loyalty to his brother the king helped keep the peace for a long period of prosperity, and for the most part his financial prudence helped alleviate the tax burden on the masses. Even his behaviour towards his unbelievably duplicitous brother Clarence shows him in a good light. Despite Clarence's repetitive treachery and his attempts to block Richard's marriage to his beloved Anne, Richard tried his damnedest to stop Clarence's execution for treason.

The close group of skilled men who Richard chose to help him govern wisely were described in one famous and irreverent rhyme of the day: 'The Cat, the Rat and Lovell our Dog rule all England under the Hog.' The Hog was clearly the king, since the boar was his emblem, Lovell and Dick Ratcliffe were old friends from Richard's time in the north, and William Catesby was his closest confidant. None were big landowners, but Catesby's father, buried at Broughton, was married to Philippa Wykeham, whose sister was married to Broughton Castle's then owner. Catesby Junior was soon to be beheaded.

*　　　*　　　*

If luck had been with him, Richard III might well have ruled long and wisely, but in the spring of 1484 he was aware that the Scots were again spoiling for trouble in the borderlands, French fleets were raiding his vital export traders, and Henry Tudor was again raising an army of invasion. But far worse than these blots on his horizon was the sudden death of his own son and heir, the Prince of Wales, who died still a child and, since his wife Anne had been barren for a decade, Richard was faced with the supreme irony of being a childless usurper. Such a status would, he knew, encourage far greater support throughout the realm for the obvious alternative, Henry Tudor. Henry Tudor's own advisers were planning the betrothal of Lancastrian Henry to Edward IV's daughter Elizabeth of York, thus binding the two warring factions forever and ending the Wars of the Roses. Such a marriage would be intensely popular in war-weary England.

In order to avoid the Hastings fate of Harold Godwinson at the hands of the Conqueror, King Richard pressed the Scots hard by land and sea until a safe treaty and a three-year truce was forced on them. He could then concentrate on the southern threat from Henry Tudor, and a coastal watch was organised, including relays of fire beacons on high ground. Richard dealt harshly with spies, including one William Colyngbourne, a former servant of his mother who was caught sending information to Henry Tudor. He was also the rhymester responsible for the Cat-and-Rat doggerel. Colyngbourne was 'drawn unto Tower Hill and there full cruelly put to death, at first hanged (partially), then straight cut down and ripped and his bowels cast into a fire. The which torment was so speedily done that when the butcher pulled out his heart he spake and said, "Jesus, Jesus."'

Bad luck continued to strike Richard, for in March 1485 Queen Anne, his wife and friend since childhood, died, and gossipmongers accused the grief-stricken king of murdering her because he wanted to remarry someone who could give him an heir. The someone in question was his own niece, the late King Edward's daughter Elizabeth, who Henry Tudor was also keen to marry. Richard denied such rumours and concentrated on strengthening all defences against invasion.

In fine weather Henry Tudor's fleet set sail for Wales on 24 July 1485. Henry had spent half his life in exile, his first invasion had failed, and this time his entire army consisted of 2,000 French mercenaries. He relied on discontent in England and Wales to swell his ranks. His banner was the red dragon of the old Welsh princes from whom he claimed descent. The two armies met at Bosworth Field, a touch west of Leicester, Richard with 7,000 men and Henry with some 6,000. The king's army occupied the high ground of a single grassy hill, and both sides anxiously awaited the decision of two nearby armies, largely from Wales and Shropshire, under the Stanley brothers. Until the very last minute they appeared indecisive as to which side they would ally themselves. The only loyalties felt by these powerful magnates (and by a great many others on the battlefield that day) were to themselves.

The Lancastrian army attacked uphill under the veteran Lord Oxford. Henry, inexperienced at war, stayed behind at the foot of the hill guarded by a troop of horse. Archers on both sides loosed arrow storms and a division of the royal army rushed downhill into close combat between men-at-arms, who could only tell who their enemy were by nearby battle standards or clothing crests.

The king's leader of the Yorkists, the Duke of Norfolk, was killed and his men retreated back uphill. Richard ordered his rear division under the Duke of Northumberland to attack, but the duke, a known waverer, refused to budge for he had noticed that down on the plain at least one of the Stanley armies was static, awaiting the main outcome. Northumberland politely told the king he felt it prudent to stay on high ground until the Stanley army decided who to attack.

Ever a man of instant action, King Richard decided that, rather than await the moves of Stanley and other hedge-sitters, that he would take the bold, but risky, move of nipping down a flank of the hill with a cavalry charge straight at the weakly guarded Henry Tudor, easily identifiable by his battle standard. If he could kill Henry, the battle would be won whatever the Stanleys did. With only ninety mounted men beside him, King Richard charged down and around the battle front and straight at Henry's bodyguards. The king fought hard, but his tiny force was surrounded and he himself was cut down before he could reach Henry Tudor. It was a close call and could well have worked.

The battle was quickly over as news spread of Richard's death. He was the last King of England to die in battle and the last of the long line of Plantagenets. He lost to a rival claimant with a numerically inferior army because of several factors. Enthusiasm for the war was at a low ebb, with many nobles ready to opt merely for the winning side of the day. Few folk cared whether Richard, the childless usurper, or Henry Tudor, the little known Welshman, held the throne. Peace was craved, not further dynastic conflict, so when all was said and done at Bosworth Field, the military skills of the Duke of Oxford for Henry's side versus those of the king's Duke of Norfolk were the factor that turned the day and King Richard's rash charge decided the outcome.

King Richard's body, stripped and flung over a

packhorse, was taken to nearby Leicester, where it was exhibited as proof that the House of York was no more. The Wars of the Roses were over and Henry Tudor was crowned King of England.

From a family point of view, it is sad that Richard III, the descendant of sister Margaret and Joanna Fiennes, died childless, but his Welsh successor soon ensured that our DNA was reintroduced into the royal line (to keep them 'on the straight and narrow', as my mother used to say) by marrying another Fiennes descendant, Elizabeth of York, whose ancestor was that William Fiennes killed at the Battle of Courtrai.

14

TWISLETONS AND TUDORS

Henry Tudor, now Henry VII, relied on his heritage for Welsh support. He encouraged Cambro-British propaganda that he was the man long prophesied to return the Welsh to the throne of Britain. His legal claim to be a monarch of dynastic descent was tortuous, being through the illegitimate line of Edward III's fourth son, John of Gaunt. He was clearly a usurper, but then so was Richard, his childless predecessor, so, between the two of them, what mattered most was the outcome of the Battle of Bosworth, since possession is nine-tenths of the law and he who laughs last laughs longest.

Bosworth also killed off a great many key Yorkist supporters not already dead from previous battles, and on a more upbeat note, there was something very attractive to the whole country about a Lancastrian and Yorkist marriage to end all wars. Especially since Elizabeth of York quickly gave Henry seven children, including an heir in 1486 who he named, with an eye to Celtic nostalgia, Prince Arthur, and in 1491 she bore the future King Henry VIII. Both princes shared York and Lancaster blood and Henry seemed doubly secure on his throne.

However, just as all seemed most rosy, storm clouds crept over the horizon in the shape of a pretender claiming to be the legitimate king, being the elder of the princes in the Tower who had managed to escape. The real identity of this pretender was one Lambert Simnel, the son of an Oxford organ-maker who had been selected by William Seymour, an eccentric priest who had dreamed that he was the tutor of the prince. To make his dream come true, Seymour taught Simnel to impersonate the prince; not difficult since virtually nobody had ever met the poor lad.

In startlingly quick time, great numbers of citizens rallied to the cause of this pretender. Died-in-the-wool Yorkists, such as the Earl of Lincoln, stirred support in Burgundy from the queen there who was Richard III's sister, hated Henry and raised a mercenary army. Sailing to Ireland, where they crowned Simnel as King Edward VI, he then landed on the Lancashire coast with a much larger army than that which Henry Tudor had wielded at Bosworth.

Luckily for Henry, few Englishmen, even in Yorkshire, had rallied to this pretender's cause by the time his army met the king's at Stoke-on-Trent.

Henry lost 2,000 men but won the day, killed Lincoln and captured Simnel. Henry clearly had a great sense of humour, for instead of beheading Simnel, he had the young man put to work as a servant in the royal kitchens, from where he was later promoted to royal falconer, and he died peacefully long afterwards.

The next pretender, Perkin Warbeck, was an even less likely specimen, since he spoke not a word of English and, the son of a Flemish boatman, arrived in Cork with a load of fine silks. His only claim to possible fame was that the mayor and good citizens of Cork were impressed by his 'royal bearing'. But that was enough. He was taught to speak English (no doubt with a Cork brogue) and how to comport himself like the prince he had become. This time the pretender's patrons decided he should be the younger prince from the Tower and, as with Simnel five years before, support came in from parties interested in causing Henry trouble, including naturally the Scots and the French. No major battle was needed to deter Warbeck's intermittent 'invasions', for he was never well supported. Nonetheless, when King James IV of Scotland hosted Warbeck, married his cousin to him and addressed him as Prince Richard of England, Henry decided to raise money for a Scottish campaign.

For some reason this new tax went down especially badly in Cornwall. A lawyer from Bodmin, ironically the son of the local tax commissioner, noised abroad that honest Cornish folk were being taxed into the ground for a fight at the far end of the land that had 'nowt to do with them at all'. Fifteen thousand Cornish men armed with bows, arrows and pitchforks marched peacefully on London, where Henry's troops killed 2,000 of them, beheaded their leaders and heavily fined the rest.

Henry, soon after the Cornish tax revolt, sent his army north to relieve the garrison of Norham Castle, under siege by James IV's Scots. Lord Thomas Fiennes of Dacre excelled himself at Norham, as he had when defending London during the Cornish troubles. Henry obviously felt that he was reliable, for he made him Constable of Calais, England's only remaining property in France, and awarded him the Order of the Bath. James IV soon caved in and signed a seven-year truce with Henry who, for the rest of his twenty-four-year reign, suffered no further threat from any direction. Warbeck lasted a lot longer than Simnel, six years to be precise, before Henry had him imprisoned and eventually, since he proved to be a compulsive escapist, executed.

Henry married his son and heir, Prince Arthur, to Catherine of Aragon, a diplomatic marriage with the newly powerful royal house of Spain but, within a few months of the wedding, Arthur died, aged fifteen, to be followed very soon after by his mother the queen. Henry, who doted on them both, never recovered from his grief and became a morose semi-recluse.

His second son, Henry, now his heir, had been kept on a very tight rein and was never the apple of his parents' eyes, as Arthur had been. He was never instructed in the arts of government, never allowed to attend councils, nor witness court attendances of foreign ambassadors. Historians usually deduce from this that Henry Tudor feared the future, sickness and death, and jealously guarded all ruling activities for himself while he still could. By the time he was fifty he was visibly careworn and withdrawn. He died of no recorded sickness aged fifty-two and on his deathbed made his son Henry promise that he would marry Arthur's widow, Catherine of Aragon.

Compared with his predecessors, Henry Tudor had things pretty easy combat-wise. Apart from the two pretenders, the Cornish marchers and border strife with the Scots, all was peaceful. Remembering the carnage of Bosworth, which he had observed close-up, he must surely have thanked the Lord hugely, devout and spiritual man that he was. So instead of evaluating his prowess at war, it seems a good time to take a quick look at an England unusually at peace at home and abroad. Henry's rule began as the Middle Ages faded away: the age of the printing press, the discovery of India and America, the Renaissance and a time when many men no longer believed that the Pope was divine, nor the church supreme.

Life expectancy was still poor, whichever class you belonged to and no matter how great your wealth. The most famous teacher-preacher of the day, John Colet, Dean of St Paul's was the only child to survive out of the twenty-two born to his mother. Few marriages lasted more than fifteen years, since by then one of the couple was likely to be dead. There were very few divorces, but people often married twice or three times. England was not especially backward in medicine or any other science, and in 1499 the famous Dutch scholar Erasmus wrote of Henry's England: 'I have met with so much learning here; not hackneyed and trivial but deep, accurate, ancient Latin and Greek. It is marvellous how general and abundant is the harvest of general learning in this country.'

*   *   *

So far I have accounted for the parts of the family name that cover the Fienneses and the Wykehams, but this is the point where the Twisletons make their entrance. The name is Saxon and means a settlement on a river bend. The family heraldic symbol is three moles, or in Old English, moldiwarps. Our ancestral Twisleton came from Darrington, near Pontefract in Yorkshire, and in all the records is nicknamed John the Baptist Twisleton. He was a farmer who, in his will, left his cow to John Twisleton of Bolton and his windmill at Wentbridge to his wife. He died in 1503, but one of his sons was named John, and in his will he named a John Twisleton as his trustee.

I cannot tell which of these two later Johns was the father of John the Goldsmith Twisleton who, three years after Henry Tudor killed off Richard III, headed south like Dick Whittington to make his fortune in London. There are fifteen generations of Twisleton in between me and the Goldsmith. Apprenticed to Robert Johnson, Goldsmiths of London, he had by 1498 become a Freeman of the Company of Goldsmiths, and four years later entered that Livery. In 1508 he was the Renter Warden. In 1515 he had twelve apprentices under tutelage, and by 1523 he was in the exalted position of 2nd Warden of the Livery.

He never made it to Prime Warden due no doubt to his curmudgeonly nature. He once accused some fellow goldsmiths of using slanderous words about him in ale houses and other places, and this despite all the years he had spent in the Company. He laid down his Company hood and announced that he would never again wear it. Told to take it up, he refused. The order was repeated or he was to sit down and shut up. He then said that he might as well take it for he had paid for it. All this is on record. Nonetheless he ended up making and repairing plate for the Royal Court, grew wealthy and bought a manor back in Yorkshire at Barlow, where a derelict part of his hall still stood in the 1980s.

The Goldsmith's son, Christopher Twisleton, married Anne Bere, a Kentish heiress, and he moved down to Dartford. Such upward mobility happened all over England increasingly during Henry Tudor's reign, for by his own appointments of top ministers due to their talents not their rank or class, he showed that he believed that ability, good service and loyalty, irrespective of social origins and background, should be the yardstick for promotion, favours and rewards.

*   *   *

Both Edward IV and, for his short two-year reign, Richard III had brimmed with financial and administrative acumen, which made life a lot easier for Henry Tudor when he took over. His own handling of the nation's finances were extremely efficient, for he was a natural and dedicated accountant who derived great pleasure from devious new methods of squeezing blood from stones. His was the time of the saying, 'The sparing were to be pressed for money because they saved, and the lavish because they spent.' His attitude on taxation, according to one of his ministers, was, 'Heads I win, tails you lose.'

Europe was seething with aggressive leaders, and Henry needed all his natural Welsh cunning to maintain English influence and involvement without actually committing expensive armies to one side or the other. France was focused on invading Italy, and so spent less time than was traditional in plotting with the Scots against England. Henry was not expected, as were most of his predecessors, to wage war on France and to extend English territory there, because the public had become accustomed to Calais being the last bastion of the English empire abroad.

Henry began the slow process of curbing the private armies of the barons, whilst not banning them altogether, since they were the only source of a national army if and when it should be needed. In Kent and Sussex, where troubles for past regimes had often originated, Henry did forbid the hiring of armed retainers, and no man below the rank of baron could raise an army.

Today's green agenda was in Henry's day mirrored by chronicled warnings of shrinking woodlands. So more coal and fewer logs were being burnt. London's air, as a result, was beginning to thicken and maybe, even then, an embryonic ozone layer hole was forming. England was exporting coal, wool and textiles, and becoming unusually wealthy, which prompted the English to focus more on the world beyond little Europe. But so did other Europeans, especially the Hispanics. Italians had powered the Renaissance, rediscovered Greek philosophy, freshly interpreted the New Testament, and encouraged humanism rather than narrow doctrinal religious obedience. All this led to new threats to the church and to bold voyages, sponsored by kings, to see what lay beyond the horizon.

The Portuguese led the way by rounding Cape Horn not long before Columbus crossed the Atlantic, found the West Indies and colonised Central America. De Gama reached India, and English fishermen, sailing ever further north with Cabot's guidance, discovered Newfoundland. From centuries of war within the kingdom and against the French, little England had begun to stir. Henry did not openly challenge the self-given rights of the Spanish and Portuguese (which the Pope described as 'God-given') to all 'the New World', but he did quietly encourage John Cabot, the Bristol seaman and others in their northerly search for a new route to the rich lands of Asia. Cabot disappeared on a voyage with five ships, one supplied by Henry, but his son Sebastian Cabot discovered Hudson's Bay before Henry died, the first of many British nudges at the great ice barrier that blocked the North-West Passage. Henry's reign saw the Spanish and Portuguese as the big winners of the new urge to colonise, along with vast wealth from the east. England, with its prowess in northern waters, ended up only with unlimited supplies of cod.

The Fiennes' local expansionism, fairly steady since Hastings, had stabilised in England with the Fiennes Dacres at Herstmonceux and the Wykeham Fiennes clan at Broughton. The wealth and the lands of the Counts of Boulogne and of the

186

Sayes had been swallowed through marriage and inheritance, but the original Fiennes family remained 'over there' (near Boulogne), as they do today. Many of my expedition friends still call me Froggy, harping back to my ancestor at Hastings, but by the dawn of the sixteenth century all the Fienneses 'over here' were as English as roast beef.

Henry died in 1509, a sick, tired and stressed king who had fought no wars, kept a tight rein on the barons and on the nation's solvency. He should definitely go down in history as a good, successful monarch. His young heir, crowned King Henry VIII, took over a throne unchallenged from any direction, despite the fact that his father, a little known Welshman, had sprung from nowhere. Henry VIII was soundly imbued with Fiennes DNA through his mother, Elizabeth of York, the direct descendant of Margaret Fiennes.

15

DEATH OF A DEER HUNTER

Henry VIII, the most famous of English kings, was the great grandson of a Welsh tradesman once wanted for murder, whose son married the French widow of Henry V. His hereditary claims on the throne were negligible but, once on it, the strength of his character and the fear that he commanded in all around him kept would-be rival claimants from making an appearance. With Henry VIII you kept your head well below the parapet at all times, or you risked losing it.

Born handsome, intelligent, physically strong and full of the joys of life, Henry remains famous (or infamous) for his serial matrimony, his dissolution of the monasteries and his schism with Rome. What linked all this was his casual brutality to all who crossed him, whether closest family or oldest friends. In rereading English history, before writing this book, with no inbuilt bias for or against any particular monarch, I have come away with an active dislike for only one of them—Henry VIII. He was in every way a right evil bastard, as we used to say in the army, and with no redeeming features. Some historians have tried to whitewash this monster but without success.

Most of my kinsmen who had the misfortune to get close to Henry soon regretted it. One who didn't was the previously mentioned John the Goldsmith Twisleton, who caught the eye of the purchasers of the fine plate Henry was wont to dole out as new year gifts. Through his goldsmith's skills, John rose to the appointment of repairing the silver of the royal household and became wealthy. Seven times he applied to become an alderman of the City, and on the eighth was accepted for the Queenhythe ward. As well as the manor of Barlow back in his native Yorkshire, he bought three more manors in Nottinghamshire, four in Lincolnshire, plus property in London. One of his two sons was John Twisleton, the vicar of Windlesham church in Surrey where I was christened 390 years later. The other son, Christopher, prospered greatly, became Comptroller of Hull, bought large tracts of land in Yorkshire and married a Kent heiress.

Within three generations my ancestral

Twisletons had elevated themselves from the lowest echelons of trade to the manorial class complete with their own heraldry. This was not an unusual shift at the close of the Middle Ages, especially for the great merchant tradesmen of London. The Hoares of Hoare's Bank began their rise soon after our Twisletons took off, and other goldsmiths, the Dunscombes, became the richest commoners in England and bought the Duke of Buckingham's prime estate in Helmesley.

But apart from this clutch of lucky Twisletons, the family, especially the Fienneses of Dacre at Herstmonceux, ended up in very deep water under Henry-the-butcher.

In his late teens Henry was, by all records, extremely handsome, spoke four languages, excelled at sports from tennis to jousting, was highly literate, a tenor of rare ability and an accomplished player of various instruments. He adored the hunt and was a skilled archer. He enjoyed elaborate masked balls, tournaments and royal ceremonies. He craved recognition on the wide European stage, especially if he could achieve it through battle, like Henry V.

He remained married to his first wife, Catherine of Aragon, daughter of King Ferdinand of Spain, for twenty years, and for the first ten appeared to be truly fond of her. In 1511 she gave birth to a son, and Henry was over the moon. But the child died two months later and Henry was desolated. His desire for a son was to rule much of his life, but fame as a warrior was surely a close second on his wish list, and for many years he dabbled in diplomatic conspiracies either with Ferdinand of Spain or Francis of France to fix a firm enough alliance to ensure a great military victory—anywhere, but above all, of course, in France.

Time and again over the next thirty years treaties were made by and between the three potentates and occasionally other parties, but treachery and double-dealing by one or all of them always interfered with Henry's ambitions. Nonetheless he built up England's navy from five to fifty ships with the latest artillery, and he has even been called the father of the Royal Navy, as have at least five other kings before him. In 1513 Henry's first invasion of France, after years of talk, successfully managed to besiege two well-defended towns and to defeat a lost group of French knights at the so-called Battle of the Spurs. The Emperor Maximilian's tiny force which had fought under Henry's command went home delighted, as did Henry. This was his first military command and also his last, although some of his army commanders did very well without him from time to time.

He learnt on his return home that King James IV of Scotland, to whom he had previously married his sister, had, with French connivance, led 15,000 Scots over the border and clashed with a smaller English army near Berwick. This battle, at Flodden Bridge, lasted only three hours but ended with 10,000 dead Scotsmen, including King James and many nobles. Henry's sister Margaret now ruled Scotland on behalf of her seventeen-month-old son, James V of Scotland, Henry's nephew.

One man who shared Henry's philosophy of the end justifying the means, no matter how cruel and ruthless they might be, was Thomas Wolsey, son of a butcher and servant of another. Due to Henry's

190

innate dislike of the mundane side of government, Wolsey was given a loose rein to rule England in all but name for fifteen years. He was very much a self-made churchman, like many of Henry's top executives, and he remained in the number one spot, a lethal position with Henry VIII anywhere near, by simply doing exactly what Henry wanted at all times.

Ferdinand of Spain had proved a treacherous ally during the French campaign, and his daughter, Henry's wife Catherine, suffered a distinct lessening of kingly affections as a result. As the years went by and she failed to produce a male heir, Henry's philandering increased and he began to realise that he must look elsewhere to obtain the required son. With no royal heir to marry off to a powerful ruler's daughter, England was in a no-win position on the diplomatic chessboard of Europe.

In 1518 Wolsey used the mutual hostility of France and Spain to convene the so-called Treaty of London, which in turn led to an agreed peace meeting between England and France to be held in the halfway house of the district of Calais, the only English possession left in France. The exact venue for this meeting was halfway between Guisnes and Ardres in the very heart of Fiennes country, and came to be known as the Field of the Cloth of Gold. Henry's court and anybody who was anybody, or thought they were, had crossed the Channel to be seen at this event and all wore clothes of rich satin and velvet under cloaks of gold. Six thousand workmen put up costly tents and prepared the food brought over, much of it from England, including 2,000 sheep on the hoof. Wine flowed freely and with trumpets blaring, the mounted hosts approached each other from either side of the field, much as they had for hundreds of years with intent to kill. But this time they put aside the long years of mistrust and fear and, dismounting, joined together in a huge love-in of feasting, dancing, music, jousting and laughing. Wonders never cease. John Fiennes, Lord Dacre, who enjoyed the fun must have felt at home, for he had been the Constable of Calais twenty-seven years before. Yet within two years of all the many oaths of eternal friendship sworn at this Field of the Cloth of Gold, the two sides were again officially at war.

After fifteen long years of relying on his chancellor Cardinal Wolsey to sort out Europe, or at least France, by his much vaunted diplomatic cunning, Henry no longer valued him and that, as Wolsey knew, was a distinctly dangerous sign. Especially as his tax collection methods back home were causing great discontent verging, in Kent of course, on armed rebellion. Wolsey's additional failure, and the one that sealed his fate, was his inability to obtain a papal annulment of Henry's marriage to Catherine of Aragon and a blessing on Henry's desired replacement wife, Anne Boleyn, who he had met at Hever Castle, which Roger Fiennes had sold to Anne's father. Anne's elder sister had for a while been Henry's mistress, but Anne kept the king panting with desire, allowing no hanky-panky without a promise of marriage.

By 1529 Wolsey's star had fallen from on high, and he was stripped of office, wealth and privilege. He died a year later on his way to the Tower and certain execution. His place was partially taken by a lowly don named Thomas Cranmer who Henry promoted to Archbishop of Canterbury, but he never gained the supreme power that Henry had once allowed Wolsey, for the king had himself grown more involved with government and especially with the church, the body that was so frustrating his remarriage plans.

With Cranmer's help, Henry identified a groundbreaking new way around his problems, while the cunning vixen Anne Boleyn unearthed a treatise penned by the reformer William Tyndale which suggested to Henry that the monarch of England could be leader of both church and state; in short, his own Pope with his own divorcing powers. Cranmer proceeded to issue dozens of proclamations which ended England's ancient allegiance to Rome, installed Henry as Supreme Head of the Church of England and saw him married to Anne Boleyn (already pregnant) in no time at all.

A longstanding friendship between Anne's family at Hever Castle and the Fienneses of Herstmonceux was to be cemented by Henry's subsequent dealings with both families. Thomas Fiennes, the 2nd Lord Dacre, had served Henry VII well and had often done diplomatic duty for Henry VIII. But in 1525 Henry's judiciaries shut him up in Fleet prison and the court record states: 'The Lord Dacre confesste the bearinge of Theuves, and his negligence in ponyshement of them, and also his famylyer and conversaunte beinge with them, knowinge them to have com'ytted felonye and dyvers other his mysdoings.'

This Dacre's seventeen-year-old grandson Thomas and his sister Mary were called to Henry's court where Mary married courtier Henry Norris, a good friend of Anne Boleyn.

As soon as Anne's first child turned out to be a daughter (the future Queen Elizabeth I), Henry's infatuation with her began to fade. He was also no longer the handsome lover of yore, having suffered from smallpox, malaria, several jousting accidents and, as a result of the latter, a pus-producing leg ulcer that, together with migraines, gave him a good deal of pain. He was vain and jealous, so Anne was courting big trouble when she openly flirted with the likes of the fashionable sonneteer Sir Thomas Wyatt, and several others. Her reputation as a flirt was well-known, and one recorded epithet given her by the public was 'the goggle-eyed whore'.

At the May Day celebrations in 1536 Anne dropped her handkerchief as a token of admiration for a jouster. Henry Norris, Mary Fiennes's husband, witnessed this and, either because he was himself infatuated with Anne or merely to curry royal favour, he snitched on her. He probably knew that Henry's first minister, Thomas Cromwell of Putney, who had previously been Wolsey's chief executive and attorney, was in the process of collecting evidence of Anne's infidelity for the king.

In addition to Henry's ailments, he had by 1536 grown so obese (over twenty stone or, in modern EU parlance, about 130 kilos) that he needed a servant-borne litter, a shire horse, or, to go upstairs, systems of ropes and pulleys. The imagination boggles at the bedtime duties of Henry's wives, most of whom were petite. Small wonder that the flirtatious Anne failed to err on the side of caution.

194

Mary Fiennes' husband made a fatal miscalculation when he told Cromwell about Anne's handkerchief, because the latter had, at a secret tribunal, decided to arrest Anne on charges of treason, adultery and incest with her own brother (patently untrue) and with half a dozen others including, ironically, Henry Norris himself. Anne was speedily put on trial in front of a jury of twenty-six peers under the chairmanship of her own uncle, the Duke of Norfolk. One of the peers, the brother-in-law and good friend of Henry Norris and his son, was the seventeen-year-old Thomas Fiennes of Herstmonceux who had to vote for the execution of Norris, the other equally falsely-charged adulterers and Anne herself. She was executed a few days later after spending a thousand days as Queen of England. Two queens down and four to go.

*   *   *

Not long before Anne's execution, ex-Queen Catherine had died a lonely death, exiled to an East Anglian priory, and, only a month after killing off Anne, Henry married one of her ladies-in-waiting, a quiet girl named Jane Seymour who, in 1537, gave Henry what he had wanted for so long, a healthy son who was named Edward. The birth was difficult, so Jane's surgeon cut her stomach wide open to ensure Edward's live exit, and this killed Jane. The king, utterly callous at the deaths of Catherine and Anne, showed genuine and long-lasting grief at Jane's death.

Thomas Fiennes of Herstmonceux was again called up from Sussex to act as pall-bearer at

Jane's funeral.

Now that he had an heir, the king could more patiently look upon future marriages with a view to cementing advantageous diplomatic alliances. He and Chancellor Cromwell contemplated various matches with a number of European princesses, eventually settling on Anne of Cleves, a duchy in the Lower Rhinelands. Henry was never content with Cromwell's suggestions on political grounds alone. His bride-to-be must also look good, and to that end he always sent out the portrait painter Holbein to capture each potential bride's likeness for him to inspect. Holbein's picture of Anne of Cleves was clearly to his liking, but following their betrothal, he was in for a shock.

Anne arrived in England early in 1540 and was met by Thomas Fiennes of Herstmonceux and the Duke of Norfolk heading a cavalcade of knights 'all in coates of velvet with chaynes of gold'. They brought her to the king, who took one look, swore at Holbein and Cromwell for having deceived him, and described Anne as a Flanders mare whose ugliness 'struck him to the heart'. Without consummating the marriage, Henry divorced her six months later. Divorce was now no problem at all, since in that respect Henry was his own Pope. The faithful Thomas Cromwell, who had done so well for Henry and for so long, was executed in 1540, largely for the crime of having advised Henry to marry Anne and for having praised her beauty.

*   *   *

Henry lived his life to the end as a devout Catholic. He did not approve of the German Protestant

196

Martin Luther, and was proud of his title, Defender of the Faith, awarded him by the Pope for writing a treatise against Luther. But the Church's wealth was quite another matter and he realised, with the earlier prompting of Cromwell, the great scope for enriching his Treasury at the expense of the hugely wealthy clerical establishment. The church, except in the north, was extremely unpopular with the population. A large percentage of the clergy led idle lives, never gave to the poor, kept mistresses in their benefices, sat on great hordes of wealth and levied heavy church taxes on their parishioners, including big fees to bury anyone in holy ground. The king used the anti-clerical mood to instigate and execute the dissolution of the monasteries. The church's wealth was now the king's. He would use it for his own ambitions, especially for any future wars against the French or Scots.

Removing England from under the power and influence of Rome had been no more unpopular than would, today, be withdrawal from the European Union. There were, of course, individuals who refused to sign declarations of loyalty to the king as head of the church. These included the famous philosopher and, briefly, Henry's chancellor, Sir Thomas More, and his friend Bishop Fisher of Rochester. Henry naturally beheaded them both, alongside a trio of dissenting Carthusian monks who were lashed to hurdles, dragged to Tyburn, hanged, cut down alive, disembowelled, mutilated and cut into quarters.

Henry wanted Catholicism without the Pope. He did not want heresy, but he lived at a time when Protestantism was on the move all over Europe.

William Tyndale was no Lutheran, but his driving passion was to translate the Bible into English and make Bibles available to all. Henry had anti-heretic spies at home and abroad, and Tyndale was eventually hunted down in Antwerp and executed.

Cromwell's purge on the church went ahead with ever increasing vandalism. Eight hundred major churches and abbeys were forced to close by 1540, and 9,000 monks and other inmates were turned out into the cold. Ancient tombs of the Anglo-Saxon kings were destroyed, as were priceless collections of books and manuscripts. Whole buildings were pulled down, while metalwork and jewellery were melted with the same determined but thoughtless vandalism as was later to be practised by the Chinese in Tibet and the Taliban in Afghanistan.

Not everyone kowtowed weakly to Henry's new laws. Various small uprisings occurred, mostly in the north, the biggest being the Pilgrimage of Grace which was led by Robert Aske and orchestrated by Thomas Fiennes' Dacre cousin, Lord Thomas Dacre of the North, in collusion with the Darcy and Hussey clans, all loyal Roman Catholics. They demanded that all powers seized by the state from the church should be returned. Together with a Lincolnshire-based rebellion, those involved were more than Henry's small available armies could hope to cope with, and Henry was lucky indeed that the main rebel leaders did not resort to armed conflict. Once they dispersed, following his vague promises to look at their grievances, his men exacted revenge with widespread hanging and burning of ringleaders.

The Catholics abroad were also incensed at

Henry's shrugging off of Rome and of his treatment of the monasteries. A holy war, bringing France and Spain together, seemed imminent and so threatening to the English in 1539 that a major building of coastal defences was begun, and the navy was placed on alert.

At the same time, Henry's long-time paranoia about rival claimants to the throne resurfaced. Since his father, the Welsh usurper, had such a feeble royal lineage, there were several families whose claim was at least as strong, such as the Nevilles, the Staffords and the Poles. Henry had been plucking them off one by one over the years as the opportunity arose. Back in 1513 he had a Pole beheaded, and in 1521, on a feeble excuse, Edward Stafford, Duke of Buckingham, was executed. Henry now learnt that for the Franco-Spanish holy war on England, the Pope had selected as their figurehead Englishman another Pole family member, Reginald, once a great favourite of Henry's but a staunch Roman Catholic. Henry, with typical ruthlessness, forced Reginald's brother to save his own skin by 'confessing' to the involvement of the rest of his family. His eldest brother Henry was beheaded, as were their cousin the Marquess of Exeter, a close Neville friend, his own mother, Margaret Pole, and his little nephew, brother Henry's son. Other Poles were locked up in the Tower. Henry sent spies armed with poisoned daggers, the forerunners of KGB umbrellas, to search Europe for Reginald himself.

When Henry's defences were fully ready, his navy patrolled the Channel on alert under three main admirals, one of whom was Edward Fiennes

Clinton, the Earl of Lincoln who eventually made it to Lord High Admiral a few years after Henry's death. The pride of the navy was the *Great Harry*, a monster with banks of heavy cannon set all along her waists and designed without the fatal flaws which caused the sinking in 1545 of Henry's equally ambitious *Mary Rose*. The *Great Harry* and the rest of the navy were not, in fact, needed because the Franco-Spanish invasion never materialised, since the two countries' leaders mistrusted each other.

This was as well, for by 1540 Henry was a great rotting hulk of a man who suffered more or less constant pain from his ever-pustulating leg ulcers. His irrational rages grew more frequent and he thrived, Stalin-like, on causing all those around him, especially his nearest and dearest, to live in constant fear of death.

His old warrior friends, the Dukes of Norfolk and Suffolk, seemed for many years to live charmed lives as year after year they arrested all Henry's top men one by one. But when Henry parted amicably from Anne of Cleves, without consummation of their six-month marriage, the Duke of Norfolk saw a chance to consolidate his royal links. He introduced his sexy, nineteen-year-old niece, Catherine Howard, to Henry, who fell hook, line, and sinker for her blatant charms. She was very soon his fifth queen but, having enjoyed sex with a number of men prior to meeting Henry, she foolishly saw no reason at all why she should not continue to entertain secret lovers now that she was queen.

Henry soon learned of the antics going on in the queen's bedchamber. One lover, her music teacher

Mannox, confessed that he 'had commonly used to feel the secrets and other parts of the Queen's body', her handsome cousin Francis Dereham that he had 'known her carnally many times'. Catherine confessed that Dereham had often 'lain with me, sometimes in his doublet and his hose but I mean naked when his hose were put down.' Two of her lovers' heads soon adorned London Bridge, and she was executed sixteen months after becoming queen.

*　　　*　　　*

Looking at the records, it is painfully obvious that many of the treason trials were utter farces. The peers who sat in judgment parroted 'Off with his/her head' in order to keep theirs. Cromwell and the king maintained control through terror.

One who knew how easily people of his rank and standing could lose their heads was Thomas Fiennes, husband of Mary Neville, granddaughter of that Duke of Buckingham who was judicially murdered by Henry VIII because of the possible threat his Plantagenet lineage posed to the throne. Thomas himself had sat on the jury at the trial of Anne Boleyn and her brother, Lord Rochford, with whom she was accused of committing incest. Thomas had also been one of the jurors who tried and found guilty the rebellious northern lords, one of whom was his own cousin, the other Lord Dacre. As well as being a pall bearer at the funeral of Jane Seymour, he had been chosen to 'bear the spice plates' at the christening of Prince Edward.

Thomas Fiennes was clearly a young man in favour at court, but also one with an unfortunate addiction. Hunting the numerous deer in his own extensive parks was not as exciting a challenge as planning night raids on his neighbours'. But deer poaching was a capital offence, and unfortunately Thomas was caught at it, more than once.

I found a creepy little note the nineteen-year-old Thomas Fiennes wrote to Thomas Cromwell after one episode:

> I have received your lordship's letters wherein I perceive your benevolence towards the frailness of my youth in considering that I was rather led by instigation of my accusers than of my mere mind to those unlawful acts, which I have long detested in secret. I perceive your lordship is desirous to have knowledge of all riotous hunters, and shall exert myself to do you service therein.

Young Thomas was volunteering to be a grass. This did not, however, stop him having another go himself in 1541. According to court records, Thomas and thirteen cronies, mostly local tearaways, met up at Herstmonceux Castle to plot a two-pronged raid on the neighbouring park of one of England's most influential nobles, Nicholas Pelham. There had been territorial wrangles between the Pelhams and the Fienneses going back to the previous century when Sir John Pelham was allowed to enclose a road which led through the middle of Herstmonceux park and Roger Fiennes enclosed Herstmonceux and enlarged its park by 600 acres of Pelham land. All this no doubt still rankled down the generations.

I can't help having some kindred feeling for

Thomas and his exploits, as in my own youth I was brought before the Assizes for night offences in Sussex, viz raiding a girls' school with smoke bombs and, on another occasion, for blowing up civilian property at Castle Combe with army property, Her Majesty's explosives. Like Thomas, I was addicted to wild behaviour at night. It must be something in the Sussex night air. Like him, I had been led astray by my colleagues. My fate was to be thrown out of the SAS. Thomas, however, was to fare far worse.

In the dark, one group of the Herstmonceux poaching party came upon three Pelham gamekeepers, which was not part of the script, and in the ensuing fracas one of the gamekeepers, John Busbrig, 'received such hurt that he died thereof'.

Everyone involved was arraigned for murder even though Thomas was not himself with the group that killed Busbrig. The lords who sat to judge him included many of his neighbours who had been co-jurors with him on previous trials. But the outcome of this trial showed him no mercy. The king himself ruled that Thomas and his three main ringleaders must die on commoners' gibbets. The London Chronicle records: 'The 29th day of June, Saynt Peturs day was my lorde Dakars of the Southe led . . . from the Tower to Tyburn and there he was hanggid . . . for robbre of ye Kingges deer and murther of ye Kepars.'

It was the talk of diplomatic circles. I found a letter from the French ambassador in London to the King of France dated 30 June, which said there was judgment on a young lord called Dacre of the South 'who, for assembling armed men with the intention of seeking a park keeper whom they wished to slay . . . was condemned to be hanged, and yesterday was executed at the common gibbet of London, called Tyburn.'

Another to the Queen of Hungary from the Emperor's ambassador ran: 'Lord Dacres . . . a cousin of this Queen, 23 yeares old and possessing a property . . . was hung from the most ignominious gibbet, and for the greater shame dragged through the streets to the place of execution, to the great pity of many people, and even of his very judges, who wept when they sentenced him, and in a body asked his pardon of the King.'

Of Thomas's friends, three were hanged at Saint Thomas Wateringe, the official place of hanging for Sussex criminals. They included John Mantel, the husband of Thomas's sister Anne, who was Controller of Customs and a member of the select group of fifty courtiers known as the King's Pensioners. Herstmonceux and its estates were confiscated by Henry from the Fiennes family so, for a while, only the Oxfordshire branch at Broughton Castle, the Lords Saye and Sele, kept the Fiennes flag aloft.

The Fiennes Clinton branch, once claiming the Lord Saye title, had now dropped the Fiennes part of their surname. Edward, the 9th Lord Clinton, backed all the right horses under King Henry. He sat on the board that decided the dissolution of the monasteries and cultivated a close friendship with John Dudley, the Lord High Admiral. Together they led a fleet to attack Scotland in 1544 and, on landing, their army stormed Edinburgh. Later Henry sent them to France, where they successfully laid siege to Boulogne. Ravaging the surrounding countryside, they razed many castles to the ground, including our family castle in the village of Fiennes.

A decade later, a local duke reconstructed the castle less than a mile away, a tower of which stands today. Local road names still reflect both castles: the *Rue de Chateau* and the *Rue de Vieux Chateau*.

*   *   *

King Henry meanwhile decided to have another go at war with France and their Scottish allies. The latter under Henry's nephew, now King James V of Scotland, pre-empted the planned English invasion by their own southerly attack. The armies met at Solway Moss, the Scots were defeated and King James died soon after the battle. His week-old daughter was crowned Mary Queen of Scots, and Henry quickly arranged for his heir, Edward, to marry her once she was of age. Henry then focused on France, leaving an army in Edinburgh to ensure good behaviour. After the siege of Boulogne, the English army's planned advance on Paris petered out, along with their supplies, near mutiny of the troops ensued and Henry had to make do with a vague peace treaty.

To conduct even these minor military meanderings cost Henry an arm and a leg and destroyed the financial independence of the crown which his father had won through his policies of peace. The resultant tax gathering did nothing to enhance Henry in the eyes of the populace. Nor did his ongoing reign of terror endear him to his nobles. Even his old friend and loyal general, the

Duke of Norfolk, forgiven over the years for tempting the king into marrying two adulterous Norfolk nieces, was finally tabbed for execution, largely due to his son's tactless arrogance.

But the night before Norfolk's head was due to roll, Henry VIII died in his pain-wracked bed in the presence of his loyal adviser, Thomas Cranmer. Before he died, Henry made clear his wishes for the future of England. His heirs, in order, must be Edward, his son by Jane Seymour, then his elder daughter Mary by Catherine of Aragon, and, after her, Elizabeth, the daughter of Anne Boleyn. His sixth wife, Catherine Parr, became queen in 1543, gave him no children, but served as a good companion for Henry's last few crotchety, inward-looking years.

Henry ruled for thirty-eight years. He started out in a blaze of popular glory as bluff King Hal. He died a wounded bull who killed many of those with whom he worked or bedded, a callous megalomaniac with a fifty-four-inch waist, weighing over twenty stone and crippled by festering ulcers. The most famous King of England he may always remain, but also, in my opinion, speaking on behalf of Thomas Fiennes, Lord Dacre, by far the nastiest.

16

STATELY HOMES OF ENGLAND

Prince Edward, son of Jane Seymour, was a sickly child, and his six-year reign as King Edward VI was punctuated by ever-worsening illness until his death from tuberculosis in 1553. His uncle, Edward Seymour, who had been appointed by the late king to act as a member of a Council of Regency during Edward's minority, seized power, became sole regent and promoted himself to the dukedom of Somerset, with the title of Protector Somerset. He could see that Edward was likely to die long before he came of age and that if, as the late King Henry had wished, Edward's elder sister Catholic Mary then took over, there would be big trouble in an England which, under the guidance of the protector with young Edward's fervent approval, had become ardently Protestant.

Anne Boleyn's daughter, Elizabeth, was brought up as a Protestant, but not fanatically so. She lived with her stepmother, Henry's sixth wife, Catherine Parr, who was good to her until a troublesome third party entered their household in the shape of Thomas Seymour, the brother of Protector Somerset, who first married Catherine Parr, and then began to flirt with the fourteen-year-old Princess Elizabeth. When Catherine found out what was going on, poor Elizabeth was sent packing, and when Somerset lost patience, his brother ended in the Tower.

Protector Somerset had bigger troubles than his philandering brother, for his rule was under threat at home and abroad. The French sent an army to Scotland, where the child Mary Stuart was queen. They took her 'to safety' in France and betrothed her to the dauphin. Various plans by the protector to avoid just such a Franco-Scottish alliance had come to nought, and embryonic Protestant England was threatened by hostile Catholic coalitions from all sides.

The protector's chief rival for power was John Dudley, who was the close friend of both Edward Fiennes Clinton and Richard Fiennes, Lord Saye and Sele of Broughton Castle. Richard was attendant to the Privy Chamber of young Edward VI. To what extent he and Fiennes Clinton were involved in John Dudley's plots to seize power from the protector is not clear, but they were certainly close colleagues, and John Dudley's faction was successful, deposing Somerset in 1549.

John Dudley, promoted to the dukedom of Northumberland, ruled in much the same manner as had Somerset, but with more efficiency and enough new regional controls to prevent the spreading anarchy. He sued for peace with the French and Scots and worked closely with the highly intelligent and precocious teenage king. From an early age, and backed to the hilt by Thomas Cranmer, still the Archbishop of Canterbury, Edward VI worked to make the Anglican church created by his father (Catholic in every sense but adherence to Rome) into a genuinely Protestant body of worship. He was described by a famous Protestant writer of the day, John Foxe, as a 'godly imp'. He loved listening to sermons by Cranmer and was proud to read at least twelve chapters of scripture daily. He reinvigorated his father's robbery of church property, and issued the first English language Book of Common Prayer, which with various revisions is still in use today. Church services were made more simple, Mass became Holy Communion and was conducted in English, altars were turned into tables, stained glass windows, icons and holy pictures were removed, and priests' robes toned down. Priests could also marry, if they wished.

*   *   *

This period of dynastic uncertainty and religious zeal was curiously also a time of great architectural expansion as the Fienneses, the Dudleys and the Seymours vied to employ the services of the top English architect, Sir William Sharington, and his brilliant mason, John Chapman. The superb quality of his workmanship at each castle, all of which are now open to the public, is as impressive today as it was back then, though Sharington turned out to be a rogue who was executed for fraud whilst Master of the Bristol Mint. My cousin Nathaniel Fiennes, the 21st Lord Saye and Sele, has lived at Broughton for much of his life and he sees the modifications made to the castle by Richard Fiennes during the reigns of Edward VI and Mary as being the most important in the entire six hundred years that our family has lived there. Richard's son, another Richard, spent most of his short life completing the works, and much of the fortune that it cost derived from the wool of the Broughton sheep.

Many of the new rooms and the ninety-foot long gallery of Richard's time were designed, not for family life, but to receive royalty. New windows were installed, along with flamboyant plasterwork ceilings and extensive oak panelling. On one chimney the date identifying the completion of the exterior building work is inscribed as 1554. The style of the work relates uniquely to the short-lived style of King Edward VI's court. Today the comparisons can be made by visiting the castles or manors of Longleat (the Thynnes), Sudeley (the Seymours), Dudley (the Dudleys) or Sharington's own Lacock Abbey. The other main patron of the style was Protector Somerset himself, and the old Somerset House, now owned by the nation, is another example which is worth viewing.

*   *   *

Quite how Richard Fiennes, a mere lord in the company of the king and his top dukes, came to occupy such dizzy heights was through his father's close friendship and family ties with the Norris family. Henry Norris, executed on the trumped up charge of adultery with Anne Boleyn, had been guardian of Richard Fiennes back in the 1530s, at which time he married Richard's cousin, Mary Fiennes of Herstmonceux. Mary had a son, Henry Norris II who, as a child, spent much time playing with his young cousin, Richard, his father's ward. When this Henry joined the court in the Privy Chamber of Edward VI, he introduced his long-time friend Richard Fiennes to the boy king.

Edward, who became seriously ill, named his fifteen-year-old cousin, Lady Jane Grey, an ardent Protestant and John Dudley's daughter-in-law, as his heir, specifically excluding his two sisters, Mary because of her Catholic tendencies and Elizabeth so he could be seen to apply the same rule to her as to Mary. Among the last recorded words of the dying Edward was the plea, 'Oh, Lord God, defend this realm from Papistry.' Richard Fiennes was one of the signatories of Dudley's 'Device for the

Succession' to nominate Lady Jane Grey as Edward's heir. So on Edward VI's death, Dudley needed to speedily ensure that Lady Jane Grey was crowned before Henry VIII's elder daughter, Mary Tudor, could, as feared, try for the throne.

Unfortunately for Dudley and for Lady Jane, Mary, the daughter of Catherine of Aragon, was a canny lady who had hidden her hardcore Catholic leanings from the general public, whose long-time expectation was that she would become their queen. So they refused to acknowledge Lady Jane, and only nine days after Northumberland's council had her crowned, Mary, with a large force of supporters, marched on London, and Jane was betrayed by every one of her supporters, even Cranmer. Mary was crowned, to the (temporary) joy of the people, and later that year the sixteen-year-old Lady Jane was executed, as were her father, her husband and the Duke of Northumberland.

The most famous 'heads' man, King Henry VIII, had gone, but folk who hovered too close to the throne of England were still living in a fairly risky environment. Mary Tudor's honeymoon period as queen did not last long, for no sooner was she on the throne than she revealed the fanatical nature of her Catholicism and her determination to return England to Rome, reversing everything her father and brother had done to reform the church. Worst of all, she announced her firm wish to marry Philip, the heir to the throne of Catholic Spain, who would swallow England in one gulp once he became King of Spain, which was at the time the richest, largest and most powerful empire in the world. The marriage went ahead.

At twenty-seven Philip was already a widower of nine years. His future as King of Spain was to be a rule of forty-two years and, thirty-four years later, he would send the Armada to attack England. Mary, at thirty-eight, was eleven years older than Philip, highly neurotic and lacking in teeth. Philip wanted England, but not her queen's body. Mary wanted his support to help her re-Catholicise England, and she desperately wanted a good Catholic son and heir. Whether or not Philip ever consummated the marriage is not known, but Mary did suffer a number of phantom pregnancies. She was to die childless, and Philip, engaged in enlarging his empire, seldom visited her or, indeed, England.

Mary became instantly unpopular on her marriage to Philip and then a figure of hatred when she started burning Protestants at the stake, 274 of them according to the records of John Foxe's *Book of Martyrs*. Sixty of the fried victims were women and several were Lollards who would probably have come up for burning sooner or later even if Edward VI had stayed around longer. Mary Tudor grew to be detested by her people, and the epithet Bloody Mary is still current today. It is also a rather evil-looking drink.

The most famous of her victims were the priests Ridley, Latimer and Archbishop Cranmer, but the *Book of Martyrs* tells the detailed sufferings of each and every known martyr. The story of the immolation John Hooper, the Bishop of Worcester and Gloucester tells of the executioner's inability to get a good fire going that would have shamed a Boy Scout. The faggots were green and the first two attempts went out.

After the second fire was spent, he wiped both his eyes with his hands, and beholding the people, he said . . . 'For God's love, good people, let me have more fire!' and all this while his nether parts did burn; but the fagots were so few that the flame only singed his upper parts.

The third fire was kindled within a while after, which was more extreme than the other two. In this fire he prayed with a loud voice, 'Lord Jesus, have mercy upon me! Lord Jesus receive my spirit!' And these were the last words he was heard to utter. But when he was black in the mouth, and his tongue so swollen that he could not speak, yet his lips went until they were shrunk to the gums: and he knocked his breast with his hands until one of his arms fell off, and then knocked still with the other, while the fat, water, and blood dropped out of his fingers' ends, until by renewing the fire, his strength was gone, and his hand clave fast in knocking to the iron upon his breast. Then immediately bowing forwards, he yielded up his spirit.

Thus was he three quarters of an hour or more in the fire.

The *Book of Martyrs* remains controversial among historians in terms of its accuracy, but the background of Mary's reign of terror is indisputable and was masterminded as chief inquisitor by the notorious Roman Catholic Bishop of London, Edmund Bonner. Foxe emphasises throughout his book that the stand of brave individuals, like John Hooper was all about freedom. Freedom of religious choice and the ability of individuals in England to read the Bible in their own language.

Quite apart from her notoriety as the scourge of Protestants, Mary was deeply despised as being responsible for the loss of Calais, England's last possession in France. Her marriage to Philip of Spain naturally involved her agreeing to help his ongoing fight with the French, and this led to the loss of Calais, despite the valiant efforts of Edward Fiennes Clinton and his garrison to withstand a determined French siege with no hope of relief. Mary came to recognise the morale-boosting effect which Calais had for so long given to Englishmen but only after she had lost it. She is reported to have said on her deathbed, 'When I die, you will find the words Philip and Calais written on my heart.' That assumes that she had a heart. Certainly she had no conscience about the torture she had loosed on so many of her citizens. She once said that a good bout of burnings enhanced her appetite for dinner. The loss of a French town may have disturbed her on her deathbed, but not the blood she had spilled.

Although she burnt up many leading Protestants, many also escaped through exile or through hiding with friends whilst promulgating subversive religious propaganda, in the manner of *samizdat* pamphlets in the darkest days of the Soviet Union.

Religious mania aside, and she was certainly not the only religious maniac around at the time, Mary was relatively successful in some ways. She reorganised and redesigned the financial system with intelligence, played cleverly with recoinage and customs taxation, and completed the more sensible financial reforms of the beheaded Duke of Northumberland.

That Queen Mary's soul was not entirely black is evident in that she failed to have her little sister Elizabeth poisoned, beheaded, smothered or anally skewered with a red hot poker. The temptation, though, must have been great, for Elizabeth was used by a number of anti-Mary conspirators as the most obvious and highly popular successor to the throne. Elizabeth was a born survivor. She knew from late childhood as heads rolled all about her, favourite uncles disappeared and the smoke from pyres of human flesh wafted over London, that she must tread with care and avoid too open a commitment to one side or another, for life at the top was a game of roulette.

In 1555 Queen Mary sickened, probably with ovarian cancer which, through the resultant bloated stomach tumour, made her think she was suffering yet another phantom pregnancy. She feared death in childbirth, and she knew her only feasible successor, due to her failure to produce her own heir, must be her sister Elizabeth, and during the last year of her life the half-sisters grew closer.

In November 1558 the Spanish ambassador, representing Philip who was as usual 'abroad on business', called together the ruling council and gave Philip's approval for Elizabeth to succeed Mary. Mary, near death, at last gave her own assent, with the pitiful request that Elizabeth maintain the Catholic religion. A week later she died, and the great Elizabethan age began.

The mad dogs of England, puppies as yet, heard the bells chime out all over their land and stirred in their kennels. Elizabeth had witnessed the loss of Calais and the last English 'empire', but she was destined to sow the seeds of the greatest empire the world had ever known. She gave the English— for they were not yet British—a sense of national pride. Here, for the first time, was a monarch who preached no overt form of religion and stood for no Red or White Rose. She preached only the glory of England.

17

BEGGING FOR A BARONY

King Alfred has been remembered for his burnt cakes, Canute for sitting on a sandy beach with the sea lapping his feet, and King Harold for the arrow in his eye. Queen Elizabeth I spawned many a myth, including the cloak that Walter Raleigh was said to have thrown over a puddle to keep her dainty feet dry. She is said to have owned two thousand magnificent dresses, to have been fluent in Greek, Latin, Spanish and French by the age of twelve and, later in life, to have plugged her cheeks daily with cotton buds to disguise her lack of teeth, made rotten by chewing sugar cane. Her face, they say, was layered with lead paint in her middle age to make her look younger and hide smallpox ravage. Yet she held the adoration of the English for forty-five difficult years and is still revered today as a highly successful monarch.

She was celebrated as Gloriana, Deborah, Virginia, Diana, Cynthia, Astrea and Belphoebe. Hers was the so-called Golden Age of England. Only moderately religious and described by the reformer John Knox as 'neither a good protestant nor yet a resolute papist', she always steered England towards the middle ground and ended with a bland form of Protestantism very similar to that of today's Anglican church. She achieved the return of the Book of Common Prayer from Latin to English, but not in time for her own coronation which had to use the traditional Latin format. The crowds outside Westminster Abbey for that service, like Beatles fans or Berlin Wall souvenir hunters, tore off strips of the carpet she had trodden to enter the Abbey.

A great many nobles, scared stiff of the late Mary Tudor, homed in on Elizabeth and her council for the righting of long held grievances. The Fienneses led the charge: the Fiennes Dacres from Herstmonceux, and the Saye and Seles from Broughton. The first Fiennes appeal reached the queen in early January 1559, and this begged that Gregory Fiennes, the son of the poacher-lord Thomas, hanged by Henry VIII, be given back all that which had been confiscated by the crown. Gregory's wife Anne was at the time the queen's lady of honour which may have helped his claim. The queen and her senior adviser, William Cecil (whose great granddaughter would marry a Fiennes), were keen to gain the support of as many of the nobles as they easily could by the simple expedient of bestowing favours. So to Gregory the queen said yes or, to be precise, '*Soit fait comme il*

217

est desiré. Gregory and Anne remained in Elizabeth's close court and were given a 'convenience house' in Westminster. Later they bought the Chelsea home of Sir Thomas More from the Bishop of Winchester, who had taken it over when Sir Thomas was executed by Henry VIII.

At the same time that Gregory had his appeal agreed, Richard Fiennes of Broughton (applying to have the dormant title of Baron Saye and Sele reinvigorated, in case of a nominal lapse) was turned down. Not taking no for an answer, he kept on pestering the queen and Cecil for decades. Although Richard was, like Gregory, an intimate of the royal court, the queen had, before her coronation, long observed how the nobles of England were often, if not always, the greatest of all pains in the neck to their current monarch. So, once she was in firm control, she did all that she could to cut down their number and created new ones only when she had no alternative.

Her religious policies were naturally less simplistic, especially since they were directly entangled with most threats to her very existence from a number of Roman Catholics, the most obvious being her second cousin Mary Stuart, Queen of Scots. Her most likely enemies were English Catholics, the Pope, the French and the Spanish, or a Catholic alliance of them all with the aim of planting Mary Stuart on her throne. England had for a long while counted on enmity between France and Spain to keep both countries occupied, but in 1562 a bloody civil war broke out in France, enabling Spain at the height of her power to focus on Elizabeth's heretical new-look

England.

The ministers that Elizabeth selected to advise her included a great many experienced councillors of the three previous monarchs, even some of Mary's. However, the man who, along with William Cecil, would be the greatest companion of all to the queen for the next thirty years was Robert Dudley, whose father and brother, the latter married to Lady Jane Grey, had been executed by Mary. Dudley's aunt married Sir Thomas Fiennes and this connection remained of value to the Fienneses throughout the reign of Elizabeth, at least until Dudley's death.

Dudley was the queen's age and, although already married at seventeen, had begun to flirt with Elizabeth even before her coronation. Although they are thought never to have made love together, they had numerous tiffs over the years, and Dudley served the queen loyally as a close adviser, admirer, and sometimes successful army commander. The queen gave him the title of Earl of Leicester, but often spoke of him as 'My dear Rob'. There was a period after his wife died in suspicious circumstances when marriage to the queen was an option, but Elizabeth declined, as she would a dozen or more ardent suitors well into her fifties.

Elizabeth's sexuality has long been a subject of debate by historians and psychiatrists, but none deny that she adored male admirers and maintained a constant flow of them at her court, delighting to play one off against the other. By far the most enduring was Robert Dudley, but if ever he acted above himself, she kept him in his place, at one time shouting, 'if you think you rule here, I will take a course to see you forthcoming. I will have here but one mistress and no master.'

The queen's other main man was her first minister, William Cecil, who she promoted to Lord Burghley. He had served in the governments of her three predecessors and was a pragmatist, survivor and, apart from one or two exceptions over forty years, totally obedient to Elizabeth. He and Dudley often sparred and held opposing opinions, but both died in their queen's service.

William Cecil's great granddaughter, Frances, was to marry James Fiennes, my great to the power of eleven grandfather. She was a woman of scandalous behaviour who had an adulterous affair with James Fiennes' steward at Broughton Castle. Still, Queen Elizabeth's William Cecil can hardly take the blame for that, and he did a truly wonderful job for his queen and for England, unsurpassed by any prime minister past or since.

In 1562 Elizabeth caught smallpox and nearly died. This caused near panic among ministers and, like worms at dawn, a clutch of claimants surfaced. Elizabeth merely instructed her anxious councillors to appoint Robert Dudley as regent, and named no successor of her choice. There was method in her apparent madness, for she had seen, when a girl, how a named successor can instantly become a rival queen bee and disrupt the hive.

One of the claimants, Henry Darnley, was the son of Henry VIII's niece. He married Mary Stuart Queen of Scots, and their son would one day become King James VI of Scotland. Darnley was an arrogant drunkard who was murdered, some say on the orders of his wife. The Protestant Lords of the Covenant forced Mary Stuart to abdicate and to appoint her Protestant stepbrother, the Earl of Murray, as regent. Mary fled to England, requesting her cousin Elizabeth's support to regain her throne. This was, of course, a major conundrum for Elizabeth, since Mary was her main Catholic rival for the throne of England, or could become so at the turn of a coin. The French and Spanish certainly rated Mary as their best chance of re-Catholicising England. Elizabeth decided not to send Mary back to Scotland, nor yet to let her loose in England. Instead she placed her under house arrest in a northern castle policed by a loyal Protestant commandant.

Two of my relations now figured as major players on the queen's chessboard, for the chief villain in her biggest English rebellion was Leonard, Lord Dacre of the North while the 9th Lord Clinton was Elizabeth's chief of staff. When Leonard Dacre and other northern Catholic lords, including, of course, the Percys and the Nevilles, ignited what became known as the Rising in the North of 1569, John Fiennes Clinton was sent north to deal with it. The danger to Elizabeth was very real. She possessed no standing army, so she shut herself up in Windsor Castle and had Queen Mary (who the northern lords aimed to crown Catholic Queen of England) imprisoned well south of the rebel forces. Luckily for Protestant England, a harsh winter thinned out the northern forces, the rising was defeated, and the Dacre lands were confiscated, as were most of the Percy and Neville estates, to be given to loyal courtiers. Over seven hundred rebels were executed, hundreds of Catholic clergy were deprived of their livings, and the previously moderate queen pronounced a repressive set of laws against all Catholics which would last into the nineteenth century.

After his defeat, cousin Leonard fled to Scotland, but his younger brother managed, fifteen years later, to retrieve some of the Cumberland estates which he believed were his. In the courts he carried on a family land feud until 1591 when, feeling his family would never receive justice under Elizabeth, he joined the Spanish army in the forlorn hope of helping to throw her out.

The next plot to overthrow Elizabeth, and many subsequent conspiracies, were foiled by England's first spymaster, Sir Francis Walsingham, previously the English ambassador in France. William Cecil spotted his counter-espionage talents which, in cunning, deception and inventive forms of torture, were at least on a level with the Inquisition. One of the queen's cousins, the Catholic Duke of Norfolk, plotted with the Spanish to put Mary on the throne. But Norfolk and his co-plotters were careless in using the sixteenth century equivalents of their own mobile phones. Walsingham discovered hidden letters, broke ciphers and then put suspects on the rack, and Norfolk was sent back to the Tower, where he had already spent nine months for a part in the Northern Rising.

Elizabeth knew now that she was beset by hidden dangers, papal poisoners and treacherous courtiers. If Norfolk, her cousin and senior peer, was mired in intrigue, who could she trust? Even Dudley had briefly involved himself with a previous plot, but had then sworn devotion and been forgiven. William Cecil and other ministers forced the queen to agree reluctantly to Norfolk's execution three full years after his intrigues were first revealed. Cecil advised Elizabeth to put a stop to the ongoing papist plots by agreeing to have her cousin Queen Mary executed, but for nineteen long years, remembering, no doubt, her own teenage imprisonment at the mercy of Bloody Mary, she stayed her hand. So the plots against her continued. Jesuit priests, the chief arbiters of the Inquisition, were sent to England under cover, but Walsingham's agents were everywhere and Tyburn awaited his annual catch.

All monarchs and presidents risk madmen with pistols, and Elizabeth had her fair share. John Somerville of Warwick was caught in the act, as was Francis Throckmorton of the so-called Babington Plot. Walsingham's agents shadowed would-be assassin Throckmorton for six months, intercepted his mail, cracked his ciphers, eavesdropped, and finally placed him on their most successful rack. Somehow he survived his first full session, but spat out everything he knew on the second, including the identity of all his colleagues. Walsingham then used a double agent to entrap the imprisoned Mary Queen of Scots into accepting the Babington Plot, and she wrote to its French sponsors stating that she would prefer Elizabeth's assassination to precede her own rescue from captivity.

Walsingham now had his trump card which, despite Elizabeth wriggling every which way to avoid such an outcome, ended with cousin Mary's Catholic head, minus its orange wig, rolling off the block. A little terrier was then found to be lurking among the petticoats of the headless body. Elizabeth, when she heard of the execution, was furious and blamed her councillors, especially

William Cecil, for acting without her go-ahead, despite the fact that she had signed her cousin's death warrant a week earlier.

The year of the Babington plot saw Europe's other Protestant monarch, Prince William of Orange, assassinated by papist agents, so Elizabeth, once she recovered from her initial fury, must have recognised the good sense of her cousin's execution.

Elizabeth Throckmorton, the daughter of the conspirator's uncle, married Sir Walter Raleigh and, after his death, carried his embalmed head about with her in a bag. This must have been upsetting for her next husband, Richard Fiennes, the 7th Lord Dacre of the South.

*   *   *

Through much of the 1570s the queen steered England along a path of peace, relying on internal troubles in France, Scotland, Spain and Holland to keep them occupied elsewhere. Nevertheless, Elizabeth sent a batch of top courtiers, including Gregory Fiennes of Herstmonceux, over to France to agree the Treaty of Blois between herself and the French regent, Catherine de Medici (an unusually merciless ruler, even for those inhuman times). This Gregory Fiennes, the son of the poacher, was sent on various political missions by Elizabeth, but historian William Camden describes him as 'a little crack-brained' and dominated by both his mother and his wife Anne, whose inherited fortunes had helped restore the depleted-due-to-poaching fortunes of the Dacres.

Elizabeth numbered two other Fienneses

amongst her tightly controlled household retinue of top ladies. One was Lady Fiennes Clinton, whose husband Edward, the Lord High Admiral, she promoted to Earl of Lincoln. Another was a French girl, Françoise Fiennes, a younger daughter of Eustache, the head of the French clan and the brother of Guislain Fiennes, Viscount de Fruges. This Guislain Fiennes was a naval officer and top-level diplomat who fought all his life against Spanish tyranny. In 1572 he commanded the Protestant fleet against the Spanish and was William of Orange's personal envoy to negotiate with the Emperor Charles IX. The King of France also engaged him to negotiate with Charles IX on the delicate matter of France ruling the lower Catholic Netherlands. Fiennes proved himself '*de beaucoup de zèle et d'habilité*', in other words, an industrious and foxy negotiator. As a reward, he was buried with great honour in Paris in the Cathedral of Notre Dame.

The English Fienneses and Twisletons, as far as I can trace, were generally inclined to Puritanism at Broughton, wishy-washy Protestantism at Herstmonceux and, up north with the Yorkshire Dacres, Catholicism. In all cases they were better off being English, since Elizabeth's religious dealings were infinitely milder than those of her contemporary rulers on the continent. Her main punishment of well-heeled determined Catholics was to make them recusants, confiscate their properties and 'imprison' them in the castles or manors of loyal Protestant nobles, forbidding the latter to fraternise with their 'prisoners'.

Like most appointed hosts, Richard Fiennes at Broughton found the recusants' unwelcome presence an extreme imposition and, since the government paid nothing towards their keep, a considerable expense. Since Broughton, despite all the new wings Richard and his father had added, was not as vast as most top noble manors, he was forced to send his wife and children to the nearby rectory to avoid accusations of fraternisation. Many of the sixteen recusants, 'men of quallitie and calling', dumped on Broughton brought their own families and servants too, so the poor Fienneses were greatly put out for at least eight years from 1589. Richard was still on good terms with his old friend William Cecil, the boss of the recusancy system, and wrote him many pleading letters, one of which states that he would gladly send ten horses for the queen's military service, rather than the five he was due to send, and even do military service himself if only he could be freed of the recusants.

Cecil's answer was to point out that Richard could charge his recusants for bed and board at a higher rate than they would have to pay the government if they were in Fleet Prison.

At no time over Elizabeth's remaining years at the helm did Richard stop pestering Cecil to officially reinstate him as Baron Saye and Sele, which title his immediate forebears had allowed to lapse into dormancy, but Elizabeth steadfastly refused. Richard sold off his remaining manors in Hampshire and Somerset to help fund his ongoing building work at Broughton. There were extensive attics where the servants who ran the household slept with their own strict *Upstairs Downstairs* hierarchy. Other manors at the time were also allotting attics or basements for their servants and,

Edward I and Queen Eleanor of Castile. William Fiennes (who was Edward's childhood guardian) and his younger brother Giles Fiennes, joined them and the French King Louis IX on the Crusade of 1270.

Battle of Sluys, 1340. The first big military move of the Hundred Years War. Admiral Geoffrey Saye, grandfather of William Fiennes, prepared the Southern Fleet for war. Twenty thousand French and 4,000 English died.

Henry VI captured by Richard, Earl of Warwick, after the battle of Northampton, 1460, during the Wars of the Roses. Both dynasties were, at some point, mothered by Fiennes DNA. On the Lancastrian side, Henry VI's grandmother was Mary, the granddaughter of Joan Fiennes. On the Yorkist side, Edward IV was Margaret Fiennes' great grandson times four.

Herstmonceux Castle, East Sussex. The greatest red brick castle in Britain in the mid sixteenth century. Thomas's family lost this castle because of his bad behaviour but Elizabeth I gave it back to his descendants.

William Fiennes, 'Old Subtlety', 8th Lord and 1st Viscount Saye and Sele. His long life was a highly successful balancing act between king and Parliament. If any single individual controlled the destiny of Great Britain during the key years before, during and after Cromwell's reign, it was William.

The devil presides over Oliver Cromwell, 'B', and his cabinet in a Royalist print. William Fiennes is shown as 'K', with his back to us (left).

Nathaniel Fiennes, William's second son, at the time of the Civil War. He was almost hanged by Cromwell for losing Bristol too easily to the Royalists, and was later Speaker of Cromwell's 'Other House'.

Major General Thomas Twisleton, great grandfather times six of the author, saved the Bank of England from the mob, killed as few rioters as possible and averted national chaos. He later committed suicide with a razor and sword.

Elizabeth Fiennes, second cousin of Jane Austen, whose mother said of her; 'poor Lady Saye is to be sure rather tormenting though sometimes amusing and affords Jane many a good laugh. But she fatigues me sadly on the whole.'

Cecil Twisleton, teenage eloper, daughter of Major General Thomas and Elizabeth Fiennes. She later divorced, committed adultery and had an illegitimate son, which naughtiness produced a good deal of gossip and rich pickings for cousin Jane's novels of the day.

Thomas James Twisleton, actor and eloper to Gretna Green aged 18, whilst still at school.

Frederick Benjamin Twisleton brought back the old family name of Twisleton-Wykeham-Fiennes by royal licence. His descendants include the author and the actors Ralph and Joseph Fiennes.

William Thomas Twisleton, a dandy and friend of the Prince Regent, Lord Byron and Beau Brummell, once said to a man-servant, 'Place two bottles of sherry by my bedside and call me the day after tomorrow'.

Eustace Fiennes (seated left) in the British South Africa Company's Police (1890–2), was just stopped by the British High Commission from chasing Portuguese troops to the sea.

Southern Command was extremely generous to Fiennes and Churchill. 'I recommend that these officers be excused this examination, Major Churchill has also to attend to official duties and Major Fiennes has a city business to look after. Both officers are natural leaders and thoroughly competent in every way.'

The author with the 2008 Master of Fiennes (the Institute) and Matron. Eustace Fiennes, Governor of the Leeward Islands 1921–9, built amenities for the sick and poor beyond his permitted budget. 'It is hoped,' noted the Colonial Office, 'that Sir Fiennes will pay more attention to Colonial Regulations.'

The author's father, Ranulph, leading 300 Royal Scots Greys, mounted, an exercise in the 1930s, prior to switching to tanks in Palestine in 1942.

The author's father after Alamein, with Royal Scots Greys and crew. He was wounded on five separate occasions before dying of wounds in Italy in 1943.

Oliver Fiennes, Dean of Lincoln, with Ronald Reagan and Magna Carta at an exhibition in United States, in the 1980s.

Nathaniel Fiennes, 21st Lord Saye and Sele, his heir Martin, and eldest grandson Guy, with the author at Broughton Castle in 2009.

Meeting of the Fiennes clan at Broughton Castle at the Millennium, 2000. The author's mother (front row, third from left) was the oldest person there.

as at Broughton, creating or appointing other rooms as drawing rooms or long galleries hung with portraits and manned by pedestal-mounted ancestral men-at-arms in full gear staring through their visor slits at their children's children. Log fires crackled from another popular new feature—brick chimney fireplaces ornamented with armorial bearings. Cooks were experimenting with new ingredients, including potatoes, and daring nobles were puffing at pipes stuffed with a weed called tobacco, both goodies which Sir Walter Raleigh brought back from his expeditions beyond the horizon and his daring, highly successful raids on Spanish treasure galleons.

*   *   *

By 1587 Elizabeth had spent a great deal of money and effort helping the Dutch against the Spanish, while both Francis Drake and Walter Raleigh had raided Spanish ports with her blessing and financial support. She had also executed Catholic Queen Mary of Scots. So King Philip II of Spain decided to undertake a holy crusade against England and to occupy the throne, this time by invasion not by marriage. He felt sure that the estimated 25,000 English Catholics would welcome his invading army under the Duke of Parma launched from Spanish-held Flanders, whilst his much-vaunted Armada ruled the Channel.

A system of high beacons was erected and tested along the cliffs of the south coast, local Dad's Armies were formed, and Drake was sent on a pre-emptive strike against Cadiz. Elizabeth had long been in the habit of nominating her oldest friend Robert Dudley, the Earl of Leicester, as commander of her military missions, and now she placed him in charge of the defence of the realm because, sixty years old and a spinster, she cared more for loyalty than military brilliance. Nor did England possess much of an army beyond the amateur volunteers who had long served in the Netherlands in support of Dutch Protestants fighting their Spanish overlords.

As it turned out, the English didn't need an army, for the navy that set out to meet the Armada in July 1588 was well led by the powerful personality of Lord Howard of Effingham, keeping under iron discipline a pack of brilliant naval commanders, including Drake, Hawkins and Frobisher. The two navies eventually met off the Isles of Scilly. The great Armada of 130 ships with 8,000 sailors and 19,000 soldiers appeared to Lord Howard to be unbeatable 'with lofty towers like castles' stationed across the entire southern horizon 'like a crescent moon'. For five days both fleets fired long-distance broadsides at one another, doing little damage and running out of ammunition. A council of war of the English admirals decided to send fireships amongst the Spaniards when they anchored off Calais. Drake offered to fire his own ship, and other commanders followed suit. Tar, gunpowder and other inflammables were duly lit or fused and drifted with a suitable wind into the Spanish lines. Chaos ensued, Howard's men excelled in close-quarter fighting, and the Spanish only avoided immediate disaster due to a sudden storm.

To escape, the Spaniards sailed right around the perilous seas off northern Scotland and Ireland,

and only eighty-six of their 130-strong original fleet made it back to Spain. Nine thousand Spaniards died en route. The English navy never chased the Spaniards, due to their own lack of gunpowder, rations and water. Some sailors were, by the time they made port, already drinking their own urine. Not one English ship was sunk by the enemy, and their subsequent victory medals boasted the legend: 'God breathed and they were scattered.'

Nobody told the queen of the victory, so she and Robert Dudley spent anxious days with their army at Tilbury. She rode about, part Boadicea and part Joan of Arc, in a shiny suit of armour making sturdy speeches. Dudley shared in the victory celebrations when news of the Armada's defeat eventually reached London. But he died the following week causing great grief to the queen, a sadness which in the course of time was mended by the new love of her life, Dudley's young stepson, the Earl of Essex.

Essex had been a close attendant of the queen since a teenager, and he was a keen soldier with handsome looks and great charm, spoilt only by his arrogance. Unlike Dudley, whose long-term loyalty and love of the queen had been genuine, Essex flattered her for his own ends. However, he was addicted to the glory of soldiering and would periodically grow bored with the honey platitudes of court life beside the old queen and, disobeying her direct orders, would sail over to the Netherlands for a quick punch-up with the Spaniards.

He upset the queen when, without telling her, he married the daughter of her old spymaster, Walsingham. She forgave him, however, and in

1596 sent him with Lord Howard of Armada fame on a second attack against the Spanish fleet in Cadiz. Henry Fiennes Dacre, the grandson of Thomas Fiennes the Poacher, went too, but I have no record of his part in the raid except that he came back alive and was knighted by Essex. By then Drake and Hawkins were both dead, but Howard's fleet nonetheless surprised Cadiz, destroyed the Spanish fleet there and captured the town. The popularity of the handsome young Essex blossomed overnight back home and remained so high that his natural arrogance overtook his meagre supplies of common sense.

On a new voyage to the Azores, he argued violently with his admiral, Walter Raleigh, and back home, encouraged perhaps by the queen's ongoing forgiveness of his ever-greater public effrontery toward senior ministers and even herself, Essex soared, Icarus-like, too close to the sun. When, at his request, Elizabeth put him in charge of an army in 1599 to subdue Irish rebels being helped by the Spanish, he not only made a mess of the mission and disregarded all her specific instructions, but, on being summoned back to England, arrived in a towering rage and entered her bedchamber unannounced, to find her wig-less and unmade-up. Anyone else would have lost their head, or certainly their freedom, but the queen merely imprisoned him briefly, removed his state titles and kept him from court.

This was too much for vain Essex who conspired in 1601 to overthrow her. He was undeniably popular, but not sufficiently so to unseat the queen. Arrested and tried for treason, he was quickly executed in a manner to which his family must have become almost accustomed. His grandfather had been executed for his support of Lady Jane Grey, and *his* father had also lost his head for treason; a triple whammy.

*   *   *

Only five years after the Armada the greatest of queens died of old age without naming her successor, other than by her answer to her councillors' urgent queries, 'Who but our cousin of Scotland.' By then there was no question in anyone's mind but that the cousin she referred to was James, the Protestant son of Mary Queen of Scots and of her husband of brief duration, Henry Darnley. James was already King of Scotland and a direct descendant of Henry VIII.

Elizabeth's chief minister of four decades, William Cecil, had been succeeded by his equally talented second son, Robert Cecil, who had long been in secret communication with King James VI so that a speedy and painless takeover would follow the queen's death. Robert Cecil, who was to become as vital a minister to James as his father had been to Elizabeth, was neither as religious nor as moral as the older man. He was out for himself, open to quiet corruption and enjoyed power, not just for itself but as a route to ever greater wealth. If anything blemishes the queen's record, it is the increase of bureaucratic corruption which flourished in her last few years.

On the plus side, her diplomacy allowed for a prolonged peace in England in which great artists could thrive, and she refused to allow the ever-growing menace of Puritanism to stifle the performing arts. Her brave new world of the arts was symbolised by Shakespeare's own Globe Theatre on London's South Bank. Elizabeth patronised Shakespeare, Ben Jonson and Christopher Marlowe and a drama company called Queen Elizabeth's Men was formed in her name. In the 1980s I sat on a committee founded by the actor Sam Wanamaker to rebuild the Globe, burnt down in 1613, on its original site.

Under Elizabeth the English also began to widen their horizons. They realised the riches of the world could be theirs. We had been local, mostly inshore, sailors for centuries, but after the Armada we found our destiny on the great seas in which, wrote Shakespeare, our realm was set like a precious stone. Drake, Raleigh, Hawkins and Howard of Effingham showed the way to make their country rich as well as great. All the English thenceforward needed was to maintain the most powerful navy in the world.

18

A FAILED POISONING

Though knighted by the queen, and a good friend of William Cecil, Richard Fiennes of Broughton never managed during Elizabeth's reign to regain the barony of Saye and Sele for which he had so frequently petitioned. But fresh from Scotland, James I of England needed all the friends he could make down south, and he readily granted his courtier Richard Fiennes the 'favour' he and his wife so fervently requested. So in 1603 we were back in the barony business, thanks to the persistence of Richard, 7th Lord Saye. He and his wife Anne had done incredibly well to keep up with the Inigo Joneses at court and still find time to manage the estate and finish the building work at Broughton. By 1597 he had been able to write to the elder Cecil saying, 'I have the estate in such order that I can free it from debt nor lose a foot of land.'

Richard Fiennes survived five straight years of poor harvests due to successful selective sheep breeding, timely consolidation of his various estates into a single Broughton-centred block, and by judicious land enclosure. Enclosure for cattle and sheep grazing purposes often involved depopulating an entire area which was naturally highly unpopular. Somehow Richard managed his enclosures without depopulation and without local resistance. He switched most of his tenants from copyhold to leasehold, thereby avoiding the countrywide reaction to enclosures which included the murder of certain landlords in Oxfordshire, not all that far from Broughton. To Robert Cecil he could eventually boast, 'Never did any tenant find himself grieved, their living being much better and now estated.'

Once Richard had the barony officially back in his hands, he quickly switched his focus to ways of increasing his income by various, usually ludicrous, schemes. He urged Cecil to have Winchester College, founded by his ancestor William of Wykeham, send him the college annual revenues worth £7,000, which were, he claimed, 'lineally descended to me as heir to the Founder's sole sister and heiress'. He offered to lead an army 'under my Royal master, to recover those lands in France which to my noble ancestor were given'. Cecil would know very well that such French lands had plenty of French Fienneses in them and that they had not been the property of any English Fienneses for at least two hundred years. So he fobbed Richard off by sending him, in an ambassadorial role, to the Archduke of Austria.

On King James's arrival in London, he had already ruled Scotland for twenty-nine hectic years, spoke with a strong Scottish accent and was in many ways the antithesis of his cousin, the late Queen Elizabeth I. She had adored and encouraged ceremony and the adulation of the common people. James shunned both and put up with them only as an unfortunate necessity. He loved to hunt and to read. His youth in Scotland had, like that of many Scottish kings, been plagued by the plots, rivalries and religious differences of clan nobles. But above all else, he believed that all kings had a Divine Right to rule and to make laws, a belief which had gone down like a lead balloon in rebellious Scotland and would fare little better in his new expanded kingdom of what he described as 'Great Britain'.

James came south with the full approval of the English people. After all, he was no usurper, and he *was* a sane male leader, adult, experienced and Protestant. What more could anyone want? He also had five children, including two sons. His rumoured homosexual tendencies did not at first worry anyone and, since he needed to make friends in his new realm, he sensibly handed out knighthoods like confetti; over two hundred of them.

The Fiennes clan did well out of this largesse. We have seen how Richard Fiennes, Lord Saye and Sele, had his barony restored, and it was on the basis that it could be inherited by 'heirs general', since the lawyers were under the impression that the original 1447 barony (of the Jack Cade'd James Fiennes) could pass through both sexes. Another relative, one of the Clinton family still using the surname Fiennes Clinton when it suited them (and about to marry back into the family), was the 11th Lord, Thomas, who was given the barony of Clinton and Saye in 1610 and who helped James greatly in his ongoing attempts to formalise the official Union of Scotland and England.

Most of today's Fienneses are adamant that this bunch of Fiennes Clintons should not have used our name and were no longer relatives, but the records of the Star Chamber during James's reign detail the trial of 'Sir Henry Fiennes, a gentleman of the King's Privy Chamber and a younger son of the Earl of Lincoln'. This identifies him as a younger brother of Thomas, the 11th Lord. The Star Chamber's jury on 19 February 1622 found Sir Henry guilty of attempting to murder his wife, Lady Fiennes, by poison, robbery and other grave charges. He was fined £2,000 and imprisoned, but was let off lightly through the intervention of King James. There is a detailed description of the trial in *The Genealogists Magazine* of March 1942 from which I have taken the gist of events.

Grace Somerville, daughter of Sir William, a Warwickshire knight, who by tradition was a friend of Shakespeare, went, when her father died, to live with her aunt, Lady Gresley, a woman of bad character, and there she met Sir Henry Fiennes, who did everything in his power to seduce her, telling her that his wife was ill and might die any day. They agreed on marriage as soon as Lady Fiennes died, and Sir Henry, who owned houses in Westminster, had two rooms furnished for Grace. He would visit her there regularly, having made a secret way from his mansion in Cannon Row, through his garden and stables, and into a shoemaker's house, where he made a special door and stairs to reach a garret with a trapdoor down to Grace's rooms. There is a letter today in the British Library written by one of Grace's uncles, Sir George Gresley, who grew suspicious and forbade Grace further entry to his own house.

After two years Grace grew discontented. Sir Henry had given her a false report of his wealth. He was, in fact, hated by his own father, Henry, 2nd Earl of Lincoln, who refused to make adequate provision for him, and he was driven to such straits that Grace had to come to *his* assistance. Her shameful life distressed her mother and her friends and, what's more, caused her to let slip many good chances of marriage. As for Lady Fiennes, she lived on and proved no more likely to die than did Grace.

Sir Henry decided to force the issue and procured from an apothecary two little gallipots full of a poisoned confection which he gave to Lady Fiennes, telling her they were special cordials against the pains of wind and stone. In June 1620 she did become very ill, and Grace began to invite her friends to her wedding, which was to be in the Tower of London. But Lady Fiennes recovered.

After four years of dashed promises, Grace began to hate Sir Henry. And Lady Fiennes, long fed up with her husband's infidelity, decided to send a petition to King James by way of her first cousin, Sir Henry Montague, who was the Lord Treasurer of England. Whether her petition ever reached His Majesty is not known, but Grace went off with an ex-Cambridge student named Harrison to the Isle of Wight, where they were married.

Sir Henry, furious, followed them there with two retainers and confronted the couple at a Yarmouth Inn, wearing 'swords, daggers, stilettos, pistols, petronels and guns'. Grace and Harrison somehow remained married, and Sir Henry, blinded by his anger and jealousy, filed proceedings against Harrison in the Star Chamber in the name of the Attorney-General. One of the witnesses that Harrison called against Sir Henry was one of the latter's own retainers called Armitage, and to keep this man quiet, Sir Henry had him murdered by contracted ruffians just before the trial.

Ironically, Lady Fiennes died a few months after the trial and Sir Henry's incarceration in the Fleet prison. Harrison, still married to Grace, was sent to the Fleet as a debtor. When Sir Henry was set free, he remarried, and his descendants fill a great deal of space today in *Burke's Peerage* in the pedigree of the Dukes of Newcastle.

*   *   *

In 1605, only two years after James's rule began in England, plotters of both ultra-Protestant and Catholic persuasions began to surface. The Protestants approved of the king's great work, the beautifully phrased Authorized Version (now called the King James Version) of the Bible, but otherwise they disliked his adherence to the middle episcopalian way, not far enough distanced, in their opinion, from Catholicism. The Catholics, for their part, despised him for retaining the penal laws against them and enforced limitations on their form of worship.

The so-called Gunpowder Plot of 1605 involved half a dozen Catholics, led by one Robert Catesby, who planned, as every schoolboy knows, to blow up the House of Lords during the State Opening of Parliament on 5 November, when the Lords, the Commons and the king would all be there. Somebody betrayed them in the nick of time, and Guy 'Guido' Fawkes, who was caught red-handed amongst the barrels of explosive, was tortured on the rack to get him to confess and name his colleagues, all of whom were subsequently executed, with the brutal sentence of disembowelment whilst yet alive and after semi-suffocation on gibbets.

That such acts of brutality should still be acceptable in the seventeenth century may seem surprising, but England's penal system was slowly becoming less harsh. This was definitely not a universal trend and, in 1616, the Japanese dictator or *shogun* united his country by subjugating the last independent province, Osaka, and beheading every single soldier who had defended it against him, lining the long road from Kyoto all the way to Fushimi with tens of thousands of severed heads.

The cruel deaths of Guy Fawkes and his fellow plotters certainly put a stop to all further meaningful Catholic plots, but King James faced a far more serious threat to his powers from an ever more rumbustious Parliament which would in thirty-seven years' time lead England into civil war. The House of Commons, especially its Puritan-inclined members led by three or four men including William Fiennes, Lord Saye, was showing ominous signs of opposition to royal authority, especially in the matter of granting tax moneys to the king.

By no means profligate in the playboy sense, James nonetheless ran up big debts by way of the many favours he handed out to his favourites, quite a few of whom had accompanied him from Scotland and were sneered at by English aristocrats. James's wife, Queen Anne, enjoyed the good life and specialised in elaborate masked balls, while James openly favoured the Scottish courtier Robert Carr, to whom he gave the Earldom of Somerset and whose lips he openly kissed, to the disgust (or jealousy) of many of his nobles. Somerset was later murdered, and the king's next favourite, and probably lover, was one George Villiers who James knighted and then made Duke of Buckingham. The king once wrote to him, 'Sweet child and wife; I naturally so love your person and adore all your other parts, which are more than ever one man had.'

Buckingham achieved very considerable influence throughout the last decade of James's life, a fact which greatly favoured William Fiennes, Lord Saye, whose sister Elizabeth married Buckingham's brother.

The most sensible minister, who had sufficient influence with James to curb his high-flown ideas of the Divine Right of Kings, was Robert Cecil, but he died in 1612. Soon afterwards the House of Commons and the king fell out in a big way. James believed in his prerogative, and the Commons, did not. So the king dissolved the 1613 Parliament in a high dudgeon. The previous year his eldest son Henry, of whom he was extremely proud and who was popular with the people, died, leaving James in a state of mourning and gloom for many months, while James's remaining male heir, Prince Charles Stuart, eleven years old at the time, became the focus of the nation's curiosity. For a long while James planned to marry young Charles off to the Spanish Infanta to complement his existing treaty with that powerful nation.

In 1614 he called another Parliament to raise much needed funds, but the members of this congress were so good at bitching about every wish of the king and made such hate-filled comments about his cabal of courtiers, advisers and ministers 'imported' from Scotland, that James, exasperated, dissolved this Parliament as he had the last, but without obtaining his badly needed funds. One tax that he did refine was his Tobacco Tax, whereby all Virginian tobacco, no matter what its eventual destination, must pass through English ports and be taxed there. This was levied with great zeal, despite his personal aversion to smoking. He once pronounced: 'Smoking pollutes men's inward parts ... with an unctuous and oily kind of soote, as hath been found in some great tobacco takers who, after their deaths, were opened up.' He added for good measure that smoking was: 'a custom loathsome to the eye, hateful to the nose, harmful to the brain and dangerous to the lungs.'

King James twice took his queen to stay in the

250

newly decorated Broughton Castle, with the newly decorated (or, to be more accurate, redecorated) Baron Saye and Sele, and there he would have met the strong-willed young William Fiennes, only heir to the barony and recently out of New College, Oxford at the conclusion of his Founder's Kin free education.

William Fiennes, my great to the power of twelve grandfather, was to become in the next reign the number one pain in the royal backside. Known to king and Cromwell alike as Saye, it was not for nothing he acquired the popular nickname of 'Old Subtlety', as his life became one long and highly successful balancing act between the Royalist and Parliamentary forces. William Fiennes took over the barony in 1613 and was soon to be one of the half dozen individuals who would help mould the destiny of Great Britain during the key years leading up to Oliver Cromwell's Protectorate.

To begin with, his friendly relationship with his sister's brother-in-law, the king's favourite, George Villiers, Duke of Buckingham, had proved of great value, but as he, Saye, felt increasingly at odds with most of the king's policies, Buckingham slowly became an enemy. The contemporary historian Lord Clarendon detested William Fiennes as the man behind all the king's worst troubles.

The Lord Saye, a man of mean and narrow fortune and of the highest ambition had for many years been the oracle of those who were called Puritans in the worst sense and had steered all their counsels. He was a notorious enemy to the Church and to most of the

251

eminent Churchmen . . . He was in the truth the pilot that steered all those vessels which were freighted with sedition to destroy the government.

Clarendon's ongoing diatribe against Saye underlines the fact that he appeared to be a self-interested hypocrite.

a man who had the deepest hand in the original contrivance of all the calamities which befell this unhappy Kingdom, though he had not the least thought of dissolving the monarchy and even less of levelling the ranks and distinctions of men, for no man valued himself more . . . His parts were not quick but so much above his own rank that he had always great credit and authority in Parliament; the more so for taking all opportunities to oppose the Court. He had with his milk sucked in an implacable malice against the government of the Church.

This refers to William's Puritanical leanings, and the problem with James I, as far as he was concerned, involved the king's desire for tolerance in his new Great Britain for all forms of religion, including Catholicism. William loathed Catholics and therefore fought every move by James for an alliance with Spain. James had married his daughter Elizabeth to the main German Protestant leader, Frederick, the Elector Palatine. Spain had later caused Frederick to be deposed, and thereafter James had to tread a diplomatic tightrope trying to become friendly enough with

Spain to have them reinstate Frederick.

At home James and his ruthless Archbishop Laud of Canterbury reacted strongly against fundamentalist Puritans who, tied to the dour ethics of the Old Testament, insisted that they, like the Jews before them, were God's chosen people and should observe every last biblical ruling, such as strict observance of the Sabbath. The most troublesome Puritans like William, Lord Saye, were imprisoned, and many fled to ultra-Protestant Amsterdam to start a community there. In 1620 another group set sail from Plymouth in the *Mayflower* to form a Puritan settlement in America.

In Ireland James pursued what he called a 'plantation policy', which dispossessed hundreds of native Irish Catholic families whom he replaced with thousands of Londoners (mostly in the region of Londonderry) and with even more settlers from lowland Scotland. By 1641, 100,000 English, Welsh and Scots settlers had arrived in Ireland, and, in Cromwell's time, another 100,000 followed them. Over 150,000 Scots settled in Ulster. Despite this ethnic flooding of the area, the majority of the population were still Catholic Irish, but whereas they made up 98 per cent of the population in 1600, the Stuart 'plantations' reduced them to 75 per cent and stored up big troubles for the future. So James, the Scotsman, was the godfather of the first British colonists. At the beginning of his reign there were no British colonies, but by his death, in both Ireland and America, they were thriving. This is the point at which, to be accurate, I will often need to switch from using the term English to British, especially when describing our activities abroad.

In addition to the Pilgrim Fathers' voyage, new settlements soon sprang up in Newfoundland, Virginia, Massachusetts, Bermuda, India and the East Indies. Scotsmen were at the forefront of many of these adventures. Trade began to flourish, which was just as well as, in the second half of James's reign, Britain suffered a sudden dire rise in the cost of living and a severe depression.

As with many leaders who strain to follow policies of pragmatism and peace, James often came to grief by upsetting extremists. This was especially true of his balancing act with Spain, for his colonial missions naturally clashed with Spain's foreign policy. He let Sir Walter Raleigh out of prison (where he had languished since Elizabeth I put him there) in order to have him search for gold up the Orinoco. Raleigh, against royal orders, clashed with various Spaniards, and on his return, at Spanish insistence, James had him beheaded. This infuriated the likes of Saye, who increasingly saw the king as a mere Catholic lackey.

When Robert Cecil had died back in 1612 and James needed a new first minister, he had chosen a friend and neighbour of Saye, Sir Walter Cope, a valuable choice for Saye's ongoing influence. The man who had thought he should get the top job, Sir Francis Bacon, was thereafter hostile to those who had helped Cope get his job. That included Lord Saye. In 1621 James needed to placate a Parliament he had called yet again to raise cash and he used the sacking and imprisonment of Francis Bacon, demanded in the Lords by Saye, as a bargaining chip. Saye had clearly become a major influence even then; a sign of what was to come.

Saye's next rebellion was over James's plan to marry off his heir, Charles, to the Spanish Infanta at some suitable future date, but only if such a union became sensible. Unfortunately for James, as he grew older and more plagued by introspective gloom and crippling arthritis, his son Charles, arrogant and self-willed, formed an alliance with the king's old favourite, the Duke of Buckingham, and the two men frequently, when requested to fulfil a mission for the king, simply waved two fingers at the old man and followed their own, usually foolish, designs. They both liked the idea of Charles's marriage to the Infanta, but without the baggage of key diplomatic conditions that James specified. They badgered the king until he allowed them to go to Madrid where they were kept waiting for many months and failed to gain any reasonable diplomatic agreement to go with the proposed royal marriage. Eventually, in disgust, they returned to England, now wanting an immediate war with Spain, which was precisely what Saye and the other Puritan lords had long been advocating.

The king wanted peace and his son wanted war. Buckingham, knowing that Saye, by 1624, was the most influential figure in the Lords, promoted him to viscount, which meant that William now had two concurrent titles, as 8th Lord Saye and 1st Viscount Saye.

Why was Saye so hostile to Catholicism and to Spain? Since he wrote a good deal which survives today but never dwelt on his feelings towards the Spanish, I can only wonder if he was deeply affected by the fear that rippled through England in the year of the great Armada threat when, aged only eight, he would have watched from Broughton the rehearsals of the beacon fire-keepers on nearby Crouch Hill and the training of the local Home Guard in readiness for the expected invasion.

A British force was, in due course, sent off to help rescue the Protestant Elector Palatine. The result was both dismal and expensive. Nobody was happy and, only months after accepting his viscountcy, Saye was openly hostile to the Buckingham faction once again. Saye began at that time to hold clandestine meetings of leading Puritan lords and others in an upper tower room at Broughton, well away from the ears of spying servants. As Clarendon's history recounts: 'Saye gave them instructions how to behave themselves with caution and to do their business with most security.'

He was not known as Old Subtlety for nothing.

19

THE SMALL ROOM WITH NO EARS

Old, sick and arthritic, James I of England died in late March 1625, having warned his heir, Charles, to call as few Parliaments as possible, for they were increasingly big trouble. He gave the same advice to his old favourite Buckingham, Charles's chief crony. Buckingham was assassinated three years later and, after a brief honeymoon period, Charles alienated a great many people by his lack of subtlety, his apparent arrogance and even his unimpressive personal appearance. Most historians paint successive monarchs as part good, part bad, like every other human, but the only redeeming features any of them allow Charles I are his lifelong chaste behaviour, patronage of the arts and the dignity of his final tragic days. Otherwise the adjectives applied to him make sorry reading: prudish, cold, shifty, runt-like, autocratic, offensive, indecisive and a stutterer with a thick Scottish accent. His better known abuses of power include arbitrary arrests, a lifelong desire to rule without reference to Parliament, insensitive and harsh taxation systems, and use of Catholic troops to enforce his will on his Protestant subjects.

For the first five years of his reign, Britain warred with the Spanish in order to regain Protestant territories which the Spaniards had taken from Charles's brother-in-law, the Elector Palatine. Charles also warred with France to make them honour a marriage treaty which had been designed to keep the two countries friendly. He married the French king's sister, Henrietta Maria, which must have been quite a sacrifice for him, judging by a contemporary account from a bitchy Bohemian royal lady following a visit to Britain. 'Van Dyck's portraits had so accustomed me to thinking that all English women are beautiful that I was amazed to find a small creature with skinny arms and teeth like defence works sticking out of her mouth.' The US state of Maryland is named after her.

Charles, like his predecessors, had to raise funds for the fighting by calling Parliament, who would, he hoped, then raise the necessary taxes. Simple but effective when it worked, but with Charles, even when Parliament approved of a particular foreign campaign, they often still refused to raise the relevant taxes unless Charles agreed to extend their powers, to the direct detriment and dilution of his own royal prerogative. This was simple blackmail and, as Charles was stubborn, the result was usually stalemate. Charles refused to hand over meaningful powers, and Parliament gave him minimal funds. As a result, a mercenary army sent to help the Protestants in Germany was a total failure, as were various naval attacks on French and Spanish coastal strongholds. Francis Drake and Elizabeth I no doubt squirmed in their respective graves.

In 1630 a number of Puritan nobles got together to launch a grand design. Those who had since the *Mayflower* landings established a tentative foothold in cold and rocky New England had done so to escape persecution from the regime of the Stuarts, which they wrongly believed to be steering the nation back to Catholicism. Lord Saye and his Puritan friends, including John Pym, Lord Brooke and the notorious semi-pirate the Earl of Warwick, all hostile to King Charles and his Spanish appeasement policy, decided to increase the colonisation process in a big way and with a long-term grand design. The chief planner was Saye who in 1630 formed the Providence Island Company to colonise the island of New Providence, 130 miles off the Mosquito Coast of Nicaragua. He and Lord Brooke also bought from the Earl of Warwick a large tract of land on the Connecticut river. They appointed John Winthrop, a close friend and neighbour of Saye, to be governor of a fort at the mouth of the river, called the new colony Sayebrook (nowadays Old Sayebrook) and sent off shiploads of hopeful colonists, including many friends, neighbours and acquaintances from the Banbury region. Then in 1633 Saye and Brooke invested in a large plantation at Cocheco, in what is now New Hampshire. Saye, Brooke and the buccaneer Warwick were among Britain's most active early imperialists and entrepreneurs for colonisation.

My godfather, Lawrence Fiennes, who first told me about Lord Saye, used to refer to this ancestor as Bill Fiennes, in an irreverent but nonetheless admiring sort of way. To me 'Bill' epitomises the sort of entrepreneur who has very big ideas and loves to plot them with a group of close friends and in the face of lots of opposition. His group included many with whom he was to engineer the launching of the Civil War in Britain.

By the mid-1630s Saye grew discouraged by the setbacks of the North American settlements and by the attitude of their local governors to his suggested system of choosing future leaders. They should, he and Brooke demanded, select governors from 'gentlemen of approved sincerity and worth'. When the governors of what is today Massachusetts flatly refused, Saye turned his back on them and focused his attentions on the Caribbean and his Providence Island colony.

Since Providence was at the epicentre of the Spanish trade routes, it was bound to be attacked, so Saye had to work extremely hard to attract settlers. The name Providence was calculated to act as a lure in the same way that medieval Danes hoped the name Greenland would entice settlers to that icy and barren island. In his zeal to attract greater numbers of settlers, Saye appealed to the experienced but often disgruntled colonists already in New England under John Winthrop. The 'Colonist Captain' Saye sent to Providence was another old friend, the ex-Mayor of Banbury, fifty-four-year-old Henry Halhed, a staunch Puritan who had imbibed from Saye many of the lessons learnt from Winthrop's experience. These included the tendencies of largely middle-class families, arriving in harsh and alien environments, to clash with one another and to need very firm leadership to avoid anarchy.

Knowing this did not stop Halhed, who spent the next eight years on Providence with his wife and young family, from experiencing constant trouble with his co-islanders. The Spanish attacked twice but were repelled, the English buccaneers who were based on Providence upset the more Puritan settlers with their ribald ways, and the successive governors, mostly ex-navy types, quarrelled with the clergy and neighbours. The last of the governors, rightly accused by Halhed of dereliction of duty during a Spanish attack, countered by putting Halhed in irons and sending him back in disgrace to England: Saye immediately released and praised Halhed and sacked the governor. Very soon thereafter a massive Spanish fleet attacked and took over Providence in order to stop further depredations on their treasure ships by the island's buccaneers.

At the time Saye's Providence dream came to this abrupt end in 1641, there were over 25,000 British immigrants settled along North America's east coast, and Governor John Winthrop agreed that 'some men should be appointed to frame a body of law, in resemblance to Magna Carta which . . . should be received for fundamental laws'. Such Magna Carta-based liberties appear today in the founding charters of Maryland, Maine, Connecticut, Rhode Island, Georgia, and other states.

Sadly, the nation failed to take advantage of Saye's colonising vision but his enterprise did lead to certain other islands being settled and developed into the British sugar islands, which formed the foundation of a great commercial empire. As for Providence Island, now part of the South American state of Colombia, my cousin David Fiennes went there in 1977 and found that the inhabitants, including many descendants of English pirates, spoke not Spanish but their own version of English, and sported surnames like Huffington, Hawkins and Henry.

The eleven years of the Providence Island Company's Caribbean survival coincided with the eleven years of King Charles's personal rule, and when the island fell to the Spanish, the board meetings of Saye and his shareholders ceased. No longer able to create their new world across the Atlantic, they switched their full attention to building a new world at home and became the leaders of the Puritan Parliaments of the 1640s. They met in secret in each other's houses, mostly in John Pym's lodgings in Gray's Inn Road and William Fiennes, Lord Saye's Broughton Castle's 'small room with no ears', which today is known as the Council Chamber. Apart from Saye and Pym, the plotters included John Hampden, the Earl of Warwick, Lord Brooke, and Benjamin Rudyard.

For five years, Charles I ruled alongside three

noisy and hostile Parliaments, but by 1629 he had had enough and decided he would rule, for as long as he could raise his own taxes, without a Parliament of any sort. The tax which had sparked off the Saye group's anger, was known as Ship Money. Its purpose was to fund the defence of the nation. Since the state of the navy was abysmal, most Englishmen were for a few years willing to pay to have the Channel cleared of Dutch privateers and of pirates from as far away as Algeria and Turkey, who were turning trade with Europe, and coastal fishing, into risky activities. But then, when the tax was extended far inland and reached Banbury, Lord Saye, his tenants and his sympathisers in North Oxfordshire all refused to pay up.

Warwick advised the king against the tax and, when this failed, Lord Saye personally sued the government. Cleverly enough the latter responded by counter-accusing Saye of enclosure and depopulation of one of his estates in Gloucestershire and summoned him to trial in the Star Chamber. The inference was that the trial would not take place if Saye dropped his Ship Money case. Saye was famous for his anti-enclosure stance and he had, years before, become a celebrity through physically tearing down hedges put up by his neighbour, a senior judge, and winning major victories for anti-enclosure laws in the Banbury area. So the accusation that he had enclosed in his own demesne was calculated to cause him maximum embarrassment.

Only one other senior peer joined Saye in suing the government, and that was Theophilus Fiennes Clinton, the 2nd Earl of Lincoln, who was married to Bridget Fiennes, Saye's daughter. He also became the only peer that year to be imprisoned in the Tower for tax refusal. His son, Thomas, was called to Parliament in 1610, and at that time he combined his title of Lord Clinton with that of Lord Saye. Despite this, he, his family and the real Lord Saye, William Fiennes, seemed to be good friends.

Here is a statement of the position from the Bulletin of the Institute of Historical Research which gives Saye his proper due:

Ship Money will forever be associated with John Hampden and his challenge to its legality. Popular history has glowingly described the courageous Hampden refusing to pay a mere 20 shillings for the sake of the liberties of all Englishmen and being dragged to trial. Closer examination reveals a much more complex picture for, surprisingly, Hampden appears to have played a passive role whereas . . . the genesis of the challenge to the King's policy came from William Fiennes, Viscount Saye and Sele, and by implication the other directors of the Providence Island Company, one of whom was Hampden. There can be little doubt that Saye, through his tenacity and through the effective manipulation of his connections, outmanoeuvred the government and finally forced a legal confrontation that Charles could neither control nor afford.

Saye was not imprisoned, but he and his heir, James Fiennes, were sacked as North Oxfordshire

Justices of the Peace. Banbury was the foremost town in Britain for tax refusal, and one of its most avid mutineers was Thomas Halhed, the son of Henry Halhed of Providence Island. Nevertheless, Charles won in the end, for 90 per cent of the tax was eventually collected, if a lot more slowly than planned.

*   *   *

By 1637 the king was at the height of his power with a balanced budget and a secure throne. His main troubles were caused by the unbending ways of William Laud, Archbishop of Canterbury, whose goal was to harness everyone in Britain to the 1559 Prayer Book. This upset pretty much every shade of Puritan in the land, whilst many of the church practices of Laud and his colleagues smacked of Roman Catholic ritual. This made Puritans apprehensive that he and the king, who supported Laud's every edict, were planning to re-establish popery and rule by bishops.

The Saye group loathed Laud and, although not keen on Scotsmen per se because Charles was, in their eyes, a Scot, they were sympathetic to their co-religionists, the Scottish Covenanters. So when in 1639 Charles, falling back on an almost obsolete prerogative, summoned his peers to York to join his army to squash the Covenanters, Saye and his friend, Lord Brooke, obeyed only with great reluctance. Once there, Charles demanded that they take a military oath committing them to the struggle. Both men refused. When his turn came, Saye 'kneeled downe and told His Majesty that he would take the Oath of Allegeance to adventur his lyfe for the defence of this Kingdome of England against any that should invade it. But to goe and kill a man in Scotland he was not satisfyed of the lawfullness thereof.' Saye went to prison for four days for this refusal.

The king's plans to invade Scotland fizzled out through poor organisation, so he abandoned the idea, which allowed the Scots to attack southwards and to occupy Newcastle late in 1640, refusing to head back home until they obtained a favourable treaty from the king.

One of Saye's four very capable sons, Nathaniel Fiennes, had gone to Geneva, where he was immersed in the Calvinist doctrine before returning home via Scotland, where he established links with the Scottish opposition which later helped his father. Saye helped Nathaniel's election as MP for Banbury so, when Charles was forced to call Parliament for funds in 1640, it was Nathaniel in the Commons who called a motion to block any taxes they raised being used against 'our Scottish brethren'. When the king found this Parliament altogether too stroppy to warrant its existence, he dissolved it and it became known historically as the Short Parliament. Saye later claimed that its dissolution was above all a strategy to block the success of his son's pro-Scottish motion.

Charles had tried to prevent Saye even participating in Parliament by not recalling him (and Brooke) to the Lords at all. This ploy failed, Saye turned up and, true to form, was the only peer who spoke out directly against an attempt by the king to distance the Lords from the Commons. This royal move was caused by Charles's worry that, whereas the Commons had long proved troublesome, only recently had there been an ominous alteration of temper in the Lords, and this he attributed to Saye, Brooke and their clique.

The king ruled largely through Lord Strafford and Archbishop Laud, and all three were keen on the re-establishment of powerful bishops throughout the land. On one occasion in the Lords various bishops had not turned up and Laud moved that 'this House adjourn because the Bishops are not present'. Saye objected, 'that the presence of the Bishops is not necessary to give legality to the proceedings. They have such absolute dependency upon the King that they sit not here as free men.' Saye then made a long speech to push a bill to restrain bishops from meddling in secular affairs.

Lord Strafford and Laud had had a bellyful of Saye at this point, so they imprisoned him in the Tower, alongside Pym, Hampden and Brooke. Men were then sent to Broughton Castle and to Saye's London house to search for evidence of treasonable collaboration with the Scots. None, of course, was found. The plotters were released due to lack of evidence against them and immediately went back to their schedule of secret meetings at Broughton. Fiennes family records simply state: 'Between the dissolution of the Short Parliament and the meeting of the Long one, there met in this room at different times Mr Pym, Mr Hampden, St John, Vane, Brooke, Bedford, Warwick, Nathaniel Fiennes and Lord Saye to take steps to oppose the arbitrary measures of the King. From this room they would pass on to the leads [the castle roof] in discussion.'

Lord Strafford continued to advise Charles to

arrest Saye when, for various reasons, Strafford was himself arrested and Saye escaped to become eminent in the subsequent Long Parliament of 1641, which impeached both Strafford and Laud, gained several powers over the king and voted Saye to be Privy Councillor, Master of the Court of Wards and Commissioner for the Treasury.

Saye heavily criticised the rigidity of the Church of England and its Book of Common Prayer and denounced Laud's attempts to impose 'certaine prayers and formes of divine service . . . upon all persons in all times to be used and none other . . . as if, because some men have need to use crutches, all men should bee prohibited the use of legges and injoyned to take up such crutches as have been prepared for those who have no legges.'

During that August of the Long Parliament, the king went north to Scotland and, in his absence, Lord Saye was appointed one of a select group of regents. By the time the Long Parliament came to a close, apart from removing the king's chief bully boys, they had also abolished the juryless royal courts which Charles had used to imprison MPs he disliked, and had secured a Bill preventing kings from dissolving Parliaments without their own consent. Saye had a leading role in all these 'triumphs of the people'.

Charles, who had called the Parliament only because he had no other way of raising the money he urgently needed, but ended up without, had to resort to desperate means. In 1641 his wife Henrietta Maria even went as far as pawning the crown jewels to raise money for the king's army.

Over in Ireland, meanwhile, the Catholics of Ulster, fearful of the huge influx of Scottish and

English Protestants the Stuarts had 'planted' there and thinking that the English were about to introduce new repressive Protestant legislation, decided to attack the Protestant settlers by way of pre-emptive action. They slaughtered over 3,000 men, women and children, the direct cause of Cromwell's subsequent retribution a decade later. Fatally for the king, the Irish Catholic killers in Ulster claimed to have acted on his authority and produced a forged document to prove it. This served to convince wavering Parliamentarians that Charles really was plotting with Irish Catholics, with the Pope, and probably with Catholic Spain to get money to invade Scotland.

This was followed by Nathaniel Fiennes' discovery that Charles was planning to dissolve the Long Parliament by force, and by the unprecedented arrival at a Parliamentary session of the king himself, with armed troops at his back, demanding the arrest of five Parliamentarians, including Pym and Hampden. No arrests were made as the five wanted men slipped away, but the next day, when news of the king's attack on Parliament was noised about, mobs roamed London in fury and Charles fled the city.

Since the king had resorted to armed threats against his own Parliament, Parliament set about raising its own troops. To this day no sovereign has ever again been allowed into the House of Commons. John Pym led a motion that Charles was unfit to reign, and over the next eighteen months a majority of the Commons and a minority of the Lords came round to Pym's viewpoint. On 22 August 1642 the king raised his standard at Nottingham, declaring war, from a Puritan's point of view, on his own country.

The bulk of the Royal or Cavalier army came from the Catholic north and the west, including Wales, with a strong contingent of Irish troops and foreign mercenaries, whilst the Roundheads, so-called due to the shaved heads of the London apprentices who supported Parliament, came mostly from the more prosperous south and east, and from the Scottish Presbyterians. This was a general rule to which there were a great many confusing exceptions. Close kin often ended up on different sides, and the Fienneses were not immune to such splits.

William Fiennes, Lord Saye, had the close support of his three younger sons, all of whom became Roundhead generals, but his eldest son and heir, James, was a shy, gentle type who would nowadays be described as apolitical or agnostic, in terms of his commitment to either side during the Civil War. If anything, his proclivities appear to have been on the Royalist side. One of his sisters, Saye's younger daughter, married into a Royalist family, but the rest of the eight-strong brood were definitely anti-Royalist.

Most people throughout Britain (for Scotland and Ireland experienced as much or more bitter internal strife) only wanted peace, but they were sucked inexorably into the conflict and followed the line of least resistance. Some areas were let off lightly, having no key defensive installations on either side. Others were constantly fought over, and life there was hell on earth for the local people. At the height of the conflict in 1643 there were some 150,000 fighting men in England, a total which dropped by the late 1640s to 25,000.

At the outbreak of war Saye was made Lord Lieutenant of Oxfordshire with the power to call out and command the militia. He lost no time and the Oxfordshire Regiment was soon 1,200 strong and his own Saye and Sele Bluecoats vied for efficiency with the troops of his friends, including Hampden's Greencoats and Brooke's Purple. Saye additionally raised four troops of cavalry, three commanded by himself, and his sons, John and Nathaniel, while a fourth was led by a Captain Francis Fiennes and his ensign, Cornet Henry Fiennes. The family today are uncertain who exactly these two rogue Fienneses, presumably brothers, were, but think they were Fiennes-Clinton cousins.

Another Roundhead colonel, and one who achieved local fame by turning up with his regiment late for the battle of Worcester, was one of the Yorkshire Twisletons who had moved south and lived in Kent where he became a Puritan militia officer. He married four times and was the third husband of Elizabeth Fiennes, the granddaughter of Old Subtlety by his heir James, and my great to the power of ten grandmother. Her father was of Royalist inclination, despite being heir to Broughton, at the very time his father was plotting the downfall of the monarchy in the upstairs room.

Poor James must have kept his politics very much to himself, for not only were his father and three brothers active leaders of the Roundhead army, but his daughter's Twisleton husband was a Roundhead colonel knighted by Cromwell, whose elder brother, Colonel Philip Twisleton, was also Cromwell-knighted and whose younger

Roundhead brother, George Twisleton, was the army colonel who settled North Wales for Parliament. He later married there and his memorial is still to be seen in the church of Clynnog, near Caernarfon.

The first real battle of the Civil War took place at Edgehill, only five miles up the road from Broughton, and was well attended by at least six Fiennes relatives, all leading Parliamentary forces.

20

OLD SUBTLETY

The king's cavalry at the Battle of Edgehill was led by his nephew, Prince Rupert, and the Roundheads' army by the Earl of Essex, the son of the longtime favourite of Elizabeth I. His title was Parliamentary General, and Saye disliked him, but Saye's fourth son, Richard, was at Edgehill one of Essex's personal bodyguard, 'one hundred men of rank and fortune'. Colonel John Twisleton also belonged to it from time to time.

I have been to the site of the battle and could see how well chosen was the start point of the Royalist army. The king himself stayed on the high ridgeline out of harm's way, whilst the prince's ill-trained cavalry swept down on the Roundhead left flank, capturing their cannon and chasing them way back. But Saye's sons in the Roundhead centre did well and forced their opponents to retreat. The Broughton Horse with Essex's bodyguard cut down Wilmot's Royalists and killed many of the gunners of the king's artillery. They then fought a pitched battle with the royal foot guards, which they won shortly before dusk.

Back at Broughton, Saye's wife Elizabeth listened to the thunder of the cannon and must have kept her fingers crossed, for three of her beloved sons were there. The sixty-year-old Saye was himself in London addressing Parliament. The reports Elizabeth heard and diarised included one that her son, Colonel John, had been seen running away from the battle. This turned out to be false, since he was merely joining the fighting late, having collected much-needed stores and ammunition.

Rupert's initial charge would have won the day, despite the Roundhead presence of over 14,000 men, but he failed to regroup to protect the royal infantry. Nonetheless, the king's men felt that they had won and the road to London, their overall goal, was at least for a while free of Roundheads. The king then directed Rupert, his cavalry and artillery to attack Saye's two castles in the immediate vicinity, Banbury and Broughton. The Royal infantry under the Earl of Northampton laid immediate siege to Banbury.

In London Saye received a message from his son Nathaniel that the Earl of Essex had withdrawn to Warwick, leaving the road to London open for the king's army. Saye reacted with a Churchillian speech to a demoralised Parliament:

My Lords and Gentlemen, that little I have to say shall not be to emphasize your approaching danger but rather to apply myself to stir up your spirits, to encourage

272

you . . . This is now not a time for men to think with themselves that they will be in their shops to get a little money . . . In common dangers let every man take his weapons in his hand, let him offer himself willingly to serve his God . . . Let every man therefore shut up his shop, let him take his musket, let him offer himself readily and willingly, let him not think with himself who shall pay me, but rather think this, I'll come forth to save the Kingdom, to serve my God, to maintain his true religion, to save the parliament, to save this noble city . . . Let every man arm himself and arm his apprentices, and come forth with boldness and with courage and with cheerfulness, and doubt not but God will assist you . . . Be not daunted, let not malignant parties that go up and down and would go about to inform you that there are these fears and these dangers, let them not make you be wanting to yourselves; fear them not at all. I shall conclude with this, that that good King said, up and be doing and the Lord will be with you.

A revealing point of this text is that Saye was not anti-king *per se*. As with different forms of worship, where he saw no particular sect as omnipotent, he viewed no particular form of government as singled out by divine commendation. Mixed monarchy seemed to him to be the best system for the Britain of that time. There must, he believed, be a king or queen, but one who ruled *with*, not against, the wishes of the people's Parliament. The aim of Saye's Civil War, as plotted with Pym,

Hampden and his other friends at Broughton, was to control, not to evict, the king.

Four days after Edgehill, the combined troops of Colonels Nathaniel and John Fiennes attacked the siege force of Royalists around Banbury Castle, especially keen to save Lord Brooke's artillery from falling into enemy hands. They failed. The Saye and Seles had for many years owned Banbury Castle and been MPs for Banbury. (I am today the 3rd Baronet of Banbury, my grandfather having chosen the town where he had long been the Liberal MP when he was made a baronet.) But that castle was extremely well built to withstand the strongest of sieges. The fact that it fell in only four days to Prince Rupert's troops and the metal cannon balls of a single small gun was entirely due to a large part of the garrison being disaffected and, after the siege, going over to the Royalists. Banbury Castle spent the rest of the war as a Royalist stronghold. Once Banbury Castle was in Prince Rupert's hands, the king ordered him the very next day to 'attack and plunder Broughton Castle'.

Personal animosity against Saye explains why the king, with a major war on his hands, should send his senior cavalry general to attack what amounted to a mere country house, for although crenellated with a moat and drawbridge, Broughton was never built with serious defensive features in mind. A Banbury complaint record states:

When our Mayor showed Prince Rupert the King's hand and royal seal that the towne should not be plundered, Prince Rupert threw it away and said, 'My uncle little knows what belongs to the wars.' And so he commanded his men to plunder which they did to a purpose. But that which touched us most is a warrant under His Majesty's hand for the plundering of Lord Saye and Sele his house, demolishing of it and invites the people to do it with a grant to them of all the material therein.

Broughton was held only by a single troop of horse whose billets were the extensive attics, still known to the family as 'the barracks', which is where cousins Nat and Mariette, the present Lord and Lady Saye and Sele, took me to locate many of the documents quoted in this book. The castle is also overlooked from rising ground nearby, ideal for cannon fire. The defenders had lashed large bales of wool along the battlements, but this proved a useless gesture and the garrison sensibly surrendered after twenty-four hours. Prince Rupert's diary for Friday, 28 October 1642 simply states, '28. My Lord Saye's howse was taken.' Cannon balls dredged up from the Broughton moat are on display to the public today, along with a coat owned by Cromwell, which is displayed in the Great Hall. Like Banbury, Broughton remained in Royalist hands for the rest of the war.

Soon afterwards, General Essex, the Roundhead army commander, ordered the Fiennes cavalry to push forward ahead of the army towards Worcester. In charge of this reconnaissance force were Nathaniel and John Fiennes with Colonel Sandys. Unfortunately, the Royalist cavalry under Prince Rupert attacked them in strength at Powyck Bridge. The Fiennes force was heavily defeated, Sandys was killed and the brothers were among the last survivors to leave the battle, Nathaniel killing a Cavalier officer with his sword. A Royalist victory song results from the Battle of Powyck Bridge:

> Thither came Fiennes with arms complete
> The town to take and Biron defeat
> Provision was made but he stayed not to eat
> Which nobody can deny'o
> Which nobody can deny.
>
> For as soon as he heard our great guns play
> With a flea in his ear he ran quite away .
> Like the lawful begotten son of Lord Say,
> Which nobody can deny'o
> Which nobody can deny.

After this setback, the Fiennes brothers with the remnants of their force were sent by Essex to other campaigns. John was commissioned as colonel of a cavalry regiment, later involved in many actions in the Oxford area. He commanded the siege of his home town of Banbury from August to October 1644, when he finally succeeded. He was singled out by Oliver Cromwell in a commendation the following year: 'His diligence was great and this I must testify that I find no man more ready to all services than himself . . . I find him a gentleman of that fidelity to you and so conscientious that he would all his troop were as religious and civil as any and makes it a great part of his care to get them so.'

When a temporary treaty was mooted in Oxford

in November 1642, the king gave his grant-of-safe-conduct to all the Peace Commissioners put forward by Parliament, with the sole exception of Lord Saye. The latter gradually grew in influence and reputation in the Lords, as did his sons, Nathaniel and John in the Commons. Saye's position was one of hostility to both religious extremes, the Presbyterians and the episcopalians. He took a middle, relatively tolerant line and became the leader of the Independents, or middle party.

His greatest friend and ally, Lord Brooke, was killed at the siege of Lichfield. Sir Walter Scott celebrates him in verse: 'fanatic Brooke, the fair cathedral stormed and took.' In fact, Brooke was merely inspecting entrenchments there when he was shot through the eye. 'That very eye,' crowed his enemies, 'with which he had said he hoped to see the destruction of all the cathedrals in England.'

Saye's main allies, fellow Independents, after 1644 were the Earl of Northumberland and Lord Wharton in the Lords and, in the Commons, his son Nathaniel and Oliver Cromwell. Cromwell was slowly ascending the army ranks and agreed with Saye that the current overall commander, the Earl of Essex, was getting too powerful and too autocratic; just like his father who Elizabeth I had eventually beheaded. Saye led the plot to deal with Essex, and when the Earl started to receive Royalist peace proposals in person rather than as head of Parliament, Saye pounced. He put forward a proposal for a joint Anglo-Scottish governing body called the Committee of Both Kingdoms. This radical new bill was engineered through

Parliament by Saye's powerful cliques in both houses. The Scots acquiesced, for Essex had arrogantly claimed jurisdiction over their army, too. The Scottish Minister, Robert Baillie, wrote: 'The proposal was gotten through the House of Lords with little difficultie, where most was expected, my Lord Say being somewhat of the General.' The proposal established an alliance between the Parliamentarians and the Scots. That is, of course, those Scots who were not for the king.

At this time Saye also proposed a bill known as the Self-Denying Ordinance, an attempt to depoliticise the army, and began the move to form an efficient 'New Model' Parliamentarian Army with Sir Thomas Fairfax as its commander-in-chief. Saye was everywhere at once and always one jump ahead of his many adversaries. To some extent the parliamentary system and its two houses made this easy for him because the politics of the English revolution were dominated by members of the House of Lords. Being at the tip of the pyramid of English society, individual lords used their power and prestige to control the government. Powerful non-peers in the Commons, such as Nathaniel Fiennes, John Pym and Oliver Cromwell, were briefed by their patrons in the Lords; secretly briefed since the Commons was proud of its independence. Hence the ongoing cabals at Broughton Castle and, later on, in Saye's London rooms. As they stood to address the Commons, King Pym, King Cromwell and King Fiennes never owned up to their co-movers in the senior house.

In February 1643 Nathaniel was sent as a troubleshooter to keep Bristol from the Royalists. The current governor's loyalty was under suspicion, the garrison had been dangerously denuded by the army of the west, and the city aldermen were openly sympathetic to the king. Nathaniel Fiennes was clearly the man for such a job. His first move once there was to execute two men caught plotting to open the city gates to Prince Rupert. Then he pestered Fairfax for more men and supplies but, only five months after his arrival, Prince Rupert's 25,000-strong army attacked on all fronts, including from the sea, for the ships in Bristol harbour declared for the king. With the citizens hostile, supplies running low and the city walls breached in several places, Nathaniel had no option but to surrender after a week of desperate resistance. His 3,000 troops were allowed to leave under 'partial arms'.

Various MPs, shocked by the collapse of such a key city in the west, accused Nathaniel of treason and cowardice. A trial before a Council of War found him guilty of improper surrender, and he was sentenced to death despite fierce support from his brother, Colonel John Fiennes, who had shared the Bristol defence with him. The prosecution made use of one Dorothy Hazzard, the Baptist leader who had established Bristol's first dissenting church three years before and who, with two hundred other women, had held the city's Frome Gate against Prince Rupert's men. Nathaniel received a last minute pardon, doubtless due to the influence of his father and other friends in high places, but his own considerable influence waned until, two years later, Prince Rupert was forced out of Bristol by a Roundhead siege, and it then became clear that the city was indefensible without huge commitment and expense. Nathaniel, fully vindicated, regained his powerful position as an Independent leader in the Commons. He is remembered in the records of Winchester, which city his men once took from the Royalists, with great gratitude for the firm hand he took with Roundhead troops found desecrating and smashing memorials, including the tomb of the city father, William of Wykeham, Nathaniel's ancestor.

After the Bristol debacle, Nathaniel's brother John returned to Oxfordshire and, in April 1644, laid siege to Banbury Castle. Letters which he sent from his siege tent to his parents in London were intercepted, as was incoming mail, by Royalist spies, and published in the public *Court Journal*, presumably by way of ridicule. One from Lord Saye said: 'Jack, I fear you must get into the Castle by a golden bridge. Try if you can get a fit instrument. Spare not cost. No matter for the clamour of bribery. £500 given were well bestowed and would soon be gotten up again.'

Another letter from Colonel John's mother runs: 'Sonne John, Whatever you want, send earnestly for it before you want it or else you will go without it when you most need it. I pray you, do not engage yourself more than in keeping them in and in keeping others from them.' That sounds like a typical worried mum, hoping her son will keep safe by taking minimal risks.

The Royalists had also managed to get hold of an executive order sent by John to the Constable of Roxton, presumably prior to a planned attack on Banbury Castle.

These are to charge and command you that upon sight hereof you gather together all the

ladders in your town with a load of hay bound hard together with thumb ropes, and one load of good brush faggots and bring the said things into the churchyard in Banbury by one of the clock this day week at the furthest; hereof fail not upon pain of death and forfeiting your whole estate.
Given under my hand the 20th April 1644
John Fiennes
Colonel

The largest battle of the war, a Roundhead victory, took place a few weeks later at Marston Moor involving 45,000 soldiers, but most Civil War engagements were mere skirmishes or sieges. At Marston Moor Prince Rupert, in admiration, called Cromwell Ironside, and thereafter his personal cavalry were known as Ironsides. 'Cromwell's troops moved to victory,' wrote historian Lord Macaulay, 'with the precision of machines and the fanaticism of Crusaders. From the time it was remodelled to its disbandment it never found an enemy who could stand its onset whether in Britain or abroad. These Puritan warriors, even contending against three-fold odds never failed to conquer, to destroy and break in pieces whatever force was opposed to them.'
The New Model Army gradually took shape as Saye's Self-Denying Ordinance removed the old commanders, leaving Fairfax and Cromwell in charge. Their chief recruitment areas were in and around London. At the beckoning finger of Cromwell, like Kitchener's subsequent 'Your country needs you', thousands of Londoners would be rapidly deployed to augment the standing army.

Cromwell wrote a condolence letter to his brother-in-law just after the Battle of Marston Moor:

The Left Wing which I commanded, being our own horse saving a few Scots in our rear, beat all the Prince's horse. God made them as stubble to our swords. We charged their regiments of foot and routed them . . . Sir, God hath taken away your eldest son by a cannon shot. It brake his leg. We were necessitated to have it cut off, whereof he died. There is your precious child full of glory, never to know sin or sorrow any more.

After the battle Cromwell was promoted to commander of all the Model Army's cavalry units. A succession of chess-like moves by both sides, various sieges, siege reliefs and skirmishes eventually led to a major confrontation near Naseby, where Colonel John Twisleton's men fought by chance alongside those of Colonel John Fiennes, both on the right wing and directly under Cromwell's command. Their forces were critical to the final outcome of the three-hour battle in which over 5,000 Royalists were killed. Fairfax's men pursued and slaughtered many fleeing Royalists and, unusual for Puritan troops, raped and mutilated dozens of Rupert's female camp followers. Those responsible later said that they did this because the women spoke Irish. In fact, they were Welsh.

After Naseby the Roundheads were all-conquering. Chester, Leicester, Taunton and other major bastions fell to Parliament. The king managed to last out until the fall of Oxford in 1646, but after Naseby he never really stood a chance.

Amongst the royal baggage coaches captured at Naseby were compromising copies of letters written by Charles seeking support from Catholic Europe. The Roundheads published these with much righteous indignation and gained popular support to carry on fighting to the finish. But there were increasing signs of anger in many regions that the war was ruining people's lives and achieving nothing. Groups of neutralists or 'clubmen' throughout the west country tried to drive both warring sides out of their area and demanded an end to the war by negotiation. In Dorset there was even an armed clubmen uprising that Cromwell had to quash.

Eleven months after Naseby the king's troops had withered away, disillusioned by constant defeat, and, unlike the Roundheads, unpaid. So Charles surrendered to the Scottish in the hope that he could enlist their support by promising to establish Presbyterianism as the official form of worship throughout Britain. But the Scots did not trust him, and anyway hoped to achieve their religious aims through Parliament. So they handed the king over to the Roundheads for £400,000. 'Cheap at the price,' was Charles's recorded comment. So he still had a sense of humour. (The £400,000 was also to pay the Scottish army to go back home.) The first Civil War was over.

*   *   *

Parliament put the king under comfortable house

arrest at Hampton Court Palace and began a series of internal squabbles between various factions. One small act by Lord Saye at that time revealed that, although an outwardly cold individual, he was kind at heart, for he was the only peer who paid for the royal children to be well looked after whilst their father was 'away' and before Parliament voted the money for their care.

To win the war, Parliament had imposed tax on two key commodities: beer and salt. People needed salt to preserve food, and they drank beer as today we drink tea and coffee. So to tax such items was a sure way of losing support. Bad weather, in fact the worst harvests for a century, led to exorbitant food prices and economic recession. The poor became desperate. Large numbers of redundant soldiers found no work and Parliament enraged the army, early in 1647, by trying to disband most of the soldiery without pay.

Parliament, by that summer, was far more unpopular throughout the land than the king had ever been and, unable to see an alternative, a majority in both houses felt that the only way forward was to restore the king to his former position with the best terms they could squeeze from him. But such a course was anathema to the many whose loved ones had died to change the system. To admit that the whole hellish struggle had been fruitless and futile by bringing back the king to his former powers would be a betrayal to God and to the dead.

The dominant faction in Parliament's Committee of the Two Kingdoms was the Scottish-orientated Presbyterian grouping who had, in order to win the war, promised their Scottish allies that they would dismantle the Elizabethan Church of England and refashion it in the Presbyterian model. This they had done with edicts throughout the land banishing the Prayer Book, the episcopacy, cathedrals, and all festivals like Easter and Christmas. Nobody was exempt from the authority of this new national church and nobody could receive Holy Communion without the approval of their minister and a Certificate of Worthiness.

The reaction of the populace to all this was to hate the source of it all: Parliament and the Puritans. Congregations everywhere chucked out ministers who tried to impose the new rules. There were riots in London. The Independents, led by Lord Saye in the Lords and, in the Commons, by Colonel Nathaniel Fiennes (his reputation fully restored since his near-hanging after his surrender of Bristol), pursued a path that led between the various radical factions. A letter sent to the king at that time by his adviser, Lewis Dye, stated: 'Cromwell and his Cabinett which are the Lord Say, St John and Vayne-the-younger, now steer the affaires of the whole Kingdome.' Only five days after the London riots, Sir John Maynard wrote to the court, 'On my knowledge the greatest enemies the King had be my Lord Say, St John, old and young Vane and Evelyn.' The Royalist publication *Mercurius* summed Saye up: 'He is as smooth as a butterbox. Oh! how the Presbyterians sneare in their sleeves to see with what dexterity this spider weaves his nets to catch the silly flies of the Army.'

The views of the Fiennes faction, which at that stage included Oliver Cromwell and the other army generals, were reflected in a document drawn up by Saye known as the Heads of the Proposals.

In this they told the king that they believed that nobody in Britain should be treated as a heretic, except aggressive papists or way-out Low Churchers, and that no one should be prosecuted for failing to attend parish services 'if he could show a reasonable Cause for his absence'. Saye believed that 'beyond ensuring order and punishing blasphemy, the State had no brief to police men's thoughts and that congregations were free to choose their ministers and forms of worship or use the Book of Common Prayer. But the old episcopal order should be abolished.'

On the monarchy, Saye's bill proposal stated that the king's executive powers were to be strictly limited. 'He himself,' Saye wrote, 'hath brought this necessity upon us; not to trust him with that power whereby he may do us and himself hurt but with so much alone as shall be sufficient to inable him to do us good.' Restoration of the king, Saye stated, was to follow immediately upon his agreement to the concessions demanded in Saye's proposals.

In such a complex and contrary environment as Parliament in 1647, Saye's proposals could only be implemented by cunning and influence. Only Saye had the necessary web of contacts and allies in the Lords, the army and the Commons.

'Colonels Nathaniel and John Fiennes,' Sir William Waller claimed, 'acted as tame draftsmen for the Lords who gathered at Saye's house'; and another contemporary observed that: 'it made little difference which of Saye's parliamentary siblings was involved [with an appointment to control the Exchequer] since, no matter which of them it is, both may do well enough with their Father's

Money Baggs.' Political prisoner in the Tower, John Lilburne, wrote in a letter: 'Cromwell is now closely glued in interest and councelle to the Lords Say and Wharton.'

In October 1647 the king's men responded that royal assent would be given to Saye's proposals as passed by the Lords, but not with the amendments applied by the Commons. The king, however, still believed that he could win the day without making any concession to anybody. He eluded his guards at Hampton Court and fled, to Carrisbrooke Castle on the Isle of Wight. Saye went to see him there, in defiance of Parliament, but negotiations came to an abrupt halt when Civil War broke out again as the army faced a Royalist invasion from Scotland and a series of regional uprisings. Charles had promised the Scots he would Presbyterianise the whole of Britain in return for their support.

This second phase of the Civil War, as bloody as the first, ended at the Battle of Prestonpans, where the Scots were crushed by the New Model Army and the king was again imprisoned. Back to square one, and Saye, Nathaniel and John Fiennes again pressed in both houses for settlement with the king. Thomas Coke wrote of Saye:

Of all the parlement commissioners, the most inward man with the King, he undertooke most on his behalfe with his interest in the Houses. The Duke of Richmond and hee were very intimate and by him the Lord Saye conveyed his intelligences still to the King. He was so confident of the successe of the treatie that he had bespoke of himselfe to be Lord Treasurer. He did all that he could to work upon the King to yield to what was proposed to him. And, afterwards, to persuade the Parliament to be content with what his majesty had yielded.

Likewise, in the Commons Nathaniel Fiennes strongly supported the king's response to the Saye proposals and, on 1 December, made a powerful speech urging that the king had 'done enough' to safeguard religion and the constitution and that therefore they should negotiate and settle with him.

The majority of the Commons clearly agreed with Fiennes, but a large section of army men, disgusted by the king's secret alliance with the Scots, pre-empted any further discussions with him by Parliament by simply raiding the Commons. Colonel Thomas Pride arrested over half the members and forcibly prevented them taking their seats. Two-thirds of the remainder, appalled, boycotted their violated house.

In the revolutionary months that followed, less than one in six of all MPs returned to the house, and many of those that did wished only to moderate proceedings. The decision to put King Charles on trial was approved by less than one in ten of those who had made war on him five years before. Nathaniel Fiennes was amongst those arrested by Pride's men who proclaimed 'a Republic' and, when released, he, like his father and brother, took no part in it. The House of Lords, meanwhile, was abolished to be later replaced by Cromwell's 'Other House'.

Saye wrote gloomily: 'Had the King only passed those Four Bills [his proposals], a Peace had been settled, safe and just to the subjects, as Honourable to himself, and all troubles and confusions ended. When they will now end, the Lord only knoweth.'

Unforgiving of the recaptured king's treasonable dealings with the Scots, Cromwell pressed for the trial of the 'tyrant, traitor and murderer, Charles Stuart'. On 2 January 1649 a bill was brought before the remnants of the Commons, known as the Rump Parliament, ordaining that 'a high court of justice for the trial of the King be erected'. All the peers were ordered to attend and, from my point of view, an interesting note was the reaction of a hitherto timid, non-participatory Fiennes relative. Lord Francis Dacre normally kept well clear of trouble, and therefore of attendance at the Lords. I have a copy of a letter he wrote from Herstmonceux some five years earlier addressed to the Deputy Speaker.

On Wednesday night last I received your lordship's of the ninth of this month, and would have most gladly obeyed the commands of the House of Peers, by coming . . . to wait on the affairs of the kingdom on the 22nd, had not the ways ever since been so extremely clogged by a very deep snow, that men pass not without much difficulty and danger: I beseech your lordship to add to this reason the weakness of my own health, not being able to endure the rigour of the journeying on horseback in such exceeding cold weather, as now it is; and to represent this to their lordships' favourable constructions; not that I intend to make long

use of any way to excuse myself from that duty, which I shall ever owe to the commonwealth, but very shortly shall give my attendance on their lordships with all willingness and readiness. And so I rest
Your lordship's
Most humble servant,
Francis Dacre

However, so strong were his feelings about the impending trial that on a cold January day he not only made it to the Lords, but was one of only twelve peers who had the courage to speak out in defence of their sovereign, an act of loyalty which so upset Cromwell's men that they suggested that the twelve lords should be impeached 'as favourers of the grand delinquent of England and enemies to public justice and the liberty of the people'. Good Marxist stuff.

Later that month the trial went ahead and the king was tried for his life. He was found guilty of treason and sentenced to death. The court decided that the king 'be put to death by the severing of his head from his body'. On a wintry morning outside Whitehall, Charles was beheaded in public which, in time, turned out to be a great propaganda mistake by his enemies. The crowd, watched over by the army, were stunned and sympathetic to their king.

Charles wore several layers of underclothes on his way to the block, for it was cold and he did not wish the public to see him shiver and mistake this for fear. One record of the event is a letter home from an Oxford student in Whitehall by chance. 'I stood amongst the crowd where the scaffold was erected. The Blow I saw given, at the instant whereof there was such a Grone by the Thousands then present as I never heard before and desire I may never hear again.' The crowd were allowed to rush forward and dip their handkerchiefs in his blood. It was the Puritan poet Andrew Marvell who wrote:

> He nothing common did, or mean
> Upon that memorable scene
> But with his keener eye
> The axe's edge did try . . .
> And bowed his comely head
> Down, as on a bed.

Four months later England became a Republic, with Oliver Cromwell the chairman of the Council of State.

21

ADULTERY AT THE CASTLE

A popular image of Oliver Cromwell, the man who killed the king and then usurped the throne, is of an angry, prudish commoner who, like Idi Amin, quickly climbed the ranks and ruled as a tyrant. But Cromwell's grandfather was a wealthy landowner who regularly entertained King James I and his court on his estates. Cromwell's father, a younger son, inherited a lesser part of the family wealth, and young Oliver, after studying at Cambridge University, farmed his land and looked after his seven unmarried sisters.

He was thirty-nine years old and suffering from depression (for which he consulted doctors) when he underwent, like St Paul on the road to Damascus, a religious conversion which was to propel him from middle-aged obscurity into national power and a fame which has remained so durable that at the millennium he was voted one of Britain's Top Ten Men in History.

Through his wife, whose family had extensive estates in Essex, he met the Earl of Warwick and through him Lord Saye, both vociferous members of the Independent party of liberal Puritans, at that time the group whose aims most tallied with Cromwell's. As MP for Cambridge by 1640, Cromwell first became known for his frequent fiery speeches in the Commons, which mirrored those of the Saye group in the Lords. He remained friends with Saye through the Civil War, and in 1647 tried to push Saye's Heads of the Proposals through Parliament. But, when the king proved recalcitrant and escaped from house arrest, Cromwell's anti-Royalist side hardened and, unlike Saye, he no longer saw a way forward that included King Charles as monarch. After Pride's Purge cleansed Parliament of MPs wishing to continue negotiations with Charles, Cromwell was one of the main architects of the king's subsequent trial and execution which so disgusted Lord Saye.

The Rump Parliament was set up after the Purge to run the new Republic. Cromwell, very powerful by now, tried at first to bring together Saye's group of Independents and to work with them, but only one participated in the Rump. The rest were too alienated by the regicide and, like

292

Saye, left Parliament. The Fiennes family was not at this stage politically split, and 1649 saw both Nathaniel and John unsympathetic to the Rump. Neither brother had anything to do with the Republic, nor did they approve when Cromwell abolished the House of Lords, leaving nobody but the blinkered and intolerant Rump to run the Republic.

Although Broughton was by then out of Royalist hands and back with the Fienneses, the seventy-year-old Lord Saye, probably because his beloved wife Elizabeth had died at Broughton the previous year, did not go back there, but spent the next three years in self-imposed exile on the Isle of Lundy, a pirates' haven for centuries in the Bristol Channel halfway between Wales and North Devon. I boated to Lundy in 2003 and noted the puffins nesting along the high cliffs, the seals in the Atlantic surf below and the total lack of trees or permanent inhabitants. I failed to find the ruins of the 'castle' where my great to the power of twelve grandfather had spent those three Cromwellian years. Yet in his day, and certainly in the first half of his century, the place was a hive of piratical activity and not the sort of place I would have chosen to bunker down in an anti-Cromwellian huff. Lundy was one of the very last Royalist strongholds in England to surrender to Parliament, the governor eventually handing the island over to Colonel Richard Fiennes, representing General Fairfax.

Richard lived there for a while, then when his father Lord Saye arrived, fed up with Cromwell and with the Lords abolished, Richard moved with his family to Broughton, where he settled, although his elder non-military brother James was heir to the castle and, while Saye stayed away on Lundy, its proprietor. The two brothers clearly enjoyed each other's company, and James was otherwise alone as his wife had left the castle due to what seems to me to have been a bad case of in-house adultery. Not exactly *Upstairs, Downstairs* so much as Upstairs and along the Corridor to the Chief Steward of the Household's suite.

At that time many great houses with estates were run by stewards, who were often younger sons of nobles with good university qualifications. Lord Saye at first took on Thomas Dudley, a scion of the famous Elizabethan favourite, but then Saye did a favour to his son-in-law, Theophilus Fiennes-Clinton, 4th Earl of Lincoln, by lending him Dudley, who did such a good job for the earl that he never returned to Broughton. He was replaced by one William Sprigge of Banbury, an excellent steward who went on to become the steward of New College, Oxford, but was the father of a prudish Puritan, Joshua Sprigge, who, behind James Fiennes' back, seduced his wife in his own castle.

The adulterous Frances Fiennes, Lady Saye and Sele, was herself an extreme Puritan of the sort who could do no wrong and made a study of hypocrisy. Lady Frances Cecil (her maiden name) was the great granddaughter of Queen Elizabeth's great statesman, Lord Burghley, and with James Fiennes she had produced six little Fienneses, including three sons. Two died as infants and the eldest, after a Winchester education that did not include swimming, went to Paris aged nineteen, where he drowned in the Seine. In his rooms in

Paris he had a miniature painting of his father which the owners kept when he died. Over two hundred years later a French family returned this miniature to Broughton. Two of his sisters survived to carry on the Fiennes inheritance.

Fiennes relations, the Verney family, are famous for having kept family letters down the centuries, and one of them in 1648 mentions: 'Your cousin James Fiennes and his wife are parted. They say the reason is they cannot agree in disputes of conscience and that she does not think him holy enough, but in my opinion there is very little conscience in parting from husbands.' Contemporary gossip-mongers described Joshua Sprigge as the 'Gallant of Lady Saye', and when James died, they married.

Quite when the adulterous goings-on at Broughton became general knowledge it is difficult to say, but James was married to Frances for at least sixteen years before she went off to live with the slimy Joshua. The scandal would have been all the greater due to the extreme Puritan prudery that they both preached. Indeed, to confuse things, Sprigge had a post as chaplain in Fairfax's army and wrote a popular account of various battles, called *Anglia Rediviva*, but he was a monarchist nonetheless and wrote a forceful argument against the king's execution as part of Saye's effort to stop the regicide.

So James, no doubt smarting in public as a known cuckold, lived at Broughton with his two surviving daughters and the family of his brother, the retired Colonel Richard Fiennes. How long their father would have stayed away on Lundy is difficult to deduce. It is said that he wrote a romantic novel there or, together with his other son Nathaniel, a famous Parliamentary tract called *Vinducii*. Either way, one of his supply ships from the mainland was in 1651 captured and a ransom was demanded, which must have turned him off Lundy.

Royalist vessels based in France routinely harassed parliamentary ships, and one Captain Will Hinton who hijacked Saye's boat sent him a ransom note on behalf of his exiled master, Charles II to be, which read:

My Lord,
Not far from that pretty island whereof your Lordship is petty prince, it was my fortune last evening to fetch up a small vessel laden with provisions of your garrison. I could wish it have been of some considerable value . . . so famous is your Lordship for your activity against your Liege Lord, the King's Majesty of ever beloved memory. Yet, as little as it was, it did me good to seize upon it by virtue of my commission from his Majesty that now is, were it but to keep it in your Lordship's memory that there still is a King.

The letter went on to threaten Saye that future supply ships to Lundy would also be liable to seizure. So Saye returned to live out his old age at Broughton and keep a jaundiced eye on his number one enemy, once his good friend, Oliver Cromwell.

The Royalists had, following the regicide, regrouped in Ireland after signing a treaty with the Irish Catholics, and Cromwell was chosen by the

Rump Parliament to lead a Roundhead army to deal with this Irish threat. First on his list of targets was Drogheda. Cromwell's first attack on well defended Drogheda was repulsed, which annoyed him, but after the defenders began to waver, all hell was let loose. By his own estimate he put some 2,000 to the sword. 'In the Round Tower they refused to yield to mercy whereupon I ordered the fire. One of them was heard to say in the midst of the flames, "God damn me, God confound me: I burn. I burn."'

Cromwell starved out some sixty defenders of another tower, and when they at length gave up, he had their officers clubbed to death, every tenth soldier shot after the Roman fashion of decimation, and shipped the rest to the Barbados. Cromwell's report added: 'I am persuaded that this is a righteous judgement of God upon these barbarous wretches who have imbrued their hands in so much innocent blood.' The final toll of the massacre included 2,700 Royalist soldiers, many of whom were actually English, anyone with arms, many civilians, Roman Catholic priests, and even prisoners. Wexford was in the process of surrendering when Cromwell's men broke into the town in his absence, killed 2,000 Irish troops, murdered 1,500 civilians, and set fire to the town.

In the conquered areas, Cromwell's officers confiscated the land of 'all rebels', as a result of which nearly 40 per cent of all Ireland was redistributed from Catholics born in Ireland to Protestants born in Britain. The public practice of Catholicism was banned, Catholic priests were killed when caught and somewhere between 12,000 and 50,000 Irish folk were sold into slavery.

Cromwell is still a figure of hatred in Ireland, his name being associated with massacre, religious persecution and mass dispossession of Catholics.

Parliament then sent Cromwell's army to Scotland, where Charles I's son had been proclaimed Charles II by the Scottish Presbyterians. Cromwell was far less harsh with the Scots, many of whom had been his allies in the Civil War. At the Battle of Dunbar the Roundheads smashed the main Scots army, killing 4,000 and taking 10,000 prisoners before capturing Edinburgh. Despite this, Charles II with a small army of Scots invaded England, hoping to gather support en route to capture London. But Roundhead armies closed on Charles near Worcester in September 1651 and surrounded his 15,000 men with twice that number. Charles had made a crucial error in assuming that traditional Royalist supporters in Lancashire and the Welsh border area would rush to his standard, but Parliament had done a successful PR job convincing the populace that this was a Scottish Presbyterian invasion first and foremost, never mind the king.

The river Severn figured strongly in Royalist Worcester's defences, but Cromwell's men built pontoon bridges which circumvented the king's defensive plan. Charles II fought with brain and bravery, but the battle was eventually lost. There were very few Parliamentary dead, but 3,000 Royalists were killed, over 10,000 captured, English prisoners were conscripted into the Parliamentary army still in Ireland, whilst 8,000 Scots prisoners were sent to labour in New England and the West Indies.

Prior to the battle, King Charles II had contracted the Worcester clothiers to outfit his army with uniforms, but the £453 bill was never paid. In June 2008 Charles, Prince of Wales, paid off the debt. Charles II managed, just, to escape, via an oak tree hide and many other adventures, to exile in France.

Three Fienneses were involved in the Battle of Worcester: the three elder sons of John Twisleton, all of whom were colonels in the New Model Army. The eldest one, Colonel John Twisleton, had two years previously married Elizabeth, the eldest daughter and co-heiress of James Fiennes, whose inheritance would include Broughton Castle. He was Colonel of the Kent Militia and had been summoned to help surround Charles II at Worcester. For some unrecorded reason he was very nearly late for this, the last battle of the Civil War. A stern order was sent to him (27 August 1651): 'Council of State to Col. John Twisleton: We are sorry that, in a time when there is such a necessity for forces, there should arise such difficulties to get out your regiment and we desire you to march forthwith with it to Lt Gen Fleetwood with all expedition to Banbury or to such place as he shall direct, and use all diligence as your regiment is so far behind.' Twisleton and his men did just make it and helped Fleetwood secure the key south bank of the river Teme, south of Worcester. Cromwell even knighted him.

The battle was Cromwell's last and his victory over the Scots contributed to his ever-growing eminence in the early 1650s. Over in Broughton, 'Old Subtlety' Saye must have thought all his life's work had been to no avail, but he was to live long

299

enough to have the last laugh.

Whilst Cromwell was in Ireland and Scotland, the Rump Parliament, with no king as a common enemy, squabbled amongst themselves and failed to convince Cromwell, when he returned to active politics, that they could effectively achieve his goals to set election dates, to unite the three kingdoms under a single government and to put in place a single tolerant, national church. In April 1653 Cromwell and other army commanders decided that the Rump was a waste of time, so they used gentle force to 'help' the Rumpers out of their Commons seats, in the shape of a squad of forty musketeers under the command of Major General Charles Wolseley (who was married to Lord Saye's daughter, Anne Fiennes). Cromwell took away the mace, symbol of parliamentary authority, and gave it into Wolseley's safe keeping.

The Rump was replaced by a group of 140 men considered by Cromwell and his army colleagues to be the 'most godly men in England'. This 'holy parliament' was nicknamed the Barebones Parliament, after one of its members, Praise God Barbon, and was tasked by Cromwell to agree upon and implement a permanent constitutional and religious settlement. After five months of useless deliberation, they gave up and voted that Cromwell take over the reins of government. At this stage the army leaders asked Cromwell to accept the crown and to rule as king, but he refused, even though he approved of monarchy in principle. He was even, at the time of Charles I's execution, discussing with colleagues the case for restoring one of his sons to the throne.

However, Cromwell did agree to become Lord

Protector of the three kingdoms, a title which brought with it most of the trappings of royalty without the embarrassment of becoming king and being known as the usurper. For the next five years until his death, he ruled through a Council of State with a sitting Parliament, but to all intents and purposes his Britain was a benevolent military dictatorship, in order to avoid being an anarchy or a monarchy. People started to address him as 'Your Highness', and he did not object. He signed his name regally as 'Oliver P', standing for 'Oliver Protector'. He was paid £100,000 per annum and would clearly remain undisputed boss of the realm so long as he stayed popular with the army.

The new constitution which he initially tried out was based on the Heads of the Proposals which Lord Saye, Pym and he himself had put together years before. When it failed to work, he tried a number of other forms of government, and none were revolutionary. He was perfectly happy to keep the country's class structure the way it was. He approved of a wide measure of religious liberty. His state church did not require folk to attend it, and all citizens (except Catholics) were allowed to follow their own conscience as to how they chose to worship. He was, like old Lord Saye at Broughton, violently anti-Quaker, but his Protectorate was, looking back, a remarkable period of religious freedom in Britain.

He even encouraged Jews to come back to Britain. Edward I had sent them all packing, but Cromwell's welcome back invitation was well-timed, since only five years before the Ukrainians had massacred 100,000 Jews and deported the rest. Cromwell saw Holland as Britain's main trade rival, and Amsterdam was full of Jews. He felt that, if tempted to Britain, they could lead an economic revival to help the country recover after the Civil War. He gave them full freedom of religion. Many soon arrived from Holland, Spain and Portugal, bringing invaluable information to assist the British trading empire in the Atlantic which Cromwell envisaged. Seventeenth-century British emigration across the Atlantic reached its peak during Cromwell's rule, many going for a better life, others for religious reasons, like the Catholic emigrants to Maryland and Puritans to New England. Thousands were also deported, often for minor crimes such as vagrancy.

Despite his policy of overall religious tolerance, Cromwell, like some fundamentalist Ayatollas of today, cracked down on what he regarded as frivolous pleasures which offended his work ethic. Many sports were selectively banned and theatres were closed. Women were not allowed brightly coloured dresses nor cosmetics, and Puritan soldiers would patrol the streets and rub the make-up off offenders' faces. Festivities at Easter and Christmas were abolished, and patrols would confiscate holly decorations and, by following their noses, roast goose and plum puddings would also be requisitioned.

In 1657 a major split occurred for the first time between Lord Saye and his two actively Puritan sons, Colonels Nathaniel and John. They had both left Parliament by the time the Rump was formed but, unlike Saye, both had made friends again with Cromwell and, when he became Lord Protector, both joined his Council of State. When they were invited to join Cromwell's Other House, a replacement for the Lords, both Fienneses agreed and became active members. Nathaniel rose to be the Speaker of the House, Keeper of the Privy Seal, and officially known as Lord Fiennes. He was one of the main movers in 1657 who attempted to convince Cromwell to take the crown because, as Protector, he officially possessed unlimited powers whereas, as king, he would be subject to legally limited authority.

In 1658 Nathaniel, as Speaker of the Commons, opened the new Parliament's first sitting with a rousing speech to both houses in which he described Cromwell as 'His Highness' and urged an ongoing war against the evil empire of Spain. Nathaniel's brother John did not shine in any way, and one Republican pamphleteer describes him as 'such a one who they call a sectary, but no great stickler and partly under the influence of his brother'.

Their father, although well into his seventies, was also summoned to the Other House by writ, but he refused and objected strongly to his two sons acquiescing with the king-killer. He also despised his son-in-law, Major General Charles Wolseley, who had become Cromwell's chief adviser and army supporter. No doubt to Saye's satisfaction, Cromwell sickened suddenly from septicaemia, some say malaria, and died in September 1658 with Nathaniel Fiennes at his deathbed strongly supporting his proposal that Cromwell's son, Richard, take over as Lord Protector.

Oliver Cromwell was buried with royal pomp in Westminster Abbey but, three years later when the monarchy was restored, his body was dug up, beheaded (on the same date that Charles I was executed), his body was hanged in chains from a Tyburn gibbet, then thrown into a pit. His severed head was displayed on a pole outside Westminster Hall for the next twenty-five years. Afterwards his head was auctioned several times, most recently in 1814, and was finally buried near the chapel of his alma mater, Sydney Sussex College, Cambridge in 1960.

His son and successor, lacking both his character and, crucially, top army support, was widely known as Tumbledown Dick. He ruled for only eighteen months of relative chaos. Army commanders with widely differing ideas of what should be done fell out with one another until the most powerful grouping under General Monck decided that there was only one answer, and that was to call back from exile the son of Charles I. Free elections were called and the man who had hidden in an oak tree after defeat at Worcester nine years before was recalled from France to be King Charles II of Britain.

As his ship brought him over from France, another vessel transferred the exiled Richard Cromwell to Paris, where he tactfully remained for twenty years before returning under an assumed name to live quietly in England until he died in 1712. His father had left Charles II a legacy of unusual religious tolerance but, after an eleven-year Republic during which he had experimented with many ways of changing the government system, nothing very much had actually happened since the killing of Charles I.

Scotland and most of Ireland were now fully integrated with the rest of Britain (under a continued dynasty of Scottish kings!) and, abroad, Cromwell's foreign policy had accelerated the road to empire. His invincible armies allied with the French to defeat the Spanish in 1658, but his grand 'Western Design' to defeat the Spanish in South America was a dismal failure. He did, however, capture Jamaica.

His 1651 Parliament passed the Navigation Act as a direct challenge to Dutch shipping. This provoked a brief naval war with the Dutch which Cromwell's powerful navy under General Monck had won by 1653. The Navigation Act confirmed Britain as an aggressively outward-looking nation, soon to become a commercial world power with an extensive merchant marine and a big-gun navy to protect it.

Cromwell was an undeniably successful ruler at home and abroad and, although originally a minor sheep farmer, he has today more roads named after him in England than anyone else but Queen Victoria.

But it is arguable that without his original friendship and political affinity with William Fiennes, Lord Saye, he would never have made it to be head of state.

22

A RESTORATION AND ELOPEMENT

My great uncle, Geoffrey Twisleton-Wykeham-Fiennes, the 19th Lord Saye and Sele, spent many years researching the history of his predecessors at

Broughton, especially Old Subtlety, and observed: 'It was Saye's rare and strange fortune after being the mainspring of the Revolution to become also the mainspring of the Restoration.' Although Saye was nigh on eighty years old at the Restoration, the king acknowledged his key role (despite the fact that Saye had been among the first to plot and take up arms against his father) and made him Lord Chamberlain of the Household and a Privy Councillor. Other ardent Fiennes Cromwellian fighters were also forgiven, including Colonels Nathaniel and John Fiennes, Colonel John Twisleton and Theophilus Fiennes-Clinton, Earl of Lincoln, whose wife was Old Subtlety's daughter.

Saye, back in his old seat in the Lords, was appointed Councillor of the Colonies and chairman of the committee to settle the government of New England. The Puritans there were naturally apprehensive of their changing status under the new Royalist motherland. Saye did his utmost to use his unparalleled influence with army, Parliament and king to ensure that the colonies were treated well under the new management. Near the end of his life he wrote to John Winthrop, the Governor of Massachusetts: 'I was loth to omit writing because it may be my last, my glass being almost run out. I have not been wanting, both to the King and Council, to advance your interest; more I cannot do but earnestly pray the Lord to stand with you.'

Old Subtlety's glass did indeed run out in April 1662, a few weeks before his eightieth birthday, and he was buried at Broughton, to be succeeded by his eldest son James, the least Puritan of his brood. Old Subtlety was undeniably the chief architect of the Puritan movement to which the United States looks for its origins and to which England owes three centuries of constitutional government.

The recalled Charles II set sail from exile in Holland in May 1660. Naval Secretary Samuel Pepys was on board the good ship *Royal Prince* (a quick name switch from *Naseby*) sent by Monck to collect the thirty-year-old king-to-be. Also on board was Charles's younger brother, James, Duke of York. Pepys was ready to weep at Charles's stories of his escape from Worcester and charmed by the king and the Duke of York's willingness to eat ship's diet of pease, pork and boil beef. He got into a barge to disembark with, 'one of the king's footmen with a dog the King loved (which shit in the boat which made all laugh and me to think that a King and all that belong to him are just as others are).'

Charles had been asked back to rule by a people who had experienced twelve years of Republican, Puritan-type experiments at government without a monarch, and so much did they hate the experience that they reverted to square one and, with great relief, welcomed back the son of the man they had allowed to be executed. They asked Charles back, surprisingly without conditions. They knew his history well enough to respect him as a man and in all probability (although you never really knew with the Stuarts) as a Protestant likely to keep the hated Catholics at bay. So the Parliament that welcomed Charles back had no greater governmental powers than it had possessed under Queen Elizabeth and the early Stuarts.

Charles would always live in fear of another

revolution and would never forget the trial and decapitation of his father, but that did not much shake his inner conviction that he should be an absolute ruler, not a parliamentary puppet. And he was shrewd enough to see that he could pretty much get away with murder, since England had witnessed life with no king. Oppression had got worse, not better. So Charles knew that he could push his Parliaments hard, and if they didn't like it, he could keep dissolving them. By the time he died twenty-five years later, he had become an expert at the king versus Parliament game.

Charles built up his regime on a broad base with power-sharing at every governmental level. Old enemies and all religions (except way-out non-conformists and, of course, Catholics), as well as Cromwellians and Royalists alike, were all to be involved in handling the future of Britain. Charles devised an act to prevent religious intolerance, but Parliament blocked it and, because he desperately needed funds (the dilemma of all English and British monarchs in the days they had to fund their own wars), he gave in to the Clarendon Code which was a good deal less tolerant to both extreme Puritans and Catholics than the king had wanted.

The first war Charles became involved in was the Second Anglo-Dutch War. The First Dutch War, back in Cromwell's time, had been caused by English interference with Dutch trade. The second was fought for similar reasons and started well for the English, who captured New Amsterdam from the Dutch and renamed it New York in honour of the Lord Admiral, Charles's younger brother, James, Duke of York.

The big problem that Charles was to face through much of his reign was his need to constantly confirm to his Parliament that he was doing nothing that might bring back Catholicism to Britain. This meant that he would have to favour the Dutch against the French and Spanish. Yet he was related by marriage to both sides, a conundrum for any ruler. Both the Dutch and the French needed British help over the years, and Charles, often at odds with his Parliament, formed secret alliances and treaties with one or other, or even both at the same time.

Jokers in the pack were the Catholic Portuguese who wanted to be independent from both Spain and France and were happy when Charles, in 1662, married the Portuguese royal heiress, Catherine of Braganza. This brought Charles a considerable and desperately needed dowry, as well as control of Tangiers and Bombay, and a lovely, modest, loyal wife whom he loved all his life and who put up with his outrageous behaviour with dozens of mistresses, and a small army of illegitimate children. The English were initially highly suspicious of their new king taking a practising Catholic wife but her obvious harmlessness soon soothed their worries. However, Charles put up another black the same year by selling Dunkirk (which Cromwell's army had captured) back to his Catholic French cousin, Louis XIV for a hefty price.

Given a choice of aligning himself with his Catholic French relations or his Protestant Dutch ones, Charles chose France, primarily because they seemed to have an exhaustive exchequer, and in return for ongoing secret alliances Charles received vital funds which enabled him to yield over lesser issues to awkward, sometimes hostile, Parliaments. He could, in essence, survive without them so long as he kept cousin Louis happy (but did so always in secret).

One of Charles's biggest problems throughout his reign was that Queen Catherine never gave him a male heir, which meant that his younger brother, James, to whom he was always loyal, even under great provocation, was destined to become king on his death. Unfortunately, James was a not-so-secret practising Catholic who did not worship openly (which was against the Clarendon Code) but Parliament was highly suspicious of him throughout Charles's reign even when he made pregnant and married Anne Hyde, the daughter of Charles's Protestant Lord Chancellor, Clarendon.

Of the king's many loves, he acknowledged seven kept mistresses and, from them, fourteen children. He was good to them all, paid their upkeep and gave many of them titles. He became known as The Merry Monarch or Old Rowley, after a stallion known for producing many fine foals. The actress Nell Gwynne was the best known of the mistresses and most popular with the public, who nonetheless objected to paying taxes that were part spent on maintaining their ruler's many mistresses and illegitimate children. Of all the royal bastards, surprisingly enough, only one was to cause big trouble, mostly after Charles's death, and that was his first son James who he made the Duke of Monmouth and was from time to time a popular choice of some Parliamentarians as a better successor to the throne than Catholic James.

Rumours of ongoing debauchery at court did

not help in 1665 when the war with Holland was going badly, and for the first time in many years an outbreak of the rat- and flea-borne bubonic plague scythed through the country. Despite being called the Great Plague at that time and ever since, it was in fact a pale image of earlier such pandemics. In London it began in early summer, and the king, court, mistresses and all fled to Salisbury, and Parliament to Oxford that July. Seven thousand people died in a single week, 75,000 in all and a fifth of the London population.

The law, unaltered since the plagues in Elizabeth's time, involved victims being sealed up in their homes along with all other current occupants, infected or not. Food and water, if they were lucky, would be put by the local watch-keepers into baskets which survivors lowered from upper windows. Doctors in fearful robes with masked beaks and waders were few and far between, as were priests to give last rites. The wealthy infected who could entice a doctor to attend them would invariably undergo vicious bloodletting, the infected blood being black, thick and vile-smelling, mixed with a green scum-like substance.

Not a good time for rumours of court debauchery, but the king and his brother received a timely boost to their waning popularity with the outbreak in 1666 of the Great Fire of London, which most people believed burnt so many rats, fleas, dirty hovels and putrid corpses that it stopped the plague, the last such bubonic outbreak to ravage England. In contrast to President Bush who received public odium for failing to react properly to the New Orleans flooding, King

Charles and James, Duke of York were greatly applauded for their reaction to the great blaze which in four terrifying days of strong winds turned 14,000 houses, St Paul's Cathedral and eighty-seven churches into smouldering cinders. Working together with groups of volunteers and dangerously close to the inferno, the royal brothers joined the chain gangs of bucket-heaving firefighters for hours on end.

The public naturally blamed the Catholics for starting the fire and making 100,000 Londoners bereft. In the long term and entirely thanks to the influence and encouragement of the king, new London was rebuilt using the talents of Sir Christopher Wren.

Soon after the fire, the Second Dutch War came to a disgraceful end, from the British point of view. Following on from a series of naval defeats (including the drowning or burning to death of 6,000 British sailors at the Battle of Four Days), a masterful sally up the Medway by the Dutch navy, guided by two traitorous English pilots, put to the flames the pride of the anchored Royal Navy. Peace was made soon afterwards, but there were growing murmurs of dissent through the land, and the main target was, as ever, the unseen but ever present Catholic menace.

The king's scapegoat for the disgrace of the Dutch war was the Earl of Clarendon, who had been at the right hand of Charles for a quarter of a century. Politics are cruel. If Clarendon had stayed he would have been impeached and probably executed. As it was, he fled to France and power passed to the largely aristocratic grouping of Clifford, Arlington, Buckingham (Charles's childhood friend in exile), Ashley and Lauderdale. Their surnames spelled CABAL, and by that acronym they became known. Some of the Cabal favoured friendship with the Dutch and others with the French. The king ignored them in a polite and crafty manner, made a Treaty with Holland and, a year later in 1670, a similar Treaty with France. The second one, like several others, he naturally kept secret.

Despite the sometime failure of the Royal Navy, often under the capable command of James, Duke of York, Britain did well during Charles's reign in terms of increasing both colonies and trade. He granted the British East India Company the right to autonomous acquisition of territories, the right to form its own armies, build fortresses, make war and peace and, in their new lands, to be solely responsible for justice. In Canada he granted a royal charter to establish the largely Edinburgh-controlled Hudson's Bay Company, which is today the oldest corporation in Canada. Based on fur trading with the Indians, it ended up governing and colonising over three million square miles of North America. Not so successful was the Royal African Company which traded in slaves.

On the strictly domestic front arranged marriages were still the main way of ensuring that your family wealth and status increased, or were at least maintained. So elopements were anathema, and often blamed on the loose living example of the court. In 1670 an elopement seemed to spell disaster for the Broughton family.

After Old Subtlety's death, his son James became the 9th Lord Saye and Sele and 2nd Viscount Saye and Sele, and his eldest surviving

313

daughter, Elizabeth, married Colonel John Twisleton who inherited Broughton. She was the only descendant from Old Subtlety's eight children to provide an heir for the barony. So the importance of who John and Elizabeth's only child, a daughter called Cecil, should marry could not be underestimated. After much consideration, John decided that the ideal match for their precious daughter would be her first cousin, another John Twisleton, who was three years older than she was. This John's father, Philip, was John Senior's younger brother, but first cousin marriages were common at the time. With Cecil marrying young John, all the Twisleton estates would be reunited in the family name.

John Senior was wont at the time to ask cousin John Junior to many merry weekend parties, and another cousin (of a poor Twisleton branch) called George Twisleton was also invited, since both he and John Junior were of a similar age and both were training at Gray's Inn to be lawyers. John Senior had lost his Cromwellian-awarded baronetcy at the Restoration, but had since been made Sheriff of Kent, where most of his estates then were. My opinion of him is of a gloomy, but kindly, status-proud man. His wife, Elizabeth Fiennes, seems to have had many of the prudish traits of her mother, the scandalous yet ultra-Puritan wife of James, Lord Saye, who had gone off with the equally prudish Joshua Sprigge. So neither of Cecil's parents were likely to have been good company for their only daughter. She may well have pined for some excitement. This may explain why sexual attraction to her poor, but exciting, cousin George far outweighed her feelings of duty to her parents to marry her rich, but boring, cousin John Junior.

The 'wicked' George waited until three days after Cecil's fifteenth birthday before pouncing. He and a group of wild friends carried Cecil away on horseback at night, and the two young cousins married before her furious parents could prevent them. Today, in America, their marriage would have been illegal, for they shared the same Twisleton grandparents. But modern medical belief claims that genetic deformities in the children of first cousins are only 2 per cent higher than those of unrelated couples. The twenty-two-year-old George and his new teenage bride proceeded to live it up in London, and Cecil's father the furious Colonel John retaliated by leaving his entire estate to his nephew, John Junior. His will read: 'Whereas I have but one child living who has been very disobedient, married without my consent and has then run into great debts above the sum of two thousand pounds, I have therefore bequeathed all estates to my nephew John Twisleton and his heirs. To my daughter and her husband George I bequeath the sum of one hundred pounds.'

Even this miserly sum had twenty-seven conditions attached to it. He also tried to make sure that even if his nephew had no children, the estates could never revert to George and Cecil's line. Fate, however, was to favour the teenage elopers in the course of time, for they bred a healthy son who survived and to whom they gave the Christian name of Fiennes. This young Fiennes Twisleton had an unfortunate childhood because, not only did he see little of his merrymaking parents but was brought up by trustees, none other than the prudish Joshua Sprigge and the runaway former Viscountess Saye and Sele, who was now merely the ultra-Puritan, elderly Mrs Sprigge. From such subdued beginnings Fiennes was to go on to great things after the reign of Charles II.

*   *   *

When he was only two years into his reign, Charles had raised enough funds to commence the Third Anglo-Dutch War jointly with the French, and with his brother James still as Admiral of the Fleet. The war went badly and, after four major sea battles lost to the Dutch, Charles made peace on reasonable terms to all parties, but to the disgust of Parliament who turned down another attempt by Charles at that time to enact a law favouring religious tolerance, and substituted for it a new act that made things even more difficult for Catholics. James, Duke of York's wife Anne Hyde died, leaving him with two daughters and the duke's next wife Mary of Modena was an ardently Catholic lady whose mother was the niece of the notorious Cardinal Mazarin. The English, horrified that the wife of their future king was so dangerously Catholic, dubbed her 'the daughter of the Pope'.

The ruling Cabal faltered in 1673 (Clifford being sacked as scapegoat for the failed Dutch War) and their power as a group was eclipsed by the rising star of the Earl of Danby. Two of the Cabal, Buckingham and Ashley (who had become Lord Shaftesbury), formed a new party consisting of all the disparate elements who were discontent with the government. This party was to become the

Whigs.

In 1677 powerful French armies attacked Holland and provoked an outcry for the English to help their Dutch Protestant neighbours. The powerful Danby agreed with this course before Charles II, bearing in mind his secret alliance with France, could procrastinate. Tiny Holland saved itself by flooding some of its sea walls and, advised by Danby, Charles made an important pro-Dutch manoeuvre by marrying his niece Mary, one of his brother James's daughters, to William of Orange.

At about this time Thomas, a Lord Dacre descended from that Thomas Fiennes Dacre hanged for poaching, and the son of one of only twelve peers who had dared to object to Charles I's trial, made a name for himself by marrying one of Charles II's illegitimate daughters. He was promised £20,000 as a dowry which was never paid, and made the Earl of Sussex. Nonetheless, in later life he was to find enough funds to improve the old Fiennes family castle of Herstmonceux. This Thomas was the last descendant of the ancient families of Herst, Fiennes and Monceux to run Herstmonceux.

In 1678 a believable weirdo named Titus Oates, who had been both an Anglican and a Jesuit in his past, gave warnings of a complex Popish plot to assassinate the king and put Catholic James on the throne. He implicated several innocent ministers, various Catholic peers and even the queen in his fantastical conspiracy. Such was the anti-Catholic hysteria of the day that Oates was widely believed. Judges and juries condemned the long list of accused plotters, all of them innocent, and many were executed. Lord Danby himself was impeached and saved from death only by the king dissolving Parliament. Danby's supposed sin was to have planned the king's secret alliance with France (which was eventually revealed to the public). The next Parliament refused to allow Danby's acquittal, and he was confined to the Tower for five years.

Parliament's next attack on Charles was known as the Exclusion Bill and was designed to legally prevent the, by then, openly Catholic James, Duke of York becoming James II on Charles II's death. The ex-Cabal member, Lord Shaftesbury, was the bill's main mover, so the Whig Party that he had formed became synonymous with the Exclusion Bill, whilst their political rivals, who came to be known as Tories, opposed the bill. Tories were named after dispossessed Catholic Irish bandits, and Whigs, or Whigamores, was a term for rebellious Scottish Presbyterians.

To avoid the passing of the Exclusion Bill, Charles dissolved Parliament four times in three years, and by 1681 popular sentiment turned against troublemaker Shaftesbury and his Exclusion-bent Whigs. The bottom line was the national fear that, if excluded from his rightful succession, James would start a new civil war, and that was just about the only thing that none of the rival factions wanted.

In the spring of 1681, Charles felt ready to make a master move because another secret alliance with Louis XIV had assured him that France would back him against Parliament, with force if need be. First Charles, by a royal prerogative never before used, summoned Parliament to meet in royalist Oxford away from the Whig crowds of London. And when they did, he surprised them all with another prerogative by turning up in full royal garb and declaring Parliament dissolved until further notice. For the rest of his reign he ruled without Parliament, supported by funds from France and the basic fact that his country was at peace and desperately anxious to avoid more civil strife. A trade boom helped, and a new plot to murder both the king and James and to re-establish a Cromwellian style government backfired and provoked sympathy for him. This led to the arrest of the alleged plotters, who included the old arch-enemy of the king, Lord Shaftesbury, and even Titus Oates.

By 1685, the year he died and the twenty-fifth year of his reign, Charles II had handed over much of the running of the kingdom to his brother James. He still signed the documents, but mainly he spent time with his many mistresses and children, with his beloved wife, and in his private science laboratory where he loved to experiment. Science had prospered greatly under Charles, the founder of the Royal Society. Anatomy, physiology and the discovery of blood circulation, along with much of Isaac Newton's work, had taken great strides. So too had chemistry, geology and the predictable movement of heavenly bodies. The country's agriculture and economy still depended on human and animal power, but the world of magic and spells had, by 1640, become outmoded and the cruel centuries of witch prosecution ended.

Charles died in his bed at Windsor Castle after a short illness and the diarist John Evelyn wrote of him, 'He was a prince of many virtues and many great imperfections, debonair, easy of access, not bloody or cruel.'

He left a nation governed by those who believed in the Divine Right of Kings, the divine right of the Church of England, and the divine right of local regions to run their own affairs. After all the traumas of the Exclusion Bill and so many hostile anti-Catholic Parliaments, Charles had the last laugh, for his brother was now secure in his succession from his Protestant rivals, the Duke of Monmouth and William of Orange.

When Charles II died and James II came to the throne, my great to the power of eight grandfather, Fiennes Twisleton, had been at Winchester College for two years but was still in the bottom form. Only four years later he would command the forces that favoured the middle way against absolutism from left or right.

23

RIDE A COCK HORSE

James Stuart, long-time Duke of York, long-time royal heir in waiting, came to the throne of Britain in 1685 as an acknowledged Catholic prepared to accept Protestant ways, and as such was just about acceptable, providing he did not rock the boat, because both his daughters were Protestant. This acceptance, grudging by many factions both religious and political, was hugely helped by all those who still remembered the bloodshed of the Civil War and the grey gloom of the Interregnum.

So when, with a reasonable amount of celebratory joy that his accession had at least been peaceful, his people welcomed his crowning, James expected to be succeeded by his Protestant daughter Mary and her Dutch Protestant husband, Prince William of Orange. He had been a loyal, if sometimes irritating, supporter of his brother Charles II throughout the twenty-five years of that reign and was already fifty-two when crowned. The basic difference between the two brothers was the degree of their attachment to and belief in the Catholic form of worship.

Once on the throne James forgave the Whig Exclusionists who had tried in vain to block his accession. He kept most existing ministers in their jobs and was granted by Parliament a very generous life income. It seemed, after a month or two, that all would go reasonably well between the new king and his Parliament, even though he clearly worked harder and paid more attention to the governance of the realm than had his brother. And he was less prepared to compromise when his ministers disagreed with his wishes.

Trouble, unfortunately, arrived only a few weeks after the coronation in the form of two co-ordinated Protestant rebellions, both of which were planned in Holland with the full knowledge of William of Orange. The Scottish rebellion was led by the powerful clan leader of the Campbells, the Duke of Argyll, who sailed from Holland and raised a meagre host of Highlanders, but was easily defeated and captured at Inchinnan. This was a mere eight weeks after James was made king, but the royal reaction was instant. Argyll's head was severed on the Edinburgh block.

The other more menacing part of the rebellion came from James's nephew, the illegitimate James,

Duke of Monmouth, who had long been personally popular in England, especially in the south-west. So with eighty-two followers he landed at Lyme Regis and had already raised over 4,000 armed men when, at Sedgemoor, near Taunton, he was confronted by the Royalist army under John Churchill (later to be the famous general and Duke of Marlborough). The Royalists won the day and King James's revenge was ruthless. Sedgemoor was the last battle ever fought on English soil and is remembered to this day.

I live on Exmoor, near Taunton, and pass the Sedgemoor battlefield twice weekly on the M5. My late wife's ancestor was King James's 'Bloody' Judge Jeffreys, who hanged suspected Monmouth men for months after the battle and left their bodies swinging at crossroad gibbets until they rotted. Local families, whose ancestors were gibbeted, still had meaningful words with my wife in the 1980s.

Monmouth himself, clearly a spirited character and thirty-six years old at the time, was clapped in the Tower, whence he sent letters to his uncle pleading mercy. He received no reply, and nine days after the battle he faced the axe-man, Jack Ketch (notorious at the time for making a mess of various aristocratic lopping jobs), and said, 'Do not hack at me as you did my Lord Russell', whereupon he gave Ketch six guineas to ensure a good clean cut. History recalls that on the fourth blow Monmouth's head came clean away and 320 others of his fellow rebels were hanged, drawn and quartered for good measure.

The king was determined to ready himself for attacks from other quarters. Maybe he had his

Protestant son-in-law, William of Orange, in mind. After all, he had been Lord High Admiral in two wars against him. So he began to recruit an enlarged standing army, something which was completely contrary to the English tradition of raising a national army only when needed (and thereby avoiding a huge drain on the exchequer). This act by the king rang alarm bells for many, even loyal, subjects: Charles II had not needed such an army, so why should James, unless he had some Popish plot up his sleeve? Worse still, many of the commanding officers of James's new regiments were practising Catholics. The previously supportive Parliament objected strongly to James's military behaviour, so he prorogued them never to meet again during his reign.

His religious activities were to trigger his downfall, and one year into his rule his true colours began to show. Previously, like Charles II before him, his attempts to help Catholics were always disguised as a search for overall religious tolerance because they were always bracketed with similar favours for Dissenters. But James was a pig-headed believer in the straightforward Divine Right of Kings. What he wanted, nobody should stop him from obtaining. Unlike Charles II, who ruled for twenty-five years through the art of compromise, pragmatism and procrastination, James was a bull let loose in a china shop. A few of his early faux pas, which alienated friend and foe alike, included allowing Roman Catholics into the highest of offices, inviting a papal nuncio to visit his court, the first such liaison since Bloody Mary's day, and replacing the holders of court offices with Catholic favourites. In 1687 he issued the

Declaration of Indulgence, which negated the effects of the existing laws that punished Catholics and Dissenters. He then, in 1688, reissued the divisive Declaration and commanded that it be read out in every church in the land. The Archbishop of Canterbury and six bishops naturally objected to the king, who promptly arrested them all for seditious libel.

In a very short time the king's insensitive, indeed stupid, behaviour had lost him the support of great chunks of the populace who he could previously have counted upon as loyal. The final crunch came in June 1688 when his Catholic wife produced a male heir. Previously, people could put up with his reign in the knowledge that his successors were his Protestant daughters, Mary and Anne by his first marriage, but not with this new threat of a permanent Catholic dynasty.

James was blind to the dangerous pit he was busily digging for himself. He believed that if he insisted that his way was best, then aristocrats, gentry and Tories would go along with him through lack of an alternative. He was, of course, forgetting that his own Protestant daughter Mary was married to Prince William, the heroic defender on mainland Europe of all Protestant states against the powerful Catholic armies of the French.

By the summer of 1688 enough was enough, and Anglican leaders secretly invited James's daughter and son-in-law to help them remove their king. Plainly speaking, they were plotting to replace the Catholic Stuarts with Protestant Stuarts. From Prince William's point of view, this was a great chance to increase his anti-French power base whilst ensuring that Britain ceased being a potential French ally. The resulting agreement by Prince William and his English wife to 'invade' England and protect the English from their king's Catholic ambitions came to be called the Glorious Revolution: glorious partly because it came about through the unlikely agreement of anti-Catholic Whigs and previously Stuart-friendly Tories in a settlement designed to avoid bloodshed. Assuming its success, England would switch from a Catholic monarch to, not one but two Protestant rulers who would, if that's what they wanted, become Queen Mary II and King William III.

When, in September 1688, it became clear that William was about to sail for England (after many rumours that had proved false), individuals had to show where their true sympathies lay. Only a minority were willing to join the invasion by taking up arms, but even fewer were willing to show any meaningful support for their king. James refused assistance from Louis XIV of France because he believed that he could deal with things himself and that he would only blot his copybook forever if he invited a French Catholic army to help subdue his own subjects.

Before James could even raise his battle standard, his hoped for adherents began to jump the sinking ship like so many rats. Importantly, John Churchill, his senior army leader, defected to join the prince's forces. The king, stricken by nosebleeds and behaving in a bizarre and erratic fashion, halted at Salisbury, and before the two armies could meet he fled back to London where he was netted by William's men. He escaped and, seeing the hopelessness of his situation, put to sea but, visiting a Kent port for vital ballast, was seized, placed under guard and presented with a summary of Prince William's proposals. This, which was probably his last chance of remaining at least a parliamentary puppet-king, he refused, and the prince, not wishing to have James made any sort of martyr, happily let him flee to France.

John Evelyn wrote: '18th: I saw the King take barge at Gravesend at twelve o'clock—a sad sight! The Prince comes to St James's and fills Whitehall with Dutch guards . . . All the world go to see the Prince at St James's, where there is a great Court. He is very stately, serious and reserved. The English soldiers sent out of town to disband them; not well pleased.'

On arrival in France James was given a palace and a pension by his cousin and ally Louis XIV, whilst back home his daughter and son-in-law set up their Protestant shop by convening a Convention Parliament. Instant deposition was not on the cards, but since James had effectively abdicated the throne, the resulting vacancy was therefore declared filled by his daughter. She was crowned Queen Mary II and her husband King William III. A Bill of Rights was quickly passed which declared James to have forfeited his crown and which stipulated that no Catholic would ever again be permitted to ascend to the English throne or be married to an English monarch. William and Mary agreed to everything put forward by the Convention, which was made up entirely of the propertied classes, and so was in no circumstances a social revolution like the one in France would be.

Nonetheless, the Declaration of Rights agreed between the new dual monarchs and Parliament in 1689 did curtail the previous royal prerogative and established a parliamentary monarchy which, with absolutist monarchs prevalent through most of the world at the time, was a huge step forward towards the ideal of genuine democracy. From then on no monarch in Britain could rule without the majority support of Parliament.

Mary had married William in 1677 when she was fifteen and he twenty-seven. She had lived in Holland for eleven formative years and learnt to treat it as her home. She and William had, after a slow start, fallen in love with one another, and when in 1688 they became King and Queen of England, they were patently homesick for Holland. Mary had to stick it out, but William escaped whenever he could to command his Dutch forces in their ongoing fight against the French and to train a fledgling British army from mostly raw recruits into, eventually, the most effective army in Europe some twenty years later.

William, already the most determined of France's enemies, now became their formidable foe, not only because he had stopped any likelihood of England joining forces with Stuart-supporting France, but whatever English forces he could now muster would definitely be used *against* the French. The direct result of the Glorious Revolution was therefore to involve Britain in major European warfare. Firstly, the Nine Years War from 1688 to 1697 and, in Queen Anne's reign, the War of Spanish Succession from 1702 to 1713, England's first continental warfare since the days of the Elizabethan struggle with Spain.

In 1689 William and Mary were forced into war with France as a matter of survival, for there was a very real danger that Louis XIV would try to restore James II to the throne. As it was, in March that year, with a powerful force of 6,000 French troops, James did land in Ireland where the Irish Parliament declared that he was still their king. In the two years prior to William's arrival in England, Irish Catholics had retained their ascendancy over Protestants, and many of the latter had begun to sell up and sail for England. By the time James arrived in Ireland with his French or 'Jacobite' army, Catholics controlled everywhere except Londonderry and Enniskillen in the far north. James ordered these towns to surrender, but neither would, so his army laid siege to both.

The key to subsequent Protestant survival in Ireland depended entirely on whether or not these two vital strongpoints could hold out long enough to provide the secure landing points for the army that William was desperately putting together in England. William decided to send a naval force to relieve the 30,000 starving and disease-ridden citizens of Londonderry and the man chosen to lead the tiny relief force was none other than young Fiennes Twisleton, sole heir of the teenage elopers, first cousins George and Cecil Twisleton. I must explain the background to his arrival at the Londonderry siege as I left him as a young lad in penury and cut out of his grandparents' will.

His CV can be found on a plain stone slab in the church at Broughton Castle, the home he loved and where he died after fighting for Britain for many years in many lands. Aged twelve, he went to live with the ultra-Puritan trustees appointed by his grandfather. Somebody must have realised that, despite the disgraceful behaviour of his parents, Fiennes could benefit from a free

Wykehamist education. So he was sent to Winchester aged twelve, and was there aged thirteen and a half when both his Sprigge trustees died and he presumably returned to his gadabout parents. School records show that, of the five years he was at the college, he spent three of them in the bottom form, so he naturally chose the army for a career.

Many years later I took my Common Entrance exam for Winchester, hoping to get some advantage in the 1950s from the long-ago family connection. But my results were so low that they would not accept me, and I had to go to Eton where, after five years, I failed to pass the A-Levels necessary for Sandhurst. The British army had obviously become a lot fussier in between Fiennes Twisleton's day and mine.

Fresh from college, Fiennes joined the Oliver Nicholas Regiment of Foot as an ensign on 25 November 1685. He rose through the commissioned ranks rapidly and, as a captain, was sent by ship to relieve Londonderry in command of a small force who ran the gauntlet of Jacobite patrols up Lough Foyle, cut the siege-force boom that blocked the river and managed, after much excitement, to deliver two ships laden with vital provisions to save the starving garrison. The Londonderry success fired up the only other Protestant garrison in Enniskillen, who broke out and beat up their besiegers. These two successes gave William a firm base in Ulster from which to start reconquering Ireland. Records show that Fiennes Twisleton married an Irish girl, one Mary Clarke, at Dublin Castle in 1692.

When William replaced the last Stuart king of

England, there was surprisingly little resulting trouble from the Scots. In the Highlands the Viscount Dundee did rally the clans, who clashed successfully with William's men at the Pass of Killiecrankie. Two thousand Highlanders with claymores charged a thicket of musket-firing troops and cut off the heads of all those who could not reload quickly enough. Sadly for the clans, Dundee was killed and his men went back to their farms, where they were ruthlessly murdered by William's patrols. There would be no further trouble with the Jacobites in Scotland until the time of the Hanoverians.

William's army, once fully established in Ireland, numbered some 30,000 and was a far more complex mix than merely a Protestant force arrived to save Irish Protestants from their Catholic oppressors. That was, of course, William's immediate aim, but the wider context was pan-European and crossed religious boundaries. The Pope had become just as worried as William by the huge territorial gains of the all-powerful King Louis XIV, the long-time friend of the Stuarts and instigator of James II's invasion of Ireland. So, weird bedfellows indeed, the components of William's army included Dutch Catholics, French Huguenots, English and Scottish Presbyterians, Italians, Poles, Danes, Germans, Norwegians and Protestant Irish.

James's force, lined up against the above mongrel horde, was mainly made up of Irish Catholics and some 6,000 French regulars with a few English and Scots Jacobites thrown in. The ensuing battle was fought around the river Boyne, and although over 50,000 soldiers were involved, a mere 2,500 were killed, mainly because when James's army retreated, William's did not follow them up, due to the difficult terrain. In purely Irish terms, the battle was the saving of the Irish Protestants. From a British point of view, the Jacobite threat—the return of the Stuarts—was from then on a lost cause. And, in a European context, the Boyne was the first victory of a multinational force of combined Catholic and Protestant groups come together to block further French control of Europe.

King James II fled back to France immediately after the battle, where he was to die a distant Jacobite menace, eleven years later. Ironically, one of the titles, bestowed on him by the French King, was Duke of Normandy. After the Battle of the Boyne, William no longer had to worry overmuch about Ireland, Scotland, the Jacobites or, indeed, lingering Stuart supporters in England. So his focus returned to the main drive of his life: to stop the spread of the French empire over Europe, especially the Netherlands.

From 1691 to 1697 he therefore spent every campaigning season on the continent, for he knew, without conceit, that only he—a simple Calvinist who was perfectly happy with any and all other forms of worship including Catholicism but hostile to domination by any one power—could hold together the international alliance which had worked so well fighting together in Ireland. In these wars Fiennes Twisleton fought for William against the French general, Maximilian-François de Fiennes, their ancestral connection going back to Henry III.

*　　*　　*

Although King William spent a great deal of his time fighting abroad (whilst Queen Mary proved a more than competent and much loved ruler of Britain in his absence) and although he kept a mistress throughout their marriage (Betty Villiers was originally one of Mary's ladies-in-waiting), William nonetheless loved his queen very much and they worked extremely well together as joint rulers. They had no surviving children and were always happy that they would be succeeded by Mary's younger sister, Anne Stuart who, married to Prince George of Denmark, also had no surviving children.

Mary's conscience was never at rest over her father's exile and the usurping of his throne by her husband, even though her motivation in going along with it in the first place had been her sincere Protestant beliefs. The public always loved her and she was revered as much as was Elizabeth I, although she was queen for only five and a half years and died aged thirty-two. Although no great beauty, several love ballads were printed during Mary's reign which featured illustrative woodcuts depicting the queen with exposed breasts. These sold in great numbers.

Her sister Anne was a shy girl who rarely responded to Mary's normal lively chatter but was for many years in platonic love with and in thrall to her childhood friend, Sarah Jennings. This Sarah later married the senior army commander, John Churchill, who had deserted James II in his hour of need. King William disliked Churchill as a turncoat, and in 1692 dismissed him from the army. When Anne continued to consort with the sacked Churchill's wife in public, Queen Mary was furious, and the two sisters never spoke again. This is the only record of 'unpleasant' behaviour by Mary. In 1694 Mary caught smallpox and took a week to die, during which a distraught William slept by her bedside and was inconsolable. When Mary died, William sacked his mistress Betty Villiers (a bit late in the day) and never married again.

William then ruled alone but was never popular. For no good reason, other than the fact that he was foreign. The country prospered under his sensible rule, as is witnessed in a uniquely valuable description of the country during his reign by a lone horsewoman who wrote meticulous notes on all her travels through every county in England. The result is still available in most bookshops as *The Diaries of Celia Fiennes.* Historians of the late seventeenth and early eighteenth centuries quote heavily from her text.

Celia's grandfather was Old Subtlety and her father was his second son, the famous General Nathaniel Fiennes (almost hanged by Cromwell for losing Bristol to the Royalists). She often stayed at Broughton. Celia was born in 1662, the year of Old Subtlety's death, and little was known about her unique travels until her remarkable and extensive diary was first printed in an unedited version in 1887. Edited versions in 1947 and 1949 suffered from nasty post-war paper and printing, but attractively illustrated versions have been constantly reprinted since 1982.

Three of her four sisters died as babies, but the survivor married a merchant who traded with the

Turks in London, and there Celia based herself after her mother died. In 1697 she decided that she would do what no other woman did at the time, never mind ones of her social class. She would travel and see the world outside London, or at least as much of England as possible, and make notes of all she saw. She set out on her first journey aged thirty-five and rode side-saddle. She put up with the most uncomfortable, dangerous conditions, being stared and hooted at in towns, sleeping and eating in filthy inns, facing up to highwaymen (who frequented wild areas like Hampstead Heath), fleeing from floods, falling into deep mud in which her horse floundered, and getting badly lost in remoter areas.

In the 1940s I was brought up by my mother to recite the nursery rhyme 'Ride a Cockhorse', and was assured that the words were based upon the travels of my ancestor, Celia. The line 'Ride a cockhorse to Banbury Cross to see a fine lady upon a white horse' I was told was a corruption of the original 'see a Fiennes lady'. This seemed all the more likely to me due to the fact that I was born the 3rd Baronet of Banbury and one of my elder sisters was called Celia. Whether or not the Fiennes version of the rhyme is true, nobody has been able to confirm.

The first official signposts were erected in England in 1697, the very year Celia set out on her first journey accompanied by her manservant, William Butcher. 'At all cross wayes,' she noted, 'there are Posts and Hands pointing to each road with the names of the great towns that it leads to, which does make up for the length of the miles that strangers may not lose their road.' Sadly, she later found many a crossroad further from London where signposts had either been removed by locals, rotated by highwaymen or simply never erected. She never explored Scotland or Wales in great depth, although arriving near Mount Snowdon, she was told that nobody knew what was 'up there' because 'there be dragons'. 'At Holywell,' she wrote, 'they speak Welsh, the inhabitants go barefoot and bare legged, a nasty sort of people.'

She also had a poor and ill-informed opinion of the Scots. 'Thence I went into Scotland . . . all here about which are called Borderers, seem to be very poor people which I impute to their sloth . . . two or three great wenches as tall and big as any women sat hovering between their bed and chimney corner all idle doing nothing, though it was nine of the clock when I came thither, having gone seven long miles that morning.'

Further south in a Durham 'chappell', she observed: 'here is the only place that they use these things in England (fine embroyder'd Coapes), and severall more Cerimonyes and Rites retained from the tymes of Popery; there are many papists in the town and popishly affected, and dayly encrease . . . I happen'd to get into a quiet good inn . . . two maiden sisters and brother kept it, at the Naggs Head.'

In Halifax her focus was on their unique system of dispensing justice, 'The town now being almost ruined . . . and the Engine that the town was famous for—to be head their criminalls at one stroake with a pully—this was destroyed since their Charter of Liberty was lost or taken from them because they most barbarously and rigourously acted even with an absolute power which they had of all the town; on these informations I resolved not to go to that ragged town.' The engine in question was used for the instant execution of cloth thieves in the local market. It was the model for the 'Scottish Maiden' which was later the inspiration of Dr Guillotine's finished article in Paris.

In Northwich Celia excitedly made a financial investment in the very first discovery of rock salt in England, 'It's not very large,' she noted of the town, 'it's full of Salt works, the brine pitts being all here and about and so they make all things convenient to follow the makeing the salt, so that the town is full of smoak from the salterns on all sides.' At Land's End she described tin and copper mining in great detail, and praised the Cornish for their cleanliness and their ales.

She loved the spas in Bath, but that of Harrogate, called 'The Sulphur' or 'Stincking Spaw', she described as 'not improperly termed for the Smell being so strong and offensive I would not force my horse near the Well.' In Bristol Celia describes an almshouse for better-off folk. 'The one side is for the women, the other for the men . . . and a middle room in common for washing and brewing . . . They have their coales and 3 shillings per weeke allowed to each to maintaine them; this is for decayed tradesmen and wives that have lived well.' Of the city itself she writes: 'The streets are narrow and sometimes darkish because the roomes on the upper storys are more jutting out, soe contracts the streete and the light . . . This town is a very great tradeing citty as most in England, and is esteemed the largest next London; the river Aven, that is flowed up by the sea into the Severn and soe up the Aven to the town, beares shipps and barges to the key.'

From the shore, Celia described the Eddystone Lighthouse. 'You can just discover a light house which is building on a meer rock in the middle of the sea. This is 7 leagues off. It will be of great advantage for the guide of the shipps.' Soon after Celia wrote this, in 1697, the resident Eddystone architect, Henry Winstanley, was captured on the rock by the French, but Louis XIV agreed to liberate him as 'a benefactor to humanity'. However, he was drowned six years later when a huge wave struck the rock.

Celia also made polite comments on the structurally brilliant design of Mount Edgcumbe, 'a seate of Sir Richard Edgcomes'. This was the magnificent manor on the Cornish coast spotted by the Commander of the Spanish Armada, who told his officers that once they had command of all England, he would reserve it for his own possession.

Celia was always at her most enthusiastic when describing the various sights and scenes in the London area. The countryside between Westminster town and London itself, she noted, had just begun to be urbanised but you could still shoot woodcock in what is now Regent Street. There were nearly one million people in the whole of the newly expanded London, out of a total English population of nearly seven million. Celia wrote: 'there is alsoe one Nobleman's house . . . Parke House, which is a very curious building.' She later noted of this place, 'Arlington, now the Duke of Buckinghams, being newly built.' She was talking about Arlington House, which was pulled down a few months later, then became Buckingham House, and finally Buckingham Palace. Of London Bridge, Celia wrote: 'The Bridge . . . with 18 arches, most of them bigg enough to admit a large barge to pass it; it's so broade that two coaches drives abreast and there is on each side houses and shopps just like any large streete in the Citty.' The houses on the bridge had been rebuilt after the Great Fire of 1666, but were again burnt down in 1758 and never replaced.

Celia visited Parliament and observed: 'Westminster Hall has appartments, the one for the House of Lords and called the Upper House, where all the Lords which are not Papists and which are of age do sitt in their order on benches covered with scarlet cloth; the Bishops likewise sitt as peers of the realme and have voice in all causes but in bloud.' This meant that bishops could not be involved in sentencing which might lead to death or mutilation. Celia observed further that these Lords 'which are peeres of the realme are born Councellors to the King and are looked on as such; it's true tho' at all tymes, they may and should give the King their advice, yet the King has power and do make choice of a Privy Councill.'

Moving on to the fashion centre of town, Hyde Park, Celia wrote: 'Hide-Park is for rideing on horseback but mostly for the coaches, there being a Ring railed in, round which a gravel way that would admitt of twelve if not more rowes of coaches, which the Gentry to see each other, comes and drives round and round; one rowe going contrary to each other affords a pleasing diversion. The rest of the Parke is green and full of deer; there are large ponds full of fish and fowle.'

All travellers made comparisons between London and Paris. Paris, the largest city in France, had 350,000 citizens, Rouen and Lyon a mere 90,000. London was bigger than the next fifty towns in England and had a near stranglehold on overseas trade, but most of the towns Celia visited offered her a wide choice of produce, including American tobacco, Yorkshire ironmongery, West Indian sugar, fancy metalwork from Sheffield, pottery from Stoke, and cloth goods from Leeds.

All this trade led to innovations in banking, which included the setting up of the Bank of England, which made big, much-needed loans to William's government in the 1690s. During William's wars these loans were vital to his ongoing success but, in the longer term, the development in London and Edinburgh of experiments in long-term credit enabled Britain to emerge from the wars more quickly than France, a country with a larger population and far greater resources. London soon overtook Amsterdam as the financial capital of Europe. For a while Isaac Newton was Master of the Mint, which reflected the fact that in both economics and scientific theory, the Britain of William and Mary led the way. The number of new patents for new British inventions also increased greatly at the time.

Despite all this, the British public never took to King William, nor did his Parliaments. He, in turn, hated them, complaining in public that 'the Commons use me like a dog'. William's military triumphs abroad were eclipsed by Commons xenophobia. They even disbanded most of the hugely efficient and experienced British army that he had fashioned. William rightly, but futilely, warned against further troubles. Parliament, he said, had done in a day to his army what Louis XIV had been unable to do in eight years. He even considered abdicating, furious at the ingratitude of the British.

After Mary's death, William, basically a kindly and polite man, reconciled his family with Princess Anne and her Danish princely husband. He gave her St James's Palace and even restored her favourites, the Marlborough family, to Royal favour. He had, after Mary's death, retired into the company of his mostly Dutch courtiers and, when he needed a society hostess, he would ask Anne to fill the role. In February 1702 William's horse tripped against a molehill whilst he was riding in Richmond Park. This led to his final illness, and vindictive Jacobites (the general term for pro-Stuart folk) were later prone to drink many a toast to 'The little gentleman in the velvet waistcoat.' William died a month later and was found to be wearing a lock of his beloved Mary's hair around his neck.

His death was not lamented in Britain, although by all he had done as king, it should have been. Daniel Defoe summed it up well. 'The dislike of the English people ate into William's very soul, tired it with serving an ungrateful nation and absolutely broke his heart.'

24

FIENNES VS. FIENNES

The childless Anne became Queen of England and Scotland in March 1702 in the knowledge that her Catholic half-brother, James III, considered himself the rightful heir. He lived in exile with his father James II, hovering like a vulture, or rather like some French-controlled hawk, just across the Channel. His supporters, the Jacobites, kept a low profile in England, but less so in Scotland and, over in France, proclaimed him loudly as the rightful English king.

The year before Anne's succession, Parliament had passed the Act of Settlement, which finalised the succession process that is still in force today. It overruled the hereditary rights of the House of Stuart (apart from Anne) and the legitimacy of fifty-seven potential Stuart Catholic claimants, and thereby gave priority to take over, as constitutional monarchs subservient to Parliament, a Hanoverian dynasty who were Anne's cousins, being the descendants of James I's daughter Elizabeth. They were middle-of-the-road Protestants with no real power base in Europe, being merely junior German princes. Parliament ignored the fact that none of them spoke a word of English, because they were the perfect answer to the succession should Anne remain childless.

Unfortunately, the Scots put their usual spanner into the works by passing their own bill in 1704 which emphasised their absolute right to choose their own ruler. The English hit back with a stick (to deport all Scots living in England) and a carrot in the shape of a huge financial settlement and an Act of Union which would unite both Parliaments. The Scots finally accepted this new joint state set-up, even though it specified, should Anne die childless, that their own independent monarchy going back to the ninth century would cease to exist. This new Anglo-Scottish state would be called the Kingdom of Great Britain, with a Union flag (designed by James I), a British government, and a British army to look after the ever-expanding British empire.

William of Orange had left Anne a legacy, in England at least, of a fairly liberal, if argumentative, political system in a reasonably free society which would become before long the wonder of eighteenth-century Europe. He had also developed the British army into a force of 60,000 men which formed the foundation of the efficient machine that John Churchill, Earl of Marlborough, would later use to conquer the mighty forces of Louis XIV.

So Anne's foreign policy was a simple continuation of William's. The Grand Alliance of Holland, Britain and the Emperor would continue to keep the greedy French in their place. In May 1702 Anne declared war on France in response to aggressive moves by Louis XIV. Her declaration of war was a fair one, but the war was to last for twelve long years and provide a main issue of contention between the grandees of the Whig and the Tory parties.

Anne firmly believed in the monarch's right to choose her own ministers, and amongst her chosen batch during her twelve-year reign was Lord Godolphin, whom she had known since childhood and who was neither Tory nor Whig, for he saw his task as managing government. As lord treasurer he sought support in Parliament from wherever he could muster it, Whig or Tory. He was a man of the centre, as was Anne's great general, the newly promoted Duke of Marlborough, who she made, to all intents, into her foreign secretary. Her third main man, Robert Harley, whom she described as dark, cunning, disagreeable and ambiguous, was selected due to his remarkable way with the Commons, where his oratory and instinct could sway the most intractable opposition.

Ambitious men wanting to be ministers would often seek out the queen's long-time favourite, Sarah Churchill, Duchess of Marlborough (often cattily called 'Queen Sarah') as the best stepping stone to royal favour. The duke did not like Sarah's Whiggish views but, being as indulgent a husband as he was fierce a warrior, he refrained from tackling her politics. Theirs was a life-long love match and it was said that on return from campaigns he would 'pleasure her with his boots on'.

In 1702 the duke's armies did well in Flanders, with Fiennes Twisleton a senior commander with his foot soldiers, and Maximilian Fiennes a brigadier of cavalry in the French army. He was later promoted to marshal. 1704 was a good year for Marlborough and his armies, starting with the Battle of Blenheim which was long, complex and vicious. Marlborough, the victor, made his name that day. The myth of French invincibility on the European battlefield was destroyed, and a grateful nation, recalling the days of Henry V and Agincourt, hailed Marlborough as their hero. His reward was Blenheim Palace, named to rub salt into French wounds.

In 1704 the French did well in Spain and their Marshal of the Army, Maximilian Fiennes, commanded at the Siege of Gibraltar. The Duke of Berwick joined him that November and the two co-operated to take the vital city of Carthagena, after which Fiennes was promoted to lieutenant general. It is confusing enough to accept that the English Duke of Berwick was a senior commander in the French army, but even more so when one remembers that he was also the nephew of the Duke of Marlborough.

In 1706 Marlborough struck back with a victory at Ramillies, during which affray a cannon ball flew between his legs and blew off his equerry's head. His army killed 15,000 Frenchmen to only 4,000 of their own dead and won back nearly all the Spanish Netherlands, gaining in a single day what all the years of William III's campaigning in the region had failed to achieve.

The next year, however, saw the Duke of Berwick and his colleague General Max Fiennes crushing the allies, including Colonel Fiennes Twisleton, at the Battle of Almanza. Cousin Max followed this up by a famous victory at Lerida. From a foreign affairs point of view, therefore, it was a bad year for Anne but, back home, her government finally concluded the Act of Union.

On 6 March 1707 parliamentary and royal assents were officially accorded to three items on the agenda of the day: to the Act to Try to Stop the Escape of Convicts; to the Act to Repair the Road between Hockliffe and Woodborne; and, almost incidentally, to the Act of Union with Scotland. In November that year the queen drove to open the very first Parliament of Great Britain which was to remain the greatest domestic achievement of her reign.

That arch-strategist, Louis XIV, did not take long to notice the considerable disquiet which the Act of Union was causing amongst Jacobites. So he energised the twenty-year-old Pretender, James Stuart, and provided him with troops and a fleet to help him on his way to rally all Jacobites and to claim his throne. In the event the whole invasion plan foundered with the French fleet off Scotland failing to co-ordinate with the Jacobites and being chased back to France by the British fleet. The scare, however, played into the hands of the Whigs, Anne's self-appointed loyalty party. They removed Anne's minister, Harley, and forced her to accept five peers she disliked. In the tussle over all this Anne received no support from those she most relied upon—Sarah, Duchess of Marlborough (now fifty and irritable in the extreme) and her husband, the duke, who simply went along with Sarah. Just before the duke left on his next European campaign, Anne wrote to him begging him to stop Sarah being so unreasonable, unfriendly and even hostile to her in public. The duke's response, unhelpfully, was that Sarah was being just as nasty to him. She has at present, he wrote, 'a resolution of living with that coldness and indifference for me which, if it continues, must make me the unhappiest man alive'. He went on to another great victory over the French at Oudenaarde, which paved the way for the allies to enter France and capture Lille, the strongest of all the French frontier fortresses. The following spring he fought the bloody Battle of Malplaquet, which he 'won' at a cost of 20,000 of his own troops to a mere 12,000 Frenchmen.

Max Fiennes, now working alongside the Duke of Orleans, took the key city of Tortona and received awards for his gallantry at the Battle of La Gudina. Thence he helped Berwick in the Piedmont and finally at the siege of Gerona. He was made head of that province and remained there until peace was agreed in 1713.

Despite his victories at Oudenaarde and Malplaquet, the Duke of Marlborough's star was on the wane back home, mostly through the ongoing rude behaviour of his wife Sarah to the long-suffering queen. In October 1708 Prince George died and Anne was heartbroken. She had nobody left who loved her, and Sarah, determined it seemed to break their friendship, continued to sour their relations, until in 1711 Anne finally snapped, dismissed Sarah from all her court positions and became more and more of a recluse.

Desire for peace with France led to the anti-war Tories taking over from the Whigs. Ministers came and went, the longest lasting being Lord Harley who Anne had grown to rely upon. Secret negotiations were continued with the French. Marlborough became less and less a key figure as these negotiations advanced, and in 1712 he was finally dismissed along with much of the expensive British army. The Treaty of Utrecht, when it was eventually signed by all parties in 1713, was preferential to Britain and resulted from the great diplomatic skills of Harley's Secretary of State,

Henry St John, Viscount Bolingbroke. It gave Britain a monopoly of the Spanish-American slave trade, Gibraltar and Port Mahon as permanent bases in the Mediterranean, and Acadia and Newfoundland in North America, as well as the restoration of all Hudson Bay Company properties and forts in Canada. The French negotiator conceded, after the treaty was signed, that its terms gave to the British 'such considerable advantages as must absolutely ruin all commerce but their own'. By his diplomatic skills, St John had laid the basis for Britain's great era of trading and supremacy at sea for the next two centuries.

By the summer of 1713 the queen was too ill to attend the great celebrations of the signing of the Treaty of Utrecht. Her health continued to worsen with ever-present pain from gout, and it was clear to all that she would soon die childless. Who did she wish to succeed her? Her half-brother James, the Old Pretender, who had been in exile all his life but who was avowedly Catholic? Or the Hanoverian Protestants, as currently represented by her eighty-year-old cousin Sophia, a fairly distant descendant of James I? Anne refused to make up her mind. In Parliament she acknowledged the existing Act of Succession which officially nominated Sophia as the next queen.

The Old Pretender wrote to Anne from France to encourage her to vote for him. He reminded her that they shared the same father (James II) and asked her 'to prefer your own brother, the last male of our name, to the duchess of Hanover, the most remote relation that we have who will leave the government of our country to foreigners of another language'. A most appealing fraternal

347

letter, but Anne did not send a reply. In June 1714 the duchess Sophia, thirty years older than Anne, collapsed and died suddenly in her garden, which handed the Hanoverian claim to her son, Prince George, who Anne had always disliked. Only two months after Sophia's death, two months of great pain for an increasingly sick Anne, she finally accepted that her own demise was imminent and announced that her choice was for the German prince, rather than her own Catholic half-brother. Her Privy Councillors immediately appointed a Board of Regency, who took rapid steps to safeguard the country against invasion by the Pretender. Coastal defences were made ready and troops placed on patrol.

In the event, the Jacobites everywhere stayed quiet when, on 1 August 1714, Queen Anne passed away, and such was the lack of panic that the new monarch, George I, took over a month before deigning to visit his new kingdom. He could speak hardly a word of English—just like William the Conqueror.

25

BANKERS, BUBBLES AND BONNIE PRINCE CHARLIE

George I took his time, but then why should he rush? No Jacobite stirred, and, aged fifty-four, he had spent his whole life in the state of Hanover which he ruled as a benevolent despot with orderly subjects who showed him respect. He had been warned that such a commodity might well be in short supply with the British Parliament and their bickering Whig and Tory set-up. So he slowly put his Hanoverian affairs in order and leisurely sailed to his new kingdom a month after Anne's death, arriving at Greenwich in a thick pea-souper fog.

Things were at once awkward for him because not all his ministers spoke French and very few spoke German, whilst he spoke virtually no English. His own past behaviour did not recommend him to his new subjects as a pleasant character, for he had imprisoned his own teenage wife for two decades for unproven adultery and had for many years refused to speak to his own son. His family seemed to consist of his two ugly German mistresses with unpronounceable names, one of whom was grossly fat and the other as thin as a string bean. The British called them Elephant and Maypole.

As soon as George arrived in London, the Regents dissolved themselves and left the king to appoint his own ministers. This he did, choosing able men from both parties on the advice of those of his Hanoverian supporters who had been in England for some time. James, Earl Stanhope was a good choice as foreign secretary, and among his most able new men were two Norfolk lower echelon nobles who were brothers-in-law, Charles Townshend and Robert Walpole. In his first few months as king, George identified himself with the Whigs and made many high-level Tory enemies. He himself put people off by his cold, uncommunicative manner and by the pack of Hanoverian courtiers with weird names who surrounded him at all times.

Two top Tories went to France and encouraged

the Old Pretender that the time was right to invade. In September 1715 the Earl of Mar raised the standard of rebellion at Braemar and marched on Perth which quickly succumbed. He sat there waiting for the expected arrival of the Pretender with French troops and when they failed to arrive, sent part of his 7,000 strong army south to join up with a force of Lowland Jacobites, to march into Lancashire, where they were confronted by a Hanoverian army. After a bitter battle at Preston, and another at Sheriffmuir near Stirling, there was stalemate, but Mar's Highlanders dispersed, as was their wont, when their leaders showed signs of getting them nowhere.

Five weeks later the Pretender himself finally made it to Scotland with 5,000 excellent troops and entered Perth where, like Mar before him, he dallied for five weeks until a powerful English force under the Duke of Argyl headed his way, whereupon he re-embarked for France, for the very good reason that the major army the French had promised him never turned up. His lack of success, whether his fault or not, was viewed as pathetic by many a Jacobite, and, his stay in France no longer being welcome, his exiled court moved to Italy.

The invasion attempt had proved that no violent anti-Hanoverian sentiment existed in England or Scotland, and this greatly strengthened the Whig/Hanoverian administration. But James was still alive, and knowing the Jacobite threat had not actually gone away but was merely latent was an ongoing incentive for the Hanoverians and their ministers to govern with moderation. Peace seemed the order of the day, both in England and in France. Marlborough and his wife Sarah retired to their glorious Blenheim Palace, whilst Maximilian Fiennes, the Marquis de Fiennes and Lieutenant General of the French army, retired to glory and awards in Paris where he died in 1716.

Colonel Fiennes Twisleton, meanwhile, had experienced many ups and downs since his famous relief of Londonderry. In 1710 he was promoted and sent as adjutant-general of the British expedition to Canada under Brigadier-General Sir John Hill, where, often in extreme weather and in arduous conditions, he fought many bitter engagements in the contest with the French for that country. Back home, Fiennes had a great stroke of luck with his Twisleton inheritance, which his grandfather had blocked from his teenage eloping mother Cecil and her descendants. By good fortune, the cousin who had inherited Broughton became a very good friend to Fiennes, and was, indeed, godfather to Fiennes' only son. This cousin, having no children of his own, had passed the inheritance back to Cecil and Fiennes, who therefore owned Broughton to which, after his extensive military career spanning two long wars, he looked forward to retiring.

Cecil had remarried some years before but when her second husband died, the sixty-year-old widow moved in with a surgeon, Will Burman, at his home in Holborn and left her entire inheritance to him. Fiennes was left not a penny, not an acre, and had to spend a good deal of money, trouble and time at the Courts to prove Cecil had no legal rights to disinherit him.

In 1718, finally living with his family in Broughton, the first Twisleton to do so, he was made assistant to the Banbury Borough Council and local magistrate under the charter of George I. What he did not do, which was years later to cause his grandson much trouble, was to reclaim his due right to the title (then in abeyance) of Baron Saye and Sele. Barony apart, Fiennes had the last laugh over his grandfather, whose measly will had, with obvious reluctance, stated that he was leaving 'an education allowance for Cecil's only son, Fiennes Twisleton, secured on the rent of the Bull Inn at Dartford, so that he may be fitted either to be an apprentice to a merchant or other trade, or to study the law, phisick or any other learning.' One way or another, Fiennes, my great to the power of eight grandfather, did pretty well for himself and his descendants.

King George meanwhile made no attempt to hide his preference for Hanover over England. He escaped there whenever he could and, once the Jacobite 1715 scare was over, he took another trip 'home'. Parliament needed to appoint a regent, if only to sign the daily paperwork, and the Prince of Wales, George's heir, seemed the obvious candidate. But George had probably always disliked, and distrusted his son, and the last thing he wanted was to entrust him with Britain while he was over in Hanover. A compromise was reached which gave the Prince of Wales a nice sounding title, Guardian of the Realm, but minimal power. Both Georges were happy with this, but in 1717 a serious rift occurred between them due to a complex misunderstanding at the christening service of a newborn son of the Prince of Wales. This ended with a furious king banishing a furious prince and his sexy wife Caroline from the palace.

352

The prince and Caroline set up a far more lively court at Leicester House, where one of the frequent attendants was the brilliant young minister, Robert Walpole. Walpole manoeuvred cleverly to close the rift between king and prince, eventually succeeding in 1720. They were never friends, but nor were they again outright enemies, and Robert Walpole was clearly responsible for this royal rapprochement. This coup leveraged him into the top all-Whig group of four ministers, along with his Norfolk colleague, Townshend, and the Lords Stanhope and Sunderland, all highly efficient and competitive men.

Quite how long these four star ministers would have survived working together without a major rift is anybody's guess, but the explosion that was to blow them apart occurred soon after the establishment of their power group, and it was known as the South Sea Bubble. In many ways it resembled a number of subsequent international, if not global, financial disasters, including that of 2008. Its history went back to 1694 when a group of City Whigs formed the Bank of England, which helped the Hanoverians to the throne since they promised Britain greater stability than did the Pretender. In 1711 the Tories, seeking a counterbalance of their own to the Whig Bank of England, agreed to the foundation of the South Sea Trading Company, which took on £9 million of the national debt in return for a monopoly of all trade to South America.

The directors of the trading company observed that a Scots banker, John Law, had in 1716 founded a bank in Paris that took on all the French national debt in return for a monopoly of all foreign trade. Law had then printed and circulated paper money so that from a deep economic depression, France had soared into wonderful (but inflationary) prosperity. By 1719 Law had founded his own trading company in which everyone bought shares which initially proved highly successful. The South Sea Trading Company in Britain followed suit, took on £30 million of the national debt and, with the deal approved by Parliament, saw its shares go sky-high, with nearly everyone in Britain and Hanover who had any money at all rushing to buy stock.

In a month or two a few wise men saw danger signals, and the so-called Bubble Act was passed to cool things down, but too late. Public confidence dropped overnight, share prices plummeted, and financial ruin was everywhere the result. The clever old Duchess of Marlborough had early on muttered, 'This project must burst in a little while and fall away to nothing,' and kept her money in the bank. But she was the exception to the rule.

Most of the king's ministers were deeply implicated in the Bubble, but Robert Walpole managed to avoid the appearance of involvement and cleverly used the disaster to overhaul his rivals and continue his rise to the top spot. Walpole was not himself a financial whizz-kid, but he knew someone who was, and in the immediate aftermath of the Bubble, this genius broker and investor saved Walpole in the same way that, years later, he would save Prime Ministers Pitt and Pelham. Samson Gideon, through a maternal link, was my great to the power of eight grandfather, and was also the first Jew to penetrate the peerage, an incredibly difficult task which he achieved through obtaining the favour of prime ministers and twice saving Britain's national debt. In the disastrous period of 1721 when the Bubble burst, Gideon was famous in the City for his lack of panic and for his positive investments. His services to Walpole in restoring the public credit gained great public admiration. From then on he and Walpole remained close and clever colleagues.

Walpole's success and the prosperity he brought to Britain naturally reflected on his king, but although the populace accepted George as a tolerable monarch, they never grew to love or venerate him. The writer John Jesse, in his *Memoirs of the Court of England*, wrote:

It may be remarked . . . that, with the single exceptions of social pleasantry and constitutional good-humour, he seems to have been possessed of no redeeming quality which reflected dignity on him as a monarch, or rendered him amiable as a man. Profligate in his youth and libidinous in old age, he figures through life as a bad husband, a bad father, and, in as far as England is concerned, a bad king. He wanted even those graceful qualifications of the Stuarts, a love for polite literature and the fine arts; he possessed no taste for the one, and extended no patronage to the other. The only thing he seems to have had a regard for was his own ease; the only being he hated heartily was, probably, his own son. Many of these unamiable characteristics were unquestionably owing to his indifferent education; for, notwithstanding his wrong-headiness, he is said to have meant well.

In the summer of 1727 the king took one of his many trips back to Hanover and overnighting in Holland, gorged himself on ripe melons and soon afterwards, with severe indigestion, suffered an apoplectic fit and died. News of his death reached London by a speedy messenger who went straight to Walpole. He, in turn, rode forthwith to Richmond Palace, where the Prince of Wales was in bed. The story goes that, irritable and holding up his breeches with one hand, he received Walpole, who managed to lower his great bulk into the kneeling position and told the prince he was now the king. The confused king, according to Walpole, responded with the words, 'Dat is one big lie.'

Nonetheless, the crown changed hands smoothly and Walpole, who had for years taken trouble to cultivate the prince and, even more so, the Princess Caroline, soon became even more indispensable to George II than he had been to George I.

*   *   *

George II was a touch less alien to the British than his father had been, and at least he spoke English, albeit with a heavy German accent. He would be the last British monarch to be born abroad. He did very little ruling in terms of dictating politics, for he left that to his all-powerful prime minister, Robert Walpole. Nevertheless only two years into his rule, and despite the urgent requests of Walpole to desist, George was itching to declare war on Spain. Walpole worked on Queen Caroline who adored him, and she managed to persuade the bellicose king to go easy with the Spaniards, but Walpole was well aware that George continued to spoil for a fight and that peace hung by a thread.

As it was, the British army had shrunk quickly after the last war and many experienced veterans of battles all over the empire had hung up their boots. This included Fiennes Twisleton, whose only son John inherited Broughton on his father's death in 1730 and lived there until his own death thirty-three years later. In 1733 John put in a petition to claim the barony of Saye and Sele, which Colonel Fiennes Twisleton had not bothered about. The petition, initially unsuccessful, was deferred and John was subsequently discouraged from following it up by his cousin, Lawrence Fiennes, the 5th Viscount Saye and Sele.

Disappointed by his failed attempt to claim what, in his eyes, was rightfully his, John Twisleton proceeded to act strangely. For an unknown reason, perhaps to ensure that his progeny were all legitimate and in strong positions for future claims on the barony, he clandestinely married one Anne Gardner at the chapel of the Fleet prison, a place then notorious for granting unchecked, pre-dated marriage licenses for small fees. John did this on 30 December 1733, just inside the year of his baronial claim, which may or may not be pertinent.

Who exactly was Anne Gardner? Family tradition over the next two centuries maintained that she was a Broughton parlourmaid. Her apron remained until very recently hung on one of the castle walls by way of evidence of her station. More recent family research has upgraded her to housekeeper. Whatever the truth behind the conundrum, Anne and John remained a devoted couple living happily at Broughton until she died aged sixty-nine, having produced three gallant soldier sons.

Such domestic harmony was not mirrored at court. The king had an explosive confrontation with his heir, Frederick, Prince of Wales, who he threatened to banish to the colonies, and did banish from the palace. Then George's beloved wife Caroline died, which greatly reduced Walpole's influence over the king who, despite his prime minister's elegant advice, declared war on Spain.

This conflict was originally nicknamed the War of Jenkins' Ear, after a sea captain, Robert Jenkins, who claimed that his ear had been sawn off by the Spanish navy and, to prove it, waved the severed organ above his head in the House of Commons, sparking an outcry for vengeance. (The Spaniards had obviously made an error of judgment in allowing Robert to keep the ear.) The resulting Anglo-Spanish conflict soon melded with the Europe-wide War of the Austrian Succession, which was to last eight years and cause a heavy national debt. Walpole, the traditional peacemaker, was powerless as the Europeans squared up to one another, and in 1742 he retired. His place was taken by George's favourites, Lords Wilmington and Carteret, and then by Henry Pelham of Herstmonceux.

Britain found herself fighting the Spanish overseas and a powerful French coalition on the continent. George's prime aim, which naturally gained him no plus points in Britain, was to protect his beloved Hanover. But there were other reasons for fighting which definitely did enhance British interests, since it gave the British ever increasing opportunities to snatch more trade from Spanish South America, more bullion and more highly attractive tropical products.

At the same time, the growing importance of Britain's thirteen great colonies in North America was becoming obvious to both the French and the British. Demand for all sorts of merchandise was huge and British manufacturers were clamouring for export markets, not just for finished textiles, but for the newer, metal-based industries, everything for the household, tools, utensils, weapons and simple machines. In short, the made-in-Birmingham products destined in time to supply the world as made-in-China goods do today. One result of the 1740s conflict was, therefore, realisation that North Atlantic dominance would soon become the big issue between Europe's main naval powers.

On the European front George II personally led his troops into the major Battle of Dettingen in 1743 (the very last time a British monarch was to fulfil this function). The battle was fierce and bloodthirsty, and once again my ancestors turned out to fight on opposing sides. General Henry Hawley, the great great grandson of Old Subtlety, led successful cavalry charges as part of the army of Sir John Cope whilst, on the French side, General Charles-Maximilian Fiennes was made colonel of the army. When the battle was over George's men had won a significant victory, with under 3,000 casualties, compared to 8,000 French dead.

Such was Henry Hawley's personal popularity with both George and his army commander and favourite son, the Duke of Cumberland, that rumours abounded that Hawley was George's natural son. This did not stop his subsequently famous brigade-major, James Wolfe, from writing: 'The troops dread his severity, hate the man and hold his military knowledge in contempt.' The war in Europe continued for four more years, and Colonel Charles-Maximilian Fiennes fought at the sieges of Menin, Ypres, Furnes, Ath and Mons. He died in 1750, but his son, Christian-Maximilian, was later also a colonel of the army.

Shrewdly, in 1745 King Louis XV of France, knowing that the bulk of Britain's army of, by then, 62,000 men was fighting on the continent, stirred up the Old Pretender's son, Bonnie Prince Charlie, with the promise of 12,000 French troops if the prince could establish an army of Jacobite supporters in Scotland. This, it appeared, should not prove too difficult, especially in the Highlands, due to the extreme unpopularity there of the recent Enclosures Act imposed by George's government. Even in southern England this law had caused much hardship, for the poor could not afford the fences, ditches and hedges needed to demarcate their tiny land plots. One southern contemporary wrote: 'The poor in such parishes may say with truth, "Parliament may be tender of property; all I know is, I had one cow and an Act of Parliament has taken it from me."' And the effects in northern Scotland were infinitely worse.

Bonnie Prince Charlie landed in the Hebrides in July 1745, raised a Highland army of 2,500, took Edinburgh and nearly all Scotland, apart from the big, industrialised towns, defeated a British force at Prestonpans and marched south into England with 5,000 men. He took Manchester at the end of November without a shot fired. Many residents waved approving crosses of St Andrew at Charlie's men, but didn't stir a finger to help. Why should they? Times for most folk in prosperous towns were at least comfortable and secure under the Hanoverians. The prince moved on to Derby, but there was still no pro-Charles or anti-George reaction. So the prince went back north to await the promised French troops. The clock was ticking and George sent a force north under his son, the Duke of Cumberland, soon to be remembered in history as 'The Butcher'.

My kinsman, General Henry Hawley, had by then been promoted first to Lieutenant General and then, in December 1745, to Commander-in-Chief in Scotland. A month after getting this top job, his army was defeated at Falkirk. Normally such a defeat would have warranted his immediate demotion, but such was his closeness to Cumberland that he retained his command and followed the prince north to Inverness, close to which, at the field of Culloden, the two armies faced off. The prince, at a desperate stage of the battle, charged his men uphill at Cumberland's centre. Yelling Highlanders were ripped by musket balls or impaled on bayonets. They died in their thousands, and when at last they turned and fled they were mercilessly hunted down by Hawley's cavalry. For weeks afterwards his dragoons continued the hunt to the north, sparing no suspects and earning the general the sobriquet Hangman Hawley in his mission to ethnically cleanse all rebel areas.

Culloden was the last battle ever fought on

British soil. The French support for the prince never arrived and there were more Scotsmen fighting under Cumberland than under the Pretender. Young Charles did escape back to Europe, but the Jacobites never rose again and the Stuart cause withered away. Unlike the earlier lukewarm Stuart rebellion, which George I had treated with leniency, retribution this time was harsh in the extreme. The last of many resulting executions, that of the famous Highlander clan leader, Lord Lovat, took place at Tower Hill in April 1747, and that was to be the last official beheading in Britain.

As for Hawley, he went back to the war on the continent and led the allied cavalry at the Battle of Lauffeld. He retired to become Governor of Portsmouth and was buried in his home parish of Hartley Witney in Hampshire, one can only hope with a clear conscience.

The War of the Austrian Succession finally ended in 1748 with Maria Theresa's accession as Archduchess of Austria being accepted by all parties (although she soon dropped Britain from her list of key allies as being too liable to shift sides). With the end of the war and with no further threat to Hanover, King George lost all interest in politics and in military matters. His son and heir, Frederick, whom he had disliked from an early age, died in 1751, so Frederick's son, George, became the new heir apparent.

A succession of French visitors to Britain at the time, including the highly critical and observant genius Voltaire, recorded their impressions of Britain compared to the rest of Europe as being far less class-bound. The social ladder, they noted, was, in Britain, there to be climbed by anyone with initiative. Aristocratic privileges were fewer in Britain than elsewhere, and they approved of peers being hanged in public for their crimes, just as commoners were. They also emphasised that, unlike on the continent, any person who cared to dress like a gent and had the money, could ape a higher rung of society and become a gent. The lower class could soon become the middle class if they were so minded in Britain but not in pedigree-conscious Hanover.

With George no longer bothered overmuch with the politics of the realm, and with Walpole no longer at the helm, there was in 1753 a vacuum and a need for a new effective supremo. Parliament was becoming a touch somnolent, especially in the House of Lords, and efforts were made in 1754 to sweep away the cobwebs. One of the officials of the Secretary to the Treasury, John Namier, drew up a list of a dozen peers who were, against the basic rules of the House, in receipt of financial assistance from the 'secret service budget'. Namier was at pains to point out that these payments were merely charitable and benevolent, and he titled them 'the aristocratic dole'.

One of Namier's Dozen, Richard Fiennes, the 6th Viscount Saye and Sele, explained to Prime Minister Newcastle that he could only afford to attend the House if he continued to receive his parliamentary handout of £600 per annum. Namier suggested that he and others in this situation would be unlikely to prove critical of government motions. One could see his point. Looking into Richard Fiennes' domestic situation, it is clear that whatever Namier's deliberations, Richard was still drawing his 'secret service benevolence' eighteen years later, despite, in 1753, having married a very rich widow, one Christobella, who had by then got through two previous and wealthy husbands.

She was descended from Sir Walter Raleigh, and married Richard when he was thirty-seven and she was fifty-eight. When he died, she was quoted as saying that she had married her first husband for love, the next one for money, and Richard for his title. When she eventually died in 1789, the *Gentlemen's Magazine* recorded: 'she tasted the good things of this world and enjoyed them long . . . she dressed, even at the close of her life, more like a girl of eighteen than a woman of ninety.' Quite how her husband, Richard Fiennes, got away with nineteen years of such a wealthy wife *and* £600 a year, due to being 'too poor to attend' the Lords, shows just how slack the Revenue had become at the time at checking MPs' expenses claims. A recurring theme.

*   *   *

However, the mid-1750s did see a considerable sharpening up of governmental and Commons efficiency with a fresh set of leaders and a new sense of urgency as another war loomed. William Pitt the Elder was the second son of a family who were often in debt, but he married the daughter of one of the great Whig families, the Temples, related by marriage to William 'Old Subtlety' Fiennes. Pitt made his name in Parliament as a fiery young orator who raged against the Hanoverians in general and George II's Hanover-protecting war antics in particular. By 1746 he was a minor minister, but 1754 saw the death of Lord Pelham, and the next prime minister was Pelham's brother, the Duke of Newcastle, then living at Herstmonceux. With the Seven Years War breaking out, the Newcastle administration started badly, missing a glaring opportunity to smash the French navy in the Atlantic and losing the key harbour of Minorca in the Mediterranean. Leadership brilliance was needed, and Pitt proved to be just the man to provide it. He was made Secretary of State but was effectively prime minister, and over the next few years, starting in 1757, became the most successful minister of war in British history.

Due largely to Pitt's brilliance, Britain won a whole series of engagements and switched the focus of the war to a global battle between the two great mercantile nations of the world—France and Britain. In North America France fought to establish a chain of influence from Quebec down to Louisiana which would cut off the east coast British colonies. In the West Indies they attacked the British 'sugar islands', and in India they made trouble for the East India Company. Somehow, against the most powerful army and navy of the day, Pitt's forces on land and sea decisively defeated the French throughout the Seven Years War.

The war was, of course, hugely expensive, and this was where my great to the power of eight maternal grandfather, Samson Gideon, saved the government by his financial wizardry. He had come a long way since boosting Walpole's post South Sea Bubble reputation in the 1720s. When Bonnie Prince Charlie invaded in 1745, panic ensued in the City with investors selling stock at any price, but Samson continued without a blip to buy good securities which doubled his huge fortune and helped calm public hysteria in the process. From 1742 onwards he was consulted by the government and loaned the nation vast sums. In 1750 he raised £1 million at 3 per cent at par, whilst at the beginning of the Seven Years War he paid a bounty from his estates to help army recruiting at a desperate time.

His main motive behind all this munificence was a peerage for his family, which for a Jew at the time would have been hitherto unobtainable. Nonetheless, in 1758 he pressed Newcastle, then prime minister, for a baronetcy, the first step up the ladder, but the PM could not oblige with such a blatant perk. As a compromise, and to keep the invaluable Samson on side, Gideon's son, then fourteen, was made a baronet in 1759 and sent to Eton. By 1754 Samson realised that however much he saved the British from financial chaos, his religion would always block his dreams of nobility. So he resigned his membership in the Sephardic congregation and raised his children in the Christian faith.

The two greatest triumphs of Pitt's colonising success were undoubtedly those of Plassey in India in 1757 and Quebec in 1759. The origins of the Battle of Plassey go back to the establishment of the East India Company which, independent of England's close control, established autonomous areas of influence on the subcontinent. The Company, in the 1750s, was violently opposed by the Nawab of Bengal who overran the Company's Calcutta headquarters and crammed 146 officials and some of their womenfolk into a small, over-hot guardroom. One survivor, the senior British official there, wrote:

> We had been but a few minutes confined before everyone fell into a perspiration so profuse, you can form no idea of it. This brought on a raging thirst which increased . . . as the body was drained of its moisture.
>
> Various expedients were suggested to give more room and more air . . . I believe every man stripped (myself and three others excepted). Every hat was put in motion to produce a circulation of air . . . Almost a quarter after six in the morning, the poor remains of 146 souls . . . came out of the black hole alive.

There were said to be only twenty-three survivors.

One Robert Clive, the son of a Shropshire squire and a soldier of the Company was told to avenge the Black Hole, and with a force of 3,200 he confronted the Nawab's army of 50,000 soldiers, including French artillery, at Plassey. By a mixture of brilliant tactics and luck, Clive's meagre force defeated the Franco-Bengali host, and even pursued them for six miles. This was the turning point in the east which stopped French ambitions in India and established the British empire there.

Pitt turned his attention to North America, where the French had made a number of incursions into British held areas of Canada. In the summer of 1757 the famous French general Montcalm attacked Fort William Henry with a force of 8,000 French regulars, Canadian militia and their Indian allies. Their aim was to drive the British out of New York State. After six days the British surrendered, and during the ensuing retreat many, including children and women, were tomahawked or dragged off into the forest to become slaves. The story of the defeat was told by Fenimore Cooper in *The Last of the Mohicans.* The French went on to many further victories until, in 1759, the tide turned when the British attacked the main French stronghold of Quebec.

The British general in charge was the eccentric James Wolfe who, at Culloden fourteen years before, had described my relative, General 'Hangman' Hawley in such hostile terms. When George II was advised of Wolfe's eccentricity, he replied, 'Oh! he is mad, is he? Then I hope he will bite some other of my generals.'

The key to the attack on Quebec was Wolfe's unorthodox planning. The French defenders had discounted any likelihood that they could be attacked from the flank known as the Heights of Abraham, protected as it was by a river and high cliffs. The battle that followed was closely fought, bitter and bloody, but Wolfe's Commando-style approach had the great advantage of surprise. He himself was killed, but his victory at Quebec secured British control of Canada and eastern America.

Twelve months later George II died suddenly at the breakfast table, and his grandson succeeded to the throne as King George III. George II, like his father before him, died unloved by the British but, thanks mostly to William Pitt the Elder, his reign saw the emergence of Great Britain as the greatest empire-builder in the world.

26

RIOT AND ROMANCE

George III is today remembered for being mad. The film of Alan Bennett's play *The Madness of King George* (shot partly at Broughton Castle) rammed this point home. But although his last nine years (1811–20) were indeed spent suffering from a cruel form of insanity, he was an active and often effective monarch for fifty-one years, during which Britain went from strength to strength, even if most of the credit for this can be put down to strong prime ministers and foreign secretaries, including the two Pitts.

The new king had one or two things going for him. He spoke good English and was married to a solid Protestant, Charlotte, a German princess of a minor state, who quickly gave him a son and heir, and as he grew older he chose very reasonable ministers when circumstances allowed. In 1770 King George selected as his prime minister Frederick, Lord North, the man who was to go down in history as having 'lost America'. British attempts to institute a revenue-raising Stamp Act had already caused the Americans to denounce King George's 'tyranny', and rioting ensued in many cities. British goods were boycotted, causing bankruptcies in Liverpool and Bristol, and the famous cry 'No taxation without representation' was raised across the thirteen colonies, leading by

1773 to the equally famous Boston Tea party when taxable tea arriving on three British ships was tossed into the Charles river. London ministers and commoners alike had failed to grasp the ability of a distant and independently-minded population of two and a half million colonials to obstruct any and all imperial edicts. The Stamp Act of 1765 led directly a decade later to the Declaration of Independence and war.

In 1778 Pitt the Elder, the last great figure from the reign of George II, had a stroke in Parliament and died. Lord North, after seven years in the hot seat, ached to retire but wanted to solve the American problem peacefully first. He offered the colonials any terms they wanted, short of actual independence, but by then they had the freedom bit between their teeth and would settle for nothing short of full severance from the mother country. The War of Independence (or what Americans call the Revolutionary War) started in Lexington in April 1775. At first the British did well, but then, with both the French and the Spanish offering the colonials their naval assistance with relish, things went from bad to worse.

Forty per cent of the immigrants, about 250,000 colonials, who settled in America in the Hanoverian century were from Ulster, and half as many again were from the Catholic south of Ireland. When the American statesman, Benjamin Franklin, for a long time very pro-British, realised that war was inevitable and travelled to Europe to raise support for his American brethren, it is hardly surprising that his first call was to Dublin in 1771. After all, nearly half of all his countrymen were of Irish stock.

On the other hand, in February 1776 an army of 1,000 kilted Highlanders with muskets and claymores, and to the sound of drums and bagpipes, attacked an American militia force at Moore's Creek, North Carolina. The Scottish were beaten and three-quarters were taken prisoner. These Highlanders were mostly recent immigrants who chose to fight as loyalists to the British crown rather than remain neutral or join their new country's forces. Many remembered the brutal aftermath of Culloden thirty years before, when most of their enemy had been from the Scottish Lowlands and Ulstermen Protestants. Many of them spoke only Gaelic and were still resolute in their hatred of these same Protestants who faced them at Moore's Creek.

Two of those imprisoned by the Americans after the battle were the husband and son of Flora Macdonald, who had led Bonnie Prince Charlie away from Culloden and his pursuers in a narrow escape to the Isle of Skye. For this deed she was later imprisoned and, when released, she and her family had eventually decided to emigrate to the New World.

In 1777 the British Army under General Burgoyne surrendered after the Battle of Saratoga and this changed the mood in Britain. War taxes were high and success was clearly evading George's generals. So Britain sought peace, especially when the French began to negotiate an alliance with Benjamin Franklin. The British quickly saw the very real threat of a French invasion whilst their navy was mostly far away supporting the troops in North America. The

Channel was vulnerable in the extreme.

So on 30 November 1782 America received full official independence and a treaty was signed between France, Spain and Britain in January 1783 which, bearing in mind the circumstances of Britain being decidedly on the back foot, was lucky to lose George only Minorca and a few islands in the West Indies. The loss of the American colonies did not, in fact, harm Britain in any way, since the ex-colonials, friendlier now they were free, continued to trade as before with the Old Country, which in turn was now able to switch its full imperial focus to the East.

After a decade of fluctuating popularity, George III had, by the early 1780s, become as canny as many of his ministers. Trade was booming, confidence—at a low ebb during the defeats of the American War—quickly returned, agricultural yields were improved, largely thanks to encouragement by 'Farmer George', as the king was affably known, and to successful new methods of farming by innovative owners of great estates, like the Duke of Bedford and Lord Coke of Norfolk.

George's reign saw Edward Jenner's discovery of vaccination against smallpox. Dockyards turned out not only revolutionary steam-powered ships, but also sail system designs so sophisticated as to rival steam at sea. The new turnpike trusts funded major repairs to all roads, especially between manufacturing cities, so that, whereas in 1745 it took a fortnight to reach Edinburgh from London, in 1796 that journey was cut to two days. In the 1760s the Duke of Bridgewater's dead-water canals and lock-gate systems revolutionised river transport, linking major coal regions with manufacturing sites.

The burgeoning middle class underwrote new manufacturing companies and then spent a great deal of their money keeping up with the neighbours' acquisitions. 'The English,' according to Josiah Tucker, 'have better conveniences in their houses and affect to have more in quantity of clean neat furniture, and a great variety of such as carpets, screens, window curtains . . . polished brass locks, fenders, etc.—things hardly known abroad among persons of such rank—than are to be found in any other country in Europe, Holland excepted.' Quality was considered of great importance, and British goods soon obtained a global reputation for excellence and reliability. Eighty per cent of Josiah Wedgwood's pottery was sold for export.

And Britain also exported her inhabitants in great numbers throughout George's sixty years as king and as the empire grew and grew. By 1803 the great Mogul Emperor of India finally capitulated to the British army in India (most of whose soldiers were Indians) and Britain thereafter ruled over forty million Indians. Many Britons settled there, mostly as bureaucrats, but thousands succumbed to the heat and disease. More popular temperate parts of the empire included Canada, Australia and New Zealand. In the 1770s emigrants flocked to these vast areas of free land, and by far the most zealous were Scots-Irish, who outnumbered everyone else six to one. The phenomenally powerful fur trading giant of Canada, the Hudson Bay Company, employed 80 per cent of its new labour force from the Orkneys alone (and when I spent months on the rivers of the North West Territories and British Columbia in the 1970s, the HBC was still hiring many of its bureaucrats direct from Edinburgh).

Meanwhile, the number of immigrants into Britain was, apart from Europeans fleeing from persecution, such as Huguenots and French aristocrats, difficult to tally. Black immigrants were counted, however, and in 1770 there were 14,000, most of whom were the servants of West Indian planters who looked after their children sent back to British schools.

Generally, and against the backdrop of bloody revolution in France, the British working class, along with various middle-class intellectual troublemakers, stuck to the occasional low-grade riot, machine-smashing and, once or twice, stones were thrown or pistols fired at the monarch. But in June 1780 a rabid Protestant, Lord George Gordon, furious with recent concessions granted by Parliament to Catholics, roused a London mob to hysterical and homicidal violence against king and government. All too easily that month, a Paris-type revolution could have engulfed London. Magistrates seemed powerless to intervene and in the face of imminent catastrophe, one man Thomas Twisleton, held the line between revolutionary madness and democracy. As he was my great to the power of six grandfather, I need to take a short diversion from the Gordon Riots to explain his place in the family fortunes.

His father was John Twisleton, Lord Saye and Sele, who had clandestinely married the parlourmaid. Their sons, John and Thomas, joined the army, serving with the Coldstream Guards during the Seven Years War. During the Battle of Brüchemühle in 1762 the enemy cannonade was so violent and the British detachment, composed chiefly of the Foot Guards, suffered so severely that the soldiers piled up the dead bodies of their slain comrades and sheltered behind them as behind a parapet. Thomas Twisleton, at the height of the slaughter, reprimanded a sergeant whom he heard utter some exclamations of horror, and was answered by him, 'Oh, sir, you are now supporting yourself on the body of your own brother.' This sergeant had been a servant in the family.

So Thomas, the younger brother, ended up inheriting Broughton and had the foresight to marry Elizabeth the eldest daughter of the chairman of the East India Company, Sir Edward Turner, which allowed him to spend money on repairing the castle's neglected state. Elizabeth Turner turned out to be an excellent, house-proud Lady Saye and Sele. She was also highly extravagant and a determined party-giver, so Thomas sold off long-held Twisleton properties to fund her fun and her updating of the castle, whilst he continued to gain high promotion in the army, reaching the exalted rank of major general by the time of the Gordon Riots.

In terms of the property market, Thomas was lucky. His own father was not long dead but, prior to his demise, the last male heir of the other Twisleton line had also died, leaving Thomas property in Dartford, Kent, which had been in the family for a century.

Then in 1780, just before the Riots, Judith Twisleton, the last Twisleton heiress, died, leaving Thomas the large Yorkshire estates east of Selby which John Twisleton, the London goldsmith, had bought in 1519. Thomas and Elizabeth lovingly redecorated much of Broughton in the fashionable gothic style, with sash windows and Chinese hand-painted wallpaper in the Star Chamber hall, which is still there today.

By 1780 Thomas had enjoyed a long period of peacetime soldiering and was stationed in the London area. All army officers were well aware of the infectious dangers of the revolution just across the Channel. Many of the country labourers who had been attracted by the Industrial Revolution had, like Chinese peasants in the early twenty-first century, wandered into the big cities and had lost their old country ways, including traditional deference to the squires. The 1780 Riots served to demonstrate to the ruling class just how quickly life could become highly dangerous.

The London riot that summer was costly in lives and property. Big English cities were ripe for riot, and any access to looted supplies of gin was fatal. On 2 June 1780 the semi-deranged George Gordon led a 50,000-strong howling mob to Westminster, from where they fanned out in a maelstrom of hatred and destruction, the result of long-simmering political discontent. They quickly destroyed the mansions of various senior ministers, including the Lords Rockingham, Devonshire, Mansfield and Savile. They violently assaulted both Houses of Parliament whilst in session. They attacked gentle folk who they caught riding in hackney carriages, including Lord Sandwich, breaking the windows, slashing his face and beating him up. He sent for a guard unit, mounted and on foot, but the mob dealt with these part-time constables in no time at all.

One witness, George Crabbe, later described what he saw:

> I met a resolute band of vile-looking fellows
> . . . armed with clubs. [I passed by to the Old
> Bailey] . . . The new prison was a very large,
> strong building, [as was the house of the
> keeper, Mr Akerman.] How he has escaped
> . . . I know not . . . they set fire to his house.
> [A mob of 500 passed by.] . . . They broke
> the prison gates with crows . . . They broke
> the roof, tore away the rafters [and let loose
> the prisoners] and they were conducted
> through the streets in their chains . . . You
> have no conception of the phrensy of the
> multitude.

Hundreds of Catholic homes were destroyed, and eventually, after three days of government paralysis, George III himself ordered the troops to go in, and a small force of three hundred under Major General Thomas Twisleton marched into the City, thirty-six bullets having been doled out to each of his men.

Cousin Thomas was the chief liaison officer between the War Office and the action force he was himself commanding. The situation was lethally confused. He tried to appeal to the Common Council of London, the same legislative body who, urged on by the inveterate troublemaker, John Wilkes, had delayed appealing for troops for three full days of rioting simply because they hoped that a really good riot would bring down Lord North's government which they disliked. Fortunately, by the time Thomas confronted the councillors they had seen the fearful results of their irresponsible behaviour, and they agreed to give him a free hand. This being settled, Thomas sent off detachments to those key buildings not yet destroyed, including the headquarters of the South Sea Company, the Navy Office, and the Excise Office.

Thomas knew that the Fleet prison and the king's Bench had been burnt to the ground the previous night, and he now received a report of growing trouble in Holborn. A family company, Langdales, had built a huge distillery there and had very recently laid in enormous stocks to avoid an imminent new duty on gin. The mob, intent on murdering Langdale and his twelve children en route to liberating the gin, had set fire to all Langdale property, and in doing so had managed to start a huge alcohol-fuelled inferno. Rioters, blind drunk and on fire from head to foot, were staggering about the labyrinthine cellars. Looters were everywhere and Thomas despatched as many men as he could spare to that part of town. On the evening of 8 June, hearing that mobs were closing in on the most vital British institution of the time, the Bank of England, and that the guards there were insufficient, Thomas made best speed to Threadneedle Street, where he commanded the defence against two mass attacks by determined mobs, by all later accounts the key actions of the Gordon Riots.

Under Thomas's direct command, his meagre troops did their best to kill as few of the mob as was necessary to avoid being overwhelmed. This judicious restraint in all likelihood saved hundreds of lives. By the end of the riot only three hundred dead were counted. Although Thomas did not trust John Wilkes, he used him to help cool down the mobs until peace eventually came back to the smoking streets of London. Various neighbourhood groups subsequently offered, if armed, to act as voluntary patrol groups, but Thomas maintained that only the War Office had the right to re-establish public order. His cool behaviour in the most stressful circumstances did a great deal to assure a good outcome to a riot that could have grown into who can tell what national chaos. A few months later Thomas was busy fighting a very different sort of campaign.

Back in 1624 his ancestor, Old Subtlety, already Baron Saye and Sele, had been made the 1st Viscount Saye and Sele, a title that could traditionally pass through male heirs only, unlike the barony which in the Saye and Sele case could go through both male and female line. Soon afterwards a male shortage of Saye and Seles meant that the barony passed to a nephew, and the viscountcy ended up with the teenage eloper Cecil Twisleton's grandson trying to claim back the barony in 1734. He dropped his claim, probably for fear of offending Lawrence Fiennes, who was at the time the 5th (and penultimate) Viscount Saye and Sele and opposed the family barony being officially resurrected. He probably liked being the only Lord Saye and Sele in the House of Lords.

In 1781, with advice from his lawyer and probably with the encouragement of his wife, Thomas Twisleton decided to try to claim back the barony himself, despite his father's failure to do so. He needed, his lawyer advised, to put his claim in quickly because the current 6th Viscount Saye and Sele was about to die without male issue, so would not be likely to object to a resurrected barony but more important, Thomas would have to prove his own legitimacy since his father had previously been unable to present the appropriate documentation. Thomas's lawyer worked out that to find suitable witnesses who would agree to remembering Thomas's birth details, they would have to hurry, since, in his words, such witnesses were very aged and infirm. They must have found such survivors for they won their claim to the barony. Seven years later, Thomas began to suffer from a violent pain in his head due to a condition which his doctors declared was incurable. He committed suicide in his Harley Street rooms by cutting his throat with a razor and falling on his major-general's sword. He was buried that summer at Broughton.

*   *   *

Apart from the Gordon Riots, 1780 was quite a good year for King George. Admiral Rodney won a great victory against the Spanish in the West Indies, went on to raise their siege of Gibraltar, already a key British port, and then, when the Dutch entered the war against Britain, Rodney trounced them, too. Ministers came and went. Then came again. The troublemaking hedonist, Charles James Fox, was up and down the popularity charts, except with George with whom he was on a permanent down, largely because he encouraged the Prince of Wales, whose loathing for his father was mutual, into dissolute ways with women, drink and obscene language.

George III was especially blessed by the arrival on the ministerial scene of William Pitt the Younger, if anything even more brilliant than his father had been. George made him chancellor of the exchequer at twenty-three years of age and, when North resigned and Rockingham died in 1784, Pitt became the youngest prime minister ever at twenty-four and the perfect political beast to work with George. For twenty-five years the king had fought hostile Parliaments, as had George I and II before him. Now at last, through guile and persistence, he had the man he wanted at the top of the tree.

For four years after his appointment of Pitt, George felt free enough to enjoy himself, although the binge-drinking and general obnoxious behaviour of his two eldest sons did upset him. Then in 1788 the same strange symptoms, which had briefly attacked him twenty-three years before, recurred. His eyes turned yellow and his urine dark purple. He rambled constantly on disconnected themes, and his eyesight deteriorated. He believed, long before his doctors did, that he was going mad; a terrible prospect for anyone, let alone a king in the prime of his life. At times he could be violent. He smashed the Prince of Wales's head against a table. The queen believed he would murder her. Doctors put him in a straitjacket. If he objected to various agonising 'treatments' to which he was subjected, he was gagged.

Then, in spite of (rather than because of) brutal treatment by his medicos, George recovered fully about five months after his first fit, and he remained fully sane for the next twelve years. The Prince of Wales and the Whigs, who had hovered hopefully in expectation of the king's death, retreated. Ironically the king's illness and subsequent recovery made him more popular and the Prince of Wales less so. By 1790, aged fifty, George had ruled pretty well for thirty years and outlived most of his earlier critics.

He was by nature an even-handed king. He hated mob violence as much as he avoided despotic government. Unfortunately, the bloody horror and absolutism of the French Revolution had, by 1792, so frightened him and a great many Englishmen, from ministers to country squires, that they became far less willing to grant any concession towards simple democracy for fear of it leading to a British version of the French anarchy. Some Whigs and most Tories, including an odd mixture of Edmund Burke and William Pitt, were, with George, amongst the alarmists, whilst Fox and Lord Gray welcomed the French Revolution and hoped it would help their quest for more liberty in Britain, not to cause a revolution but to prevent one.

For a while, whilst Austria and Prussia took up arms against Revolutionary France to crush the frightening incubus of the infant Republic, Britain hung back, for Pitt was a good peacetime leader. In 1790 the Revolution had still seemed relatively harmless to most British and many liberals thought the French were merely conducting a modest constitutional movement. Then came 1792, the year when the tumbril carts, with their abattoir-bound loads of condemned aristocrats, first rumbled their sad way towards the guillotines. George wept when he heard that King Louis XVI himself had lost his head to the 'blue blood blade'.

But his grief was tempered by his recent anger at the way the French monarchy had given armed support to the American revolutionaries.

The European monarchies, far more vulnerable than sea-girt Britain, declared all out war on the French Revolution in 1792, and the French retaliated with their newly indoctrinated people's armies. In 1793, believing Britain was herself ripe for revolution, France declared war and began plans for an invasion. George's army of 45,000 men was unprepared, and less than a tenth of his navy was seaworthy. The new French armies were proving invincible against their continental opponents, and by 1797 only Britain still held out against them. The Royal Navy defeated the French at Ushant and prevented one of three major invasion attempts in as many years. In 1798 the French fleet again confronted them at the Battle of Aboukir Bay, near Alexandria, and this battle of the Nile gave Britain dominance in the Mediterranean. It also brought to the fore a new British hero—Admiral Horatio Nelson. Three attempts by the Revolutionary army were made to land in Britain, two via Ireland, where the French force spent two weeks before being chased away, and one at Fishguard in Wales, the last invasion of the British mainland, where on one occasion a French patrol mistook Welsh women in their black hats and red flannel for redcoats and beat a hasty retreat.

In Ireland, as the nineteenth century dawned, the Protestant ascendancy sought political union with the rest of Britain on the same terms as had the Scots in 1707. Irish MPs thereafter went to Westminster, and a new Union Jack was unfurled that included the Irish cross of St Patrick. This new sense of British togetherness was well timed because in February 1800 the glamorous thirty-one-year-old Corsican general, Napoleon Bonaparte, who had won glory for the Revolution in Italy and in Egypt, became Consul of all France. Whilst he consolidated his position, his forces and his territorial empire, Britain enjoyed a brief peace. The Revolutionary War was over but the Napoleonic Wars, which would last until 1815, were about to begin.

Britain had already spent the incredible sum of £1,500 million on the war, on the navy, on foreign subsidies and on creating a complex coastal defence including a ring of Martello towers, some of which still stand. Whilst the war went on, British trade continued to expand worldwide, and as the Royal Navy blockaded French ports, the midlands textile industry achieved such a global lead that British manufacturers were soon clothing the French army.

Although Trade Unions were treated like revolutionary societies and suppressed, as were all attempts to achieve a minimum wage, serious social consequences were avoided, largely by the traditional and relatively generous poor relief systems adopted by many rural and urban parishes after the 1790s.

Suddenly, during the 1801–3 spell of peace, King George again became sick, or temporarily 'mad', returning to normal after a short while. But the Prince of Wales, impatient as ever to rule, stirred up ministerial animosities. Pitt was out; then back in again, and in October 1803 Napoleon invaded Hanover and prepared again to invade

Britain. At sixty-six and going blind, the king struggled on with Pitt, despite perennial quarrels.

1805 brought better news through the naval victories of the amazing Horatio Nelson. His famous advice to a newly reporting midshipman is recorded as: 'There are three things, young gentlemen, which you are constantly to bear in mind. First, you must always implicitly obey orders, without attempting to form any opinion of your own respecting their propriety. Secondly, you must consider every man your enemy who speaks ill of your king. And thirdly, you must hate a Frenchman as you do the devil.' During his formidable victory at Trafalgar over the combined French and Spanish fleets, the enemy lost twenty-two ships, the British not one. Nelson was killed, but Britain literally ruled the waves for the next hundred years and well beyond.

Sadly, in 1806, the greatest of all war ministers, Pitt the Younger, witnessing Napoleon's invincibility on land, died aged forty-six, to be followed as prime minister by a relatively minor man. His long-time opponent Fox, then foreign secretary, tried to make peace with France but found Napoleon far too shifty to deal with and he also died that year. George, for a blind man of sixty-eight, was doing quite well in between mad spells and the scandalous behaviour of his unpopular sons, two of whom were soon to become Kings of England. The king himself was by now a national treasure, like a favourite and much valued piece of fine furniture that you have grown up with. He was more popular than ever before, trade was booming, and so he could afford to relax. He loved to read novels or, when his eyesight worsened, to be read to.

His favourite novelist, Fanny Burney, was also the second keeper of the robes to the queen. Burney became a great gossip, but always restricted herself to praiseworthy comments when writing of the royal family. About others she could enjoy letting rip. Some years before his heroics at the Gordon Riots, she was asked to a party by Thomas Twisleton and his wife Elizabeth, Lady Saye and Sele, to celebrate the completion of their redecoration of Broughton. Of the forty-one-year-old Lady Elizabeth Burley she wrote with typical author's venom:

I met Lady Saye and Sele who seems pretty near fifty—at least turned forty. Her head was full of feathers, flowers, jewels and gee-gaws, and as high as Lady Archer's. Her dress was trimmed with beads, silver, persian sashes and all sorts of fine fancies. Her face is thin and fiery, and her whole manner spoke 'a lady all alive'. She gushed and condescended to me, 'I think your novel is the most elegant I have ever read.' Her sister Cassandra was there, to whom she introduced me saying, 'She has a novel herself, so you are sister authoresses, a most elegant work it is, I assure you, almost as pretty as yours but not quite so eloquent.' The authoress then proceeded to quote to me from it as follows, 'If, when he made the declaration of his love, the sensibility that beamed in his eyes was felt in his heart, what pleasing sensations and soft alarms might not that tender avowel awaken!'

This younger sister, Cassandra, Lady Hawke, was clearly not to Fanny's liking either, for her letter continued in an equally catty vein: 'I took the first opportunity of Lady Hawke's casting down her eyes and reclining her delicate head to make away from this terrible set, but not before a square man, middle-aged and humdrum was introduced.' This last 'square' character turned out to be Thomas Twisleton, Lord Saye and Sele.

All my life I have admired two large oil paintings owned by my grandmother and passed to me on her death in the 1950s, which are portraits of Thomas and Elizabeth Fiennes, and I neither agree with Fanny Burney's description of them, nor with the following extract from a 1795 letter between two local neighbours: 'When you do me the favour to write next, do mention Lord Saye and Sele's family who live at Broughton Castle, near Banbury. I am anxious to know how they go on. I know the late good-humoured Weak Man and his romantic Wife.'

Thomas could never have been described as weak, active soldier as he always was, but Elizabeth loved life and, from her portrait, you can spot the twinkle in her eye. So romantic is perhaps an apt adjective for her. Her second cousin through the Leigh family was the novelist Jane Austen, who used various Twisleton scandals to flavour her novels. The Saye and Seles and the Austens would often visit one another. In 1806 Mrs Austen, Jane's mother, wrote a family letter at the time when Thomas was long dead and Elizabeth was sixty-four: 'Poor Lady Saye and Sele is to be sure rather tormenting, though sometimes amusing, and affords Jane many a good laugh. But she fatigues

387

THE TWISLETONS AFFORDED JANE AUSTEN A GOOD DEAL
OF MATERIAL FOR HER NOVELS

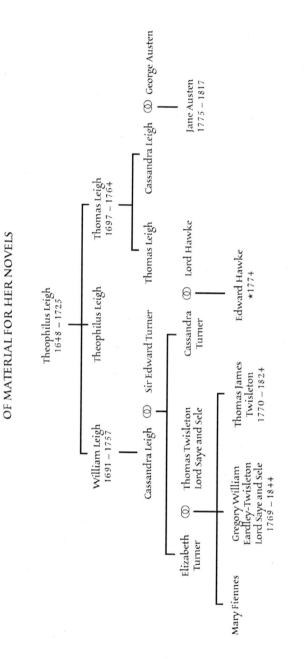

me sadly on the whole.'

The Twisletons not only afforded Jane Austen a good laugh, but also a good deal of material for her novels, including *Mansfield Park* and *Lady Susan*. Jane, who recognised a good scandal when she came across one, included them, hook, line and boudoir, when they came her way in her own family circle. The Twisletons were most obliging.

Thomas Twisleton's suicide was too serious a subject for Jane's pen, but eighteen years later, by which time Jane's novels were in full flow, her favourite sister Cassandra recalled: 'We offered Lady Saye and Sele some boiled chicken, to which she firmly replied, "No, I cannot. When my husband destroyed himself I ate nothing but boiled chicken for a fortnight in my chamber and haven't been able to touch it since."'

More in the Austen line was Thomas Twisleton's younger son, Thomas James, while still at school, eloping with an actress to Gretna Green. This spawned much high society gossip and confirmed Jane Austen's opinion that theatricals, especially conducted in private manors (such as young Twisleton and his co-eloper had frequented), were a breeding ground for dalliance of an unhealthy manner. Shortly after this scandal Jane's own parents stopped their long and excellent tradition of producing plays in their rectory home. As for Eloper Thomas James, his actress wife later proceeded to commit adultery and to produce an illegitimate son, so he divorced her and became a priest. All very rich pickings for Miss Austen's novels.

If you thought the Twisletons had run out of copy for Jane Austen at that point, you would be sadly wrong, for the disgraced young Twisleton had two sisters, the elder of whom married one of Jane's cousins, and the younger, Mary Twisleton, conducted her own highly publicised adulterous affair and, at sixteen, eloped with and later married a Mr Ricketts at a society wedding in Marylebone. Seven years later Ricketts discovered incriminating letters between Mary and her lover, one Charles Taylor MP of Cavendish Square. Ricketts instigated divorce proceedings in the House of Lords and at the hearing, a popular event for the media, several witnesses swore they had seen Mary visit her lover's home by night, others mentioned her ruffled and unkempt state as she left his house, and her maid testified that Mary had often bragged in minute detail of Taylor's prowess as a lover, compared with Ricketts' performance as a husband.

Some years later Jane Austen went to a party in Bath, knowing that the fairly large family group there would include her adulteress cousin Mary, whom she had never met. She wrote to her sister Cassandra: 'By 9 o'clock [we] entered the rooms ... and I am proud to say I have a very good eye at an Adultress, for tho' repeatedly assured that another in the same party was *She*, fixed upon the right one from the first! She was not so pretty as I had expected, her face has the same defect of baldness as her sister's, and her features not so handsome. She was highly rouged and looked rather quietly and contentedly silly.'

As a Twisleton myself, I met my future wife of thirty-six years when she was nine, and started to take her out, contrary to the forcefully expressed wishes of her father, when she was thirteen. We did not elope, but we did enjoy a good dinner in Gretna Green some years after marrying. The DNA elopement gene has obviously faded over the generations.

*   *   *

George III's family scandals were forgotten in 1810 when his many children put their differences behind them and turned up in strength at Windsor to the celebrations of his fiftieth year on the throne of Great Britain. But in January 1811, aged seventy-three and exhausted, he finally gave in to his rapidly declining health and yielded to the appointment of the Prince of Wales as regent of the realm. On 21 May that year, the old king made his very last public appearance, after which he was never seen again outside the walls of Windsor Castle, although he lived on, insane, for another nine years. In 1814 he was said to have had a brief interlude of clarity, when he was overjoyed to be told that various allied victories over Napoleon had included the recapture of Hanover. His life's work, and that of his great premier, William Pitt, had not, after all, been in vain. Whether or not in the following year George ever comprehended the crowning glory of the victory at Waterloo, history does not relate.

George's queen died in 1818, sadly estranged from her mad husband, who followed her to the grave in February 1820. He had brought his country safely through sixty years of great change and great danger. It is surely a travesty of fate that such a ruler should merely be remembered as 'mad King George'. Abroad, the gains of his reign had been immense. Britain's grip on India was tightened, Ceylon was conquered, Singapore and the material rich Dutch East Indies were dominated, South Africa was seized from the Dutch, and trading rights were secured with all the former Spanish colonies of Central and South America. The Prince of Wales, who for so long had waited impatiently in the wings, was now King George IV and, arguably, the most powerful man in the world.

27

A DANDY ROAD TO RUIN

Just as there was a lot more to George III than his years of madness, so there were other achievements to George IV's reign beyond the dandy image of the Beau Brummell period, the works of Byron and the domes of Brighton Pavilion.

His Regency had taken him through stirring times, starting in 1811. This period saw Wellesley invade Spain and drive the French out of the Peninsula with some bloody sieges; it saw Napoleon and his Grand Army wasting their substance in Russia at the wrong time of the year for an invasion; it saw Napoleon's decline and exile to Elba, followed by his escape and the final showdown with Wellesley, now Duke of Wellington, at Waterloo.

My own regiment, the Royal Scots Greys, gained their cap badge of the Napoleonic Eagle, still worn today, at Waterloo by seizing the Imperial Eagle standard of the French 45th Regiment in the heat of the battle. The Greys had charged with Gordon Highlanders clinging to their stirrups, a novel combination attack. (In 1916 my uncle was killed leading a company of Gordon Highlanders and in 1943 my father was killed commanding the Scots Greys.) Eighteen years after my father was killed commanding the Greys, I commenced eight years serving the same regiment (in Centurion tanks, not on grey horses and ranged against Marxist, not Nazi or Imperial forces).

Here is an account of the fighting at Waterloo from a young infantry officer, Ensign Wheatley, who was in the thick of that momentous fight:

About 10 o'clock came the order to clean our muskets and fresh load them. Half an allowance of rum was then issued and we descended into the plain, and took our positions in solid Squares . . . we were ordered to remain in our position but, if we liked, to lay down . . . [Behind us I saw the cavalry and artillery] in excellent order as if by a magic wand. [Including all] the horse Guards . . . A Ball whizzed in the air. Up we started simultaneously . . . It was just 11 o'clock, Sunday . . . In five minutes a stunning noise took place and shocking havoc commenced. One could almost feel the undulation of the air from the multitude of cannon shot. The first man who fell was five files on my left. With the utmost distortion of feature, he lay on his side and shrivelling up every muscle . . . in acute agony, [he died] . . .

393

A black consolidated body was soon seen approaching and we distinguished . . . the iron-cased cavalry of the enemy. Shouts of 'Stand firm!', 'Stand fast!' were heard from the little squares around and very quickly these gigantic fellows were upon us . . . No words can convey the sensation we felt on seeing these heavily-armed bodies advanced at full gallop against us, flourishing their sabres . . . the sun gleaming on the steel . . . We dashed them back [with] sharp-toothed bayonets . . . and we presented our bristly points . . . like porcupines . . . The horse Guards then came up and drove them back . . . The French made repeated attacks . . . for two long hours . . . [Then] the warfare took a new turn. In order to destroy our squares, the enemy filled the air with shells, howitzers and bombs so that, every five minutes, the whole Battalion lay on its face, then sprang up again when the danger was over . . . An ammunition cart blew up near us, smashing men and horses. I [was] shocked at the sight of broken armour, lifeless bodies, murdered horses, shattered wheels . . . Here and there a frightened horse would rush across the plain trampling on the dying and the dead. Three or four poor wounded animals standing on three legs, the other dangling before them. We killed several of these unfortunate beasts and it would have been [as well to do likewise to] the wriggling, feverish, mortally lacerated soldiers as they rolled on the ground.

About 4 o'clock the battle was renewed . . . We still stood in line. The carnage was

394

frightful. The balls which missed us mowed down the Dutch behind us [or the] cavalry behind them. I saw a cannon ball take away a Colonel of the Nassau Regiment so cleanly that the horse never moved from under him . . . [I kept] the men firm in their ranks, closing up the vacuities as the balls swept off the men, inspecting the fallen to detect deception. A regiment of Cuirassiers came like a thunderbolt among us. At the instant, a squadron of horse Guards dashed up to our rescue. In the confusion of the moment I made for the Colours to defend them. And we succeeded with infinite difficulty in rallying the men again.

Ensign Wheatley was injured soon after this, and his colonel killed. Captain Kincaid of the Rifle Regiment describes the end of the battle:

Our Division [had numbered] 5,000 men but . . . had gradually dwindled down to a solitary line of skirmishers. The 27th were lying, literally dead, in square, a few yards behind us. My horse had received another shot through the leg and one . . . in his body, sending him a step beyond the pension list. The smoke still hung so thick about us that we could see nothing. I walked . . . to each flank . . . to get a glimpse of what was going on, but nothing met my eye except the mangled remains of men and horses. I had never yet heard of a battle in which everyone was killed, but this seemed likely to be the exception.

Presently, a cheer which we knew to be British commenced far to the right . . . It was Lord Wellington's long-wished-for orders to advance. It grew louder . . . We took it up by instinct, charged [downhill] and [our enemy flew before us.] Lord Wellington galloped up . . . and our men began to cheer him; but he called out, 'No cheering, my lads, but forward and complete our victory.'

Napoleon was imprisoned finally on the island of St Helena, the twenty-year war against expansionist Revolutionary France was won and the British empire continued to expand.

As for the Regent Prince George, he was still king-in-waiting, for his mad father was still alive. In 1817 his only child, a daughter called Charlotte, died along with her stillborn son. The nation had been following her pregnancy closely in the press and was now furious, blaming the doctor (who committed suicide) and even Prince George for not being at his daughter's side when she died. The tragedy changed the prince, who suffered a nervous breakdown. It also sparked off a worry about the royal succession as the prince had long been separated from his hated wife Caroline of Brunswick, so there was no other offspring. This accelerated the marriage intentions of George's younger brothers, three of whom quickly married German princesses.

In January 1820, George III finally died after a sixty-year reign, and George IV was crowned, although unpopular, obese and almost certainly addicted to the laudanum which staved off the agony of his gout.

Six months prior to George III's death, the Tory government was over-harsh with prevalent industrial unrest. In Manchester 50,000 people rallied in St Peter's Fields. The yeomanry were sent in by the local magistrates and, at the subsequent 'Peterloo Massacre', eleven of the crowd were killed and four hundred injured.

Only four weeks after George IV's succession a group of revolutionaries was seized, the Cato Street conspirators who planned to assassinate all the cabinet ministers. Five were quickly executed, but the general atmosphere was menacing and the new king stayed away from London with its threat of mob violence. Into this uncertain scene Queen Caroline trod centre stage. She and the king still loathed each other. Both had had numerous adulterous affairs, but she had remained mostly abroad. Nonetheless, she was still popular and George's refusal to recognise her as queen and allow her to attend his coronation did not go down well with the people. George tried to obtain an official divorce through a parliamentary bill and an enquiry into her past adulteries. Neither move succeeded but, by fate (some said by poison), Queen Caroline died and saved the king a good deal of trouble.

George IV's coronation turned out to be an unexpectedly popular event and very soon after the ceremony, George, aged fifty-nine, became the first monarch since Richard II to pay a state visit to Ireland. The visit went well and the king followed it up with a fifteen-day jaunt to Scotland, entirely organised and orchestrated by the novelist, Sir Walter Scott. The King wore full Highland apparel, including the Stuart tartan. In earlier, less obese years, he had been adept at Scottish reels and was a well known lover of the bagpipes.

After Scotland and Ireland, George visited his other kingdom, that of Hanover, but thereafter until the end of his reign he retired, forever plagued by gout, to the seclusion of Windsor Castle, from where he continued to interfere with politics. One of his brothers, the Duke of Kent, died seven months after the birth of his daughter, the future Queen Victoria, of whom Uncle George grew very fond. The issue that filled his last years was that of Catholic emancipation, which he and most Whigs were against. The Tory premier, George Canning, tried to push it through on the retirement of Lord Liverpool. When Canning died, and the Duke of Wellington eventually became prime minister in 1828, he persuaded the king, against his will, to finally sign the Catholic Relief Act, which certainly soothed the southern Irish for a while.

Wellington, the great general, did his best as prime minister, but leopards do not change their spots and, in office, he spent a good deal of time suppressing democratic reforms and generally favoured elitism over enfranchisement. This made him a prime target of the London mob, many of whom had once toasted his victories. He acquired his nickname of the Iron Duke from the metal shutters he subsequently fitted to protect the windows of his London House—Number One, London. According to tradition, after his first cabinet meeting he remarked to an aide, 'It was an extraordinary affair. I gave them their orders and they wanted to stay and discuss them.'

Another minister of George's, very able but

over-sensitive and, like Wellington, from Ireland, was Robert Castlereagh, briefly a superb foreign secretary who, overworked, had a nervous breakdown and slit his own throat with a penknife, provoking the following epitaph from Lord Byron who was less than a fan:

> Posterity will ne'er survey
> A nobler grave than this.
> Here lie the bones of Castlereagh:
> Stop, traveller, and piss.

The king, as his gout worsened, spent most of his last three years in bed. His waistline by then was fifty-eight inches and his weight in excess of 350 pounds. A massive stroke finally killed him, aged sixty-seven, in the summer of 1830. *The Times*, always critical of George since his very early days, commented: 'There never was an individual less regretted by his fellow creatures than this deceased King.'

As for Broughton, it did not fare well over this period, despite Maria Twisleton following the royal fashion of marrying an extremely wealthy Prussian count. Maria's mother, Maria Marow, was the daughter and heiress of Samson Eardley, the son of the famous Samson Gideon, who saved the nation by paying off the National Debt and converted to Christianity in order to establish an Irish peerage for his son. Through his friendships with Walpole, Pelham and Pitt he had a private act passed by Parliament which enabled him to buy the magnificent manor of Belvedere in Kent, which he stocked with great art, largely bought from Walpole. Unfortunately, for all this dynastic planning by Gideon, his son Samson died without male issue, and so his eldest daughter (Maria Marow), or rather her husband, Gregory Twisleton, Baron Saye and Sele, inherited Belvedere and other large chunks of Gideon's rich estates. Gregory, being the heir of the late Thomas Twisleton of Broughton, could have chosen to live at either place but, having selected Belvedere, he let Broughton become dilapidated and rented it out to a succession of careless tenants.

Gregory had a fetish about his surname and changed it more than once. Even before meeting and marrying Maria, which enabled him to take on her family name which was Eardley, he had already appended his own old ancestral name of Fiennes. Gregory ended up as Baron Eardley-Twisleton-Fiennes and sat in the House of Lords as a Whig peer, which was consistent with the Fiennes and Twisleton political tradition, with one Tory exception, since pre-Cromwell days. Gregory also supported the Reform Bill of 1832, was offered and declined an earldom (despite marrying his daughter off to a Prussian count), and was a founder member of the Reform Club, in the entry hall of which you can still see his portrait. He lived to be the oldest member of the Whig party in the House of Lords and was greatly favoured by both the Grey and Melbourne administrations. He was also a famous patron of the boxing ring, and is still mentioned in descriptions of the sport of that time.

Gregory died in London aged seventy-five, and was buried at Broughton which, in its uncared for state, he left to his only son, William Thomas, who was unmarried, a Liberal and the Provincial Grand Master of Freemasons of Kent. He was also, to use the term as politely as possible, a dandy after the image of Beau Brummell. He was close friends with three famous bon viveurs, the Prince Regent, Lord Byron and the Count d'Orsay. William needed constant financial support for his merry life from father Gregory, who usually obliged, if necessary selling off more of the Gideon lands in Kent or Lincolnshire.

William, like Gregory, let Broughton go to the dogs. He was, after all, a distinguished member of the prestigious Royal Thames Yacht Club and a leader of fashion, both in style of clothing and in the latest cuisine. Belvedere's magnificence was a great deal more in keeping with his image than the Puritans' old country rendezvous of Broughton Castle. A report in the 1820s on the state of Broughton mentioned that the coat of arms of the Fiennes family had, in a great gale, fallen from the front of the castle's walls and lay smashed below. The walls themselves were covered in a profusion of destructive, creeping ivy, the living rooms were 'daily dilapidating from misuses', and by 1837 William Eardley-Twisleton-Fiennes had sold off all the saleable contents, even the swans on the moat, to pay off debts. (Many of the portraits he sold were subsequently bought back by later Saye and Seles and can be seen today in the Long Gallery.) William survived his father Gregory by only three years, dying aged forty-eight and much loved by his many friends, including the well-known gossip Count Gronow, who wrote of him in his *Reminiscences and Recollections*:

Twisleton Fiennes, the late Lord Saye and Sele, was a very eccentric man, and the greatest epicure of his day. His dinners were worthy of the days of Vitellius. Every country and every sea was searched and ransacked to find some new delicacy for our British Sybarite. I remember, at one of the breakfasts, an omelette being served which was composed entirely of golden pheasants' eggs! He had a very strong constitution and would drink absinthe and curaçao in quantities which were perfectly awful to behold. These stimulants produced no effect upon his brain, but his health gradually gave way under the excesses of all kinds in which he indulged. He was a kind, liberal and good-natured man, but a very odd fellow. I never shall forget the astonishment of a servant I had recommended to him. On entering his service, John made his appearance as Fiennes was going out to dinner, and asked his new master if he had any orders. He received the following answer. 'Place two bottles of sherry by my bedside and call me the day after tomorrow.'

The next king, William IV, sandwiched for seven brief years between his brother, the unlamented George IV, and his niece, the great Victoria, is rarely remembered and there is little to be said about him. He was, at sixty-four, the oldest person so far to become a British monarch. Being the third son of the long-lived George III, he never expected to be king. He was happy in the Royal Navy which he joined as a midshipman aged thirteen, and he was often known as the Sailor King. He saw very little action, although he was at the Battle of Cape St Vincent in 1780, and, when based in New York during the American War of Independence, George Washington agreed to a plan to kidnap him, since he would often walk around the city alone. British spies learnt of the plan and appointed a detachment of guards to watch over him. The problem of what to do with heirs to the throne in the British armed forces is still to be resolved.

In the Caribbean he became great friends with Horatio Nelson, who respected him for his naval proficiency. They often dined together and William gave away Nelson's bride at his wedding. William greatly improved the standard of naval gunnery and banished the cat-o'-nine-tails as a punishment, except for mutiny.

For most of George III's reign, William was overshadowed by his two fractious elder brothers, while living in semi-poverty with his actress mistress, Mrs Jordan, by whom he had ten illegitimate children. He was an affable old seadog, much given to loud obscenities and unregal behaviour. Eventually, sorely needing cash, he left Mrs Jordan and married Princess Adelaide of Saxe-Meiningen, with whom he was happy but had no children. He was as surprised as most people when his elder brothers produced no heirs and he inherited the throne.

William IV sacked all George IV's French and German chefs and artisans, gave most of George's art collection to the nation, and often walked about in town markets without his court in order to chat to anyone he met. He was for a year very popular, but then became mixed up with the Reform Bill to extend the suffrage by 50 per cent, which the Commons had passed but which the Lords blocked. Wellington resigned and Lord Grey, who took over, advised William to simply pack the Lords with new peers who would pass the bill. For various reasons William refused, so it looked to the public as if he was the chief bill wrecker. In 1832 the bill was passed anyway, and William soon regained his popularity. The bill refashioned the national electoral system and lost the Lords a good deal of credibility.

Most of William's ministers found him to be a sensible, hard worker. Wellington said that he could deal with more business in ten minutes with William than in ten days with the late George. A later premier, Lord Brougham, said William would always ask good questions when wanting advice, whereas George IV never did, for fear of revealing his ignorance, and George III had asked many questions but never listened to the answers.

On foreign affairs William, unlike his aggressive foreign secretary Lord Palmerston, was naturally non-interventionist, distrusted the French, and had a flair for flattering those foreigners he could see were important to Britain, including important visitors from the former colonial America.

He disagreed with Wilberforce about abolishing slavery, on the grounds that the slaves he had observed whilst in the Caribbean had a higher standard of living than many Highlanders. But, on other issues, he was clearly liberal, pushing for the removal of all penalties against religious Dissenters, for a bill to allow adulterers to remarry if they so wished, and child labour was drastically restricted during his reign.

Although, compared to his predecessors, he very

rarely engaged in political fracas, he was the last monarch in Britain to appoint a prime minister of his own choice against the will of Parliament. He died of a heart attack aged seventy-one and the crown passed to his favourite niece, Victoria, the only child of the eldest of his younger brothers. No other subsequent monarch was related to William, but he had many illegitimate children.

*   *   *

In Oxfordshire the future of the barony of Saye and Sele, plus ownership of poor dilapidated Broughton, were once again up for grabs on the death without issue of the extravagant William Thomas, he of the golden pheasant egg omelettes. The heir should have been the issue of William Thomas's uncle Thomas James, T.J., as I shall call him to avoid confusion and because letters to his family were always signed 'T.J. Twisleton'. But there was a snag caused by his early behaviour.

T.J.'s passion was acting, which he indulged both at school and in the holidays, at private theatres like the one at Adelstrop House, the home of Jane Austen's family, the Leighs, who were, over the years, thrice married to the Twisletons. These plays were described in *The World* as 'Lady Saye and Sele's Theatricals'. She had her son T.J. sit for a large oil painting dressed for his part of Phaedra in *Eunuchus* by the Roman playwright Terence, and when the painting, today in the Long Gallery at Broughton, was cleaned some few years ago, the cleaner exposed handcuff chains on the young T.J.'s wrists. Nobody quite knows why these were there in the first place (or, indeed, why they were later painted over), since they were in no way applicable to that play.

In 1788, shortly after his father's death, T.J. eloped to Gretna Green, aged eighteen and still at school, with an amateur actress, Charlotte Anne Wattell, with whom, after marriage, he then had five sons and a daughter. Within ten years all of the sons had died. Soon after his elopement T.J., in deep disgrace with his family, had stopped acting and went to Oxford where he matriculated in Divinity and became a poor curate with his brood of children in deepest Northamptonshire. Charlotte hated the life; not what she had expected when marrying the second son of a baron with a castle. So she fled the nest for the excitement of the professional stage. She acted, according to still existing handbills, under the name of the Hon. Mrs Twisleton, first on the Dublin circuit and then in Edinburgh, where she committed adultery with a Mr John Stein and had a baby boy. This boy was either the illegitimate son of Stein, or he just could be T.J.'s own son and a later heir to the Saye and Sele barony.

T.J. divorced his errant wife, suffered further scandal in doing so, and married again, this time to the suitably and boringly devoted Anglo-Irish Miss Anna Ash, whose ex-Bengal army father was Governor of Bath prison. In 1804 Anna and T.J., together with their first son Fred (Frederick Benjamin, my great great grandfather), went to Ceylon, where nine years earlier a British naval force had landed at Trincomalee and occupied Colombo. Quite why T.J. took up a job in such a place is not difficult to guess, because in England he was clearly an embarrassment to his lordly

Whig brother, Baron Gregory Twisleton.

Gregory was a good friend and, at Broughton, a close neighbour to Lord North who, in 1802, was appointed the first Governor of Ceylon when the Treaty of Amiens with Napoleon attached the coastal zones of Ceylon to Britain. So pushed in all likelihood by his big brother, T.J., Anna and little Fred landed in Colombo, where T.J. became initially the minister of the British garrison church and then the first Archdeacon of Colombo. For twenty years he was priest, local JP and director of forty-seven new schools he helped set up, with a salary of £2,000 a year.

Apart from their own children, T.J. and Anna also looked after T.J.'s surviving daughter Julia from his marriage to Charlotte, the actress. Julia married an English Captain James Brown, but he was shot dead in a duel by another officer after a petty argument. T.J., as judge, had the sad job of putting the surviving duellist in jail for a week and burying his son-in-law. Julia and her fatherless son, Tom Brown, returned to England on the breadline where Tom went to Winchester College and New College Oxford (as Founder's Kin) and became a priest in Dorset.

T.J. and Anna's other children after Fred included Edward who married Ellen Dwight, the daughter of the Senator for the State of Massachusetts (part founded by Old Subtlety). Edward was commendably involved in one of the most productive areas of social progress towards the end of William IV's reign, the reform of the Poor Laws. Much of the research and hard work behind their subsequent success was down to him and he went on under Queen Victoria to become leader of the 1843 enquiry into the Scottish Poor Laws, and in the terrible years of famine and repression (1845–9) he was the Chief Commissioner of Poor Laws in Ireland. He served on more government-appointed commissions than anyone else in his time. The situation in Ireland, however, was so dreadful for the poor and so apparently intractable that Edward resigned his top post in despair. Edward and his American wife Ellen had no children, but his elder brother Fred was destined to be the saving grace of the Saye and Sele line and of Broughton. Aged six, he was sent back from Colombo to Britain to be educated. He travelled alone. (His younger sister, Anna, on a subsequent voyage was shipwrecked and drowned.) On that childhood voyage, Fred's passenger ship, with its great square sails, would have been part of an armed convoy, for fear of the Napoleonic navy, and en route from Ceylon would have called at Cape Town (as I did, aged two in 1946, and stayed there for ten years).

Back in England, Fred's Saye and Sele cousins and his aunt, having discussed what was best for young Fred, earmarked him for the church, like his father in Ceylon and, funds for him being short, they took advantage of the Founder's Kin free education available. At Winchester he became a notable scholar being brilliant at memorising Latin. He won the King's Silver Medal for English and later gained his Doctorate of Civil Law at New College. He was ordained in 1823, became rector of Adelstrop and Broadwell and joined the staff of Hereford Cathedral in 1825, just after his father, T.J.'s death from typhoid in Ceylon.

In 1827 William Eardley-Twisleton, lover of

golden pheasant eggs and 16th Baron Saye and Sele, died a bachelor and, in normal circumstances, the barony would have passed directly and without question to his first cousin Fred who by then had married a daughter of Lord Powerscourt, who had given him five sons and two daughters. Fred had meanwhile advanced up the hierarchy of Hereford Cathedral, via treasurer to canon residentiary, and was forty-seven years old when William died. But because of the complication of his father, T.J.'s first wife having had an adulterous relationship and possibly an illegitimate son, he was forced by law to claim the barony at an official proceedings at the House of Lords.

This he did by hiring good barristers to locate first Mr John Stein, late of Edinburgh, who had run off with T.J.'s first wife and, secondly, the lad Charles himself. Not an easy task, but Stein, well into his eighties by then, was duly located and confronted by Fred's barrister. It must have been quite an ordeal for the old man, but he was still clear-headed and he stated the facts as he remembered them. A boy had, indeed, been born to Stein and T.J.'s wife up in Edinburgh and they had looked after him until he was fourteen when, since Stein and Charlotte were then on the breadline, he had been sent to sea. Stein had met him only once since then and remembered that he was in common sailor's garb at the time. Mr Stein repeated all this under oath before the Committee of Privileges. The barristers' agents then located exact dates from the Advocates' Library in Edinburgh, where all playbills of the Theatre Royal had been preserved for a century. So they knew exactly when T.J.'s errant actress wife had been in that city.

To locate the lost sailor son involved searching the Register of Seamen kept at Custom House. The full family name was not, of course, found, but the adopted one supplied the clue and the sailor, whether Charles Stein or Charles Twisleton, was traced on to an outward-bound ship. He was then met on his next return to England and happily, in a guileless fashion, told the story of his youth and birth as he knew it. The case was submitted to the House of Lords by Fred's lawyer where, upon investigation of the dates involved, the Lords decided that the child was Stein's, not Twisleton's. Stein and his now proven-to-be-illegitimate son gave evidence, no doubt delighted to have been reunited. So Fred became the 17th baron Saye and Sele without the ever-lurking fear of some unknown claimant appearing one day out of the blue.

Fred did not simply forget sailor Charles Stein and his old father, whose honesty had been the key to the outcome of the case. In 1863 Stein's solicitor wrote to Fred:

Many thanks for your cheque for £20 for the poor sailor. A short time since I thought the little annuity would have ceased. He had a very severe illness, with erysipelas, but the constitution of his old father seems to have descended to him and he rallied and now walks here from the region of the Docks near Limehouse every Monday morning to receive the allowance and then walks back. He is of a peaceable contented disposition, gives no trouble, his wants being satisfied by the occasional gift of a second hand coat or pair of shoes, and a little meat at Christmas. I often think the history of his life would make good materials for a novel—he used to say of himself that his existence and identity was always a subject of doubt and perplexity to himself, and he never could understand who or what he was, or where he came from.

The very next year, having begun long overdue restoration work on Broughton, Fred and his family grew to love the place and to revere the generations of their ancestors who had lived and loved there. In honour of all the Twisletons, Wykehams and Fienneses whose blood ran through Fred's veins, as the Sore brook runs through Broughton's moat, he altered his surname to Twisleton-Wykeham-Fiennes, which all my ancestors since have happily born, as, until she marries, will my daughter Elizabeth. The same year Fred re-established the close relations the family had long held with Broughton's nearby town, when he was appointed High Steward of Banbury.

Following the death of his first wife, Elizabeth, Fred married again in 1857 the much younger Caroline Leigh of the Jane Austen family, into which previous Twisletons had also married. Since the Leighs were from Adelstrop and Fred had long been their rector, he had actually baptised Caroline when she was a baby. In 1863 he became Archdeacon of Hereford (where a stained glass window commemorates him to this day) and still found time to take his duties at the House of Lords very seriously.

When he was seventy-nine and on his way into the House of Lords to discuss the highly unpopular County Franchise Bill, a riotous mob gathered outside the House to hustle and jeer the lords as they entered. Fred might well have tried to avoid the unpleasant attention of the hecklers, but instead he shouted back, 'Here is one of the Lords you are hooting—aye, and one who has always been a friend of the people.' This, in tones so hearty and with a bearing so upright that the crowd made way and cheered as he passed into the courtyard.

Sometimes when checking how repairs were going at Broughton, Fred would go up the curved stone steps to the roof immediately outside the council chamber where Hampden and Pym had plotted with Old Subtlety, and stand by the parapet. His staff below would hear his stentorian tones, well practised in Hereford Cathedral, ring out with his favourite watchwords, 'Peace, Retrenchment and Reform!' and 'No Taxation without Representation!' But life is never perfect. A nightmare gradually unfolded for Fred in his well-earned old age.

When in 1847 Fred inherited Broughton, he and his second wife, Caroline, took on the challenge of restoring the castle to its former glory. The entire contents had been auctioned off in 1837 by Gregory, probably to pay off his dandy son William's debts, and he had then rented the castle out unfurnished. Fred and Caroline had to spend a great deal over many years in their labour of love, renewing beams, replacing baths and basins, opening blocked doorways, replacing rotten

412

woodwork, and redecorating walls. They did not neglect Broughton's church, either. As the work went on, so the clouds of bankruptcy gathered. Huge imports of North American wheat had drastically cut the annual agricultural income from the Saye and Sele's farm estates, as was the case all over Britain at the time. Then to add to the ongoing costs of the restoration, there was the inexcusable behaviour of Fred's eldest son (he had four), John Twisleton-Wykeham-Fiennes, the heir to Broughton and my great grandfather. In the recent words of the 21st Lord Saye and Sele, 'John, I regret to record, was a *bad* man.'

As early as 1855, when John was only twenty-five, Fred had to bail him out of Oxford prison, whence he had been committed by a moneylender to whom he owed £3,300. He gambled heavily and Fred's lawyers were constantly having to pay off his debts. He borrowed large sums to buy racehorses under an assumed name, and was inordinately proud of his one real success. He owned one brood mare, his only stud, and by her he bred Placida who won the Oaks in 1877, which gained John £10,000 in stakes and, when he sold her, a further £2,000.

John hid much of his borrowing from his parents in expectation of his inheritance. Fred's three other sons were at least honest about their ongoing requests to their bankrupt father for funds he didn't have. One letter of 1886 from his fourth son, Wingfield, who was at the time the Rector of Milton Keynes and with five children, ran:

My Dearest Father
. . . The chief problem at the present time is

how to live at all, and it is my opinion that if the country is misgoverned much longer by the Grand Old Goose, only bankers and brewers will survive the general wreck. Every day brings some fresh application for money, and as there is so little incoming I fear it will before long end in a grand smash so far as I am concerned—and yet we have not even a pony trap, and drink no wine or beer, and have hardly a rag to our backs except what is handed over to us as old clothes . . . it is the inevitable result of Gladstonism! My son Alberic is cramming . . . for the examination required for a clerkship in the Bank of England. I am told that, if he does well, he may be able to secure £500 a year when he is sixty years old!

Your very affectionate son,
W.T.F.

Things must have looked truly dire for poor Fred. Huge debts and no remaining funds. Every inch of land mortgaged to the hilt and beyond. But tradition and family loyalty from Fred's brothers and cousins eventually paid the debts and saved Broughton. When Fred died, John took over, but tenants remained in occupation of the castle throughout his lifetime. He deserved it.

Under Queen Victoria, Broughton must have hoped the family would do better.

28

UNCLE GEOFFREY IN ZULU LAND

When King William IV, the Sailor King, died in 1837, his little niece, aged eighteen and less than five feet tall, became queen of the greatest empire in the world. She looked very unimpressive and her nickname was Drinny. She had slept all her life in the bedroom of her mother, who was convinced that her wicked uncles, the previous Kings George IV and William IV, wished to kill her.

One of her later prime ministers, the Tory Benjamin Disraeli, wrote in 1847 in his novel *Sybil* that Victoria reigned over two nations, the Rich and the Poor; 'between whom there is no intercourse, and no sympathy; who are as ignorant of each other's habits, thoughts and feelings as if they were dwellers in different zones, or inhabitants of different planets; who are formed by a different breeding, are fed by a different food, are ordered by different manners, and are governed by the same laws.'

The basic problem was that Victoria coincided with a time of huge and ever-accelerating change, but she was saddled with a tried, tested but inflexible framework of governmental machinery. The political system, into which the young Victoria found herself slotted, had been designed over the centuries for the benefit of landowning aristocrats in a rurally based nation. It had not kept up with the recent and startling transformation of Britain into an urban industrial society. The ever expanding working class had few non-violent ways of expressing their frustrations legally available to them, and there was an increasingly uppity middle class with a great capacity for radicalism but still without the vote. The Reform Act of 1832 had only extended the franchise to certain categories of adult males, so a great many workers still felt voiceless and betrayed.

Parliament's frightened response to these people's increasing agitation was to clamp down on them. Six Dorset labourers were sentenced for transportation merely for trying to organise a trade union, but countrywide protests eventually secured their pardon. They were known as the Tolpuddle Martyrs. Old-fashioned Tories, like the Duke of Wellington, believed in holding a tough line on these 'troublemakers', but such rigid views were on the way out. The Whigs, soon to metamorphose gradually into Liberals, believed there were two main social classes—property owners and rabble—and that the former must stick together or be overrun by the latter.

A factor of change which did help the urban poor in very real terms was the Municipal Act that empowered urban councils to raise local taxes and spend the results as they felt best. This sparked many an ambitious and aggressive council in the 1840s and 1850s to greatly improve the lives of their tax-paying citizens. Cities such as Liverpool and Bradford spent millions of pounds on water and sewerage schemes. Glasgow's city fathers spent £1.5 million to stop cholera epidemics caused by the filthy waters of the Clyde. But the shiny new water closets of the middle-class streets often drained into the workers' water supplies.

1858 in London was known as the Year of the Great Stink when the Thames, according to Disraeli, became a 'stygian pool reeking with ineffable and intolerable horrors'. The foul stench pervaded the Commons and forced the Metropolitan Board to spend £4 million on the construction of an eighty-two-mile, multi-levelled sewer to take London's sewage to the sea.

In the latter half of Victoria's reign, great hospitals were built in many cities, and in forty years the supply of doctors increased from 14,000 to 23,000. Chloroform stopped surgery from being the terrible experience of earlier times, but faulty hygiene practices and overzealous use of forceps still meant that 10 per cent of pregnant women who entered maternity wards left them in coffins. The safest place for delivery was still at home.

Strangely enough, in the mid nineteenth century crime figures dropped, despite the industrial tensions and the rapid population growth in crowded cities. An explanation of this phenomenon may well have been the Education Boards, instituted by the Liberals, making it compulsory for schools to be set up wherever no church schools existed.

Such was life in Victoria's great new cities in the mid- to late nineteenth century where, despite a background of poverty, the Tory party under Disraeli and later Lord Salisbury did very well through the 1870s onwards. This started with Disraeli's realisation that political success was becoming as much a matter of presentation as of actual policy. The beginnings of what we now call spin.

Victoria's greatest and longest serving minister

was the Liberal coalitionist, aggressively patriotic Lord Palmerston, who personified the arrogant self-confidence of his country, which he described, accurately enough, as the 'only world power'.

One of many examples of how British forces in the mid-nineteenth century reinforced this view was that of my first cousin Lord Nigel Napier's ancestor, General Sir Charles Napier and his 1843 successes in India. There is a bronze statue of him in Trafalgar Square.

When Hindu priests had a go at Napier for upholding the British law against their ancient *suttee* practice of burning widows alive on the funeral pyres of their husbands, he replied: 'You say it is your custom to burn widows. Very well. We also have a custom: when men burn a woman alive, we tie a rope around their necks and we hang them. Build your funeral pyre; beside it my carpenters will build a gallows. You may follow your custom. And then we will follow ours.' Later that year Napier led a force of four hundred British and 2,200 sepoys to decisively defeat 30,000 Baluchi soldiers at Miani, fighting hand-to-hand (and Napier was sixty at the time) before entering and gaining control of all Sind Province. His cable back to army headquarters simply read 'Peccavi', the Latin for 'I have sinned.' (The general was descended from the John Napier who invented Napierian Logarithms, still in use today.)

Back home, a stable Britain took in the French royal family fleeing the Parisian mob in 1848, and also two middle-class German revolutionaries, who had fled to London after involvement in a failed revolution back home, and in the calm of the British Museum produced a joint work entitled

The Communist Manifesto. Karl Marx was twenty-nine and Friedrich Engels only nineteen, but their London scribblings were, over the next hundred years and more, to spawn the monstrous Marxist-Leninist nightmare that caused countless millions to die in misery, especially in Eastern Europe. I spent five years with a tank troop of the Royal Scots Greys, waiting for the Communist Warsaw Pact armies to pour over the East German border in the early 1960s. Now, thank the Lord, the *Manifesto* has proved a mere failed political experiment.

In London Marx despaired at the resistance of the working classes to the socialist ideas of middle-class intellectuals such as himself. In 1851, the Great Exhibition in the specially built Crystal Palace in Hyde Park, set up by aristocrats to celebrate the dominance of Britain's goods in the global marketplace, was visited by great numbers of honest proletarians who, far from voicing even the mildest revolutionary themes, beamed with monarchic chauvinism and revelled in the popular London ballad of the time, which ran: 'O, surely England's greatest wealth is an honest working man . . . ' Over six million tickets were sold for the exhibition, and for many it was their first visit ever to London thanks to the special trains that brought in visitors from all over Britain. The profits were used to build the museums of South Kensington.

The next year over a million people lined the route of the Duke of Wellington's funeral procession from Horse Guards to St Paul's Cathedral. People remembered his great victories over 'Boney' of forty years before, his prickly ministries and, much later, his quaint behaviour, in his seventies, patrolling the London streets on horseback with cocked pistols on his belt as he searched for Spring-Heeled Jack, a serial killer who slashed his female victims with metal claws.

Victoria's Crimean War army of the 1850s could have done with a commander of Wellington's stature, but it seems to have suffered instead from a series of lordly buffoons, the most infamous of whom, Lords Raglan and Cardigan, sent Britain's finest cavalry into murderous cannon fire at Balaclava. The Crimean War had a complex background, but was mainly caused by Russian determination to take over the sprawling and weakening Ottoman empire of the Turks. France and Britain agreed to send armies by sea to prevent such Russian expansionism in the Crimea, and the result was extremely bloody, with the Russians doggedly holding on to a number of key coastal towns, such as Sevastopol. I have the 1850s diaries of Frederick Fiennes, 16th Lord Saye and Sele-to-be, which for 1855 simply states: 'Left Broughton and joined the depot of The 23rd [Royal Welsh Fusiliers] at Winchester . . . Left England for Malta in the *Great Tasmania* troopship . . . [joined the headquarters] in Balaclava harbour [on 16 June] and from that date there was nothing but hard fighting. Spent the Christmas in Camp before Sebastopol.'

A few months prior to Frederick's arrival, the famous cavalry charges took place. My own regiment of the 1960s, the Royal Scots Greys, together with the Enniskillens—three hundred men in all—charged uphill against a dense mass of Russian cavalry over 3,000 strong. This, the charge of the Heavy Brigade, has since been described by many war historians as the most desperate but successful cavalry versus cavalry charge in history. The tragic charge of the Light Brigade, which took place later the same day, was made famous by Tennyson with the words:

> Theirs not to reason why,
> Theirs but to do or die.
> Into the valley of death
> Rode the six hundred.

Six hundred and seventy-three of Britain's elite cavalry charged thirty Russian guns, which scythed them down as they kept coming along a mile of open ground. Survivors reached the guns, killed the crews and rode back. Only 198 lived to tell their tale. A French general who watched, said, 'It's magnificent but it's no way to fight a war.' George Orwell commented later: 'The most stirring battle-poem in English is about a brigade of cavalry which charged in the wrong direction.'

The Times pioneered a new method of telling folk back home immediately what was going on. This was the telegraph dispatch, and a new breed of war reporters were quick to expose how ill-equipped and poorly led were many of our troops. The scandal of the charge was soon overshadowed by the conditions in Crimean field hospitals, where more soldiers were dying from infections contracted in the wards than from their battlefield wounds.

Florence Nightingale, whom news reports immortalised as 'the lady with the lamp', vastly improved sanitation. Until her arrival, bedding was never washed, rats and fleas abounded and water sources were polluted. Nurses up till then were considered little better than prostitutes, and certainly never came from respectable families. Florence Nightingale, when officers obstructed her hospital reforms, simply contacted Queen Victoria direct, and Victoria always backed her requests and complaints. The queen visited the wounded and created the Victoria Cross to honour the brave. She personally knitted scarves for many an army veteran, gave nursing her full approval as a career for any caring female whatever her background, and helped Miss Nightingale establish nursing career structures at King's College and St Thomas's Hospitals.

For all the improvements in hospital care, it was typhoid from the cesspits of Windsor Castle that killed the queen's consort, Prince Albert, in 1861. Victoria wore only black for the rest of her long life and for years avoided public appearances to the point where she became very unpopular with her own subjects.

At the time of Prince Albert's death, the profligate owner of Broughton Castle, John Fiennes, the 17th Lord Saye and Sele, was renting out the castle and estate to pay for his horse racing addiction and gambling debts. He married the diminutive Lady Augusta Hay-Drummond, who gave him ten children, the second of whom was my grandfather, Eustace, born in 1864. Tradition dictated that Eustace, as second son, would end up as a priest, a soldier or an upholder of the empire in some faraway colonial outpost.

The year he was born, the papers were full of tales of the American Civil War, an affray Queen Victoria kept well clear of and indeed clear of all involvement with the ultra-sensitive ex-colonies, particularly after a recent diplomatic incident instigated by my grandfather's cousin, Sir John Fiennes Twisleton Crampton, minister plenipotentiary and envoy extraordinary to the United States. Lord Palmerston was in the process of instructing all his ambassadors to recruit foreign corps who would be paid by Britain to fight the Russians in the Crimea. These included German, Swiss and Italian legions, and Crampton recruited actively in the United States. President Franklin Pierce, in order to gain popularity and a fresh term of office, complained bitterly against such recruitment and demanded the immediate recall of Fiennes Crampton 'as prime mover in a scheme which he knew full well was contrary to the law of the United States and that he continued to recruit after it had been pronounced unlawful.' Despite Lord Palmerston's initially robust response to Pierce's posturing, he then relented and withdrew the offending diplomat. Trade, Palmerston ruled, was master of all else and master of the empire.

London sometimes instituted small imperial beginnings, the thin end of new wedges, by way of chartered companies, trading bodies with governmentally guaranteed rights to trade and administer a given region. Rhodesia, East Africa and Nigeria all came under British rule in this insidious manner. Following the Indian Mutiny in 1857, the East India Company was wound up and all its vast territories became British-administered with, in 1876, the queen as official Empress of India.

Self-rule of colonies followed sooner or later (sometimes much later). Canada became a

Dominion in 1867, and Australia a Commonwealth in 1900, but the latter half of the nineteenth century witnessed the annexation by Britain of vast new parts of the Pacific, East Africa and the Far East. World trade on the high seas was absolutely dominated by British shipping, and this carried over into the twentieth century, well after British dominance in trade goods had declined. Religious indoctrination by a thousand British missionaries, including David Livingstone, backed up trade activities, and by the 1880s a quarter of the entire world was coloured British pink on the map. In those days German tourists did not put their towels on British sunbeds.

Tory claims to be the only effective and dedicated empire party were severely dented by their handling of wars in Afghanistan where two expeditions were costly and catastrophic failures, and in South Africa where first Zulus, then Boers gave the great British army a very bloody nose. In 1879 some 5,000 British troops crossed into Zululand intent on forcing the Zulu king to accept the status of a British protectorate. Whilst the troops were camped at Isandlwana they were attacked by 10,000 Zulus with spears. The British fixed bayonets but were soon massacred. The Zulus swept on to the isolated garrison of Rorke's Drift, held by 120 mostly Welsh soldiers who somehow repulsed the attacking horde and earned eleven Victoria Crosses before breakfast, a greater number of medals for extreme gallantry than ever awarded for any other single engagement.

My great uncle Geoffrey, 18th Lord Saye and Sele, was part of Disraeli's response to the massacre, a second army of 23,000 men sent out to avenge the dead of Isandlwana. He was decorated for bravery in the fighting which captured the Zulu King Cetshwayo. On his return home he was appointed Comptroller of the Royal Household and High Steward of Oxford, and later wrote a family history called *Hearsay*.

Geoffrey, his younger brother, my grandfather Eustace, and their eight other brothers and sisters grew up spending their winters at Broughton and their summers in London. This was because family fortunes remained at a low ebb and dependent upon intermittent rental income. Broughton was rented out throughout the period from 1885 until 1912 to society figures like Lord and Lady Gordon Lennox who entertained the royal family there. Fienneses had long since learnt that they must go out individually and earn a living. They could no longer rely on the current head of the family inheriting or marrying oomph—oomph being the Fiennes slang for lots-of-money.

My grandfather Eustace decided to avoid the regular army and priesthood and to head instead for the other traditional second-son option of a colonial career. He had read of the romantic life to be found in northern Canada as a fur trapper, mining for gold on the side, and so in 1882, aged eighteen, he arrived in Alberta and tried his luck with pick, sieve and snares. He ran out of money long before finding even fool's gold and had to sign up with the North West Mounted Police as a trooper. After training and happily receiving his first salary, he picked up his first medal for his part in a campaign to quell the Plains Indians and métis of mixed race in the wilds of Saskatchewan. But there was little other excitement and he began to

425

yearn for a more colourful existence somewhere where the pine forests or prairies did not stretch to the horizon, where summers did not mean clouds of mosquitoes and winters long months of white wilderness.

So he resigned in 1888 and hitched his way to Egypt with the job of news reporter for the *Morning Post*. There he joined the staff of General Kitchener, who was busy retaking Sudan after the rebellious Dervishes of the Mahdi had earlier killed General Gordon at Khartoum. Eustace fought with Kitchener's army at the Battle of Gemaizah but it would be ten years before the final defeat of the Mahdi's successor, the Khalifa, at Omdurman and the annexation of all Sudan by Britain. Eustace left Kitchener's forces in March 1890 and joined the British South Africa Company's police as a sub-lieutenant in Kimberley. This force had been formed by Cecil Rhodes the previous year to help protect pioneers travelling north into Mashonaland (now part of Zimbabwe). Eustace did well and was soon promoted to full lieutenant with his own police troop.

Just as the East India Company in India and the Hudson Bay Company in Canada preceded British territorial gains in those countries, so Cecil Rhodes' British South Africa Company expanded British territory in southern Africa. Hence Rhodesia. Eustace did his bit. The *History of the British South African Police* described Eustace (spelling his surname ffiennes) as: 'Not a regular soldier, he was the son of a lord and a member of the London Stock Exchange although he had served, by some unexplained circumstances, in the

Canadian militia.'

Pennyfeather's Column of Pioneers to Southern Rhodesia, which began in late June 1890, made a confrontation with Portugal, Britain's oldest ally, inevitable because Portugal had laid claim to the whole area through which the Rhodes pioneers had to travel to reach Rhodesia, and many of his men, including Pennyfeather and, later, grandfather Eustace, were dead keen to grab territory for the motherland wherever they could. Shortly before Eustace joined the BSAP, an energetic Portuguese soldier, Major Paiva d'Andrada, formed a Rhodes-type commercial company and established a fortress at Massi Kessi, twenty miles from where Eustace's police were based at Umtali.

In November 1890, a small armed force under Eustace attacked three hundred Portuguese levies on the ridge above Massi Kessi. Andrada was captured and his fort seized. Andrada was sent back to Portugal where he caused a great stir against British aggression on Portuguese territory. Later, when four separate Portuguese forces arrived to retaliate, including a thousand volunteers with artillery, they found overland travel a harder foe than the British. It was easy to get lost in the dense tropical vegetation. Rations were meagre. Malaria and dysentery struck men daily. Horses died or contracted tsetse fly-induced sickness. Rivers had to be crossed, swollen and full of crocodiles. Tracks were deep in mud. The heat and humidity were exhausting.

In March 1891, according to the book *Men Who Made Rhodesia*, Eustace was stationed at Umtali when he received a messenger. Two of his men were down with fever at an outpost.

Fiennes at once called for volunteers who were good swimmers, and selected [two. The three] set out on a 23 mile journey over slippery mountain paths at the height of the rainy season when all rivers were in flood. Rain had fallen incessantly for months, and 52 inches had been recorded for the season against a normal 30 inches. When they got to the Revue River they found it to be 'raging like a miniature sea, mountainous waves roaring like thunder'. In spite of this, Fiennes attempted the crossing alone; he was carried down the stream for half a mile and was once entangled in reeds. Nevertheless he managed to gain the far bank after half an hour in the water.

At the outpost he found that one man had been dead for a week and Glover, the other, was in a dreadful condition. He began to dig a grave with his own hands. Building a small raft, Fiennes and another man got Glover back over the crocodile river and, in a rough litter, over the mountains to their base. Glover lived until 1950. The account continued: 'Fiennes' part in the rescue was one of calculated courage of the highest order; the odds in favour of his crossing the Revue were very slender.'

On 11 May Eustace took part in the Battle of Chua Hill when a Portuguese attack was repulsed. Next day the Macequece Fort's garrison was found to have fled and Fiennes was sent forward with six mounted men along the paths towards Beira to follow up the enemy and keep going east to the sea. At Chimoio, 130 miles from Umtali, he located a manned Portuguese fort, observed it and decided to attack the next day. Whilst preparing the attack he was surprised by a white man whom he nearly shot for a Portuguese. But this was the British Bishop of Mashonaland who told him not to attack the Portuguese as the arrival of Major Sapte, the Military Secretary to the British High Commissioner, was imminent. This man duly arrived and ordered Eustace not to attack because peace had been made by the two governments the previous day.

According to the official *History of the British South Africa Police*: 'when Rhodes heard what had happened, and that the swashbuckling attempt to add Portuguese East Africa to his territories had again been abandoned, he said, "Why didn't Fiennes say Sapte was drunk and put him in irons?"' On 30 May Lord Salisbury and the Portuguese government finally signed an agreement, which has lasted until the present day. At the time, Queen Victoria was greatly relieved, being closely related to the Portuguese king. Eustace, unaware of the narrow scrape he had experienced in sparking off a potentially major international embarrassment, was sent back to Umtali.

That July, Rose Blennerhassett, in charge of a group of nursing sisters posted to the Umtali region, wrote in her book, *Adventures in Mashonaland*: 'Foremost amongst our friends was Lieutenant Eustace Fiennes whom we came to regard as a special providence. He saved us as far as possible from difficulties, was kind, courteous and helpful, to say nothing of being a very jolly young fellow and excellent company.' In December however, Eustace's health broke down and he resigned his commission.

His subsequent attempts to buy stakes in the Kimberley gold mines and to start a farm in Matabeleland quickly came to nothing. He was a bad businessman. He ran out of funds, as he had in Canada, and sought work in Cape Town. There, in 1894, he met and married my grandmother, a South African of Prussian descent, born Florence Agnes Rathfelder, whose first husband, a Scotsman named Arthur Fletcher, had been thrown from a horse and killed, leaving Granny Florrie fairly wealthy. My godfather, Lawrence Fiennes, told me with great mirth how well he remembered the breakfast when he and the rest of Eustace's large family at Broughton read aloud the telegram from Eustace in Cape Town, which simply proclaimed, 'AM MARRYING OOMPH. EUSTACE'. In 1895 Eustace and Florrie had their first son, my Uncle Johnnie, and they returned briefly to England until Eustace again became bored.

Two years later, Queen Victoria's Diamond Jubilee confirmed that, after sixty years on the throne, and despite abandoning her people during her long period of mourning, she was still highly popular. She wrote in her diary after the Jubilee celebrations: 'The crowds were quite indescribable, and their enthusiasm truly marvellous and deeply touching. The cheering was quite deafening, and every face seemed to be filled with real joy. I was much moved and gratified.'

In 1899 Eustace, back home with his little

family, various medals and tales of derring-do, contested North Oxfordshire as the Liberal candidate. He was defeated by some 700 votes. That same year, in the nearby parish of Chipping Norton, the local vicar experimented with the medical properties of willow bark, and the aspirin was invented, still the most popular and useful drug in the world. Since his political aspirations had not initially worked out, Eustace kept his ears attuned to the South African scene. In October that year the Dutch, or Boer, leader in South Africa formally declared war on Britain unless British troops were withdrawn from the twin Boer republics of Transvaal and the Orange Free State. Since one of Britain's main geo-political goals was to bring both these gold-rich Boer provinces under direct British rule, war was exactly what Prime Minister Salisbury wanted, especially (PR-wise) if the Boers were seen to make the first aggressive move. Militarily Britain was confident of quickly defeating them. Eustace, along with many other Liberals, did not approve in principle of the idea of fighting the Boers to gain their gold. So he said so in public and was promptly labelled 'pro-Boer' by prominent Tories.

Originally the Cape, already settled by the Dutch, had been occupied by the British to safeguard the route to India. Various plans to incorporate the Boers into a federation were discussed and then, in 1877, imposed on them, but four years later the Boers had rebelled and their two states were given a loose independence. This had worked until both gold and diamonds were discovered on Boer land, and Cecil Rhodes goaded the Boers' leader, Paul Kruger, into his 1899 declaration of war.

Eustace, fresh from his electoral defeat as the great white hope of the North Oxfordshire Liberals, and despite his personal views on the Boers, discussed joining up for the Boer War with a friend, Winston Churchill, who had a similar background of fighting in various foreign wars, including the Sudan, and had also reported on them for the *Morning Post*.

Churchill's family, the Spencers, owned the Blenheim estate close to Broughton, had inter-married with the Fienneses years before and, although Winston was at this stage a Tory, before switching to Liberal and then back again, he thought along similar political lines to Eustace on most things. They would later work well together but, back in 1900, Eustace was attracted by Winston's war stories, not his politics. The previous year Winston had achieved brief fame through his own *Morning Post* reports by rescuing an armoured train from the Boers and then, after being captured, effecting a daring escape. So Eustace, like Winston, signed up with the local regiment, the Oxfordshire Imperial Yeomanry, said goodbye to Granny Florrie, Uncle Johnnie and all his brethren round the Broughton log fires, and shipped back to sunny South Africa to kill Boers instead of Portuguese.

Unfortunately, things did not go as planned for the British army. The superior mobility, field skills and firepower of the Boers led to many embarrassing British defeats and the siege of various garrisons, including Mafeking. Britain's enemies all over the world sniggered and gloated, though Eustace did well and was twice mentioned in dispatches, adding to his colourful collection of medals. Such had been the humiliating effect on the British public of the previous long history of defeats by the Boers that the May 1900 relief of Mafeking was greeted by nationwide rejoicing. The garrison commander, Colonel Robert Baden-Powell, who years later founded the Boy Scout and Girl Guide movements had saved many lives during the siege by boiling whole horse corpses in vats to provide 'the Colonel's Soup'.

At the close of 1900, Kitchener of Khartoum took over in the Cape with a Commonwealth army of half a million troops to clean up the remnants of a Boer army that never exceeded 50,000 soldiers. The latter resorted to the guerrilla tactics at which they were adept and to which the terrain was ideally suited. To retaliate, the British invented concentration camps and long lines of blockhouses, 8,000 of them, connected by tangled hedges of barbed wire. Boer farms were burnt and civilians shut up in the camps, where 25,000 died of disease. Finally, in May 1902 Kitchener signed a peace treaty with the Boers, whose two states became British colonies but with internal self-government.

Forty-two years later, when I arrived in Cape Town to spend my youth there, Brits and Boers lived happily together. But, in the words of historian Thomas Pakenham, the Boer War 'proved to be the longest (two and three- quarter years), the costliest (over £200 million), the bloodiest (at least 22,000 British, 25,000 Boer and 12,000 African lives) and the most humiliating war for the British between 1815 and 1914'.

Queen Victoria died before the war ended (in

January 1901) aged eighty-one and after sixty-three years on the throne. Although the British empire peaked in every way during her reign, its economic decline also began in her time. By 1900, Britain's share of world manufacturing output had dropped from over 60 per cent fifty years before to 18 per cent, with America at 23 per cent and Germany rapidly catching up. Victoria's nine children's progeny included her two grandsons, George V of England and Kaiser Wilhelm II of Germany, whose nations were to fight each other at great cost in human lives and misery.

29

EUSTACE AND WINSTON

Victoria's eldest son, Edward, like our own Charles, Prince of Wales today, had, since coming of age, waited over forty years in the shadow of his mother's rule. So he was well known to the nation and, aged sixty, unlikely to provide any nasty surprises when, on Victoria's death, he became King Edward VII. His Danish wife, Alexandra, was well loved, innocuous and seemingly inured to Edward's ongoing stream of scandals and mistresses, including Mrs Keppel and Lillie Langtry. Edward seldom interfered with home politics but was often useful to his ministers where foreign diplomacy was concerned, since most relevant heads of state were his first cousins; the most important and troublesome being his nephew, Kaiser William II of the ever more menacing Germany. Over the next nine years Edward used his charm and his cousinly links to encourage various treaties and alliances between Britain, Germany, Russia and France.

In the 1870–90 period, France had seemed, as ever, to be Britain's looming enemy and Germany Britain's ally, but that changed when in 1898 Germany's great naval construction programme and global ambitions preceded German encouragement of and backing for the Boers. Britain secured treaties or alliances with the Japanese in 1902, the French in 1904, and the Russians in 1907. Gradually, as German military power flexed its muscles on parade grounds, tensions mounted in Europe, and Britain sided increasingly with the Franco-Russian alliance against Germany and Austria. In a series of incidents in the Balkans, Turkey and North Africa and, in its ongoing naval build-up, Germany grew ever more hostile to Britain.

Edward, a long-time fan of the exotic delights of Paris, became popular with the French people and is credited with beginning the process still known as the Entente Cordiale, a diplomatic agreement that put an end to a thousand years of intermittent warfare. It did not, of course, stop the two nations constantly sniping at each other because it is difficult to break an enjoyable habit. Two reasons for traditional Francophobia were suggested by the actor Robert Morley in 1974: 'The French are a logical people, which is one reason the English dislike them so intensely. The other is that they own France, a country which we have always judged to be much too good for them.' A worthy riposte about the English came from Jacques

Chirac: 'You can't trust people who cook as badly as that. After Finland, it's the country with the worst food.'

When Victoria died, she drew her last breath in the loving arms of her grandson, the Kaiser, but Edward, though always polite, never liked his German nephew. He agreed with Admiral Fisher, in charge of the Royal Navy, that, 'Our only probable enemy is Germany. We must therefore keep a fleet twice as powerful concentrated within a few hours of Germany.' Not long before his own death in 1910, Edward noted: 'If the Kaiser goes on in that way [refusing a naval limitation agreement], a conflict between us and Germany is only a matter of time.'

Eustace returned from the Boer War with many medals. Of his nine brothers and sisters, he was definitely the most romantic. He stood for Parliament again in 1906 and this time won Banbury for the Liberals, a seat he held until 1918 through the period of his party's major social welfare reforms, including old age pensions, free school meals, sickness and unemployment benefits, national insurance, and many other rights that are now taken for granted.

His elder brother Geoffrey became a Liberal peer in 1908 on the death of their spendthrift father, John, my great grandfather, thanks to whose early debts Broughton was still, until 1912, rented out in summer to the Gordon-Lennox family. One visitor who was given the run of the castle by Lord Saye was the Baroness Orczy, whose most famous novel was *The Scarlet Pimpernel*. Keen to write about Broughton and its Parliamentarian experiences at the time of Old

Subtlety and his sons, Orczy chose the Royalist-inclined eldest son and heir, James Fiennes, as her hero and called the book *The Honourable Jim*. Lord Saye disliked the resulting novel intensely, and told her so. He subsequently wrote about the Orczy visit to Broughton: 'The Baroness and her husband stayed here at my invitation to get, as she prettily put it, "the local colour". On the morrow she came down in a picturesque muslin frock and going into the garden, she sat on one of our newly painted seats and got "the local colour".' He was also very cynical about Tories in general, even when he liked them as individuals. He once wrote: 'I crossed the Channel with an intimate friend, a Tory peer, who remarked to me that, as a Liberal, I was sure to get some office quickly, for we had so few among us who could be trusted not to steal the spoons—a cheery specimen of Tory mentality.'

Brother Eustace was basically bored with life as a Liberal MP commuting between Banbury and Westminster, so he joined the local Territorials (the Oxfordshire Huzzars Imperial Yeomanry) along with his friend and fellow Liberal MP, Winston Churchill. Judging from correspondence that I have been sent by Churchill College, Cambridge, both men received 'special treatment' from relevant authorities. Here is a note from a senior officer in Southern Command dated January 1907:

With reference to your letter asking for a report on the case of Major Winston Churchill MP and Major the Hon. Eustace Fiennes MP and their failure to present themselves for examination for Field Rank on promotion, I recommend that these Officers be excused this examination for the following reasons . . .

Both officers have exceptionally long and meritorious experience on active service. Both officers are occupied with Parliamentary duties. Major Churchill has also to attend to official duties and Major Fiennes has a City business to look after. Both officers are natural leaders and thoroughly competent in every way.

Some sixty years later, with the British Army of the Rhine in Germany, I requested permission to miss my captain to major promotion exam, owing to special circumstances (an expedition to Africa). I was refused and subsequently failed the exam. It's all right for some.

The Fienneses and the Churchills of Oxfordshire, were traditional peers whose status came largely from the great estates they had inherited. However, during Edward VII's reign new peers in the Lords were no longer necessarily large landowners. Landed estates all over Britain were fragmenting and being sold off to previous tenants; a true sign of the times. In Edinburgh in 1900 half of Scotland was for sale in the hands of a single Edinburgh lawyer. By 1910 eighty of the hundred wealthiest families in Britain had made their fortunes from manufacturing and not, as had been the case at Broughton for centuries, from rental and wool.

Churchill, Lloyd George and their Liberals, the Fiennes clan included, were in the vanguard of a raft of proposed taxes, including a super tax on the incomes of the very rich, and various taxes on property. Forty years earlier, governments had treated Britain's poor as 'those vast, miserable, unmanageable masses of sunken people' and 'that enormous mass of paupers'. Only in Edward's reign did the Liberals believe that they could actually alter the status of the truly poor by clever handling of the economy. Poverty was neither inevitable nor a necessary result of capitalist societies. Edward's reign also saw the trades union movement double its membership to over four million, with the new Labour party gaining ground against both Tories and Liberals.

Edward VII was the first ruler to experience the full development of the national political parties and a franchise which included the greater part of the adult male population. He no longer held any royal veto on governmental legislation, could no longer sack ministers he disliked, nor alter the direction any Cabinet had decided to take on any matter at home or abroad. He once wrote to an adviser: 'The Cabinet is apparently so powerful a body that neither I nor the Prime Minister can gainsay them.' Edward died of a series of heart attacks in May 1910 and was much mourned, as was summed up in a note by one of the secretaries of state: 'The feeling of grief and personal loss throughout the country, indeed through Europe, is extraordinary. It is in a way deeper and keener than when Queen Victoria died—more personal. He had just the character that Englishmen, at any rate, thoroughly like and understand. He combined regal dignity with good nature and strict regard for form with entire absence of pomp.'

The Prince of Wales was crowned King George V and was to prove as popular over his twenty-five-year reign as his namesake, George IV, had been unpopular. As prince he had been sent by his father on a good many royal tours of the colonies and dominions. He was politically savvy but content to be a constitutional monarch, much as is Queen Elizabeth, his granddaughter, today.

Two years after George's accession, Geoffrey Fiennes, Lord Saye, finally moved his family back permanently into Broughton (after twenty-five years of on-off rental), but then the Great War broke out, so both Geoffrey and three of his sons joined up, as, once more, did Eustace. By then Eustace had spent two years (1912–14) in the crucial pre-war period as principal (parliamentary) private secretary to the First Lord of the Admiralty, his old friend, Winston Churchill. In the new world of the early twentieth century, Churchill's star had definitely begun to shine, though it was to suffer a good number of ups and downs. Never afraid of switching his stance (or even his party), Winston was a good friend of Eustace down the years. Both men were of the Victorian era, but the great personalities of those times were, by 1914, long dead: Gladstone, Salisbury and the old queen herself. Those years and their prevailing views were quickly eclipsed by the roar of the new century. Now there were telephones, electricity, typewriters, fast cars and good roads, wireless and aeroplanes. Even public cinemas. And everyone who did not have them, wanted them, or so it seemed. The biggest changes of all were to be the results of the catastrophe of the Kaiser's war.

The month before the war began, July 1914, was not exactly peaceful on the home front, either. Miners, railway and transport workers were threatening mass strike action, 200,000 men were under arms in Protestant Ulster and in the Catholic South, with civil war imminent. Nationalist groups were fermenting rebellion in Egypt and India, all of which demanded a strong, calm response from government and a reliable, sympathetic monarch as figurehead for a nation under threat. Lloyd George and King George V were to provide both.

Nobody in Britain wanted war. Of the various countries involved, she had less to gain from the fighting and less to fear from staying out of it. As the world's first industrial nation, Britain had evolved a liberal, capitalist, democratic system that needed both world peace and free trade to thrive. Its success on a global basis was thwarted by the Kaiser and his Prussians. The spark that kindled the Great War, as many a schoolchild has been taught, was the assassination in Sarajevo of an Austrian archduke. But the tensions which finally exploded in the summer of 1914 had accumulated over many years.

Herbert Asquith, the Liberal prime minister, voiced his thoughts on 1 August 1914, the day Germany declared war on Russia:

I am quite clear in my mind as to what is right and wrong. 1. We have no obligation of any kind either to France or Russia to give them military or naval help. 2. The dispatch of the

441

Expeditionary Force to help France at this moment is out of the question and would serve no object. 3. We must not forget the ties created by our long-standing and intimate friendship with France. 4. It is against British interests that France should be wiped out as a Great Power. 5. We cannot allow Germany to use the Channel as a hostile base. 6. We have obligations to Belgium to prevent it being utilized and absorbed by Germany.

All over Europe young men volunteered to fight the Germans. Britain had not fought a major war for over a century. Her few professional soldiers were less excited and their favourite song of the day was:

Send out the Army and the Navy
Send out the rank and file
Send out the brave Territorials,
They'll face the danger with a smile
Send out the boys of the old brigade
They will keep old England free
Send out my mother, my sister and my brother,
But for Gawd's Sake, don't send me

Eustace left Winston's department on the outbreak of war and went to fight with the Oxfordshire Yeomanry in the Flanders mud. His son, my uncle Johnnie, joined the Gordon Highlanders fighting nearby. Johnnie's younger brother, born in 1902, was my father Ranulph (named after our ancestor killed at Towton in 1461) but he was, of course, too young to sign up. He and Johnnie had spent happy times at

442

Broughton, but were brought up at Studland Bay in Dorset. Their South African mother, my grandmother Florrie, was always the centre of a hive of activity and opened two convalescent homes for the war-wounded, one in Dunkirk and one in her own Studland House. Her French hospital was shelled by the Germans, after which she had to close it down and escape. She was awarded a French medal and the OBE.

After being fortunate enough to survive Flanders, Eustace was sent as intelligence officer of the Royal Naval Division to help defend Antwerp for the Belgians. Eight thousand men of the division went with him, and Churchill arrived that October to assess the situation. His report to General Kitchener summed up the Belgian army as 'weary and disheartened and the ground so waterlogged, nobody can dig trenches'. With the division cooped up in the city, Eustace borrowed Churchill's driver (Lord Bellew) and headed south to meet informants. To his surprise, he found that the German chief, von Moltke, had decided to surround Antwerp and his divisions were already on the move. Eustace rushed back to alert his bosses, General Paris and the Belgian General de Brockville. Thanks entirely to his initiative and to his brave Belgian informers, most of the Royal Naval Division escaped the German trap two days before the city surrendered.

The original plan of the Kaiser, to finish his lightning war in only forty days, foundered due to unexpected Belgian resistance which slowed down the German advance, so that by the time they did reach France, the French army and British Expeditionary Force were there to meet them.

And thereabouts they stayed for the next four years of murderous trench warfare.

In 1915 Churchill and Lloyd George, against the advice of Kitchener, Admiral Jackie Fisher and others, encouraged an alternative front to be opened up by the navy against Germany's Turkish allies in the Dardanelles. Eustace was heavily involved with Churchill in the planning and execution of the subsequent Gallipoli campaign. In the spring of 1915 Eustace wrote with an optimistic tone:

My dear Winston

Everyone is pleased with what you've done for the Division, not only getting it into this show but having supported us in every way. Three ships are already here in Malta and others expected tomorrow. The men's health is excellent. All inoculated. Strenuous training and lectures on board. I will write and keep you updated. They talk a lot about the Canal here, but I think that is just a clever Turk move to detain a large force here. The division should do well.

Eustace

The whole Gallipoli idea was intended to circumvent the stalemate and huge loss of life on the Western Front but, due to gross mismanagement, the plan failed dismally and Churchill was sacked. The main problem with the Gallipoli plan was that, when Eustace and his naval force arrived there and the army contingent landed, they found themselves unable to break out of a narrow bridgehead on a rocky, sun-beaten, disease-ridden peninsula overlooked by enemy artillery. Naval bombardment did little to help. One Leonard Thompson, a farmhand from Suffolk, wrote about landing as an infantryman at Gallipoli:

The first thing we saw were big wrecked Turkish guns, the second a big marquee . . . [like at a] village fête . . . we all rushed to it, [but it was] laced up. We unlaced it . . . It was full of corpses. Dead Englishmen, lines of them with their eyes wide open . . . I'd never seen a dead man before and here I was looking at two or three hundred of them . . . I was very shocked [and] thought of Suffolk . . .

[One night] we had to move on to the third line of trenches . . . but, when we got to the communications trench, we found it so full of dead men we could hardly move. Their faces were quite black and you couldn't tell Turk from English. There was the most terrible stink, and for a while there was nothing but the living being sick on to the dead. I did sentry again that night . . . I knew the next sentry up quite well. I remembered him in Suffolk singing to his horses as he ploughed. Now he fell back with a great scream and a look of surprise—dead. It is quick anyway, I thought. On June 4th we went over the top . . . On June 6th my favourite officer was killed and no end of us butchered . . . Of the sixty men I had started out to war with, there were only three left.

We set to work to bury people. We pushed them into the sides of the trench but bits of them kept getting uncovered and sticking out, like people in a badly made bed. Hands were the worst; they would escape from the sand, pointing, begging—even waving. There was one which we all shook when we passed, saying, 'Good Morning', in a posh voice. Everybody did it. The bottom of the trench was springy like a mattress because of all the bodies underneath. At night, when the stench was worse, we tied [anti-gassing] crêpe round our mouths and noses . . . the flies entered the trenches by night and lined them completely with a density which was like moving cloth. We killed millions by slapping our spades along the trench walls but the next night it would be just as bad. We were all lousy and we couldn't stop shitting because we had caught dysentery. We wept, not because we were frightened but because we were so dirty.

When the survivors were evacuated along with their nightmares, they left 46,000 bodies behind. Eustace was on one of the last ships to depart back to the hell-hole of the Western Front, which the Gallipoli experience had been designed to circumvent.

For Eustace's many activities for the empire over several decades and for his dedicated years as a Liberal MP in Banbury (but presumably not for his part in the planning of the Gallipoli debacle), Eustace was made a baronet by the king. He chose to be Baronet of Banbury, the title I inherited at birth. Edward Heath put a stop to hereditary titles in the 1970s, so we baronets are a dying breed.

At fifty-two Eustace was a touch old for the

front, so he accepted the job of quartermaster general of the Royal Naval Division in Plymouth. In August 1917 he wrote to Winston, complaining about the leader of their party. 'There are no two men I have fought harder for and stuck more faithfully to than Lloyd George and yourself, but the former has treated me very badly and I cannot make out why.' I have tried to unearth the facts of Lloyd George's dislike of Eustace, but without success. It is unlikely to have been due to Gallipoli since, like Churchill, he was fully in favour of that campaign.

In July 1916 the British army chief, grim Scotsman General Haig, commanded the great offensive of the Somme, which broke all manner of appalling casualty records by insanely attacking the strongest German defences, barbed wire, machine guns and massed artillery with 100,000 British and Commonwealth soldiers. By nightfall on the first day 20,000 British corpses festooned the wire and another 40,000 were injured or (the lucky ones) in German hands. For this ghastly toll, the greatest recorded one-day loss ever sustained by an army in history, two miles of pock-marked mud was the total gain. The entire four-month Somme offensive gained the British seven miles and cost them 420,000 casualties.

Germany's chief allies, the Turks, were eliminated by a clever campaign waged under General Allenby (with help from Colonel T. E. Lawrence 'of Arabia') and launched from Egypt through Palestine into Syria. But the Western Front continued to stagnate, and in May 1916, in order to counter the ongoing death toll, conscription was imposed. Each British attempt to crack the stalemate in the trenches ended in yet more carnage. Eventually huge financial, material and manpower support from the United States enabled the allies to overwhelm the Germans who, by the war's end, had committed eleven million men, of whom 1,774,000 were killed and four million wounded. British dead totalled 750,000, with 2,500,000 wounded, and many disabled for life. European, Commonwealth and American casualties were also huge. It is surprising, therefore, that in Britain at least, steady support for pursuit of the war lasted throughout the four years of the conflict.

In 1917 at the Battle of Arras, my only uncle, Captain John Fiennes, led a company of the 2nd Battalion of the Gordon Highlanders against German trenches and was killed, aged twenty-one. Eustace and Florrie were devastated.

When Lloyd George formed a two-party coalition to conduct the war through an all-powerful war cabinet, a mighty state war-machine enervated the nation and brought about massive industrial and social change. Collectivist control and state power dominated, to the extent that Ramsay MacDonald, the first Labour prime minister, noted with irony that the war had achieved far more for social reform than had all the campaigns of the trades unions and of progressive do-gooders over the previous half century. Social welfare, housing policy, the status of women: all were affected, to the benefit of the poor. Coal mines, railways and the merchant navy were placed under state control. Edward VII's Liberal Britain was now an evolving corporate state. Marxism was not needed. A new Ministry of

Health was set up to co-ordinate health and national insurance. Women, and they were numerically in the majority after the slaughter, were at last given the vote with universal suffrage for all men over twenty-one, but for women over thirty.

Abroad, the colonies, whose citizens had died in their thousands for the empire and the king, naturally flexed their muscles for greater independence from the mother country. But the empire did not shrink. In fact, due to the many secret treaties between the Allies during and after the war, Britain gained vast new territories in the Middle East, oil-rich Mesopotamia and the Persian Gulf. Meanwhile, thanks to the insatiable demand for wartime munitions workers and merchant seamen, there were well over 10,000 black citizens in Britain by the war's end.

Germany, and all things German, remained unpopular for a long while, and the king sensibly switched the title of the royal family from Saxe-Coburg to Windsor. At the same time, at Crufts dog show, German Shepherds were renamed Alsatians.

The coalition government of Welshman Lloyd George, the great wartime leader, triumphed in the first post-war election. But soon after, he lost his reputation with Labour when he responded to mass unemployment rallies and strikes by using troops as strike-breakers. There were many minor strikes between 1919 and 1922. Then, after Baldwin's Conservatives' defeat of Lloyd George, a period of peace until, in 1925, Baldwin fell out with the miners and the Trades Union Congress (TUC). The General Strike followed, with the unions challenging the government with their full economic strength. This was billed as an all-out class war, but there was no violence either from or against the police or armed forces. Coppers and strikers played football together and the middle classes enjoyed the novel excitement of strike-breaking by driving buses and lorries. After nine days the TUC called off the strike, acknowledging the abject failure of its main aim (to achieve a subsidy for the miners), despite having brought Britain to a virtual standstill. Britain's class war had been a brief, but bloodless, event at a time when, throughout Europe, governments were being toppled, workers rebelling and fascists menacing. At the very time Lenin was the great hero of the people in Russia, King George V was all-popular in Britain.

Lenin died of a stroke in 1924, his corpse was reverently swathed in a red flag saved from the bloody Paris Commune of 1871 and his brain was removed for Soviet studies to identify the precise location of the cells responsible for his revolutionary genius. So died the man who replaced one form of Russian tyranny with another that would keep his (and many other) people oppressed for eighty long years. He once said: 'Liberty is precious—so precious that it must be rationed.'

The British National Debt, largely caused by the need to pay for wartime loans, soared by 1920 to £7,875 million. Irish troubles, renewed with vigour by the Fenians in the Easter Rising of 1916, led to vicious repression by the crown, but in 1920 Lloyd George granted the Republic of Ireland Home Rule, a concession eagerly noted by nationalists in

India.

After the war Eustace joined the Colonial Office and was appointed Governor General of the Seychelles. He had hoped for New Zealand because he felt he had got on well with the New Zealanders at the Dardanelles but he was told not to be over-ambitious when he not very tactfully applied for a transfer after only two months in the Caribbean. Settling down in the Seychelles, he was shocked at the lack of humane provision for the poor and the lepers and began to institute all sorts of social legislation to look after them, which included building a poor house which survived right up until 2006, and a hospital. While his good works put the Seychelles in the forefront of British colonies in their care for the destitute, the Colonial Office was to note that the major criticism of my grandfather's administration was his propensity to embark on projects without considering how they would be funded. His successor found he had been left with the bill for the imported building materials for the hospital.

In 1921 Churchill, recovering his Gallipoli-dented reputation, became colonial secretary and turned part of the remains of the defeated Turkish empire into Iraq. He promoted Eustace to Governor-General of the Leeward Islands. Granny Florrie, still mourning my uncle's death at Arras, had persuaded Eustace to ask my father Ranulph (then sixteen and at Eton) whether he would prefer to stay there or have a tutor and shark fish in the Caribbean. He chose the latter and was sad when the time came to head for home and Sandhurst, aged eighteen. Eustace and Florrie loved Antigua and the Antiguans. They stayed there far longer than most governors' families, from 1921 until 1929, and both worked to relieve the poor, the homeless, the sick, and those left bereft by the perennial hurricanes, with sleeves rolled up in the heat personally administering inoculations in little villages.

And Eustace continued to spend money without permission. Sir Samuel Wilson, Head of the Colonial Service, was quoted as saying: 'What can we do with Fiennes? He asks to spend thousands of pounds on village water services. We tell him to wait. He cables back, "Could not wait. Money spent. Villagers drinking water."' Once more his passion for improving the lot of the islanders took over, regardless of economics. As well as the water supply, he introduced electricity and a radio link with other islands, he built a jetty and encouraged tourism. Bakers had to have health certificates and the first city bus service was inaugurated—the first bus being named Florrie. There was also another home for the poor which was such a success that it was soon grossly overcrowded. An island historian records how Eustace and Florrie dealt with this:

The Governor and Lady Fiennes, who were both keen dancers, arranged for a dance to be held there, during which those who were seen to be dancing in too sprightly a manner were later told to leave and find work. It was a method of weeding out the unworthy which annoyed no one, greatly appealed to the population at large, and only enhanced the Governor's reputation as a man of the people. His impact on ordinary black Antiguans was summed up by one of them, a man named Samuel Smith, whose colourful and often moving memoirs provide a unique record of estate life in the first half of the twentieth century: 'He [Fiennes] was a melle (well-informed) man. He love nega (black people's) business and he got to know what was happening in the island. I think he very well understood the feelings of the negas. He took pride in his work and he wanted that his term of office would mean something to the people. For me, he was entirely different to all the governors that reach the island before and I believe he will remain the best ever.'

Eustace retired, aged sixty-seven, and raised funds for the Hammersmith Hospital, of which he was the appeals chairman. He remained an ardent Liberal in an age of Labour and Tories. He was very proud of my father, Ranulph, who joined Scotland's only cavalry regiment, the Royal Scots Greys in India and was in 1929 appointed aide-de-camp to the Governor General of Canada. They spent many happy weekends, when my father was on leave, at Broughton. He used to swim round the moat for exercise. That was a time, the late twenties, when in southern England and the midlands there was growing contentment and prosperity. Suburban middle-class estates sprang up in mushroom clumps, subsidised by Neville Chamberlain and Stanley Baldwin. By 1930 there were over a million privately owned cars, wirelesses over which the BBC spread the news in prim voices, whilst bad memories of war and the General Strike grew dim. The danger of a Marxist revolution in Britain faded as Stalin and his gulags alerted would-be radicals against the perils of the left and, down in Munich, Hitler had only just begun to rant. Forty-three million folk lived in Britain, and many were simply content with the status quo. The empire was still, just, loyal to the king, and Kipling, still churning out his wonderful prose and verse, assured the nation that this was so.

In 1929 and the early thirties a worldwide downward spiral of trade and employment hit Britain hard, followed by despair in declining industries, hunger marches, and life on the dole. Nonetheless, the monarchy remained popular at all levels of society, and George V's annual pilgrimage to the Wembley Cup Final continued to be greeted with deafening applause and folk stood proud for the National Anthem. Meanwhile, 'over there', totalitarianism engulfed Germany, Italy and Austria, whilst France and Spain writhed painfully within their republics. Never mind the hell of Eastern Europe.

My father, back from Canada in 1931, met and married my mother, Audrey Newson, whose parents lived much of the time in Calcutta, for her father was Governor of the Imperial Bank of India. My parents had three daughters in the thirties and lived wherever the Royal Scots Greys needed my father. In 1934 he was posted to MI5 and did a stint of spying on Britain's French allies whilst attached to a French cavalry unit in the Pyrenees. His spying spree continued into 1936, and a later note in my mother's diary mentions a connected incident.

Eustace had been entertaining Hitler's great

friend, the Princess Hohenlohe. He [Eustace] was not one of the Anglo-German Fellowship but, like them, he believed the Nazis were a key obstacle to the Soviets. They were all later shocked when the two countries made a pact.

Eustace asked Ranulph to invite the Princess and her colleague Hauptman Weiderman, Hitler's equerry, to the Aldershot Military Tattoo. They accepted with alacrity, clearly hoping to gain information on the latest military tactics and equipment. Weiderman even refused an invitation he had that evening for dinner with Neville Chamberlain, our Prime Minister.

As it turned out, the theme of the tattoo that year was the Cromwellian period, so the 'latest technology' on show was frock coats and muskets. Scotland Yard arrested the princess soon after and she was imprisoned in the USA. Despite all this, Eustace, in his eighties, developed a hatred of the Soviets and decided 'that German chappie Adolf is the best thing since sliced bread to halt the Commie advance'. A lot of people shared his view until too late. Even his old friend Churchill had, at the Treasury, been keen to encourage naval cuts and other savings from the War Office budget.

In 1936 George V died, his eldest son, the Duke of Windsor, briefly Edward VIII, soon abdicated in order to marry an American divorcee, and Edward's younger brother became King George VI, a nervous, shy man with a bad stutter, chronic gastric problems, knock knees and a lovely Scottish wife, later to become Queen Elizabeth the Queen

Mother, who died, beloved by the nation, in 2002.

30

COLONEL OF THE GREYS

The utter horror of the Kaiser's War lived on in the
nightmares, the burnt lungs and the limbless
stumps of many millions, especially the Europeans,
in whose midst that trouble had begun. Surely, a
mere twenty years later, nobody would be stupid
enough to risk causing a repeat performance? And
yet Germany, one of the most civilised, culturally
brilliant nations on earth, the home of Einstein
and Beethoven, voted for Adolf Hitler and his
Nazis to govern them.

In the year of King George VI's succession to
the throne of Great Britain, on 18 July 1936 to be
exact, Hitler found a wonderful way of testing
tactics and military equipment for his coming
Apocalypse—the Spanish Civil War. All those
Spaniards who hated their country's republican
status joined General Francisco Franco's side,
including monarchists, Catholics, all branches of
the army, the Fascist party, the landowning class
and the bourgeoisie. Franco's opposition, who
supported the Republic, included the unions, the
Socialists, the Communists and the Anarchists. As
in all civil wars, brother killed brother and the
bitterness echoed down the generations. After
three long years, Franco eventually triumphed and
signed a five-year friendship treaty with Hitler.
Five hundred thousand people had died, including

100,000 from disease or starvation and 100,000 by murder or execution.

For the Germans, the interlude provided excellent practice for the Second World War. Meekly the British and French failed to react (except for loud calls for military intervention by an isolated, unpopular, back-bencher in Britain called Churchill). For the rest, the way forward was appeasement and non-intervention at all costs. Chamberlain clearly favoured this craven policy, and Hitler certainly believed that Britain would stay out of any conflict he caused that did not involve its precious empire.

Eustace and Florrie joined my mother and three sisters in bidding my father goodbye as the Royal Scots Greys, complete with their five hundred grey horses, were sent out to Palestine in 1938. Nobody, even then, had seriously considered the sacrilege of 'mechanising' Scotland's Waterloo-famous and only cavalry regiment. So, while just about every other cavalry unit everywhere slaughtered their horses and taught professional horsemen the theory of cogs and pistons, the Scots Greys settled down in Rehovot, one of the oldest Jewish settlements in Palestine, helping the local police keep the peace between Arabs and Jews and search for known rebels and hidden arms caches. My father was the major in charge of 'B' Squadron (which I joined twenty-four years later), and my mother joined him in a 'very hot bungalow' for a while in between his patrols, cordons and searches.

Meanwhile Churchill's call to arms caused Chamberlain to begin rearmament in a rush and to commit Britain to defend Poland, should Hitler attack it. When he did so that September of 1939,

Chamberlain declared war on Germany with the full support of all the British nations and dominions. As twenty years before, the British found unity at the last moment and plunged with full commitment into the fray.

For six months of Phoney War nothing happened, which allowed Britain feverishly to get its act together just in time. Then, in April 1940, Hitler took Norway and Denmark with his fearsome *blitzkrieg* or 'lightning war', followed four weeks later by equally crushing victories in the Low Countries and France. The Nazis seemed utterly invincible, as all-powerful as the Mogul hordes of Genghis Khan or Caesar's legions. Britain's entire army in Europe and the French military remnants were forced to retreat in confusion towards Dunkirk, and only just escaped thanks to a flotilla of naval and civilian craft which removed them from the snapping jaws of the Nazis at the very last minute.

With all mainland Europe under Hitler, co-Fascist Mussolini sensibly joined the war as his ally, which overnight made the Middle East a new theatre of war, since Italian forces in Libya and North East Africa posed an obvious threat to key Allied strategic features, including the Suez Canal. My father and his fellow Scots Greys eventually (in September 1940) received the long awaited news that they would not, after all, have to attack German panzers with a cavalry charge. A telegram from an ex-cavalry officer, the new prime minister, Winston Churchill, to the chief of staff stated: 'I am very pleased about the Cavalry in Palestine. It has been heartbreaking for me to watch these splendid units waste away for a whole year. The sooner they form . . . armoured units the better. These historic regular regiments have a right to play a man's part in the war.' As training major, my father had the job of removing the horses that his men loved, and most of which had names as well as mere army horse numbers. He also rented bicycles and had the Jocks learn basic tank tactics and troop formations, as per the relevant British army training manual.

After Dunkirk, Britain herself was Hitler's next target and Churchill was everybody's choice to stand up to Hitler, for he embodied the national sense of patriotic unity which none of his contemporaries could match. His famous oratory of June 1940 was an example of his ability to inspire:

> Even though large tracts of Europe and many old and famous States have fallen or may fall into the grip of the Gestapo and all the odious apparatus of Nazi rule, we shall not flag or fail. We shall go on to the end. We shall fight in France, we shall fight on the seas and oceans, we shall fight with growing confidence and growing strength in the air, we shall defend our island, whatever the cost may be. We shall fight on the beaches, we shall fight on the landing grounds, we shall fight in the fields and in the streets, we shall fight in the hills; we shall never surrender.

It's a familiar quotation but worth pondering still. And he continues:

What General Weygand called the 'Battle of

France' is over. I expect that the battle of Britain is about to begin. Upon this battle depends the survival of Christian civilisation. Upon it depends our own British life and the long continuity of our institutions and our Empire. The whole fury and might of the enemy must very soon be turned on us. Hitler knows that he will have to break us in this island or lose the war. If we can stand up to him all Europe may be free, and the life of the world may move forward into broad, sunlit uplands; but if we fail then the whole world, including the United States, and all that we have known and cared for, will sink into the abyss of a new dark age made more sinister, and perhaps more prolonged, by the lights of a perverted science. Let us therefore brace ourselves to our duty and so bear ourselves that if the British Commonwealth and Empire lasts for a thousand years men will still say, 'This was their finest hour.'

But the destruction of Hitler was a long way off in the summer of 1940. In June he took the Channel Islands and ordered Operation Sea Lion, the invasion of Britain. The Luftwaffe would first neutralise the RAF to ensure the safety of the invasion fleet, and Air Chief Goering, with over 3,000 aircraft only twenty-five minutes away from Britain's key airfields, was confident of success in the skies. On 15 September, seventy-five German fighters were shot down to a loss of thirty-four RAF planes. The Battle of Britain was under way; Spitfires and Hurricanes against Messerschmidts. Goering's prophecy that he would crush the RAF in four days proved hollow for, by late September, the air was still full of Spitfires, and Hitler, knowing when he was beaten, switched to a massive night blitz of London and other major cities to crush British morale.

In mid-September, the Luftwaffe lost sixty bombers on one London raid. The 2,500 pilots of Fighter Command had by then shot down 1,268 aircraft for the loss of 832. Hitler cancelled the invasion, having suffered his first defeat. Britain and her dominions stood alone against him until, eventually, the Soviet Union and then the USA joined in. The king and queen stayed at Buckingham Palace throughout the blitz, although the building was damaged during nine different raids. On one of many royal visits to the bombed areas of London, the queen remarked, 'I'm glad we've been bombed at the Palace. It makes me feel I can look the East End in the face.'

At Broughton, Lord and Lady Saye and Sele were in mourning from the spring of 1941 when their second son, Ingelram Fiennes, was killed in action aged nineteen, flying with the RAF Volunteer Reserves.

Rommel and his Afrika Korps grabbed Libya in 1941, while Greece and Cyprus were lost to Axis forces and a pro-German government took over Iraq. A detachment of the newly-armoured Scots Greys was immediately sent from Haifa to Baghdad to tie up with troops from India who landed at Basra. Between them they achieved the surrender of Baghdad before new Axis troops could reach that key city. This Scots Greys' success was rewarded by the delivery of their brand new 'General Stuart' light tanks to replace their grey

461

horses. The Jocks, hardly a man of whom had not been a highly proficient horseman, soon became efficient as gunners, loaders, radio operators and drivers.

That December the Japanese attacked Pearl Harbor and, three days later, came across the two finest battleships of the Royal Navy leaving Singapore with no air cover. Dive bombers sank both ships and, two months later, Japanese armies reached Singapore where they forced the surrender of 80,000 British and empire troops. Churchill described the event as 'the worst capitulation in British history'. Malaya and Hong Kong also fell to the Japanese.

Two days after the fall of Singapore my father took command of the Scots Greys, by then consisting of two heavy squadrons of Grant tanks and a light squadron of Stuarts. They were part of the Eighth Army and confronted Rommel's Afrika Korps veterans, whose dreaded 88 mm anti-tank guns could pierce the armour of my father's tanks at ranges of 3,000 metres. My father wrote home, using careful phraseology to appease the censors: 'I am now taking care of the baby, and you know what trouble they can be when they are teething.' I wonder if he meant the men or the tanks.

Rommel's aim was to break through the British lines in order to seize Cairo and Suez. But thanks to superior strategy by General Montgomery, Rommel was halted in the region of Alam Halfa and largely cut off from his fuel supply lines. At the end of August Rommel attacked with cover from Stuka dive-bombers and using many of his Mark IV special tanks with their highly effective new 75 mm guns. A tank regiment of the London

Yeomanry was soon wiped out by the Mark IVs, leaving a vulnerable gap in the British defence line. My father ordered the Scots Greys to 'charge' downhill to close the gap at the critical moment, and thus prevented further German progress. By nightfall twenty-six German tanks, 'bagged by the Jocks', burnt fiery red in the desert dusk, but at dawn Rommel attacked again. This time, still unable to break through, he gave up his attempt, and the Battle of Alam Halfa was won. The Scots Greys had done well in their first major fight with no horses.

Rommel's toll in the battle was 53 tanks, 700 motor vehicles, 70 anti-tank guns and 4,500 soldiers killed or wounded, against 1,600 casualties on the British side. The battle proved critical to the whole desert war, for it lost Rommel the last good chance he had of overall victory in Africa before Montgomery's build-up would make such an outcome impossible, even for Rommel.

In October the far better known, but actually less crucial, Battle of El Alamein again involved my father and the regiment in the key tank role against Rommel. My father, directing operations from his turretless Stuart tank, 'Astra', was slightly wounded in the neck and leg. With only slight exaggeration, Churchill later commented: 'Before El Alamein we never had a victory, after El Alamein we never had a defeat.' Various vicious tank battles then followed in quick succession as the Scots Greys caught up with detachments of Rommel's men. 'I had to move very fast to keep in front of the Colonel,' one Scots Grey officer wrote in his post-Alamein report. My father was known throughout his army days as 'Lugs' Fiennes, presumably on account of his slightly prominent ears. At the later Battle of Nofilia, as one squadron leader reported: 'The going was all soft sand. All the time I was getting stick from Lugs over the air for not coming on quicker . . . How Lugs ever managed to find his way round, up and down wadis, over about four miles of country, and arrive in the right place plumb on the flank of the enemy, I don't know. However, I am sure his quick decision and quick action won the day.'

My father wrote home to my mother:

19.7.42 When will this cursed war be over? When I see the things going on around me I can't help thinking that most of us must be mad. Why we ever allowed these filthy Germans to get up again after the last war, I can't think. I hope they give them hell for all the misery they've caused . . .

18.8.42 I've slept the last 2 months under the stars and on the ground, whether sandy, stony, hard or soft. No bother with those lilo things . . .

6.9.42 If the Russians can hold out a little longer, the winter will arrive and I very much doubt that the dirty Huns can last out another. Anyhow I doubt whether they will survive the 2nd Front which I daresay will start next spring.

29.10.42 I'm in a Casualty Station 12 miles back. I will go back up tomorrow. It is like having been peppered by a shot gun. I have small wounds all the way up my thigh, right side and arm. We had no sleep for 3 nights. My knee swelled up. I was about to take a pot at an Eyetie outpost with the Browning when an explosive bullet hit its side and the bits got me. But it was fun seeing the Eyeties bolting from their holes like rabbits. I don't think many of them waited long enough to get killed.

23.12.42 I am in No. 9 General Hospital Heliopolis. I have a deep wound in the thigh on the inside; it missed the femoral artery although it laid it bare for 2 inches, *just* missed other vital parts and ruined my beautiful green cord trousers. It was caused by a bit of a shell which penetrated the tank. A second direct hit missed me but killed Mark Bodley's son, my operator, outright. I also have a gash in my forearm.

Against this we got 200 German prisoners, 6 anti-tank guns and 4 big German tanks. I'll be in bed, they say, for ten days. I've got a steel bit travelling round my neck. When it comes out, I'll keep it for the children . . .

My father was sent to America for two months whilst recovering from his wounds, in order to lecture to US troops about desert warfare, but he returned to the regiment in time to command it for the Eighth Army at Salerno, the toe of Italy and the key to attacking the soft underbelly of Europe.

As at Alam Halfa and El Alamein, the Scots Greys' role at Salerno proved critical to the outcome of the fierce battle for the beachhead. The regiment withstood German counter-attacks, fought hard and knocked out a great deal of German armour. At one point two Jocks, briefly captured by Germans, escaped to rejoin the regiment and reported that their interrogators, following their capture, had wanted to know the correct pronunciation of the names of each of the three colonels of the Greys: Twisleton, Wykeham and Fiennes.

One Greys' counter-attack forced a large enemy contingent to retreat, another killed two hundred enemy by night, and the Jock tank gunners generally outgunned their German counterparts at most close and long distance encounters. Although they did not know it at the time, this four-day battle just inland from the beaches had seen off a real pending crisis, for the Germans had succeeded in driving a wedge between the key British and American units and almost defeated the Fifth Army before the Eighth Army could cement their post-landing link-up.

My father now needed to find the regiment a safe route through the mountain pass overlooking the Bay of Naples, so he went with the brigade commander and his intelligence officer to check the road. A shell burst near them and all were hit by shrapnel. My father was, as before, not badly hurt, although by that time his body was host to a fair number of steel splinters. Two battalions of American infantry were put under his command for the next advance, but his tanks were unable to support them closely, due to rough lava beds spawned by Vesuvius, so the enemy was not dislodged. Eventually they made it to and through Naples city and were much kissed by Italian girls.

North and west of Naples, the country was hilly, wooded and dangerous for tanks. So my father reconnoitred every part of the route prior to letting any of his tanks advance. He found one bridge fully prepared for demolition and surprised three German sappers resting in a nearby cave. He had forgotten his revolver, but pointed his briar pipe at them and said, *'Hände Hoch!'* Their hands duly shot up and, taking them prisoner to his driver, he retrieved his gun and made them remove the bridge explosives.

Unfortunately, his habit of going out ahead ended on 11 November when he and one of his officers both trod on S-Type anti-personnel mines and were wounded. My father died of his wounds in Naples General Hospital twelve days later. He had briefly come home on leave four months earlier, and I was conceived then. So I never met my father; nor my grandfather Eustace, for he died earlier in 1943.

My father was awarded the Distinguished Service Order for his leadership at Salerno. The colonel who took over the Greys from him, wrote:

Lieutenant-Colonel Sir Ranulph Fiennes will always be remembered by those who served under him as an outstanding leader and a vivid personality with a keen sense of humour . . . he had played a major part in the Regiment's conversion to armour . . . He nursed the Regiment successfully through its early battles and made it a confident and effective fighting instrument, with a high reputation both on and off the battlefield . . . A Royal Horse Artillery Commanding Officer . . . said that he had supported many armoured regiments, from the earliest days in the desert, but had never seen one fight like the Greys. To him [Lugs] more than to any other individual it was due that, when mechanisation came at last, the traditions of the cavalry trooper who fought under Marlborough, Wellington and Haig were carried over to the trooper of the armoured regiment, who was soon to fight again on the same well-worn battlefield of the Low Countries, confident that he belonged to a Regiment, which in its old role, but with new weapons, was still 'second to none'.

One of his lieutenants, Lord Althorp, the father of Princess Diana, told me years later that my father had been the best commanding officer any man could hope to serve under. I dearly wish I had met him. I grew up with only one ambition: to command the Royal Scots Greys, as he had.

A psychologist would probably say that my growing up without ever meeting my father or grandfather, nor having had brothers, uncles or any other male relatives, was bound to make me keen to trace my forebears. Whether or not that is so, I have no idea, but I do know that I have enjoyed every minute of rootling about with the history of my ancestors, of Broughton and of my country. You should give it a go, as you never know whose blood may run through your veins. It could be Genghis Khan, Florence Nightingale, or even Caligula.

Here are a couple of generalisations about England that would be accepted by almost all observers. One is that the English are not gifted artistically. They are not as musical as the Germans or Italians, painting and sculpture have never flourished in England as they have in France. Another is that, as Europeans go, the English are not intellectual. They have a horror of abstract thought, they feel no need for any philosophy or systematic 'world view'. Nor is this because they are 'practical', as they are so fond of claiming for themselves. One has only to look at their methods of town-planning and water-supply, their obstinate clinging to everything that is out-of-date and a nuisance, a spelling system that defies analysis and a system of weights and measures that is intelligible only to compilers of arithmetic books, to see how little they care about mere efficiency.

George Orwell, *England, Your England* (1941)

ACKNOWLEDGEMENTS

A very big thank you to everybody who made it possible for me to write this book, especially for the hospitality and patience of Nat and Mariette Fiennes (Lord and Lady Saye and Sele) who made available boxes full of documents, letters and old books from Broughton, many of which came from the attics where once the Parliamentary soldiers of Lord Saye's Bluecoats slept prior to the Royalist attack on the castle.

Also to Martin Fiennes, eldest son and heir to the Saye and Sele barony, for his kind agreement to check the details of the family history (but not the national history!), and to Martin's family for their time and patience. (Go and visit Broughton some time. It is near Banbury and open to the public, www.broughtoncastle.com.)

To the Reverend Oliver Fiennes who gave me details of his tour of the USA with Magna Carta, and to my surviving sister Gillian who gave me details of our South African heritage. I am also grateful for useful input received from various members of the extended family. My wife Louise spent many months involved in travel, research and photography for the book, and I must also thank our family, Alexander (14) and Elizabeth (3) for their patience and for tuning down the background noise at home (drum beat stereo and screams respectively).

For producing the book, my thanks to Ed Victor, Maggie Phillips, Rupert Lancaster, Maggie Body and Jonathan Boff and, above all, to Jill

Firman.

For South African data and photos, my thanks to Ian Johnstone, Andrew Field, Fraser Edkins, Bob Manser, James 'Tackie' Bannerman, Tim Tanser, and other members of the History Society of Zimbabwe.

For Churchill data, my thanks to Lynsey Robertson (Churchill College Archives Centre), Colonel Tim May and Harry Staff and all of the Oxfordshire Yeomanry Trust and Hugh Babington Smith and Stanley Jenkins of Soldiers of Oxfordshire.

For Herstmonceux data, my thanks to Angela Minchin, Dr Scott McLean and Ann and Cheryl Friar. For Broughton and related Banbury data, to Jeremy Gibson of the Banbury Historical Society and editor of *Cake & Cockhorse*, and Brian Little. Also to Major Robin Maclean of the Royal Scots Dragoon Guards Museum. To Ralph Fiennes, William McAteer, Robert Stewart, the Archivist and members of the Derry City Council Heritage and Museum Service, and the archival staff from the Bristol Museum City Record Office.

Also, for making it possible to complete research work (between climbs from the Everest Base Camp in 2009), Henry Todd who had all the research books, maps, etc. yak-carried up from Lukla and fixed up a tent with heat and light. And to Mark Georgio of BBC News, who patiently photographed 360 pages one by one, despite snow and wind, to send back to the UK just in time.

Plus big apologies to anybody else who helped but is not mentioned above.

RTWF

PICTURE ACKNOWLEDGEMENTS

Author's collection: 233 top and bottom, 234 top and bottom, 235 top and bottom.

© The British Library Board 2009. All rights reserved: 227 top (Cott Nero D II f179v), 227 bottom (Roy 14 E IV f276), 228 (Harl 7353), 230 top (G3538).

© Cheryl Friar: 229 top.

© Nigel Owen: 236 bottom.

© Graham Trott: 229 bottom, 230 bottom, 231 top, 231 centre, 231 bottom, 232 top, 232 bottom, 234 centre, 236 top.

Family trees © London Calligraphy Lettering.

SOURCES

The Life and Times of series (Weidenfeld & Nicolson/Book Club Associates): *Alfred the Great* by Douglas Woodruff, *William I* by Maurice Ashley, *King John* by Maurice Ashley, *Richard I* by John Gillingham, *Edward I* by John Chancellor, *Edward II* by Caroline Bingham, *Edward III* by Paul Johnson, *Richard II*, by Michael Senior, *Edward IV* by Gila Falkus, *Henry V* by Peter Earle, *Richard III* by Anthony Cheetham, *Henry VII* by Neville Williams, *Henry VIII* by Robert Lacey, *Elizabeth I* by Neville Williams, *King James VI of Scotland & I of England* by Antonia Fraser, *Charles I* by D R Watson, *Charles II* by Antonia Fraser, *James II* by Peter Earle, *William & Mary* by John Miller, *Queen Anne* by Gila Curtis, *George I* by Joyce Marlow, *George III* by John Clarke, *George IV* by Alan Palmer, *Edward VII* by Keith Middlemas, *George V* by Denis Judd. *The Reign of King Henry VI* by Ralph A Griffiths (Sutton Publishing). *Queen Victoria, A Personal History* by Christopher Hibbert (HarperCollins). *England: The Autobiography* ed. John Lewis-Stempel (Penguin). *A Leap Year of Great Stories from History for Every Day of the Year* by W B Marsh & Bruce Carrick (Icon Books). *The Tribes of Britain* by David Miles (Phoenix). *England: 1000 Things You Need to Know* by Nicholas Hobbes (Atlantic Books). *A History of Antigua* by Brian Dyde (Macmillan). *To Be a Nation*, by William McAteer (Pristine Books). *A Brief History of Medieval Warfare* by Peter Reid (Running Press). *Holy War* by Karen Armstrong (Macmillan). *The English* by Jeremy Paxman (Michael Joseph). *Churchill* by Roy Jenkins (Macmillan). *Peerage & Family History* by J Horace Round M A (Archibald Constable). *The Oxford Illustrated History of Britain* ed. Kenneth O Morgan (BCA). *Britons: Forging the Nation 1707–1837* by Linda Colley (Yale). *Hearsay* by Lord Saye and Sele (Nisbet & Co). *The Agincourt War* by Lt-Col Alfred H Burne (Wordsworth). *Second To None* by Lt-Col R M P Carver (McCorquodale & Co). *The Vikings* by Jonathan Clements (Muramasa Industries). *A Brief History of The Magna Carta* by Geoffrey Hindley (Running Press). *The Day of the Barbarians* by Alessandro Barbero (Walker). *The Journeys of Celia Fiennes* ed. Christopher Morris (The Cresset Press). *Jane Austen The Woman* by George Holbert Tucker & John McAleer (St Martin's Press). *Cake and Cockhorse* Banbury Historical Society Mags. *Foxe's Book of Martyres* by John Foxe. *The Men Who Made Rhodesia* by Col. A S Hickman (Memories of Rhodesia, Inc). *Studies in Peerage and Family History* by J Horace Round. *Oxford Dictionary of National Biography. Sussex Archaeological Collections relating to the History and Antiquities of the County* (The Sussex Archaeological Society). *The Battle Abbey Roll* by the Duchess of Cleveland (John Murray, London 1889). *Complete Peerage of England, Scotland, Ireland, Great Britain & the United Kingdom, Extant, Extinct or Dormant* ed. G E C (William Pollard & Co.). *Royal Descents and Pedigrees of Founders' Kin* by Sir Bernard Burke, LLD (Harrison, 1864). *Proceedings of the Massachusetts Historical Society 1873–75. The Genealogists'*

Magazine, March 1942. *Topographer and Genealogist,* vol. 3, 1858. *Aristocratic Century: The Peerage of 18th Century England* by John Cannon (Cambridge University Press). *Settlements in the Americas* ed. Ralph Bennett (University of Delaware Press). *Dictionary of National Biography* ed. Leslie Stephen (Macmillan & Co., New York). *The Genealogist Magazine* ed. H W Forsyth Harwood (George Bell & Sons). *The Original Baronage of England 1066–1885* by James E Doyle (Longmans, Green & Co. 1886). *Genealogie de la Maison de Fiennes* (Pere Anselme on the House of Fiennes). *The Peerage of England, Vol. VI* by Arthur Collins. *The History and Antiquisities of the County of Buckingham* by George Lipscomb (J & W Robins, 1847). *Bulletins of State Intelligence, etc. 1848* (F Watts). *Journal of San Diego History,* vol. 25, no. 1, 1979 (San Diego Historical Society). *The Principles of the Christian Religion Explained* by William, Archbishop of Canterbury (T Cadell, 1827). *The Historic Lands of England* by J Bernard Burke (E Churton). *Dictionnaire de Biographie Francaise* by Roman d'Amat (Librairie Letouzey et Ane). *The Baronage of England 1387–1676* by William Dugdale (Tho. Newcomb, 1676). *The Vindiciae Veritatis* by J S A Adamson. *Marshall's Genealogists' Guide. Histoire Genealogique et Chronologique de la Maison Royale de France. Medieval Kent Wills at Lambeth,* Book 26. *Patronage, Culture and Power: The Early Cecils* ed. Pauline Croft (Yale University Press). *The Commune of London* by J H Round (Archibald Constable & Co). *St James's Magazine and Heraldic and Historical Register, 1850. The House of Lords Cases on Appeals and Write of Error, Claims of*

Peerage, and Divorces 1847 and 1848 by Charles Clark & W Finnelly (Little Brown & Co. 1870). *The Antiquary,* vol. III (Frederick William Monk, 1873). *English Genealogy* by Anthony Richard Wagner (Oxford, Clarendon Press). *The New Century Cyclopedia of Names* by William D Halsey (Appleton-Century-Crofts, Inc). *Heraldry of the Royal Families of Europe* by Michael Maclagan (Clarkson N Potter, Inc). *A Genealogical and Heraldic Dictionary of the Peerage and Baronetage* by Sir Bernard Burke (Harrison & Sons). *The Herald and Genealogist* ed. John Gough Nichols (J G Nichols & R C Nichols, 1870). *Alumni Oronienses: The Members of the University of Oxford 1500–1714* by Joseph Foster (Parker and Co). *The New England Historical and Genealogical Register 1962* (N.E . Historic Genealogical Society). *Burke's Peerage & Baronetage. Dictionnaire de la Noblesse. The Pedigrees of the English Peers,* vol. II. *Bibliotheque de l'Ecole des Chartes,* vol. III (J B Dumoulin). *The Great Governing Families of England* by John Langton Sanford & Meredith Townsend (William Blackwood & Sons). *The Publications of the Harleian Society. The English Nobility and the Projected Settlement of 1647* by J S A Adamson.